VISUAL MESSAGES

VISUAL MESSAGES

Integrating Imagery into Instruction

David M. Considine
and
Gail E. Haley

A Teacher Resource for Media and Visual Literacy

1992
TEACHER IDEAS PRESS
a division of
Libraries Unlimited, Inc.
Englewood, Colorado

We proudly dedicate this book to our children, Geoffrey and Marguerite, who grew up to be critical viewers and thinkers and who continue to question.

TEACHER IDEAS PRESS
A division of
Libraries Unlimited, Inc.
P.O. Box 6633
Englewood, CO 80155-6633

Library of Congress Cataloging-in-Publication Data

Considine, David M., 1950-
    Visual messages : integrating imagery into instruction / David M.
  Considine and Gail E. Haley.
    xv, 269 p. 22x28 cm.
    Includes bibliographical references and index.
    ISBN 0-87287-912-7
    1. Visual literacy--United States. 2. Mass media and children-
  -United States. 3. Activity programs in education--United States.
  I. Haley, Gail E. II. Title.
  LB1068.C66 1992
  371.3'35--dc20
                                               92-6111
                                               CIP

Contents

Preface

In July 1991, with understandably little coverage from network television, the American Academy of Pediatricians recommended that the practice of targeting children with food advertisements be stopped. Throughout the year, Surgeon General Antonia Novello took on the brewing industry and its practice of targeting minorities and adolescents. Secretary of Health Louis Sullivan consistently criticized the tobacco industry and the way it uses advertising to target some of the most vulnerable groups in U.S. society. In December 1991, further evidence was provided to document the impact of tobacco advertising on impressionable children and adolescents. In a series of research studies reported in *The Journal of the American Medical Association*, doctors said: "Cigarette advertising may be an important health crisis for children whether advertisers intend it or not" (Fischer et al. 1991, 3148) and argued that "tobacco advertising promotes and maintains nicotine addiction among children and adolescents" (Di Franza et al. 1991, 3152). In the strongest statement, researchers wrote, "public policy should, as a matter of urgency, extend the ban on tobacco advertising to cover not only electronic media but also all forms of cigarette advertising and promotion" (Pierce et al. 1991, 3158). While many people argue that advertisers have a constitutional right to express themselves and communicate through their campaigns, others suggest that the right also includes responsibilities. Is it responsible to deliberately target young people, who have not yet developed the cognitive skills to understand the marketing techniques used to persuade them to purchase particular products? Is it responsible to target sections of society where disease and illness related to the consumption of these products is higher than in the dominant culture? How manipulative is it to use symbols such as the cobra, bull, dragon, or tiger "to sell wildness and power to the powerless" (Leo 1991, 18). The concerns expressed by the nation's highest health officials create a climate and context in which teachers and librarians can effectively make a case for the inclusion of media literacy in the curriculum.

In the final decade of the twentieth century, whether we know it or not or like it or not, Americans live simultaneously in two different cultures. The first culture is the physical world that surrounds us, which we experience directly through our daily interactions, whether we live in a big city, a suburb, or a small town. The values, goals, and ideals of this environment are imparted to our children through the curriculum in the nation's public school classrooms. For the most part, the form and content of that curriculum challenges the left hemisphere of the brain, stressing the logical, sequential, and linear order of a print-dominated culture. The second culture in which Americans live, and increasingly the most influential culture, is the wired world that is mediated by the pervasive and persuasive vehicles of the communications revolution. The form and content of this "real-world" curriculum are strikingly different from the world students encounter in the nation's public school classrooms. Essentially affecting the right hemisphere of the brain, this real world is mosaic, imagistic, fluid, impressionistic, and profoundly capable of influencing children's feelings as well as their thoughts. Whereas the classroom nurtures hard work and long-term goals, the mass media promote consumption, instant gratification, and impulse—the necessary motivators of a consumer culture.

The clash between these cultures confronts children with mixed messages and provides little mechanism for resolving the conflict. While the curriculum promotes nutrition and positive eating habits, advertising assails children with the taste treats of the fast-food industry; in the ultimate capitulation, school cafeterias and lunchrooms frequently contradict the classroom by feeding students what they want rather than what they need. While parents, teachers, and the clergy counsel sexual abstinence or safe sex, the mass media serve up a steady diet of sexual gratification without responsibility or consequence. While lesson plans address the dangers of alcohol and tobacco, skillful and well-financed media campaigns find ways to convince young people that consumption of these products will make them cool, macho, and sexy. While we tell children not to judge books by their covers, the media consistently suggest that how we look is more important than who we are and play on peer pressure to coerce impressionable adolescents into buying designer jeans and outrageously priced sneakers. While the nation's public schools claim to prepare students to become responsible citizens in a democratic society, the social studies curriculum seldom addresses the impact of television and advertising on the political process, where image frequently triumphs over issue and style is more important than substance. The result is not only a steady number of school dropouts, but also an increasing number of dropouts from democracy as more than 50 percent of the electorate fail to vote.

The time has come to recognize and reconcile the two cultures in which U.S. children live and learn. This step has already been taken in Australia, England, Scotland, and Canada, where media literacy is an accepted part of the educational curriculum. While U.S. schools continue to acquire new technologies and U.S. homes overflow with the latest appliances, we must begin to distinguish between what we have and what we do with it, between product and process, between media *in* education and *media education*. Some efforts are now underway to do this. In the summer of 1991, the National Endowment for the Arts drafted a Media Arts Education Philosophy and Suggested Goals statement. The report concluded among other things that "the importance of media in our culture makes it crucial to incorporate its study in the K-12 curricula" (National Endowment 1991, 1). While organizations like this seek to help young people understand and analyze the role of media in our society, others remain technological ostriches intent on protecting by censoring. In December 1991, President George Bush complained that the American public was subjected to graphic descriptions during the William Kennedy Smith trial, suggesting that the news media should not have covered the proceedings. Bush's comments prompted an editorial writer in *U.S.A. Today* to respond, "Mr. President, leash the taste police. People can make choices for themselves" (December 20, 1991, 10A).

Throughout the war in the Persian Gulf, much was made of the instant information and live coverage. But instant access to information is not necessarily consistent with the ability to comprehend that information. Dwelling as it does on conflict, images, and clichés, television news tends to affect our emotions without providing us with a clear and objective set of facts. Despite all the yellow ribbons, flags, and well-intentioned support of the troops, evidence suggests that the U.S. public did not understand the issues involved in the war and had little comprehension of the Arab culture.

As the leading world power, the United States has the ability to affect the lives of millions of people all over the globe. If U.S. policy is formulated on the basis of public opinion and perception, our classrooms must begin to address the role news and the mass media in general play in affecting those perceptions. We must reconcile the highly emotive response fostered by the media with the need for higher order cognitive thinking skills. If Dodge profits from patriotism by declaring, "Our Pride Is Showing," or Coors markets alcohol through military metaphors, we must recognize the cumulative nature of the process and its ability to subvert different perspectives or points of view. If the evening news resorts to cultural clichés and stereotypes to explore another society, we must question the ethnocentric nature of the presentation. Reporting the attempted coup in the Soviet Union in 1991, for example, Dan Rather said, "Boris Yeltsin played the part of John Wayne." Such language, along with weighted words and prejudicial pictures, is part of a trend that is referred to as "infotainment." In educational terms, it might be called the "dumbing down" of news. Our need to recognize the process is heightened by the fact that the vast majority of Americans now receive their ideas and impressions about the world they live in and the issues confronting them from television, not from newspapers. Journalists themselves question how much we can depend on the world we see through television news. Dan Rather said, "We have by and large accepted the proposition that people don't care about foreign news, don't really care much about hard news at all—that 'feel-good' news, entertainment, 'infotainment,' features and gossip sell better than anything serious and certainly sell better than anything disturbing" (Rather 1990, 6). If our schools intend to develop students who are literate and critical thinkers, they must teach students to comprehend the form and content of information in all media, including news, advertising, television, and motion pictures.

These are not easy times in which to foster change, but a window of opportunity does exist, and educational innovators must struggle with the institutions of inertia. The very nature of change intimidates and frightens many people. It is clear, however, that if we do not initiate change ourselves, based on our expertise and work with children, change will be imposed on us from the outside, by politicians and others more intent on changing test scores than addressing the skills and competencies needed in the twenty-first century.

School reform and restructuring promise an opportunity to create a more progressive human- and child-centered system of education. Those who embrace that reform will have to nurture the skeptics and the opponents in education and society. They must also show the benefits of the proposed changes. Many proposals are already being subverted by superficial media coverage that dwells (as is its nature) on conflict. Nowhere is this more evident than in the case of multicultural education or the curriculum of inclusion. The 50th anniversary of Pearl Harbor and the 500th anniversary of the landing of Columbus highlight the division and the dilemma. One group looks back on "a day which will live in infamy" and sees a United States that was strong, resourceful, and united. They also see a new Japan striding about the world stage, and they are uneasy with the implications. For many, particularly those who fought in or lived through World War II, Pearl Harbor invokes nostalgia that fosters a dangerous inclination to believe the answer to today's problems is to assert yesterday's values and perceptions. Such a response creates a climate that resents and resists questioning. The controversy surrounding Christopher Columbus's discovery of the New World is one example of how difficult it is for many people to reexamine the beliefs and principles with which they were raised. In an interesting article in *The New Advocate*, author Milton Meltzer discussed the need for children to be taught to explore and question the Columbus conventions, balancing fact with myth (1992, 1-9). Whether American society is prepared to question and challenge some of its most treasured myths remains to be seen.

New ideas and approaches inevitably foster division. But there is disturbing evidence that social fragmentation and polarization are actively being promoted for political gain. Although politicians did not invent racial and economic antagonism in this country, advertising campaigns that pit one group against another or that sell fear, such as the infamous Willie Horton spot or the racial quota issue, divide rather than unite our society. Evidence of this division is all around us. The aggressive questioning during the Senate hearings to approve Clarence Thomas as a Supreme Court justice showed the darker side of the national political process. When women looked at the heavily male-dominated Congress and declared "they just don't get it," they accurately recognized how difficult it is for the diverse groups in our culture to see things from the perspective of other groups.

When Hollywood reworked the traditional buddy theme in 1991's *Thelma and Louise*, many critics assailed the film for male-bashing. The divisions facing this society were perhaps best summed up by *Time*'s 1991 cover story that divided the nation into two opposing camps, the "busy-bodies" and the "cry babies." The 1991 World Series provided further evidence of the division. Stereotyped for years by Hollywood and the mass media, Native Americans objected to the tomahawk chop performed by Atlanta Braves fans. War paint, the headdress, and the icons of violence continued to invoke a stereotype that was seen by millions of children all over the United States. When members of the American Indian Movement (AIM) objected to these practices, their complaints were largely dismissed by a dominant culture that, once again, "didn't get it." But, if the media shape stereotypes, they can also be used to challenge and change those stereotypes. New technologies afford minorities in our society the opportunity to tell their own story through their own words and pictures, rather than being filtered through the textbooks and media of the predominant culture. In Deer River, Minnesota, for example, students such as Michael Fairbanks and a group of Christa McAuliffe Fellows are utilizing interactive video to preserve Ojibwa customs and culture.

It is against this background that school reform and restructuring are taking place. Those interested in integrating media literacy and visual literacy into this movement need to look at the history of innovation in U.S. education and the relatively poor record of educational media and instructional technology, which is outlined in the early chapters of this book. As recently as October 1991, *U.S. News and World Report* wrote:

> There is too little systematic training of teachers in the use of technology ... only a smattering of education schools prepare new teachers to take full advantage of it in their classrooms. And many school systems put technology in schools without training teachers in the new classroom strategies they will need to adopt (1991a, 79).

In *Whole Language: What's the Difference?* Carole Edelsky et al. note the tendency of U.S. education to subvert innovation without a thorough understanding of the change or its broad implications for teaching: "With its materialist consumer culture, the United States tends to consume innovations, to gobble up the latest idea, not tasting or digesting the substance, using it up, spitting it out and on to the next" (1991, 2). In preparing this book, we have attempted to look at the context of the classroom, the curriculum, and the culture, explaining media literacy in terms of how it is consistent with traditional and emerging educational goals while also addressing traditional paradigms and perceptions. The individual chapters on film, television, news, and advertising provide a rationale for studying each medium along with a variety of strategies. The early chapters provide a clear argument for media literacy and look at problems in the areas of educational media and instructional technology.

Responses to media literacy that we have attempted to circumvent include the idea that it must be a course or that schools struggling with traditional literacy cannot find time to address the new literacies. We believe very strongly that media literacy can be integrated into the existing curriculum and that, properly implemented, both media literacy and visual literacy can strengthen traditional literacy. In addition, we find the idea of media literacy compatible with educational reform. In July 1991, for example, the secretary of labor received a copy of the *Secretary's Commission on Achieving Necessary Skills* (*SCANS*). The document pinpointed skills that the commission believed U.S. workers would need in the twenty-first century. Among these were the ability to evaluate, process, and use information and the ability to use and understand technology. These skills embrace both information in all of its forms and an awareness of how information technology affects society. In 1989, the *Turning Points* report on middle schools also articulated goals that media literacy can facilitate (Carnegie Council 1989). According to *Turning Points*, the nation's middle schools should create literate, critical thinkers who are healthy, responsible citizens with respect for other cultures. The movement toward multicultural education acknowledged in *Turning Points* must do more than change textbooks. For multicultural education to have an impact, it must examine students' perceptions of various races, cultures, religions, and ethnic groups and explore how media representations contribute to these perceptions. If media literacy is conceptualized as a competency rather than a course, it also becomes consistent with outcome-based education, which focuses attention on the skills students should have upon completing school rather than the courses they have covered. If students cannot think critically about the information they receive in a multimedia world or the decisions they make on a daily basis as consumers, whether selecting a product or a politician, can we really claim to have prepared them for the world they live in?

In organizing the book, we specified a particular grade level for each activity as a general guideline *only*. Although we took this step, we hope teachers will heed the advice of Canada's *Media Literacy Resource Guide*: "While all students have a great deal of experience with the media, their experiences are varied. For this reason the ideas and activities contained in this document are not specifically assigned to any grade. Only classroom teachers can determine how media literate their students are" (Ontario Ministry, 3). In this vein, we avoided developing specific objectives for each chapter or unit. Although this book can be used to teach a course on media literacy or media studies, we believe the most appropriate approach in the United States is to integrate media education into the existing and emerging curriculum. That means this book and the activities in it may be used by social studies teachers, art teachers, health educators, and others, each selecting themes, strategies, and activities that can be integrated into areas as diverse as sex education, U.S. government, aesthetics, and civil rights. History teachers, for example, could utilize the "Cinema and Civil Rights" section of chapter 7 to help students see the relationship between motion pictures and society. Health educators could draw heavily on the advertising chapter (chapter 5), helping students understand the persuasive techniques used by the marketers of alcohol and tobacco. English teachers could have students compare and contrast the elements of the novel and the motion picture (see chapter 7). Business education classes could study depictions of various occupations and professions on television, analyzing them for accuracy and representativeness.

Chapter 1, "Education, Media, and Mindsets," is particularly useful for media specialists and program coordinators. It provides a broad overview and rationale for integrating media literacy and visual literacy into the curriculum. It also includes research that demonstrates how the culture and climate of public schools have undermined educational media and innovation. Those who seek to introduce media literacy into the nation's schools on any systematic basis must be familiar with the issues raised in this chapter.

Chapter 2 introduces workable definitions of both media literacy and visual literacy and demonstrates how they can be related to traditional print literacy. The chapter explores broad educational reform movements such as multicultural education, critical thinking skills, and outcome-based education, showing how media literacy and visual literacy can facilitate these goals.

Chapter 3, "Getting Started: Ways of Seeing, Ways of Saying," defines the concept of integration and provides a lengthy list of the materials we include in the term *imagery*. This is also the first chapter to introduce strategies and activities to use with students, including a storyboard, a rebus, and visual/vocabulary exercises. This chapter also introduces specific motion pictures to be integrated in instruction and offers the unique feature of describing specific scenes, so teachers can fast-forward tapes and readily locate the most useful sequences.

The book is then divided into specific chapters studying various aspects of the media. Each chapter includes a rationale for integrating the study of that format into education. Activities are clearly designated by the use of a code (**ELEM, MID, HIGH**: elementary, middle, high) on the left-hand side of the page. Teachers are encouraged to examine the activities and modify them for their own students. Many of the chapters are clearly divided so teachers from various subject areas can readily locate relevant activities. In chapter 7, for example, film is analyzed in terms of its application to literature, art, history, and social studies. Chapter 4, on television, also contains extensive activities specifically related to health education, history, social studies, and English. In addition to the activities, most themes are presented with a broad range of research and supported by extensive references for further reading. The activities include a mixture of teacher-centered lessons and group work for cooperative learning. Although some activities involve in-class viewing, many draw upon the viewing students are already engaged in at home. Many other activities do not require viewing, so teachers do not need access to a lot of equipment that is often in short supply in individual classrooms.

When we discuss media literacy with teachers and librarians the conversation invariably gets around to the question of copyright. In our experience, ignorance of copyright laws tends to discourage teachers from using materials that the law permits them to work with. Certainly, existing laws allow teachers to copy broadcast programs and use them for instructional purposes so long as such programs are used and erased within the required time. Although some of the activities in this book involve working with broadcast materials in the classroom, many of the activities are based on viewing that students do at home. Advertising can be studied through magazines, packages, and products that children can bring to class with them. One of the most exciting areas now opening up to teachers is the world of television, which is increasingly being turned into video format and sold through educational catalogs and other sources. Television news broadcasts and current affairs programs are increasingly making transcripts, tapes, or both available to teachers. Miniseries and television movies such as "The Winds of War," "I, Claudius," "The Civil War," and others are now available on tape for schools to add to their collections. Vintage television programs such as "Star Trek," "The Twilight Zone," "Gunsmoke," and "I Love Lucy" are now available on videocassette. Ways of using these in education are addressed in the television section of this book. Even relatively new programs such as "China Beach" and "Beauty and the Beast" are also available for purchase at a relatively affordable price, and they can begin to take their place in school media centers alongside copies of movies such as *Romeo and Juliet, The Great Gatsby*, and *The Red Badge of Courage*. Regular viewing of quality television can also link the living room with the classroom. The trials and tribulations of Kevin, Winnie, and Paul ("The Wonder Years") or Alan and Katie ("Brooklyn Bridge") can fuse the worlds of the teacher and the student, providing rich material for discussion. Media specialists and librarians will find extensive listings of films and videotapes throughout this book that can facilitate the integration of media into education. We hope they will share those ideas and materials with teachers and promote an understanding of copyright laws that will protect the copyright owners while promoting a wider use of media in education. Copyright Information Services in Washington, D.C., is a reliable source of all information related to this issue.

In preparing this book, we have had the chance to talk to and work with teachers, librarians, media specialists, children, and administrators all over this country. We have presented lectures and keynote addresses to library groups and conducted workshops with parents, teachers, administrators, and librarians. We have also had the opportunity to make presentations to school boards, defining media literacy and showing how it can fit into educational reform and restructuring. Over and over, we have received positive responses. Those who work with children on a day-to-day basis know how important the media are in their lives. They see the T-shirts children wear, the lunchboxes they carry, and the pictures in their notebooks. They hear children talk about the latest record, the best MTV video, or a movie or program they have just seen. As parents themselves, many teachers and media specialists are also concerned about the amount of time children spend with the media and the images of violence and sexuality they are exposed to. But schools of education and library science programs have done little to prepare teachers or media specialists to help children process the mass media and understand the impact the media have on their lives. When media are addressed in this training, they are invariably educational or instructional media and not the electronic environment that children interact with for five or more hours each day. The training of teachers and media specialists must change. But this book and organizations such as the National Telemedia Council in Madison, Wisconsin; Strategies for Media Literacy in San Francisco; and Canada's Association for Media Literacy can make a major contribution to helping concerned teachers and media specialists integrate media literacy into the curriculum and win the support of parents and administrators.

If democracy is to have meaning, citizens must be encouraged to participate, and they must believe that their votes and voices have value. Clearly, for many Americans that is not the case today. Increasingly the political process is a pictorial process. As the 1992 presidential campaign begins, images are already in the ascendancy over issues as "substantive choices take a back seat to well choreographed confusion, designed strictly for winning not governing" (*U.S. News and World Report* 1991b, 29). In the 102nd Congress, the *Washington Post* said, "symbolism triumphed over substance to a greater degree than ever before" (Dewar 1991, 12). Unless the nation's classrooms begin to address this process, our educational system becomes an accomplice, a co-conspirator in our own victimization, and we render our children increasingly vulnerable to the visual environment that surrounds and shapes them.

ACKNOWLEDGMENTS

Many thanks to Lee White at Appalachian State University for his help with original and photographic reproduction in preparing this book.

REFERENCE LIST

Carnegie Council on Adolescent Development, (1989). *Turning Points! Preparing American Youth for the 21st Century*. New York, Carnegie Corporation.

Dewar, Helen, (1991). It's Better to Look Good Than Do Good, *Washington Post Weekly Edition*. December 28, 12.

Di Franza, Joseph et al., (1991). RJR Nabisco's Cartoon Camel Promotes Camel Cigarettes to Children, *Journal of the American Medical Association*. December 11, 266:22, 3149-3152.

Edelsky, Carole, Bess Altwerger, and Barbara Flores, (1991). *Whole Language: What's the Difference?* Portsmount, N.H.: Heinemann.

Fischer, P. M. et al., (1991). Brand Logo Recognition by Children Ages 3 to 6 Years: Mickey Mouse and Old Joe the Camel, *Journal of the American Medical Association*. December 11, 266:22, 3145-3148.

Leo, John, (1991). Hostility among the Ice Cubes, *U.S. News and World Report*. July 15, 18.

Meltzer, Milton, (1992). Selective Forgetfulness: Christopher Columbus Reconsidered, *The New Advocate*, 5:1, 1-9.

National Endowment for the Arts, Arts and Education Program, (1991). *Media Arts Education: Philosophy and Suggested Goals*. Washington, D.C.: National Endowment for the Arts.

Ontario Ministry of Education, (1989). *Media Literacy Resource Guide*. Ontario: Queens Printer.

Pierce, John et al., (1991). Does Tobacco Advertising Target Young People to Start Smoking?, *Journal of the American Medical Association*. December 11, 266:22, 3154-3158.

Rather, Dan, (1990). Journalism and the Public Trust, *The Humanist*. December, 5-7, 42.

U.S.A. Today, (1991). Public Doesn't Need to Be Protected from TV Trials. December 20, 10A.

U.S. News and World Report, (1991b). Confronting America's Great Divide. September 23, 26-29.

U.S. News and World Report, (1991a). Wired for Learning. October 28, 77-79.

Chapter 1

Education, Media, and Mindsets

MASS MEDIA AND U.S. SOCIETY

As the last decade of the twentieth century began, education systems in the Western world continued to focus attention on the role mass media played in society and the need to help students recognize and utilize it as a source of information and as a communication tool. In 1990 Canadian educators met in Guelph, Canada, to examine the emerging media studies curriculum. In the same year, Australian Teachers of Media (ATOM) met for their national conference in Melbourne, Australia. In London, the British Film Institute and the International Visual Literacy Association sponsored conferences on media education. Toulouse was the site of Unesco's 1990 international conference, "New Directions in Media Education."

In the United States, the late 1980s and the early 1990s provided ample evidence of the impact of images on society and the controversial relationship between the mass media and the public. Perhaps no single image so enraged Americans as the sight of an individual setting fire to the flag. When the Supreme Court ruled that the act was protected by the Constitution as freedom of speech, widespread support was expressed for a constitutional amendment. The flag itself had become a major political symbol throughout the 1980s, with both Ronald Reagan and George Bush managing to transform the national symbol into a partisan icon to the benefit of the Republican party. The political process was increasingly a pictorial process, with images replacing issues and negative advertising like the Willie Horton spot subverting serious political debate through distortion and distraction.* Beyond the political sphere, the nation's health also seemed to be affected by the media. While press and politicians focused attention on the drug war, the consumer culture continued to suffer from the consumption of legalized drugs. In 1989 Surgeon General C. Everett Koop recommended a ban on alcohol advertising because of its impact on impressionable adolescents. Koop also objected to the association between sporting events and alcohol, suggesting that this sponsorship be terminated. His successor, Antonia Novello, supported by Secretary of Health Louis Sullivan, condemned the tobacco industry's advertising methods and the practice of targeting vulnerable groups such as Blacks and young women.

The art world and the entertainment industry were also embroiled in the debate about what Americans should be able to see and hear. The director of the Cincinnati Contemporary Arts Center went to court to defend the center's right to exhibit the controversial photographs of Robert Mapplethorpe. The exhibit had been at the center of a firestorm of protest about artistic expression, censorship, and national funding of art. The rock music industry, no stranger to attack since its inception in the mid 1950s, was faced with a movement to put labels on albums containing lyrics considered too explicit, and more than one court case claimed listening to rock or heavy metal music had caused young people to kill themselves. The arrest of the rap group 2 Live Crew on obscenity charges caused *Time* magazine to run a cover story entitled "Dirty Words—America's Foul Mouthed Pop Culture." In the classroom and the curriculum, any attempt to introduce commercial media seemed to induce suspicion, if not outright hostility. When Whittle Communications offered "Channel One," a 12-minute daily news program, many educators and administrators objected because the program contained 2 minutes of advertising. When the issues, the images, and the pictures are controversial, the historical American response has been a knee-jerk reaction to legislate not educate. Although school systems in much of the Western world have

---

*Willie Horton had been a convicted felon in Massachusetts released under a general amnesty program by then Governor Michael Dukakis. Horton committed a capital offense a short time after his release. The Bush campaign used this incident to undermine Dukakis's credibility as a presidential candidate.

developed media studies to create critical thinkers, viewers, and consumers, the reaction in this country has been to ban or blind or gag.

One major irony is that American education has failed to develop a philosophy or pedagogy based on the role of visuals in instruction at the same time that it has spent an increasingly larger share of its budget on iconic technologies such as computers, VCRs, video cameras, and interactive video. These technologies are much more than electronic envelopes for delivering the old curriculum in a marginally new way. They represent a new curriculum requiring new competencies and a new definition of what constitutes learning as well as how and when it takes place. Neil Postman argues that the mass media and television in particular now represent the major American educational institution, to the detriment of school: "The major educational enterprise now being undertaken in the United States is not happening in its classrooms but in the home, in front of the television set, and under the jurisdiction not of school administrators and teachers but of network executives and entertainers" (1985, 145).

Throughout the 1980s, the power of the picture in the wide world beyond the classroom continued unabated as video technologies became more and more accessible to the public. Home movies entered a new era courtesy of the camcorder, and "America's Funniest Home Videos" became one of the most popular programs on television. But this video technology has had far-reaching and often unanticipated consequences. Ted Koppel's "Nightline" devoted an entire program to what was called "revolution in a box." The program documented the role this new technology played in the democratic revolutions that swept China, the Soviet Union, and Eastern Europe. Portable cameras provided an opportunity for alternative points of view to be expressed in countries dominated by state-controlled media. The official story could now be challenged by images smuggled out of a country, images that could be transmitted around the world. The presence of the roving eye of the camera unsettled both the Israeli and the South African governments, which were both very conscious of the court of public opinion. In the United States, media restrictions were imposed during the invasion of Grenada. The war in the Persian Gulf provided further evidence of the need to teach students to analyze the form and content of the information they receive. The Persian Gulf required a critical discussion of the way the information was packaged, presented, and processed. By consistently invoking media metaphors or sporting images, segments of the press used language that distracted from the reality of war. An ABC reporter said that "it looked like *Top Gun* and it sounded like halftime at the superbowl." Dan Rather closed the CBS news one evening with "an expression of solidarity for the families of servicemen everywhere." Social studies teachers studying propaganda techniques and English teachers looking at the language of persuasion could integrate analysis of the news into the curriculum to build both media literacy and traditional literacy. In *The Media Monopoly*, Ben Bagdikian warns about the nature of information in the United States and the public's need to be able to critically evaluate its content, form, and ownership: "Instead of control by governments, public opinion is increasingly controlled by a small number of corporations ... it is time for Americans to examine the institutions from which they receive their daily picture of the world (1990, xxiii). If schools are to achieve the goal of creating responsible citizens for life in a democratic society, they must help students understand and question the ownership, origin, form, and content of information in that society.

MASS MEDIA AND EDUCATION

If we believe *information* refers only to facts in a book or current affairs reported in various news formats, we ignore the news about the world that young people receive from film, television, video games, and popular music. Whether we like it or not, these elements of popular culture construct representations of the world and serve as socializing agencies, providing young people with beliefs about behaviors and the world. If they derive information from these sources, it is important for parents and teachers to know what these messages tell them. What do they learn or can they learn from watching Bart Simpson or seeing Madonna on MTV? What do movies like *The Neverending Story*, *Glory*, or *Dances with Wolves* tell them about reading, the Civil War, or the roles of Blacks and Native Americans in this country's history? If young people derive information from these sources, it is important for parents and teachers to evaluate this information and to help young people think about it and put it in context. When concerned teachers and librarians attempt to do this by integrating mass media into instruction, they are often rebuked and rebuffed by a system that resents the intrusion of popular culture into the school. In part the media and press create the climate and content in which this rebuff occurs. *The Christian*

Science Monitor, for example, was critical of what it termed "edutainment," which it misguidedly believed was incompatible with "that old fashioned learning process called reading" (September 6, 1989, 12-13). In a curious contradiction, the January 22, 1990, issue of *U. S. News and World Report* warned about the propaganda skill of "the PLO as image-maker," and the same issue described "the entertaining of America" and lamented that "many school teachers have evolved into entertainers using magic tricks, rock music or frivolous field trips to win the hearts of students." A 1990 essay in *Time* admitted, "we are creatures of the screen," (98) and then warned of forgetting to teach students about the world beyond television. The same issue worried about "effortless affluence, racial harmony and other troubling myths fostered by the networks" (3). Nor is the academic press any kinder or less confrontational. An article by Harriet Shenkman in *Educational Leadership* invoked a military metaphor for the war with the media. The time has arrived, the author said, "to marshal forces against the electronic demons that are having a damaging effect on the literacy of our students" (1985, 29). Never mind the fact that a substantial body of research suggests that when properly used, this media can actually foster traditional literacy. Research psychologist Kathy Pezdek has attempted to debunk some of the myths commonly associated with television and other media. Much of the opposition, she says, "comes from the aspect of human nature that causes all of us to split the world into halves—love and hate, safe and dangerous, good and evil" (1985, 41). In *The Closing of the American Mind*, Allan Bloom showed himself particularly hostile to popular music: "It ruins the imagination of young people and makes it very difficult for them to have a passionate relationship to the art and the thought that are the substance of liberal education" (1987, 79). Such elitist nonsense fosters conflict rather than cooperation between youth culture and school culture. This climate of hostility and confrontation does nothing to help young people understand mass media and its impact on their lives. Bloom claims MTV makes life "a nonstop commercially prepackaged masturbational fantasy" (1987, 75). Although he bemoans that situation and its impact on "the great tradition," he turns his back and closes his own mind to the idea of critical analysis of the media. Pop culture product is left to triumph over pedagogical process. This situation is part of a wider belief system that surrenders to the mystique of the machine and technology in our culture rather than recognizes that machines are created by humans and that what affects us is the decisions we make about the machines. Recognizing that media representations may affect our opinions, attitudes, and behaviors implicitly involves recognizing that we may not control our lives as much as we want to believe. Mark Crispin Miller suggests that many Americans do not recognize the media's impact on their lives: "Most Americans still perceive the media image as transparent, a sign that simply says what it means and means what it says. They therefore tend to dismiss any intensive explication as a case study of reading too much into it" (1988, 49).

Those who speak most loudly against the media invariably see only one side of the issue. In many cases such people seek to protect children from the media by banning or denying children access to certain forms of media rather than by teaching children critical thinking and viewing skills. Many of them, knowingly or otherwise, are also defending their own territory and traditions. These traditions and perceptions actually prevent them and their students from benefitting from these technologies and programs. Describing this situation, George Comstock said, "educators have a tendency to be literary snobs, regretting the passing of an old order in which people really knew how to read and write. This attitude has prevented us from seeing the revolutionary promise of the electronic media that give new cognitive possibilities to disadvantaged groups" (1984, 46).

Despite the negative climate that has traditionally impeded media in education, media literacy is not without support in the educational mainstream. In *What Do Our 17 Year Olds Know?* Chester Finn, Jr., the assistant secretary of education, noted that in some households "television has even more influence than either school or the family" (Ravitch and Finn 1987, 237). The study discussed educational values of series such as "Roots" and "Holocaust," noting that some viewing by minority students actually improved their general knowledge of the dominant culture. The study also clearly stated that the nature and needs of students raised in an electronic environment necessitated the use of television and other technologies as teaching tools: "Weaned on television and movies ... it takes more than a textbook and a lecture to awaken their interest and grab their attention" (1987, 241). Ernest Boyer, president of the Carnegie Foundation for the Advancement of Teaching and former U.S. commissioner of education, has also acknowledged that students need media competencies to respond to the increasingly complex communication choices in this culture: "It is no longer enough simply to read and write. Students must also become literate in the understanding of visual images as well. Our children must learn how to spot a stereotype, isolate a social cliche and distinguish facts from propaganda, analysis from banter and important news from coverage" (quoted in Palmer 1988, xxiv).

Dr. George Gerbner, dean emeritus at the Annenberg School of Communication, has begun to explore the concept of a cultural environmental movement and to look at media's part of a highly integrated global system.

From Gerbner's perspective, the media actually represent an environment that affects us all. Gerbner believes today's children are born "into a cultural environment largely independent of the parent, the school, the church, the community, the local culture and often even of the native country. Most of the stories are told—mostly on television—by distant transnational conglomerates with something to sell as well as to tell" (1991). The traditional definition of literacy centered on print because that format was the dominant means of communication in our culture. Today's technology has created an iconic information system that communicates most powerfully and persuasively through pictures. Preparing students to be competent in such a world necessitates teaching them to comprehend and create visual messages. But are U.S. schools ready to redefine literacy? Elliot Eisner suggests that current educational priorities are narrow and shortsighted: "We think about literacy in the tightest most constipated terms. We need a more generous conception of what it means to know and a wider conception of the sources of human understanding" (1991, 15).

A decade has passed since Unesco's International Symposium on Education and the Media drew up the Grunwald Declaration of Media Education. That document (1982) called upon competent authorities to:

- initiate and support comprehensive media education programs from preschool to university

- develop training courses for teachers to increase their own knowledge and awareness of the media

- stimulate research and development in the area of media education

Although the educational establishments in England, Scotland, Australia, and Canada have moved in that direction, little systematic development has occurred in the United States. Important resources and support groups, however, are available for teachers to use. These include Strategies for Media Literacy in San Francisco; The National Telemedia Council in Madison, Wisconsin; and the Center for Media and Values in Los Angeles. In addition, the Public Broadcasting System (PBS) has created an outstanding four-part series with Bill Moyers called "The Public Mind." Two programs, "Consuming Images" and "Illusions of News," are excellent for high school seniors. The Center for Defense Information in Washington, D.C., also provides important videotapes and other materials that analyze the political practice of using misleading language to shape public opinion and determine national policy.

Although these materials are useful, even if large numbers of teachers incorporated them into the curriculum, they would represent no fundamental change either in the way the educational establishment regards media literacy or in the relationship between media and education. Until the structure and organization of U.S. education give teachers greater choice, voice, autonomy, and professional respect, media literacy and visual literacy can and will proceed only in piecemeal ways. After more than a decade of spending money on the new technologies, little has changed in the content, form, and structure of the U.S. school system. In 1990, James Mecklenburger, director of the Institute for the Transfer of Technology to Education, reported that chalkboards, lectures, and textbooks continue to dominate instruction (106). Technology cannot be injected into education and become successful. Change cannot be imposed on teachers by a top-down management system. Although restructuring promises change, developments such as site-based management may actually require teachers to do more with less and stifle instructional innovation. The changes required by the media literacy movement are holistic changes that require relinquishing mindsets about media, students, and education. For these changes to succeed, they must grow out of an understanding of the organizational attributes and administrative attitudes that control U.S. education. Those who wish to facilitate change, including those who wish to address the need for media literacy and visual literacy, would do well to examine the nature of the system they are trying to change.

Philip Cusick (1973) analyzed the structure and organization of high school and concluded that its key elements were the following:

- subject matter specialization

- vertical organization

- doctrine of adolescent inferiority

- downward communication flow

- batch processing of students

- routinization of activity

- dependence on rules and regulations

- future reward orientation

- supporting physical structure

Clifton Chadwick's (1979, 7-19) analysis of the traditional model of education said it included:

- the teacher as main decision maker

- passive students

- verbal presentations

- teaching to groups

- teaching to time blocks

- evaluation through repetition

These elements are neither neutral nor passive. They represent an organizational culture and climate in which innovation must be either accepted or rejected. Individual self-paced learning through technology such as computers or interactive video is a direct challenge to this model of education. It removes the teacher from the center of decision making and changes that role from information dispenser to resource facilitator. It removes students from the role of passive absorbers of information, transforming them into active decision makers learning and growing at their own rate. It is hardly surprising that teachers and administrators are suspicious of such changes. Nor is it surprising that the history of technological innovation in education shows a recurring pattern of systems subverting the inherent promise of new technologies, absorbing them instead into the old way of doing things. Thus, throughout the 1980s we saw widespread evidence of computers used for drill and practice, with everybody doing the same thing at the same time, despite the promise of individualized self-paced learning.

A Nation Prepared: Teachers for the 21st Century (Carnegie Forum on Education and the Economy 1986) clearly recognized that the new technologies were more than delivery systems or electronic envelopes for carrying the curriculum. They were instruments for changing the very way learning occurred. "These technologies should make it possible to relieve teachers of much of the burden of imparting information to students, thereby freeing them for coaching, diagnosing learning difficulties, developing students' creative and problem solving capabilities and participating in school management" (Carnegie Forum 1986, 94). Although such changes are possible with the new technologies, they can only take place with appropriate needs analysis and planning. In the absence of such systematic strategies, technological promise is undermined by managerial mindset and organizational constraints. Richard Hooper saw this when he said, "educational technology ends up doing little else but perpetuating the traditional system of education. It is an abiding irony of the new media that despite their ability to revolutionize and upgrade the quality of education, they can be the same token mirror and prolong what is already going on" (1969, 249). Some fifteen years later, Leigh Chiarelott warned that educators seemed unaware of the potential for change promised by the new technologies: "The electronic media, by their nature, have the potential to change the way we interpret and reflect upon experience, and as a result, the way we think. While there is latent acknowledgment of this by educators, only cosmetic adaptations have been manifested in the schools" (1984, 19). In the mid-1980s, *Popular Computing* reported that computers were being imposed on the schools with such haste that no real plan of implementation existed: "Changes are taking place so rapidly that it's not at all sure who's in charge. The frightening answer might well be that no one is in charge. There's no master plan, no one at the helm, just innovation for its own sake" (August 1983, 83).

In an era of budget cuts and freezes, it is essential that school administrators, teachers, and media specialists work cooperatively to ensure that purchases are cost-effective and educationally sound. As part of a consumer culture, however, school personnel and entire school systems are often stampeded by the marketplace into making purchasing decisions without fully understanding the impact or the benefits of the technology. This system is perpetuated because higher education fails to provide these administrators, teachers, and media specialists, who must work together, with common courses, common competencies, and common expectations about how technology can transform and restructure U.S. education. Higher education itself is riddled with inertia and resists technology at the same time that it is charged with preparing the teachers of tomorrow. Michael Waggoner has said, "the organizational attributes and dynamics of the American college and university that have evolved since the late 1800s generally discourage innovative applications of new technologies in teaching. The degree to which the pervasiveness of these adverse conditions is understood is a necessary precondition affecting change in an institution" (1984, 7). The failure of the public schools to fully benefit from technology is not an accident. It is the logical outcome of most teacher training, which fails to help teachers comprehend or question the system in which they function. It is the predetermined outcome of a consumer culture that imbues technology and machinery with a mystique that denies us an opportunity to question its impact or implications. Thus, we become prisoners of our perceptions. Liberating ourselves from the mystique of the machine is a necessary pre-requisite for examining the culture and context in which machines operate. In the case of media and technology, we must recognize that it's not the hardware or the software but the underwear that counts. Until we focus on those underlying policies and procedures necessary for the successful acquisition and application of technology, the traditional school system will continue to subvert innovation.

THE TYRANNY OF THE TEXT

One major element controlling the culture of the school and limiting teacher choices is the domination of instruction by textbooks, worksheets, and prepackaged materials. A 1990 report by A. Woodward and D. Elliott suggested that textbooks structured and defined the scope and sequence of 75 percent to 90 percent of classroom time. It would be one thing if these materials were well written, well researched, and current. Often, however, their form and content have been watered down and damaged by the assumptions of publishers, the dictates of pressure groups, and ignorance about the relationship between picture and text. When Francis Dwyer studied illustrations in texts, he concluded that they were often based on subjective feelings of the designer as to what is best, the accessibility of visual materials, the cost, and the attractiveness of the finished product (1978). In other studies, a combination of illustrations and words in social studies textbooks were blamed for giving students misleading impressions of Australians and other groups. It is no accident that ineffective and inappropriate text-books find their way into classrooms where teachers are required to use them. The process is part of what Michael Apple refers to as the "depowering" and "deskilling" of the U.S. teacher. More and more teachers find themselves denied decision making about what they teach and how they teach. Educational materials and curriculum packets are created outside the classroom and imposed upon teachers. Apple suggests that the agenda implicit in many of these materials has more to do with the demands of the marketplace than it has to do with the nature and needs of children:

> The more the new technology transforms the classroom in its own image, the more a technical logic will replace critical, political and ethical understanding. The discourse of the classroom will center on technique and less on substance. Once again "how to" will replace "why", but this time at the level of the student (1986, 171).

Robert Muffoletto (1988) has also questioned the impact of a packaged and standardized curriculum that reduces teachers to product dispensers. Teacher education programs that do not teach teachers to be critical evaluators of media give them no criteria for making judgments. As a result they must unquestioningly use what is available and pass it on to students with little critical analysis. The origin and authenticity of the message is not questioned. The production process and the dissemination of the ideology are rendered invisible. In short, neither teachers nor students are encouraged to question the text. As mass media and new information forms continue to dominate our lives and the lives of our students, it is essential that we have teachers who can critically analyze these representations and help students think critically about them. To achieve this, teacher education programs must make sure they create what Carl Grant calls *reflective teachers*: "Reflective teachers actively reflect upon their teaching and upon the educational, social and political contexts in which their teaching is embedded" (1984, 4). Although such a state is desirable, there is no shortage of evidence to suggest that teachers often lack power and decision-making opportunities in the very system they work in. When teachers are denied control of the curriculum, it is hardly surprising that large numbers of U.S. students find school alienating and irrelevant.

THE MEDIA AND STUDENT-CENTERED LEARNING:
Dropouts or Push-Outs?

In 1972 the Coleman Report, *Youth: Transition to Adulthood*, noted that schools deny students responsibility, as a result of which they become irresponsible. The following year Cusick's study, *Inside High School*, said high school "has systematically denied their involvement in basic, educational processes and relegated them to the position of watchers, waiters, order-followers and passive receptacles for the depositing of disconnected bits of information. They in turn have responded by paying only a minimal amount of forced attention" (1973, 222).

Three years later the New Secondary Education Task Force reported "schooling of adolescents is often conducted in ways contradicting the nature and demands of human growth and development. Consequently, it loses power as a setting for learning" (Gibbons 1976, 49-50). Noting the impact of the media on adolescents the task force said that schools "cannot ignore the hours adolescents spend dormant before television and other media. This time can be used by cultivating student involvement in action programs, by teaching students to relate actively to the media and by involving commercial television in the community's educational enterprise" (1976, 65).

By the late 1980s *Turning Points* said adolescents are exposed to "massive, impersonal schools" and "unconnected and seemingly irrelevant curricula" (Carnegie Council 1989, 13). With the 1990s underway there is little evidence that the public schools have attempted to address the gap between the world students live in and the culture of the classroom. Marieli Rowe, executive director of the National Telemedia Council, put it succinctly when she said "task forces of two national commissions have looked at education in depth and with painstaking detail. What they have failed to consider is the child of the television age" (1985, 24). In the 1960s Marshall McLuhan said children of the television era could not function within the confines of the traditional classroom. Two decades later *A Pedagogy for Liberation* (Isa Shor and Paulo Freire 1987) continued to see a mismatch between the world children live in and the world they are schooled in. Shor and Freire noticed what they called "student resistance to the official curriculum." They also saw teachers and administrators refusing to change a curriculum that alienated students. Although officials viewed student response as "mediocrity," the authors said it was actually "a performance strike" and that students "withdrew into passive noncompliance or offensive sabotage in response to disempowering education" (1987, 121-41). Elaborating on the gap between school and society, Shor and Freire said that

> the world of American education, the school, is increasing the separation of the words we read and the world we live in ... the world of reading is only the world of the schooling process, a closed world, cut off from the world we live where we have experiences but do not read about those experiences (1987, 135).

Anyone listening to the White middle-class youngsters who appeared on Barbara Walters's October 1988 special, "America's Kids: Why They Flunk," knows these kids were flunking because they regarded the curriculum as meaningless and irrelevant. Walters lamented that they had not read *The Old Man and the Sea* or *Moby Dick*. She was surprised that they could not locate the nation's capital on a map of the world and that many of them were ignorant about politicians and issues including the greenhouse effect and the nuclear accident at Chernobyl. She also noted that some information was getting through. These students who knew little about the Vietnam War or the Civil War were not uninformed about AIDS, condoms, or pop stars such as Michael Jackson. The simple fact is that students are aware of the issues, developments, and individuals that are meaningful to them. The traditional response of education has been to draw a sharp and clear line between popular culture and the classroom. In the process, we have essentially told children that what happens to them at school has nothing to do with the world they return to each afternoon. In the words of Ray Browne, "we have been living in a democracy but educating towards an aristocracy of ideas and aesthetics" (1980, 12). In such a context it is hardly any wonder that 30 percent of our students choose to leave or that many others who stay on at school fail to fulfill their potential. Whereas administrators talk about dropouts and at-risk students, a legitimate case can be made to suggest that many of these students are actually "push-outs," alienated by a system that resolutely ignores their nature and needs. Some evidence from Australia and other countries that have introduced media studies suggests that retention rates have been improved by this decision. Two obvious reasons for this should be mentioned. First, many students are able to discuss, think about, and work with information from

Symbols and national icons from yellow ribbons to the stars and stripes can evoke patriotism. They can also evoke emotionalism and distract voters and citizens from debating the serious issues confronting the country. (Cartoon copyright 1990 by Herblock in the *Washington Post*.)

Editorial cartoons in newspapers offer a cheap and readily available resource to link visual literacy and current affairs. (Auth copyright 1990 *Philadelphia Inquirer*. Reprinted with permission of Universal Press Syndicate. All rights reserved.)

their own experiences. Their involvement with film, advertising, television, music, and magazines is an integral part of this curriculum and gives them something they can relate to. Second, many students are motivated by creative opportunities afforded by hands-on production in various media formats. In Melbourne, student photography projects are turned into calendars for the Australian Teachers of Media.

When media studies is discussed in this way, it is not unusual to find parents, teachers, and administrators who are concerned about watering down the curriculum or indulging students by catering to their interests. But the concept of child- or student-centered education is consistent with good communication skills and with solid practice in both business and industry. If we think of students as our clients rather than our captives, we begin to focus attention not just on what we teach but also on how we teach it. We begin to emphasize not just the content but also how we communicate that content, the instructional choices we have, and the context in which students will understand and value instruction. In business we attempt to meet the needs of the client to make the sale or be awarded the contract. If we expect to win the hearts and minds of students, we must attempt to tailor the instructional process based on what we know about how they learn best. By linking the world in which students live with the world of the classroom, teachers are also enriched. Canadian media pioneer Barry Duncan has said, "once teachers confront the popular culture of young people, they find media-generated issues are one of the best bridges to the world of their students" (1988). One warning: Although students are motivated by exploring the media in the classroom, it is not uncommon for some of them to feel that by talking about it, school spoils it. For many young people, media is an escape, a catharsis, a release. There is a mindlessness to it, and denial and resistance can be expected in the early stages of media education. When students say, "You've ruined it for me," or "My boyfriend won't go to the movies with me anymore because I'm always talking about it and showing him things," listen carefully. Beneath the complaints, you're hearing the voices of students on the way to becoming critical viewers and thinkers.

REFERENCE LIST

Aiken, Michael, and Jerald Hage, (1966). Organizational Alienation: A Comparative Analysis. *American Sociological Review*, 31, August, 497-507.

Apple, Michael, (1979). *Ideology and Curriculum.* Boston: Routledge and Kegan Paul.

_____, (1983). *Ideology and Practice in Schooling.* Philadelphia: Temple University Press.

_____, (1986). *Teachers and Texts.* New York: Routledge and Kegan Paul.

Bagdikian, Ben H., (1990). *The Media Monopoly*, 3d ed. Boston: Beacon Press.

Birchall, Gregory, and Gavin Faichney, (1985). Images of Australia in Elementary Social Studies Texts. *Social Studies*, 76:3, 120-24.

Bloom, Allan, (1987). *The Closing of the American Mind.* New York: Simon and Schuster.

Boyer, Ernest L., (1988). Preface in Edward Palmer, *Television and America's Children: A Crisis of Neglect.* New York: Oxford University Press.

Browne, Ray, (1980). Libraries at the Crossroads: A Perspective on Libraries and Culture. *Drexel Library Quarterly*, 16:3, 12-23.

Carnegie Council on Adolescent Development, (1989). *Turning Points: Preparing American Youth for the 21st Century.* New York: Carnegie Council.

Carnegie Forum on Education and the Economy, (1986). *A Nation Prepared: Teachers for the 21st Century.* New York: Carnegie Corporation.

Catello, James, and Kyle Peak, (1990). Media-Based Programs for At-Risk Students. *Media and Methods*, September/October, 26, 28, 82.

Chadwick, Clifton B., (1979). Why Educational Technology Is Failing and What Can Be Done to Create Success. *Educational Technology*, 19:1, 7-19.

Chiarelott, Leigh, (1984). Cognition and the Media-ted Curriculum: Effects of Growing Up in an Electronic Environment. *Educational Technology*, 24:5, 19-22.

Christian Science Monitor, (1989). Video Games Children Play. September 6, 12-13.

Cochran, Lida, (1982). Visual Literacy: The Most Basic Skill. *Readings from the 13th Annual Conference of the International Visual Literacy Association*. Roberts Braden and Alice Walker (eds.). Bloomington: Indiana University, 73-86.

Coleman, James, (1972). *Youth: Transition to Adulthood.* Report of the Panel on Youth of the President's Science Advisory Committee. Chicago: University of Chicago Press.

Comstock, George, (1984). Mind over Media. *Television and Children*, 7:3 and 4, 46-48.

Considine, David M., (1990). Media Literacy: Can We Get There from Here? *Educational Technology*, December, 27-32.

Crowther, Sandra, (1977). *A Study of the Media Program of Lawrence, Kansas, Public School System.* Ed.D. dissertation, University of Kansas.

Cusick, Philip, (1973). *Inside High School.* New York: Holt.

Duncan, Barry, (1988). *Media Beat Education Forum*, Autumn.

_____, (1989). Media Literacy at the Crossroads: Some Issues, Problems and Questions. *History and Social Science Teacher*, Summer, 205-9.

Dwyer, Francis, (1978). *Strategies for Improving Visual Instruction.* University Park, Pa.: State College Learning Services.

Eisner, Elliot, (1991). What Really Counts in Schools. *Educational Leadership*, 48:5, 10-11, 14-17.

Gagne, R., (1980). Learnable Aspects of Problem Solving. *Educational Psychologist*, 15:2, 84-92.

Gans, Herbert J., (1967). The Mass Media as an Educational Institution. *TV Quarterly*, 16:20.

Garcia, Jesus, and David Tanner, (1985). The Portrayal of Black Americans in U.S. History Textbooks. *Social Studies*, September/October, 200-204.

Gerbner, George, (1991). Draft correspondence. January.

German Committee for Unesco, (1982). Grunwald Declaration of Media Education.

Gibbons, Maurice, (1976). *The New Secondary Education: A Phi Delta Kappa Task Force Report.* Bloomington, Ind.: Phi Delta Kappa.

Grant, Carl, (1984). *Preparing for Reflective Teaching.* Boston: Allyn and Bacon.

Hooper, Richard A., (1969). Diagnosis of Failure. *Audiovisual Communication Review*, 17:3, 245-64.

Levie, H., and R. Lentz, (1982). Effects of Illustrations: A Review of Research. *Educational Communication and Technology Journal*, 30:4, 195-232.

McLaurin, M., (1971). Images of Negroes in Deep South Public School States History Texts. *Phylon*, 32.

Mecklenburger, James, (1990). *Phi Delta Kappan.* October, 105-8.

Miles, T. T., (1973). *An Analysis of Personality Factors, Life Experience Items and Attitudes toward Media as Related to Innovativeness for Selected Iowa Teachers.* Ph.D. dissertation, University of Iowa.

Miller, Mark Crispin, (1988). *Boxed In: The Culture of TV.* Evanston, Ill.: Northwestern University Press.

Muffoletto, Robert, (1988). Reflective Teaching and Visual Literacy: Teacher Intervention and Programmed Instruction. *Journal of Visual Literacy* 8:2, 53-66.

Naisbitt, John, (1982). *Megatrends.* New York: Warner Books.

National Committee on Excellence in Education, (1983). *A Nation at Risk: The Imperative for Educational Reform.* Washington, D.C.: U.S. National Commission on Excellence in Education.

Palmer, Edward L., (1988). *Television and America's Children: A Crisis of Neglect.* New York: Oxford University Press.

Pezdek, Kathy, (1985). Is Watching TV Passive, Addictive or Uncreative? Debunking Some Myths. *Television and Families*, 8:2, 41-46.

Pico, Ives, (1990). History, Education: Zap! Pow! Cut! *Time*, May, 98.

Popular Computing, (1983). Computers, the Next Crisis in Education. August, 83-84.

Postman, Neil, (1985). *Amusing Ourselves to Death.* New York: Viking.

Ravitch, Diane, and Chester E. Finn, Jr., (1987). *What Do Our 17 Year Olds Know?* New York: Harper & Row.

Rowe, Marieli, (1985). Educating Children in the Television Age. *Television and Families*, 8:2, 24-27.

Shapiro, Walter, (1990). What a Waste of Prime Time. *Time*, May 14, 90-96.

Shenkman, Harriet, (1985). Reversing the Literacy Decline by Controlling the Electronic Demons. *Educational Leadership*, 42:5, 26-30.

Shor, Isa, and Paulo Freire, (1987). *A Pedagogy for Liberation.* South Hadley, Mass.: Bergin and Garvey Publishers.

U.S. News and World Report, (1990). The Entertaining of America. January 22.

U.S. News and World Report, (1990). The PLO as Image-Maker. January 22, 76.

Waggoner, Michael, (1984). The New Technologies Versus the Lecture Tradition in Higher Education: Is Change Possible? *Educational Technology*, 24:3, 7-12.

Washington Post, (1990). Waiting in the Wings: The Doofus Generation. July 9-15, 37.

Winn, William, (1982). Visualization in Learning and Instruction: A Cognitive Approach. *Educational Communication and Technology Journal*, 30:1, 3-25.

Woodward, A., and D. Elliott, (1990). Textbook Use and Teacher Professionalism in *Textbooks and Schooling in the U.S.*, 89th Yearbook, Part 1, of the National Society for the Study of Education. D. Elliott and A. Woodward (eds.). Chicago: NSSE.

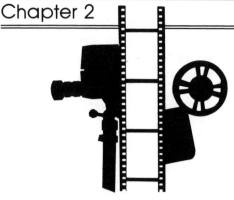

Chapter 2

Media Literacy and Visual Literacy: Instructional Imperatives in a Wired World

If we are to provide students with communication skills for today and tomorrow we must help them to comprehend and communicate through both traditional and emerging technologies of communication. Making these changes requires that teachers are trained in the emerging literacies and that principals, superintendents, and administrators value and respect the relationship between the literacies. By 1991, some evidence was beginning to emerge that suggested that administrators were focusing on these issues.

In a 1991 issue of *Educational Leadership*, Elliot Eisner said: "School programs ought to develop literacy, that is, the ability to secure meanings from the wide range of forms that are used in culture to express meaning. This surely includes far more than the literal use of language, or the ability to write precise 'standard' English" (1991, 14-15).

WHAT IS MEDIA LITERACY?

In defining media literacy it is necessary to come up with language and concepts that can be readily understood by teachers, librarians, administrators, and parents who may initially feel that children spend enough time with media at home without wasting valuable time on it at school. The definition must, therefore, be simple but at the same time must provide some context and rationale that explains the need for it. In 1989 the Association for Media Literacy in Canada suggested that the goal of the media literacy curriculum must be to develop literate individuals able to read, analyze, evaluate, and produce communications in a variety of media. Len Masterman of the University of Nottingham (England) believes media education is about empowerment and strengthening society's democratic structure. Central to media education is recognizing and helping students understand that media mediate, which means the media do much more than merely record reality and reflect it. Media—including film, television, advertising, and the news—*create* representations of reality. Although the images and the stories may seem real, or "true to life," they are always structured to represent a particular point of view, perspective, ideology, or value system. The evening news, for example, even when it claims to be "world news," does not accurately represent the news that occurred in the whole world that day. The news is filtered, edited, packaged, and presented. The stories that run, the sequence they are shown in, and the running time of each story all reflect that station's or network's priorities and its judgments about what the public needs to know, as well as about the most entertaining way to present it. In making those decisions, the media also deny the public access to other news. This concept is clearly addressed in Australia's response to media literacy. The Tasmanian Education Department wrote that "It is not always apparent to students, particularly in the case of the news and current affairs reporting, that media construct reality by selecting and composing words, images and sounds which recreate and represent the world" (1988, 2).

The following text suggests approaches that can be used at various levels of education and in a variety of classes to help students develop media literacy. These students should be confident and competent consumers and creators of media messages. They should be able to comprehend the media and to analyze and evaluate media messages. In addition, they should be able to design and produce media products that successfully communicate information and feelings.

Content Analysis. Students should be able to analyze and evaluate media messages. At its most basic level this involves a simple outline or description of the plot or topic. At a more sophisticated level students should be able to recognize themes, morals, or lessons embedded in the story, program, or advertisement, such as "crime doesn't pay," "hard work is rewarded," "there's no place like home," or "cleanliness is next to Godliness." This approach is not unlike examining themes in literature. Literary elements such as plot, conflict, character, setting, and resolution can be applied to study media genres, codes, and conventions. Content analysis also has important implications and applications in history and social studies, particularly because so much of today's education stresses multiculturalism and the curriculum of inclusion. Content analysis offers an opportunity to examine the way the media represent minorities. This includes the actual depictions as well as consideration of groups, individuals, institutions, and ideologies that are ignored or derisively depicted. Racial, sexual, religious, occupational, and other stereotyping can be analyzed in content analysis. Although content analysis can be applied within single programs, the media message is often best understood by looking at the cumulative nature of communication, which reveals recurring patterns, themes, and ideologies.

Form and Style. Students should be able to recognize the way the form and style of the message affects it and us. Persuasion, propaganda, and advertising all work on our eyes as well as our ears. A strong and logical link exists between what the media say and the way they say and show it. The music that introduces the news anchor and the high-tech set around the anchor carry and convey a sense of authority, immediacy, and competency that suggests the anchor is on top of the story. As a result, we are encouraged to accept and believe what we are told. Lighting, camera angle, posture, props, and other elements contribute to the composition and communication. The aesthetics and design of advertising, film, television, news, and picture books are part of the message, and students need to be taught how to read them.

Influence and Audiences. In studying the media students should look internally at the form and content of the image, but they must also look externally and think about the impact media messages and media technologies have on society as a whole and on audiences and user groups. A good concept here is to start with the students. By conducting simple surveys teachers can ascertain what media their students prefer, what programs they watch, whom they view with, how much time they use media each day, and so on. This information provides evidence about the media the students use. It also suggests the conditions and contexts in which media use occurs. This data can be valuable in helping teachers integrate student interests into classroom discussion. It can also be correlated with patterns of high and low achievement to see if any significant connections emerge. A more sophisticated approach to media influences might examine the nature and needs of specific audience groups, such as children, adolescents, elderly, Blacks, or Hispanics to see what relationship exists between these groups and the media. This type of study looks at media messages and also looks at the way various groups use the media. Teachers should be careful about approaching social influence studies by suggesting the media "make" people do things. Social learning theory suggests that children can imitate and identify with media models. Studies also suggest that influence is modified or magnified by a nexus of interacting variables including age, race, gender, education, and socioeconomic status. Influence is likely to be greatest when no other source of information is available and when the media message is repeated and reinforced. An isolated message or image in one program may not cause a result, but a message repeated in various programs is highly likely to have an impact. This suggests that rather than simply considering a media message in isolation, it also should be studied in terms of how it is used and who uses it. This approach prevents us from thinking about a one-way "hypodermic" model of the media that suggests the media inject us with images and information and we react. The hypodermic model usually engenders an adversarial attitude toward media, seeking to immunize students from the media's infectious imagery and ideology. By focusing attention on user gratifications and expectations, we can see how media are utilized and processed. This provides teachers with a chance to change how students perceive the media's role in their own lives. This role includes everything from what music students buy to the television programs they prefer, the movies they go to, and the posture and expression they assume when posing for a photograph.

Sources and Structure. Perhaps the most political of all media literacy issues is examining the organization and ownership of the media in an attempt to understand where the messages come from and how the source might affect the message. In recent years, takeovers and media mergers have placed our information and entertainment in the control of fewer and fewer corporations. Our access to information and alternative points of view is therefore potentially limited. Students must be able to place the media message in the context of its origin and ownership. If content analysis suggests bias, distortion, misrepresentation or underrepresentation, students need to examine the issue of ownership to see if it could affect these areas. Although some people are uncomfortable with this approach, it is quite consistent with the study of the role of media in George Orwell's *1984* or the study of persuasion and propaganda in democratic versus totalitarian societies. It is also common sense. Any student will admit that he or she pays attention to the source of information in everyday decision making. For example, the advice, "This is the best CD I've ever heard; you should get it yourself," will be dismissed or followed by a young person based on whether it came from a parent, a younger sibling, a teacher, or a best friend. Such parallels provide a framework that helps students comprehend the media and their impact in our society. This framework offers a context that permits consideration not only of media images but also of the industry, the ideology, and media's influence in carrying and conveying information. Put more simply, the framework poses H. D. Lasswell's questions by helping students to ask:

Who?
Says what?
To whom?
In what way?
With what effect?
And why? (1948)

Production. If we limit media literacy to analyzing and evaluating media messages, we deprive students of the opportunity to transfer what they have learned to the practical design and production of their own media projects. Production makes students active learners, recognizes their different learning styles, and develops their communication skills. Hands-on activities are also very much heads-on activities that promote cognitive and affective objectives. In addition to understanding how to operate equipment proficiently, students should also know how to apply concepts and techniques they have learned in other areas of media literacy. To develop a successful advertisement, for example, they must apply concepts of graphic design, with audience analysis and market research. The pitch or persuasion process they use requires an understanding of language and supports traditional literacy because of the research and writing required in scripting. Production integrates many areas of the curriculum and can include complex video productions as well as simple advertising posters and displays.

In Australia, the production component of media literacy has been linked to the economy and employment opportunities. Production skills help students participate more effectively in a workplace that increasingly relies on complex communication systems.

WHAT IS VISUAL LITERACY?

Despite the fact that the International Visual Literacy Association (IVLA) has promoted visual literacy for more than twenty years, and despite the increasing demand that computers, VCRs, and interactive video create for visually literate designers, producers, and users, the concept and the competencies implicit in visual literacy have not had a major impact on the U.S. classroom. One basic reason for this has been the complexity of the field and its language. *The Journal of Visual Verbal Languaging*, for example, sounded more off-putting than engaging. Happily it has changed its name to *The Journal of Visual Literacy*. As an interdisciplinary concept and organization, visual literacy and the IVLA embrace a wide number of areas. These include the psychology and physiology of vision, aesthetics, instructional technology, metaphoric thinking and language, media studies, and communication. The literature of the field ranges from simple to complex and is not widely known by classroom teachers. Recently the literature was centralized in the Visual Literacy Collection, which is housed in the Department of Archives and Manuscripts at Arizona State University. This collection should help to preserve and disseminate visual literacy concepts that have crucial instructional implications. Another problem associated with visual literacy is the fact that it has often been mistakenly regarded as synonymous with critical viewing skills. Although critical viewing skills are part of visual literacy, much more is involved. At its most basic level, visual literacy can be defined as *the ability to comprehend and create information that is carried and conveyed through imagery.* Although it is related to media literacy, it concentrates on visual information and would not, for example, explore newspapers, radio, or popular music, which are clearly part of media literacy concerns.

Comprehending and "Reading" Images. Like traditional literacy, visual literacy has what might be termed a *reading* component. Students can be taught to recognize, read, recall, and comprehend visual messages. This includes an understanding of the medium and the message, the form as well as the content. It can, for example, be used to facilitate children's understanding, processing, and perception of the art in picture books. Because the text in picture books is usually limited, information is often embedded in the illustrations. Students can be taught to decode and decipher this information. By drawing attention to the images and posing questions such as, "Why did the artist use this technique?" or "What do you think will happen next?" the teacher can help children understand the way visuals are used to communicate. This process can be applied to all visual media including computer graphics, cartoons, art, advertising, film, photography, and television. Analyzing the design and composition of visual media is akin to the concept of critical viewing skills. Both visual literacy and critical viewing skills encourage thinking critically and looking critically at images. Unlike media literacy, however, analysis is often based on the internal composition of the picture or frame and does not always look at the industrial, ideological, or sociological context of the image. By its nature, visual literacy also tends to focus more on educational and instructional media than it does on mass media.

Creating Images. Like traditional literacy, visual literacy embraces what might be termed a writing component. Students who understand the design and composition of visual messages can utilize this in their own projects and programs. Visual messages can include photographs, art, cartoons, advertisements, computer programs, and videotapes. The object is not simply to create visually, but to successfully communicate through visual means. It is this production and communication component that makes visual literacy more dynamic than critical viewing skills, which do not have a production component.

Thinking Visually. In media literacy most discussion centers around the way we think *about* images. Visual literacy also offers some clues about how we can think *through* imagery. Robert McKim's *Experiences in Visual Thinking* remains a landmark book in this area. In his opening McKim writes: "Many words link vision with thinking. Insight, foresight, hindsight and oversight. Visionary and seer. The word 'idea' comes from the Greek 'idein' to see. A sound thinker is sensible, or possesses common sense—a creative thinker is imaginative or far-sighted" (1972, 1). McKim believes education that develops thinking skills through visualization has several advantages:

- It vitalizes sensory and imaginative abilities often ignored by traditional education.

- It provides vehicles that are often more suitable to the thinkers' needs than are language symbols.

- It encourages flexibility in thinking levels.

- It encourages the thinker to utilize operations that are not within the realm of language thinking.

Pattern seeking, filling in, finding, matching, categorizing, and pattern completion are all visual strategies that foster thinking skills. Although these strategies all center around the analysis of external images, internal representations or pictures can also be used to link imagery to thinking. The STAR concept (stop, think, act, review) develops decision-making skills in children by asking them to think about their actions and the outcomes. STAR requires that the child project, plan, anticipate, foresee, and imagine. By asking children to put themselves in a projected position, teachers use mental imagery to help children understand the consequences of their thoughts and actions. Although this technique is often used in values education, it also has application in history and social studies. Asking students to "put yourself in their shoes" gives them a chance to see how and why historical figures made various decisions. Given all the information available, students might decide to change history. This leads to the "What if ..." scenario, in which students project alternative outcomes to history. What if President John Kennedy had not gone to Dallas? What if Harry Truman had not dropped the atomic bomb on Japan? What if the South had won the Civil War? Language arts teachers could utilize the same approach to explore characters, actions, and motivations in novels, plays, and poems.

These strategies foster a holistic approach to learning, connecting all subject areas by promoting an understanding of decision making, contexts, outcomes, and the cause and effect chain. Students begin to see bridges, not walls, between traditional disciplines. Other strategies are also available to promote critical viewing and thinking. The AIME (amount of invested mental energy) model, developed by Gavriel Salomon and Tamar Leigh (1984), improves processing. J. A. Hortin and F. A. Teague (1984) assert that some empirical evidence indicates that visual thinking can be used to help students solve problems. Gerald Bailey and John Hortin (1983) have also found success with mental rehearsal by developing planning strategies through projection, anticipation, and visualization. B. J. Minor and H. Cafone's DVTA (directed viewing teaching activity) model (1977) helps students draw inferences and develop hypotheses based on filmstrip versions of stories. Seth Kunen and Edward Duncan (1983) have also demonstrated that students can be taught to draw inferences from visuals and to verbalize these inferences "to significantly enhance children's awareness of the meaning that underlies visual events" (370). For these techniques to work and for students to benefit from the visual material available, teachers must be exposed to methods and procedures that have been shown to enhance visual learning. That requires a much more comprehensive and systematic integration of imagery into all teacher-education courses. It also requires a much more unified and cooperative approach to educating principals, media specialists, and teachers. All three groups must value the role of imagery in instruction.

Critical thinking skills and critical viewing skills should foster intellectual flexibility and encourage other perspectives and points of view. (Calvin and Hobbes cartoon copyright 1990 Universal Press Syndicate. Reprinted with permission. All rights reserved.)

Television is often regarded as hurting reading. When properly used, however, it can promote language acquisition and actually foster interest in reading. (Cartoon reprinted from the *Saturday Evening Post* © 1990.)

CRITICAL THINKING AND
CRITICAL VIEWING SKILLS

The need for critical thinking skills has long been acknowledged by educators. Jean Piaget believed that schools had to help students think independently in order to find alternative ways of doing things, rather than simply repeating what had been done in the past. R. Gagne has said that the creation of good thinkers has been central to the goals of education. He also suggested that although many educators believe this, we have not been very successful in achieving it. A 1987 report, *What Do Our 17 Year Olds Know?* concluded that the current generation of students is ignorant of important things that it should know and that generations to follow are at risk of being gravely handicapped by ignorance upon entry into adulthood, citizenship, and parenthood (Ravitch and Finn 1987). A 1990 *Washington Post* report cited a study conducted by the Times Mirror Center for the People and Press. The study indicated young people were less aware of events, policies, and personalities that shaped the world than previous generations have been. The study concluded that "sound bites and symbolism, the principal fuel of modern campaigns, are well suited to young voters who know less and have limited interest in politics and public policy. Their limited appetites and aptitudes are shaping the practice of politics and the nature of our democracy" (1990, 37). Dr. Mortimer Adler, editor of *Encyclopaedia Britannica*, has had a chance to see these students for himself. Adler interviewed students for scholarships. The candidates were all ranked at the top of their class, all highly motivated, and all earnestly interested in serving their community and country. The problem, however, was the students were more schooled than learned. They had been "stuffed full of facts to be memorized in order to get good grades on tests ... they were all top notch test takers, scoring high grades but they were all culturally illiterate.... None of them regarded the school library as one of its important educational resources" (Adler 1989). Throughout the 1980s one national report after another indicated that students were performing poorly and were not capable of simple or sophisticated tasks in many instances. With the changing nature of the workplace and fierce competition from overseas markets, flexibility and adaptability have become increasingly important components in this country's economic, scientific, and industrial strength and survival. But those in the business world and their leaders have been raised in the classrooms that Adler and others are so critical of. Management literature points to procedural problems, outmoded perceptions, and mindsets that impede change. In *The Third Wave*, Alvin Toffler said "old ways of thinking, old formulas, dogmas and ideologies no matter how cherished, no longer fit the facts. The world that is fast emerging from the clash of new values and technologies, new geopolitical relationships, new lifestyles and modes of communication, demands wholly new ideas" (1980, 2). In *Megatrends*, John Naisbitt also saw a problem with our ability to process information.

> Helped by the news media, especially television, we seem to be a society of events just moving from one incident to the next, rarely pausing or caring to notice the process going on underneath. Yet only by understanding the larger patterns or restructuring do the individual events begin to make sense (1982, 2).

The Art of Japanese Management saw Americans as prisoners of their past and perceptions: "We are defeated by our assumptions about the problem ... we need a different understanding of the problem which helps us to cope better with it ... our problem today is that our tools are there but our vision is limited" (Richard Pascale and Anthony Athos 1981, 22). In short, our classrooms and boardrooms provide evidence that our way of thinking and our decision making often hurts rather than helps us.

Gagne (1980) advanced three reasons for the education system's failure to produce good thinkers: (1) not enough teachers believe in it, (2) nobody knows how to do it, and (3) it can't be done. Although these may be useful ideas, Gagne fails to examine the context and climate in which they occur. Linda McNeil's *Contradictions of Control* (1986) suggests that schools are actually self-defeating institutions that create contradictions between school knowledge and the knowledge students need about their world. Schools claim to create responsible citizens able to participate in a democracy, yet much of what happens to students actually contradicts democratic principles and process. Students have little control over their own lives and learning while they are at school. In part the very size of most institutions mitigates against such self-direction. The more students in a school, the less chance there is for individuality and divergence. The operations of the school tend to take over the function of the school as an educational institution. Crowd control, traffic flow, bus schedules, late passes, hall passes, and a blizzard of paperwork often bury the democratic goals the school established. Naisbitt notes that in the classroom individuality is sacrificed to conformity, control, and the three R's, "remedial, repetition and rote" (1982, 121). This climate is not conducive to critical thinking skills. Grant's (1984) writing on education and reflective teaching suggests that teachers themselves are often unaware of the organizational climate in which they operate, as a result of which they seldom challenge its functions or methods even though many know intuitively that something is wrong. It is highly likely that schools cannot foster critical viewing or thinking skills unless they accept that their very existence may be challenged if it is viewed critically.

Much of the recent writing about critical thinking skills has centered on analysis, synthesis, problem solving, evaluation, and higher order cognitive objectives. Little has been said about helping students think critically about their information sources and the forms information comes in. In other words, the current widespread movement toward critical thinking skills seems to include little related discussion of what should be thought about critically. If the critical thinking skills movement does not embrace its allies in media literacy and visual literacy, students will remain unable to think seriously about the impact of media on modern society and on their own lives. In an interconnected global economy we receive the vast majority of our perceptions about the world and our place in it through the intermediary of the mass media. New technologies make it increasingly difficult to tell the difference between illusion and reality. In 1990 the *New York Times* said "computer imaging calls into question the belief that photographs are neutral images of reality" (August 12). Our willingness to accept visual representations as accurate reflections of reality is evident in expressions such as "the camera never lies," "seeing is believing," and "what you see is what you get." The problem is that in the absence of critical thinking or viewing skills, we seldom "get"—understand—what we see. The first thing we need to understand is the relationship between reality and media images or representations of that reality.

Media images in film, television, advertising, and even children's books can be deceptive because of their familiarity. Many of these representations are so powerful and appealing because they resemble a world we are familiar with. This similarity predisposes us to think the representations are realistic. The question of how representative they are of society as a whole is seldom considered. Dr. George Gerbner's (1987) research with television suggests that in that world, men outnumber women three to one; violence occurs six to eight times an hour; and doctors, lawyers, law enforcers, and entertainers outnumber all other working groups. The seemingly harmless area of children's books also structures a window on the world and conditions the way children think about that world. Susan Kessler Rachlin and Glenda Vogt (1974) studied coloring books and found that the images and ideologies represented were extremely conservative and failed to keep up with changes in the real world. Unless we begin to seriously consider the way the media influence how children and adults think, we are in danger of becoming a "soma" society of couch potatoes distracted by the latest program. Critical thinking and viewing skills offer an opportunity to prevent this. At the moment, however, Michael Parenti suggests we are actually participating in our own brainwashing. The media, he suggests,

> influence how we appraise a host of social realities, including our government's domestic and foreign policies ... rather than being rationally critical of the images and ideologies of the entertainment media, our minds—after prolonged exposure to earlier programs and films, sometimes become accomplices in our own indoctrination (1990, 19).

RESTRUCTURING, INNOVATION, AND MEDIA LITERACY

The restructuring movement underway in U.S. schools creates a potentially conducive climate for integrating media literacy into the educational process. If restructuring is reality rather than rhetoric—if the changes that occur fundamentally redefine and reinvent education—then media literacy may yet flourish. If, however, the changes are cosmetic adaptations with no systematic overhaul of traditional philosophy or pedagogical practice, schools will continue as institutions of inertia that impede innovation. One useful way of fostering media literacy during this transitional period is to demonstrate how media literacy relates to traditional and emerging concepts of education. Individuals and institutions that are change resistant need to understand that media literacy can support and strengthen many of the accepted goals and objectives of U.S. education. Those who are looking for change and progressive policies need to be shown how media literacy can facilitate those trends. In

1989, *Turning Points*, a report of the Carnegie Council on Adolescent Development, outlined the need for changes in middle schools. The report said schools need to create students who are "literate ... who know how to think critically, lead a healthy life, behave ethically and assume the responsibilities of citizenship in a pluralistic society" (1989, 9). These goals are totally consistent with competencies fostered through media literacy and visual literacy.

Literacy. Throughout the 1980s major changes occurred in the way our society produced, stored, processed, and accessed information. Computer literacy, which includes word processing competencies, clearly relates these new technologies to the traditional concepts of reading and writing. Research also suggests that the effective integration of imagery into instruction can facilitate students' ability to read, recall, and comprehend. Visual literacy can therefore support traditional literacy. The definition of reading means more than recognizing words and includes the ability to comprehend the meaning of those words. Media literacy helps students recognize, read, comprehend, and question ideas and information whether conveyed through print or picture.

Critical Thinking Skills. In *The Harvard Educational Review*, Stephen Brookfield identified what he refers to as "ideological detoxification." This is the process by which adults are "weaned from dependence on and adherence to simplistic explanations" proferred by the media (1986, 151). If adults need to be taught to critically analyze and evaluate media messages for simplification, distortion, bias, and propaganda, children, too, must be provided with these skills. Rather than seeing media literacy as an elective on the periphery of education, we need to recognize that it is central to lifelong learning and gives students the ability to think about the views and values the media presents to them before, during, and after school. In *Practical Strategies for the Teaching of Thinking*, Barry Beyer writes that critical thinking "analyzes persistently, and objectively, any claim, source, or belief, to judge its accuracy, validity or worth" (1987, 33). Media literacy means evaluating and analyzing the form, content, origin, and impact of media messages, a task that can only be accomplished by embracing critical thinking skills. Schools that do not integrate media analysis into the curriculum abandon impressionable children and adolescents to potential media manipulation and fail to provide them with skills necessary to understand the impact of media in a democratic society.

Multicultural Education. The movement to multicultural education liberates teachers and students from the tyranny of a single perspective. It recognizes and celebrates ethnic diversity, identity, and integrity. It promotes respect for differences while also acknowledging common bonds. It offers a new lens through which to view the past and the present. One example is Project REACH (Respecting Ethnic and Cultural Heritage). Although it is controversial, multicultural education incorporates a key tenet of media literacy by recognizing that the views and values of the traditional curriculum have reflected the ideology of the dominant culture. Those who control the messages received in school or society, whether in textbook or television, have imposed their own ideology and identity on the classroom and culture. The mass media and educational materials have filtered reality, distorted history, stereotyped groups, ignored issues, and misrepresented much. Courses and textbooks throughout the United States are now changing to redress some of these problems. Teachers can and should take this opportunity to focus attention on the windows on the world that the mass media provide for students. How do these frames filter reality? What do these windows conceal or reveal? What groups are underrepresented? What issues, individuals, and institutions are misrepresented? Addressing multicultural education in the classroom without also turning our attention to the images promulgated in the living room will not fully prepare students for the tolerance, respect, and cooperation necessary in a pluralistic society and a global economy. Television is becoming more sensitive to multicultural representations. In December 1991, "Northern Exposure" and "The Trials of Rosie O'Neill," for example, explored Christmas traditions and beliefs from other cultures.

Outcome-Based Education. Outcome-based education (OBE), or mastery learning that is tied to accountability, offers the opportunity to move our schools from courses to competencies, replacing content-centered classrooms with child-centered classrooms. Potentially these developments offer an opportunity to think of education not in terms of what students need to know (information accumulation) but in terms of what they should be able to do. In essence it provides a forum and a focus for determining what it will mean to be a competent citizen in the twenty-first century. Although such a definition has room for flexibility and variety, it seems evident that certain core competencies should be embodied in all statements. Communication skills are almost always cited. Although these include the ability to read, write, and speak effectively, the role of media and technology in our society would also imply that our students should be able to comprehend media messages and communicate through them by employing design and production skills. The ability to think critically is also generally included in most OBE discussions, which provides another opportunity for integrating media literacy into these outcomes. One lifelong skill necessary for all members of our society but almost never discussed can be termed "consumer competence." All members of the consumer culture make purchasing decisions everyday. But are these informed, rational decisions, or are they impulses prompted by sales pitches and the seductive persuasion of Madison Avenue? Our ability to think critically about our purchasing decisions—whether buying a car or an appliance or electing a president—is tied to advertising and media literacy. Health educators are particularly aware of the concern the surgeon general and the secretary of health have expressed about the negative consequences of advertising. But consumer competency extends well beyond the issues of tobacco and alcohol. In July 1991 the *Time* cover story was "Misleading Labels: Why Americans Don't Know What They're Eating." If the aim of school is to create literate individuals capable of being responsible and productive citizens in a democracy, consumer competency must be addressed. The decisions we make represent much more than the purchase of products. They represent the acceptance of values and lifestyles that may actually be harmful to ourselves and others.

Cooperative Learning. Media literacy and many of the activities described in this book lend themselves to group investigation and student team learning. Students have their own established repertoire of attitudes, behaviors, and gratifications associated with the role of media in their lives. Because they already have a knowledge base they are in a unique position to be involved in negotiation and decision making about what aspects of the media to study. Cooperative learning research suggests that groups working together learn more, often because of the motivational aspects of group work. Given students' natural interest in and inclination toward the media, this motivation is likely to be enhanced by utilizing cooperative learning strategies when exploring media. This approach not only promotes critical awareness of the role of mass media in modern society, but also fosters democratic values through peer reinforcement, cooperation, and accountability. The fusion of media literacy and cooperative learning offers an opportunity to restructure teaching, fostering a responsive and nurturing educational environment based on the nature and needs of students (see Figure 2.1).

Fig. 2.1. At a glance: Linking media literacy to traditional and emerging educational subjects—competencies and goals.

Literacy	The ability to read and write remain crucial competencies. A body of research from the field of visual literacy indicates that the effective integration of imagery into instruction can promote writing and improve student recall and comprehension. The significant thing is to realize that the new literacies are compatible with traditional literacy. Media literacy also addresses the ability to read and write. In this case it suggests the need for students to be able to comprehend and create information in non-print forms.
Critical Thinking Skills	Research suggests that most Americans now receive their information and impressions about the world from television and other electronic media, not from print. But television is not given to in-depth analysis or exploration of issues. Pictures and rapid cutting dominate. What impact does the format have on our ability to analyze and comprehend media messages? Given that our students spend four or five hours a day watching television, and that the picture is likely to have a greater impact than words they read at school, they need to be taught to evaluate media messages for authenticity, accuracy, bias, and distortion.
Multicultural Education	Media literacy implies analysis of the way the media construct social representations. It involves analyzing both the content and the origin of media messages, focusing attention not just on what groups are represented and how but also on why those patterns of production exist. Those who attempt to understand stereotyping, bias, and prejudice in the media or in the curriculum must focus on the issue of ownership. If schools are to seriously develop multicultural education, they must also examine the windows on the world that television and other media have become for children. Representations of minorities in the media, whether onscreen or in the industry itself, are an integral part of this process. For history and social studies teachers, media literacy offers a dynamic way to explore the construction of history and social representations in everything from picture books to advertising, television, and film.
Health Education	The advertising industry and the mass media in general have created a consumer culture. We are bombarded with powerful tools of persuasion telling us what to buy, what to believe, and how to look. These messages have the potential to affect our lifestyle, our self-image, and our sense of self-worth. If the media constantly depict images of instant gratification or sexual indulgence, it may be difficult to encourage adolescents to be sexually responsible and safe. If advertising constantly promises instant chemical solutions to complex social and emotional problems, it may prevent us from treating the real causes of such problems. If the media create an idealized, unachievable body image for women or men, they can contribute to the cult of dieting, which has been shown to be potentially harmful. If we wish to achieve the goal of a smoke-free society or address the growing problem of alcoholism in this country, we must also look at mass media's role in promoting cigarettes and alcohol.

(Fig. 2.1 continues on page 22.)

Fig. 2.1—*Continued*

Responsible Citizens in a Democracy	U.S. schools have prided themselves on creating good citizens to participate in a democratic society. The political process in the United States is a pictorial process. Presidential historian Theodore White has said that television and politics are now inseparable. Social studies teachers and English teachers in particular need to help students analyze the impact that television news coverage and advertising have on the political process and the relationship between the exploration of issues and the exultation of images. How democratic is a society if citizens cannot understand the form, content, or control of political information?
Consumer Competency	The ability to think about the purchasing decisions we make is one of the most basic tasks confronting each of us in everyday life. It affects our income, our lifestyle, our political choices, the food we eat, and the products we choose. Those decisions in turn have an impact on other members of society and, in fact, on the ecosystem. The ability to think critically before making a purchase is a central element of "green" consumerism. It focuses attention not just on the product but also on the packaging, enabling us to understand the consequences of actions that otherwise remain invisible to us. Our own health is clearly affected by the products we use and consume, and the health of the planet is also affected. Any attempt to study ecology should also examine the impact that media and marketing have on the environment.
Interdisciplinary Education and Integrated Studies	The mass media are part of the electronic environment, or envelope, we are born into. We all have experiences with the media, and these experiences are a constant in our life. By focusing upon our experience of the media, teachers in all subject areas can integrate media into instruction to discover how the media have shaped students' perceptions and attitudes about individuals, institutions, and issues. By creating continuity of process in media exploration, this integrates the living room into the classroom and unifies a curriculum traditionally fragmented by narrowly defined subject areas.
Learning Styles	Media literacy offers teachers an opportunity to develop various teaching strategies utilizing a range of materials to appeal to the dominant learning modality of students. Media materials can be selected to appeal to visual, auditory, and tactual kinesthetic learners. In the process students may learn more effectively, and some at-risk students may be retained.

REFERENCE LIST

Adler, Mortimer, (1989). Our Students Must Learn to Think, Not Just to Take Tests, editorial. *Charlotte Observer*, September 23.

Bailey, Gerald D., and John Hortin, (1983). Mental Rehearsal, a Method to Improve Classroom Instruction. *Educational Technology*, 23:8, 31-34.

Beyer, Barry, (1987). *Practical Strategies for the Teaching of Thinking.* Boston: Allyn and Bacon.

Brookfield, Stephen, (1986). Media Power and the Development of Media Literacy: An Adult Educational Interpretation. *Harvard Educational Review*, 56:2, 151-70.

Canning, Christine, (1991). What Teachers Say about Reflection. *Educational Leadership*, 48:6, 18-21.

Carnegie Council on Adolescent Development, (1989). *Turning Points: Preparing American Youth for the 21st Century.* New York: Carnegie Council.

David, Jane, (1991). What It Takes to Restructure Education. *Educational Leadership*, 48:8, 11-15.

Dwyer, Francis, and Carol Dwyer, (1989). Enhancing Visualized Instruction: A Research Overview. *Readings from the 20th Annual Conference of the International Visual Literacy Association.* Roberts Braden et al. (eds.). Blacksburg: Virginia Polytechnic Institute.

Eisner, Elliot, (1991). What Really Counts in Schools. *Educational Leadership*, 48:5, 10-11, 14-17.

Gagne, R., (1980). Learnable Aspects of Problem Solving. *Educational Psychologist*, 15:2, 84-92.

_____, (1991). Personal correspondence with the authors.

Gerbner, George, (1987). Television: Modern Mythmaker. *Media and Values*, Summer, Fall, 40 and 41.

Grant, Carl, (1984). *Preparing for Reflective Teaching.* Boston: Allyn and Bacon.

Hortin, J. A., and F. A. Teague, (1984). Use of Visualization in Problem Solving: A Comparison of American and African Students. *International Journal of Instructional Media*, 11, 135-40.

Howard, Gary, (1989). Multicultural Education in Action. *Middle School Journal*, 21:1, 23-25.

Kunen, Seth, and Edward Duncan, (1983). Do Verbal Descriptions Facilitate Visual Inferences? *Journal of Educational Research*, 76:6, 370-73.

Lasswell, H. D., (1948). The Structure and Function of Communication in Society. In Lymon Bryson (ed.), *The Communication of Ideas.* New York: Harper and Brothers.

McKim, Robert H., (1972). *Experiences in Visual Thinking.* Monterey, Calif.: Brooks Cole Publishers.

McLuhan, Marshall, and Quentin Fiore, (1967). *The Medium Is the Message.* New York: Bantam.

McNeil, Linda, (1986). *Contradictions of Control.* Boston: Routledge and Kegan Paul.

Martin, David., (1989). Restructuring Teacher Education Programs for Higher Order Thinking Skills. *Journal of Teacher Education*, 40:3, 2-8.

Minor, B. J., and H. Cafone, (1977). Reading Techniques Make Media Meaningful. *Audiovisual Instruction*, 20, 19-20.

Naisbitt, John, (1982). *Megatrends*. New York: Warner Books.

New York Times, (1990). Ask It No Questions: The Camera Can Lie. August 12, section 2.

Parenti, Michael, (1990). The Make-Believe Media. *Humanist*, 50:6, 18-20.

Pascale, Richard Tanner, and Anthony G. Athos, (1981). *The Art of Japanese Management*. New York: Warner Books.

Rachlin, Susan Kessler, and Glenda Vogt, (1974). Sex Roles as Presented to Children by Coloring Books. *Journal of Popular Culture*, 8:3, 549-56.

Ramsey, Inez, (1989). Using Filmstrips to Develop Reading Comprehension Skills. In Roberts Braden et al. (eds.), *Readings from the 20th Annual Conference of the International Visual Literacy Association*. Blacksburg: Virginia Polytechnic Institute.

Ravitch, Diane, and Chester E. Finn, Jr., (1987). *What Do Our 17 Year Olds Know?* New York: Harper & Row.

Sadler, William A., and Arthur Whimbey, (1985). A Holistic Approach to Improving Thinking Skills. *Phi Delta Kappan*, 67:3, 199-203.

Salomon, Gavriel, and Tamar Leigh, (1984). Predispositions about Learning from Print and Television. *Journal of Communication*, 34:2, 119-35.

Seels, Barbara, (1982). Variables in the Environment for Preschool Television Viewing. In Alice Walker and Roberts Braden (eds.), *Readings from the 13th Annual Conference of the International Visual Literacy Association*. Bloomington: Indiana University Press.

Sharan, Yael, and Shlomo Sharan, (1990). Group Investigation Expands Cooperative Learning. *Educational Leadership*, December/January, 17-22.

Slavin, Robert E., (1990). *Cooperative Learning: Theory, Research and Practice*. Englewood Cliffs, N.J.: Prentice Hall.

Tasmanian Department of Education, Curriculum Development and Evaluation Section, (1988). *Mass Media Draft Document*. Hobart, Tasmania: Tasmanian Department of Education.

Toffler, Alvin, (1980). *The Third Wave*. New York: Bantam.

Toronto, Ontario, Ministry of Education, (1989). *Media Literacy*. Toronto, Canada: Ministry of Education.

Washington Post, (1990). Waiting in the Wings: The Doofus Generation. July 9-15, 37.

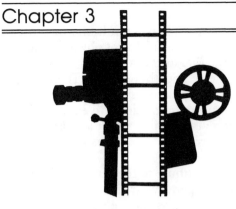

Chapter 3

Getting Started: *Ways of Seeing, Ways of Saying*

Although each chapter in this book provides strategies, resources, and a rationale for integrating the study of specific media into the traditional curriculum, teachers might also want to introduce students to the broader theme, which might be called "Ways of Seeing, Ways of Saying." Like all of the activities in this book, the following approaches are designated by age levels, but teachers are encouraged to modify these based on the attitudes and aptitudes of students.

WHAT DO WE MEAN BY IMAGERY?

In this day and age the phrase *imagery in instruction* often conjures up sophisticated computer graphics, interactive video, or videotapes and videodiscs. These are obviously all part of the vast array of materials available to educators. In this book we concentrate on advertising, television, news, and motion pictures. We also want to stress the use of nontechnological, easy-to-use, relatively cheap visuals. Research related to these methods is found at the end of this chapter and throughout the book.

Research indicates that children can be taught to read illustrations in picture books and that the pictures contain information that is not in the text. Properly utilized, these images can facilitate comprehension and recall. (Copyright © 1971 Gail E. Haley from *A Story, A Story*.)

Art. Because art is taught as a subject at school, it is often left to art teachers, as a result of which other teachers seldom reinforce it by integrating it into the curriculum. Paintings and other art forms obviously can be studied in terms of composition and design. They can also be analyzed as social artifacts and historical documents that provide evidence of the time in which they were created or the period they depict. These representations may be accurate or misleading. They may also reflect a patriarchal culture and a social mechanism that narrowly defines the role of women. Art education must include the opportunity for students to express themselves and communicate through their own creations. Visual communication also has important applications in therapy and counseling, providing nonverbal children with a chance to express their inner fears or concerns.

Body Language or Posture. Facial expressions, gestures, and posture all contribute to the way we communicate. Our posture changes according to our mood, our energy level, and the company we are in. Children can be helped to express themselves nonverbally by learning about body language. They also can transfer this concept and analyze meaning conveyed by body language in various forms including advertising, picture books, art, puppetry, film, and television.

Cartoons and Comic Strips. Cartoons and comic strips provide an outstanding opportunity for the development of both media literacy and visual literacy. Students can be taught to analyze editorial cartoons in daily newspapers and to create their own cartoons dealing with current or historical events. Language arts skills can be promoted through the use of comic strips and storyboarding techniques. Long-running strips such as "Superman" or "Blondie" can be analyzed to reveal the changing nature of society. Art teachers can look at the impact of comic strips on movements such as Pop Art. Literary genres such as science fiction, fantasy, and westerns can also be related to comics. *Comics in the Classroom* (Inge 1989), a publication of the Smithsonian Institution, is one of many resources available to demonstrate educational applications of comics.

Computers. Sophisticated computer software is now available that allows children to develop hand-eye coordination and critical thinking skills. The Oregon Trail gives them a chance to experience pioneer times. The Carmen Sandiego series encourages students to develop thinking strategies as they search through time and space, utilizing history and geography in the process. When students program computers to create images, visual-verbal thinking is enhanced. The rapid proliferation of computer software unfortunately has meant that a lot of inadequate software has been put on the market. Teachers who use computer graphics and software with students must give attention to the relationship between print and picture so that these work together to communicate effectively.

Flags, Trademarks, Logos, Signs, and Advertising. The extensive advertising section in this book teaches students to think critically about the packaging, pitch, and persuasion used to sell products. The activities include analysis as well as the design and creation of their own advertisements. This concept can be applied to a number of other areas as well. Young children can be taught to recognize and read street signs, traffic signals, and medicine labels. Older students will need to be familiar with some of these for driver education classes. When students study a particular state or country, they could be introduced to the flag or symbols such as the state bird, flower, or shield or coat of arms. Students could be asked to analyze the colors, symbols, and design of a flag in terms of what these factors say about the country or state. Why, for example, does the U.S. flag have fifty stars? How many were there in 1776? What is the design of the Australian flag, and why does it have two separate elements? Some students may have a family coat of arms. Students with a Scottish background would have clan origins, and these are clearly represented through traditional heraldic shields and coats of arms. Students might also be encouraged to design flags, shields, logos, or trademarks for imaginary products, countries, or states. Their design decisions should always be aligned with their description of the country or state.

Games: Boxed, Board, and Others. Boxed and board games have been part of U.S. culture for more than a century. Everyone is familiar with Monopoly. In recent years games such as Pictionary, Trivial Pursuit, and Risk have come onto the market. Each of these is educational in its own way. Many games not widely available in stores also have educational value. These include Made for Trade: A Game of Early American Life, Pilgrimage: A Medieval Game, and By Jove: A Classical Adventure. These games allow students, eight years and older, to explore various cultures and times in history. Jigsaw puzzles and various block games can foster everything from geography skills to mathematical problem solving. In addition to playing commercially produced games, students can study the games of various cultures, such as the ancient Egyptian game Senat (also Senit or Sen't). Students can also be encouraged to create their own board games to tie in with units they are studying. An inexpensive magazine such as *Games* can provide students and teachers with a wide range of educational activities.

Guided Imagery. Properly used guided imagery can be a powerful agent for affecting physical and mental health as well as intellectual acuity. Guided imagery can help children experience success and personal growth and explore their inner feelings. When children close their eyes to the outside world, a teacher or a recording can help them take inner journeys that can stimulate their imagination and be used for activities such as creative writing.

Hieroglyphics, Pictographs, and Rebuses. Picture writing can be a useful way of promoting left- and right-hemispheric learning. Students can be asked to translate examples of rebus writing as well as to compose stories in rebus form. These activities can be extended to history and social studies, where students can study cave drawings, cliff pictographs, ancient hieroglyphics, or the picture writing of Native American tribes. To untrained eyes these images often appear childish and simplistic. However, if we know how to read them properly, we can see that Plains Indian pictographs employ signs, symbols, and graphics for various informational purposes.

Music. We usually think of music as sound and seldom conceptualize the impressions, images, and information it carries and creates. Research suggests that music affects adolescents and socializes them into sexual behavior and attitudes. MTV is a powerful fusion of sight and sound capable of reaching teenagers on both cognitive and affective levels. Students can listen to a variety of musical styles such as classical, jazz, big band, rock, reggae, and rap, drawing and painting according to the mood, beat, tempo, and rhythm. Students can take photos or slides to document songs or make their own music videos. History and social studies teachers can use song lyrics as historical documents. Students can be taught to analyze song lyrics such as "Buddy, Can You Spare a Dime?," "The Times They Are A'Changin'," or "Ohio" as a reflection of events such as the Great Depression, the civil rights movement, or the Kent State killings. Various regions of the country or various ethnic groups can be studied through country music, bluegrass, and blues. Students can consider what pictures we get of people from the music they play and the songs they sing.

Patterns, Shapes, and Forms. Discovering and discerning patterns is an important intellectual activity that can be encouraged and utilized in many areas of the curriculum. Students can examine patterns in nature by studying natural shapes and forms. They might look at recurring patterns in leaves, trees, or rocks. Students can be taught to read their environment, study clouds, and anticipate weather as part of camping and orientation activities. Origami, block building, and other visual manipulation activities can also utilize patterns in math. In history, students can look for recurring problems and patterns of human behavior. In social studies, economics, and marketing they can look at demographics. This data can be used to make projections. How, for example, does the growth and decline of state populations reflected in a census affect political redistribution and the balance of power? What impact can be expected in our society from the browning and graying of the U.S. population? How will these changes affect institutions such as schools, hospitals, and Social Security?

Photographs and Postcards. Photographs contain a wealth of information if only we take the time to look at them and teach children to read them. Photographs are compositions in which the photographer has done more than capture a particular moment in time. What does the composition say? What is its mood? What point of view does it convey? What has been left out? How does the choice of color or black-and-white affect our reactions? When students study different countries, we usually begin with textbooks and printed information. The use of photography allows children to visually explore new cultures. Books such as the Day in the Life photography series can be used to help children visually analyze Australia, Japan, China, the Soviet Union, and other countries. By drawing attention to simple things such as clothes, transportation, food, families, and housing, teachers can help children build up a picture of the differences and similarities between a new culture and their own. Postcards can be collected and displayed to help students visualize everything from national monuments to state maps, presidents, works of art, and native flora and fauna. History and social studies teachers can collect postcards of historical figures such as Billy the Kid or Buffalo Bill. Actual portraits can be compared to Hollywood depictions of these characters. Photographs can also be used to study history. Dust bowl images in books such as *Let Us Now Praise Famous Men* (1939) or *In This Proud Land* (1973) provide strong evidence of conditions at the time. The portfolios of Edward Sheriff Curtis and other photographers document the cultures of North American Indian tribes and provide richer detail than most Hollywood movies. Photography has also proved useful in photo therapy, and Bowen Family Systems Theory (Entin 1983) provides a context for interpreting family relations and roles using family photo albums. Photography can be used with physically handicapped students to help them improve their self-image and self-concept. When using photography in instruction, teachers can help students recognize objects and draw inferences from the images. Students' ability to read and process pictures depends upon the viewing and reading guidance they receive. Finally, students can also be encouraged to explore their own environments and communicate through photographs they take themselves.

Visualization often facilitates comprehension of verbal or printed language. The ambiguous sentence "she dropped the plate on the table and broke it" can create more than one mental picture. Have students draw the image the sentence suggests to them. (Copyright © 1991 Gail E. Haley.)

Picture Books. Illustrated children's books and their filmstrip versions offer a relatively cheap and extremely versatile way of promoting visual literacy and encouraging children to become critical viewers and thinkers. Teachers and media specialists can focus on the various artistic techniques used to create the illustrations, or they can discuss the pictures as representations of various groups or cultures. The informative as well as decorative images can facilitate comprehension and provide details not referred to in the text (Considine 1986; Stewig 1992).

Puppetry and Masks. Puppetry and masks offer teachers a dynamic teaching tool that can be utilized at all levels of education and in many areas of the curriculum, including social studies, counseling, English, language arts, and art education. Hand puppets, shadow puppets, marionettes, rod puppets, and other styles provide a challenging and engaging educational experience for teachers and students.

Self-Image and Stereotyping. Unless students feel good about themselves, it is likely that their poor self-image will hurt their academic achievement and their social development. In working with children and adolescents, we must do more than deal with facts. How students feel about themselves has an impact on how they feel about school. Many times their sense of self and security are influenced by external forces, some of which are beyond our control as teachers. Many of these forces, however, can be related to media studies and visual literacy. The teenager who feels inadequate because he does not have the right designer label on his jeans needs help in thinking about peer pressure and the consumer culture. The young woman who diets excessively to conform to the fashion industry's idealized image of beauty needs intervention before she has a major health problem. David Elkind (1981) asserts that the media distort childhood, and Stanley Baran (1976) suggests that the media place pressure on adolescents about their sexuality. The minority student who sees few positive images of his or her culture in the media needs help in analyzing media representations. Students who feel good about themselves but accept negative stereotypes of other groups and cultures have to be taught to recognize and reject these media representations. Such stereotypes create visual victims, and the group that is represented is maligned. Those who see and accept these images develop attitudes and behaviors based on inaccurate information and impressions. Stereotyping cuts across all aspects of society. It deals with occupations, age groups, sex roles, religions, nationalities, and racial and ethnic groups. Stereotypes appear in comics, picture books, films, television, art, and music. They are also evident in a lot of educational software. The PBS series "Square One," for example, was criticized by one group of researchers for sexism, racism, and blatant bias (DeVaney and Elenes 1990). How we feel about ourselves and others is affected by how others see us. An isolated image here or there may not have an impact. Stereotyping, however, has a cumulative impact by reflecting, repeating, and reinforcing inappropriate and even unfounded prejudices and perceptions. Recognizing and challenging stereotyping in all its forms is a crucial component of media literacy and visual literacy in all areas of the curriculum.

WHAT DO WE MEAN BY INTEGRATION?

Clearly, an integrated approach to media literacy and visual literacy implies recognizing the importance of these competencies and including them wherever possible in the existing curriculum. The concept of integration focuses attention on reinforcing key themes and learner outcomes across the curriculum rather than trying to create new courses. Any attempt to create a course called "Media Studies," for example, although a positive step on the surface, seems to be bogged down in old assumptions about education. These assumptions cause knowledge to be divided into discrete units that create fragmentation, not integration. This framentation, according to some researchers, causes disintegration, reflected in the number of students who withdraw from the official school curriculum. Integration attempts to unify a fragmented curriculum by stressing the common themes and competencies among subjects. Media literacy and visual literacy are central to the entire notion of communication and therefore cut across all subject areas. The aim is also to integrate the world of the classroom with the world of the child and society as a whole. When students say they are bored or question the relevance of a subject or course, they are telling us that they don't see how the information relates to them. Barry Duncan, President of Canada Association for Media Literacy, and other media educators believe the study of popular culture begins to build bridges between school and society and between students and teachers. These bridges are a key component of the holistic teaching and learning implicit in an integrated approach to education. The whole language movement represents this holistic approach to language development and utilization. So, too, does the growing movement toward schooling based on competencies and learner outcomes rather than on course requirements and grades. Certain unifying themes can integrate key concepts. Hence, students might cover traditional disciplines through a unifying theme such as power. The program of study might analyze physical power, natural power, economic power, military power, political power, and personal power. The 1987 study *What Do Our 17 Year Olds Know?* saw the need for integrated teaching and learning. "Wherever possible," the authors wrote, "history teachers should enrich their courses with literature, and literature teachers should enrich their courses with history" (Ravitch and Finn 1987, 229). The study recommended teaching history in context with an emphasis on people, their myths, folktales, traditions, art, literature, and accomplishments. Integration also encourages cooperative learning and teaching. In England, the Open University has defined integration as the exploration of themes or problems requiring the use of more than one school subject for its meaning and the interest of more than one teacher in achieving this. "Thus integrated studies has a double concern, the cooperative use of subjects and cooperation between teachers to make this possible" (Open University 1976). Finally, we believe integration is key to the success and survival of media literacy and visual literacy in U.S. education. Critical viewing skills and visual literacy have been tried before, but the pockets of progress failed to become widespread. In part that failure was because of the way the effort was organized. Barbara Dobbs says, "Those curricula died a slow death because they were not global in their approach. The visual literacy skills that were taught in those isolated classes were not transferred to other curricula and more importantly, were not transferred to the students' world outside the classroom" (1988, 12). If media literacy and visual literacy are to succeed in U.S. education, we believe they must be addressed as competencies, not courses. In this book we attempt to integrate the world beyond the classroom, the pop culture world of the student, with the content and concerns of the curriculum. We attempt to show how these competencies are consistent with traditional literacy and with the need for critical thinkers in an information age. We attempt to address the dichotomy between the dominance of mass media in society and their near absence in the classroom. Finally, we look at the traditional response to teaching and technology and argue that future success depends upon breaking these patterns and paradigms. In part that means integrating technology into teaching, rather than simply injecting it. To a very large degree, however, it depends upon a more integrated approach to the way teachers, media specialists, and principals are taught about media and technology in school and society. The fragmented approach to teaching these professionals and to this topic remains one of the greatest impediments to improving education through an integrated approach to imagery and all forms of media.

A HELPING HAND FROM HOLLYWOOD: Movies for the Mind

Utilizing motion pictures in the classroom can help stimulate problem solving by developing critical thinking and viewing skills. The following films offer short excerpts that teachers can use to help students think about ways of seeing and ways of saying.

"Labyrinth" (1986)

(ELEM/MID/HIGH)—This is an interesting fantasy adventure film produced by George Lucas and directed by Jim Henson. The plot has similarities to Maurice Sendak's *Outside Over There*. Astute viewers will notice several Sendak books early in the film as the camera pans across Sarah's bedroom. The story centers around an unhappy adolescent who resents babysitting her young brother. When she wishes the goblins would steal the baby, her wish is granted. Sarah must then find her way through a maze to the castle beyond the goblin city to rescue Toby. Although this may seem suitable only for children in elementary school, the first section can be used to address the concepts of problem solving and critical thinking.

From the opening credits to the end of the first labyrinth sequence the film takes 20 minutes. If the film is fast-forwarded to Sarah's encounter with the fairies and Hoggle, outside the labyrinth, the clip takes only 8 minutes. Sarah's attempt to solve the labyrinth to find her brother is the key to this clip. Tell students that Sarah wished for something, and then when she got it realized she had made a mistake. Now she has to correct that mistake. And looking at the castle for the first time, Sarah makes another mistake. "It doesn't look that far," she says. But Sarah has time as well as distance to struggle with, for the goblin king has given her only 13 hours to solve the labyrinth before her brother becomes a goblin.

As Sarah approaches the outside of the labyrinth she sees fairies flying through the air. "How sweet!" she says. The teenager is dismayed when a character called Hoggle begins to spray the fairies as though they were flies. "How could you ... you monster!" Sarah says. Imagine her surprise when she reaches out to a fairy and it stings her! Sarah's perceptions come from a different culture, and her rules and logic do not apply in this new world. It is a lesson she will have to learn. "What did you expect fairies to do? ... shows what you know, don't it?" Hoggle says to her.

Sarah wants Hoggle to show her how to get into the labyrinth, and she asks but gets no answer. "It's hopeless asking you anything," she says angrily. "Not if you ask the right questions," he replies. Hoggle shows her how to enter the maze, but she still looks at things the wrong way. "You know what your problem is?" he asks her. "You take too many things for granted." Sarah begins her journey along the seemingly endless miles of the labyrinth. Suddenly, something Hoggle said gets her attention. "Maybe it doesn't go on forever," she says to herself. "Maybe I'm just taking it for granted that it does."

Sarah has started to think differently, but she still sees things the same way, and all she can see is walls, barriers, and obstacles. Frustrated by her lack of progress she sits down, only to be greeted by a wise worm who offers good advice. "You ain't looking right. It's full of openings. It's just that you ain't seeing them. Things are not always what they seem in this place, so you can't take anything for granted." Armed with a new way of seeing and thinking, Sarah is now able to do battle with the goblin king.

"The Gods Must Be Crazy" (1984)

(ELEM/MID/HIGH)—This interesting and humorous anthropological story shows how different cultures perceive the same things in totally different ways. At its most basic, it asks when a Coke bottle is not a Coke bottle. On a more sophisticated level, it challenges our assumptions about the whole notion of primitive and civilized societies. From the title to the end of the sequence described in this unit, the clip runs 15 minutes.

The opening of the film addresses the relationship between illusion and reality. "It looks like a paradise, but it is in fact the most treacherous desert in the world, the Kalahari." In this desert we meet the "dainty, small, and graceful bushmen." To Western eyes, surviving in such inhospitable terrain would be impossible. But the bushmen take life in stride. "In this world of theirs nothing is good or evil." Students will be amazed to see how the bushmen locate water, hunt, and deal with ownership.

After about 6 minutes the film cuts to a big city, where we are introduced to "civilized man." Civilized humans, we are told, managed to make their lives more complicated by trying to make them easier. By contrast, the bushmen have a very simple life—until the Western world intrudes upon it. "One day, something fell from the sky," dropped from "the noisy birds that fly without flapping their wings." The bushmen believe the gods have sent them a wonderful gift. The Coke bottle becomes a tool, a musical instrument, and ultimately a weapon. But the bushmen's perception of the gift quickly changes and they soon call it "the evil thing." They determine to "take it to the end of the earth and throw it off." (See photograph, page 249.)

"Dead Poets Society" (1989)

(ELEM/MID/HIGH)—This is a very interesting story of instruction and individuality, conformity, and creativity. Set at Welton Academy in 1959, the film looks at how an unconventional teacher inspires a group of adolescent males. Almost the first image in the film is a candle, "the light of knowledge." From the outset, the school and the boys see things in different ways. The school believes that the four pillars are Tradition, Honor, Discipline, and Excellence; the boys' pillars are Travesty, Heart, Decadence, and Excrement. The boys and their teacher John Keating view the world differently. It is 1959. The Eisenhower years are about to end and the torch will be passed to a new generation of Americans led by John Kennedy. The boys Mr. Keating teaches will be the bankers, lawyers, and doctors of tomorrow. But for the moment Keating wants them to enjoy their youth. "Gather ye rosebuds while ye may," he advises them. "Carpe diem. Seize the day!" Keating helps the boys think about their own vulnerability—"we are all food for worms, lads"—by helping them see the link between their own lives and all the boys who have gone before them ("they are not that different from you, are they?"). Several key scenes can be selected to examine individuality, creativity, conformity, and critical thinking.

1. The poetry class: Keating has the boys rip out the introduction of their books and tells them, "In my class you will learn to think for yourselves. No matter what anybody tells you, words and ideas can change the world. The powerful play goes on and you must contribute a verse. What will your verse be?" Keating links life and learning and shows the boys how poetry challenges them to live and think. Henry David Thoreau said, "Suck out all the marrow of life." Alfred, Lord Tennyson said, "To strive, to seek, to find and not to yield."

2. Standing on the desk: Keating stands on his desk and invites the boys to join him so they can change their perspective. "Why do I stand up here? I stand upon my desk to remind myself that we must constantly look at things in a different way. See, the world looks very different from up here. Just when you think you know something, you have to look at it in another way. Even though it may sound silly

or wrong, you must try. Now when you read, don't just consider what the author thinks, consider what you think. Boys, you must strive to find your own voice. Don't just walk off the edge like lemmings. Look around you. Dare to strike out and find new ground."

3.   Marching to the beat of a different drum: Keating takes the boys out into the courtyard. "There's no grades at stake, gentlemen, just take a stroll." Fairly quickly the boys begin to march in time, while other boys clap time. Keating has demonstrated his point, "the point of conformity, the difficulty of maintaining your own belief in the face of others." Again he resorts to poetry, advising them to "swim against the stream," telling them that Robert Frost chose the road less travelled.

Miscellaneous Movies

Almost any Hollywood movie contains scenes that can be used to help students develop critical thinking and viewing skills. The cueing and retrieval strategies that teachers provide and the questions and discussion after the screening will determine how much children get out of such excerpts. Cueing and retrieval can only work when teachers have previewed key scenes. Then they can prepare children for the key things to look and listen for. Research suggests that this preparation will result in greater recall and processing (Salomon and Leigh 1984). The following list touches on just a few films that can help students find new ways of seeing and saying.

To Kill a Mockingbird (1962)

(ELEM / MID / HIGH) — Usually studied in English as classic literature. A central theme is perspectives and points of view. The children learn that their father is much more than they think and that the neighborhood bogeyman is not half as frightening as they believe. Atticus Finch believes people would understand each other and be more tolerant if they could just get inside each other's skin or walk a mile in each other's shoes.

A Patch of Blue (1965)

(ELEM / MID / HIGH) — Contains some very interesting scenes that can show children what it might be like to be blind. The theme of racial prejudice also links to ways of seeing and thinking.

The Point (1971)

(ELEM / MID / HIGH) — This animated story tells about Oblio, the first and only child with a round head born in the land of Point. Oblio and his dog, Arrow, are banished to the Pointless Forest because they look different.

The Blackboard Jungle (1955)

(ELEM / MID / HIGH) — Fast-forward to the scene when Mr. Dadier uses a movie to reach very difficult students. Examine how the movie motivates and how "Jack and the Beanstalk" becomes a learning experience for these students.

Inherit the Wind (1960)

(ELEM / MID / HIGH) — A dramatization of the celebrated Scopes "monkey" trial, it examines small-town prejudice and the struggle between science and faith. "The right to think is on trial," one attorney declares.

PROVERBS, ADAGES, AND POPULAR EXPRESSIONS

(ELEM / MID / HIGH) — The following list provides proverbs and adages that deal with seeing, thinking, and perception. The list includes simple and sophisticated concepts, and parts of the list could be used at all levels of education. Select several appropriate expressions for discussion. Alternatively the teacher can give the students one or two examples and then have them come up with some of their own.

Seeing is believing

Don't judge a book by its cover

There's more to it than meets the eye

The camera never lies

What you see is what you get

A picture is worth a thousand words

You can't see the forest for the trees

Seek and ye shall find

All that glitters is not gold

Look before you leap

Still waters run deep

A case of the blind leading the blind

Beauty is only skin deep

In the land of the blind the one-eyed man is king

There are none so blind as they who will not see

Mutton dressed as lamb

Your eyes are bigger than your stomach

If thine eye offends thee, pluck it out

A nod is as good as a wink to a blind man

The apple of his eye

VISUALEYES VOCABULARY

Variations on this activity can be developed to expand students' vocabulary by asking them to conceptualeyes word/image, print/picture, and verbal/visual relationships. This exerceyes provides opportunity for encoding and decoding information conveyed iconically. The teacher can duplicate the "Visualeyes Vocabulary" handout (see Figure 3.1) and have students identifeye the "eye" word each picture refers to. Students can use dictionaries to locate the meaning of words they are unfamiliar with. The expanded list of "eye" words can be given to individual students, who must then draw a picture to represent one of the words and seeing if other class members correctly interpret the image. Students may also be asked to come up with their own list of "eye" words.

Expanded Vocabulary List

liquifies	tribalize	occupies	prophesize
pasteurize	humanize	televise	fortifies
exercise	memorize	individualize	hospitalize
crystalize	terrorize	stabilize	fossilize
dignifies	legalize	testifies	hypnotize
harmonize	popularize	standardize	economize

Fig. 3.1. Visual*eyes* vocabulary.

Each drawing on this page represents a word that ends with the syllable "eyes," although it may be spelled "-ize" or "-ise."

Look carefully at each panel and see if you can guess what the word is. A dictionary might be useful.

Then reverse the process: Think of words that end with "eyes"/-ize and develop a picture to illustrate each word.

Answers

a. canonize
b. unionize
c. advertise
d. deputize
e. immunize
f. lionize
g. equalize

PICTURE PAIRS

For this activity, the teacher can duplicate the half page above the answers on the "Picture Pairs" handout (see Figure 3.2) and have the class work on the project. Other examples to develop could include stout trout, legal eagle, sunk junk, cranky yankee, and spruce goose.

REBUS

The rebus is an interesting visual exercise that can be used to develop vocabulary skills. It can also be linked to the study of hieroglyphs and pictographs. Kidstamps in Ohio (P.O. Box 18699, Cleveland Heights, OH 44118. 1-800-727-5637) has an excellent rebus kit of rubber stamps, with each image designed by a leading illustrator of children's books. These can be time-saving for teachers and fun for children, but there is no substitute for conceptualizing your own image and creating it from linoleum block or other materials.

Introduce your students to the concept of the rebus by using an appropriate example from the "Rebus" handout (see Figure 3.3). See if they can correctly translate the example. Give them more practice and then have each student write a story using a rebus. Ask other members of the class to translate the stories to see how successfully the students communicate through visuals.

STORYBOARDING

Duplicate the "Storyboard Squares" handout (see Figure 3.4) and utilize it throughout this book for exercises related to visualization and communication. It can be used in activities related to advertising, television, and motion pictures. It can also be used for further verbal/visual exercises such as those found in this chapter.

Fig. 3.2. Picture pairs.

Each picture on this page represents an idea that has been expressed visually. The answer to each picture consists of two words that rhyme. Sometimes slang or incorrect pronunciation is used to achieve the rhyme. See if you can correctly identify the ideas expressed in the illustrations, and then try to draw your own picture. A good place to start would be with a picture to represent the phrase *soggy doggy*.

Answers

a. mobster lobster
b. mouse house
c. beaver fever
d. flower tower
e. cryin' lion
f. narrow sparrow

Fig. 3.3. Rebuses.

Answers

#1 I can see that you are happy.
#2 To be or not to be ...
#3 A stitch in time saves nine.

Fig. 3.4. Storyboard squares.

SUPPORT ORGANIZATIONS

The following organizations provide support materials and strategies that can be utilized in developing media literacy, visual literacy, and critical thinking skills. Additional organizations and resources are contained at the end of each subsequent chapter.

Action for Children's Television, 20 University Rd., Cambridge, MA 02138

Dedicated to improving television programming for children. Publications are useful for teachers, media specialists, librarians, and parents.

Association for Media Literacy, 40 McArthur St., Weston, Ontario, M9P 3M7 Canada (416)-923-7271.

An important contact group. North America's most successful media education association. They can provide the whys, whats, and how-tos necessary to develop media literacy courses and competencies. Membership approximately $20 Canadian.

Center for Media and Values, 1962 S. Shenandoah St., Los Angeles, CA 90034 (213)-559-2944.

A nonprofit educational organization. Publishes *Media and Values*, a very professional quarterly magazine for media awareness. Each issue centers on a specific theme. Individual membership approximately $30.

Cultural Information Service, P.O. Box 786, Madison Square Garden Station, New York, NY 10519.

Excellent planning resource. Subscription runs approximately $60 per year. Publishes *Living Room Learning* and *Reviews and Overviews*. Excellent for library media specialists because it announces upcoming broadcasts and provides tie-ins and other instructional links for integrating programs into curriculum.

International Visual Literacy Association, Virginia Tech, Educational Technologies LRC, Old Security Building, Blacksburg, VA 24061-0232.

Membership approximately $25. Publishes *The Journal of Visual Literacy* and regular newsletter. Archives housed at University of Arizona, Tempe. Holds conferences in different area of country each year, usually in October. Research and publications are very valuable but has had limited success in attracting membership and support of classroom teachers.

National Telemedia Council, 120 E. Wilson St., Madison, WI 53703 (608)-257-7712.

Membership approximately $20. Founded in 1953 to promote a media-wise society. Main focus currently is *Project Look-Listen-Think-Respond*, a classroom activity that uses students' television knowledge to foster critical viewing and thinking skills across the curriculum. Kits and guidelines available for participating teachers, media specialists, and librarians.

Strategies for Media Literacy, 1095 Market St., Suite 410, San Francisco, CA 94103 (415)-621-2911.

A small but very interesting and influential organization with a regular newsletter containing practical activities and resources.

REFERENCE LIST

Baran, Stanley, (1976). Sex on TV and Adolescent Sexual Self Image. *Journal of Broadcasting*, 20:1, 61-88.

Benson, George, (1982). Visual Media Utilization at the Kentucky School for the Deaf. In Roberts Braden and Alice Walker (eds.), *Readings of the 13th Annual Conference of the International Visual Literacy Association*. Bloomington: Indiana University Press. Pp. 259-60.

Brizee, Sandra L., (1983). Plains Indian Pictographic Painting: More Than Art. In Roberts Braden and Alice Walker (eds.), *Readings from the 14th Annual Conference of the International Visual Literacy Association*. Blacksburg: Virginia Polytechnic Institute and State University. Pp. 69-76.

Brown, Lyva Morgan, (1975). Sexism in Western Art. In Jo Freeman (ed.), *Women: A Feminist Perspective*. Palo Alto, Calif.: Mayfield Publishers. Pp 309-21.

Considine, David M., (1986). Visual Literacy and Children's Books: An Integrated Approach. *School Library Journal*, September, 38-42.

DeVaney, Ann, and Alejandra Elenes, (1990). "Square One": Television and Gender. In Roberts Braden et al. (eds.), *Readings of the 21st Annual Conference of the International Visual Literacy Association*. Conway: University of Central Arkansas. Pp. 39-49.

Dobbs, Barbara, (1988). Video Friend or Foe: How to Teach the Reading of Seeing. In Roberts Braden et al. (eds.), *Readings from the 19th Annual Conference of the International Visual Literacy Association*. Blacksburg: Virginia Polytechnic Institute and State University. Pp. 12-16.

Durden, Joan, (1989). Masks as a Vehicle of Communication. In Roberts Braden et al. (eds.), *Readings of the 20th Annual Conference of the International Visual Literacy Association*. Blacksburg: Virginia Polytechnic Institute and State University. Pp. 113-16.

Elkind, David, (1981). *The Hurried Child*. Reading, Mass.: Addison-Wesley.

Entin, Alan D., (1983). The Family Photo Album as Icon: A Family Systems Approach to Reading Photographs. In Roberts Braden and Alice Walker (eds.), *Readings from the 14th Annual Conference of the International Visual Literacy Association*. Blacksburg: Virginia Polytechnic Institute and State University. Pp. 107-13.

Freudiger, Patricia, (1978). Love Lauded and Lamented: Men and Women in Popular Music. *Journal of Popular Culture*, 6:1, 1-10.

Frith, Simon, and Angela McRobbie, (1979). Rock and Sexuality. *Screen Education*, 31, 3-22.

Garoian, Charles, (1989). Teaching Visual Literacy through Art History in High School. In Roberts Braden et al. (eds.), *Readings from the 20th Annual Conference of the International Visual Literacy Association*. Blacksburg: Virginia Polytechnic Institute and State University. Pp. 151-59.

Gaylean, Beverly, (1983). Guided Imagery in the Curriculum. *Educational Leadership*, 40:6, 54-58.

Hunter, John Mark, (1989). Visual Literacy and Political Cartoons. In Roberts Braden et al. (eds.), *Readings from the 20th Annual Conference of the International Visual Literacy Association*. Blacksburg: Virginia Polytechnic Institute and State University. Pp. 222-28.

Inge, M. Thomas, (1989). *Comics in the Classroom*. Washington, D.C.: Smithsonian Institution.

Jacobs, Amy, (1983). Visual Confrontation in Working with Chemically Dependent Adolescents. In Roberts Braden and Alice Walker (eds.), *Readings from the 14th Annual Conference of the International Visual Literacy Association*. Blacksburg: Virginia Polytechnic Institute and State University. Pp. 83-85.

Mills, Janet Lee, (1983). Men and Women Speak Different Body Language. In Roberts Braden and Alice Walker (eds.), *Readings from the 14th Annual Conference of the International Visual Literacy Association*. Blacksburg: Virginia Polytechnic Institute and State University. Pp. 49-61.

Nath, Jyan, (1983). The Use of Still Photography as Learning Assistance for the Language Handicapped in the Classroom. In Roberts Braden and Alice Walker (eds.)., *Readings from the 14th Annual Conference of the International Visual Literacy Association*. Blacksburg: Virginia Polytechnic Institute and State University. Pp. 115-19.

Open University, (1976). *Curriculum Organization*. Walton Hall, Milton Keynes: Open University Press.

Ragan, Tillman J., and Judith Blitch, (1983). Visual Literacy and the Microcomputer: Children, the Apple Computer and Logo. In Roberts Braden and Alice Walker (eds.), *Readings from the 14th Annual Conference of the International Visual Literacy Association*. Blacksburg: Virginia Polytechnic Institute and State University. Pp. 209-15.

Ravitch, Diane, and Chester E. Finn, Jr., (1987). *What Do Our 17 Year Olds Know?* New York: Harper & Row.

Salomon, Gavriel, and Tamar Leigh, (1984). Predispositions about Learning from Print and Television. *Journal of Communication*, 34:2, 119-35.

Seidman, Steven, (1984). What's in a Face? Facial Expression as a Key Variable. *Newsletter of the International Visual Literacy Association*, 13:3, 61-64.

———, (1985). Music Videos: Why They're Effective and What We Can Learn from Them. *International Journal of Instructional Media*, 12:1, 61-64.

Sherarts, Karon, (1987). New Approaches in Media Education for Physically Handicapped Adolescents. In Roberts Braden et al. (eds.), *Readings of the 18th Annual Conference of the International Visual Literacy Association*. Commerce: East Texas State University. Pp. 75-86.

Sleeper, M. E., (1975). A Developmental Framework for History in Adolescence. *School Review*, 84:1, 91-107.

Smith, D. Larry, and Nancy L. Smith, (1985). The Visual Medium: A Curriculum Model for Learning, Growth, and Perception Art. *International Journal of Instructional Media*, 12:4, 331-40.

Stewig, John Warren, (1992). Reading Pictures, Reading Text: Some Similarities. *The New Advocate*, 5:1, 11-22.

Taylor, Jenny, and David Laing, (1979). Disco Pleasure: Discourse on Rock and Sexuality. *Screen Education*, 31, 43-51.

Zaccaria, M. A., (1978). The Development of Historical Thinking: Implications for Teaching History. *History Teacher*, 11:3, 323-40.

RECOMMENDED READING

Adams, Dennis, and Mary Hamm. *Media and Literacy: Learning in an Electronic Age.* Springfield, Ill.: Charles C. Thomas, 1989.

Brody, Philip J. A Research Based Guide to Using Pictures Effectively. *Instructional Innovator* (1984) 29:2, 21-22.

Burbank, Lucille, and Dennis Pett. Eight Dimensions of Visual Literacy. *Instructional Innovator* (1983) 28:1, 25-27.

Champion, Dean J. Learning from the Stars: Do Motion Pictures in the Classroom Make a Difference in Student Performance? *Journal of Popular Film and Television* (1987) 15:1, 43-50.

Considine, David M. Movies and Minors. *Top of the News* (1984) 40:3, 253-65.

_____. Popular Music in the Classroom and Collection. *Top of the News* (1986) 42:3, 251-59.

_____. Visual Literacy and the Curriculum: More to It Than Meets the Eyes. *Language Arts* (1987) 64:6, 634-40.

_____. The Video Boom's Impact on Social Studies: Implications, Applications and Resources. *Social Studies* (November/December 1989), 229-34.

Duncan, Barry. Media Literacy at the Crossroads: Some Issues Problems and Questions. *History Social Science Teacher* (Summer 1989).

Elwell, William, and Marta Hess. Visual Literacy and the Social Studies. *Social Studies* (1979) 70:1, 27-31.

Fredericks, Anthony. Mental Imagery Activities to Improve Comprehension. *Reading Teacher* (1986) 40:1, 78-81.

Gantz, Walter, et al. Gratifications and Expectations Associated with Pop Music among Adolescents. *Popular Music in Society* (1978) 6:1, 81-89.

Grady, Michael P. Students Need Media for a Balanced Brain. *Audiovisual Instruction* (1976) 21:9, 46-48.

Greenfield, Patricia Marks. *Mind and Media: The Effects of Television, Video Games and Computers.* Cambridge, Mass.: Harvard University Press, 1984.

Hade, Daniel. Literacy in an Information Age. *Educational Technology* (1982) 22:8, 7-12.

Hendry, Leo, and Helen Patrick. Adolescents and Television. *Journal of Youth and Adolescence* (1977) 6:4, 325-36.

Johnson, Janice. How to See a Visual Perception Problem. *Early Years* (April 1984), 66-68.

Kilpatrick, W. Kirk. McLuhan: Implications for Adolescence. *Adolescence* (1971) 6:22, 235-57.

King, James. Using Media in Teaching. *Teaching at University of Nebraska, Lincoln* (1990) 2:3, 1-3.

Kundu, Mahima Ranjan. Visual Literacy: Teaching Non-Verbal Communication through Television. *Educational Technology* (1976) 16:8, 31-33.

Levin, J. R., and Alan Lesgold. On Pictures in Prose. *Educational Communications and Technology* (1978) 26:3, 233-44.

Lloyd-Kolkin, Donna, and Kathleen Tyner. *Media and You: An Elementary Media Literacy Curriculum.* Englewood Cliffs, N.J.: Educational Technology Publications, 1990.

Orderindi, Namu. Pictorial Assessment and Selection. *Audiovisual Instruction* (1975) 20:1, 20-26.

Politis, John. Rock Music's Place in the Library. *Drexel Library Quarterly* (1983) 19:1, 78-92.

Robinson, Rhonda. Learning to See: Developing Visual Literacy through Film. *Top of the News* (1984) 40:3, 267-76.

Rubin, Alan. The New Media: Potential Uses and Impact of the New Technologies for Children's Learning. *Educational Technology* (1982) 22:12, 5-9.

Salomon, Gavriel, and Akiba Cohen. Television Formats, Mastery of Mental Skills, and the Acquisition of Knowledge. *Journal of Educational Psychology* (1977) 69:5, 612-19.

Sharan, Yael, and Shlomo Sharan. Group Investigation Expands Cooperative Learning. *Educational Leadership* (1989) 47:4, 17-21.

Spillman, Carolyn, Jean Clayback Linder, and Frances Goforth. Visual Communication in the Classroom: Concepts and Applications. *Contemporary Education* (1983) 54:4, 295-98.

Tyson, Harriet, and Arthur Woodward. Why Students Aren't Learning Very Much from Textbooks. *Educational Leadership* (November 1989), 14-17.

Chapter 4

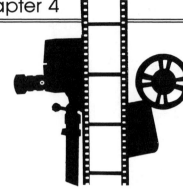

Making the Living Room a Learning Room by Using TV Effectively

> This instrument can teach, it can illuminate; yes, and it can even inspire. But it can do so only to the extent that humans are determined to use it to those ends. Otherwise it is merely wires and lights in a box.
>
> —Edward R. Murrow

WHY STUDY TELEVISION?

Television has now been present in the nation's classrooms for almost half a century, and the growth of the video industry continues to increase the potential impact of imagery in instruction. Despite this, we have still done little as educators to help children become critical consumers, active viewers, and clear thinkers able to understand television's impact on their own lives, on the lives of their friends and families, and on U.S. society as a whole.

Although students now routinely watch television and videos at school, their formal education tends to ignore the informal learning that takes place at home when they watch television. Many of our students have viewed some television before coming to school in the morning, and many go home from school to an afternoon and evening of television viewing. Research suggests that by the time they begin school, and at the very time when their brains are at their most formative developmental stage, young children have been exposed to 5,000 hours of television. Ignoring the presence and power of television in their lives is equivalent to ignoring the students themselves. Television is much more than mere entertainment for these students: It is their window on the world, with the potential to shape and influence their perceptions of that world, their moods, their attitudes, their language acquisition, and their concentration span, among other factors. Despite the enormous potential television has for influencing students, our education system has done very little to address this medium and its impact.

> Not enough time is spent in our schools helping students to cope with the symbology of visual media; few relationships between television viewing at home and teaching in the school have been established. The resultant "cultural gap" leads to misunderstandings between students and teachers as well as reduced learning (Barton and Miller 1977, 229).

Teachers need to be aware of how much their students watch television and what they watch. Drawing on these existing viewing patterns and behaviors provides a valuable insight into our students' lives beyond the classroom. It provides a common reference source that can be a potential teaching tool, enabling us to integrate the living room into the classroom. By utilizing children's existing viewing patterns and perceptions we can begin to shift the focus from how much they watch and what they watch and place emphasis instead on how they watch. By emphasizing the process, not simply the programs, teachers can begin to develop both critical thinking and critical viewing skills. The most basic concept children can think about is the way television constructs culture. *The Harvard Educational Review* has said that television "does contribute to forming this social system" (Leifer 1974). Television is clearly much more than mere entertainment. It creates an electronic environment, a social milieu, a familiar family. "To the extent that television does not reflect reality, it socializes children into a fictitious social system, where criminals are always caught … minorities and the elderly are rarely seen and problems are solved in an hour and things usually work out for the best" (Leifer et al. 1974, 221).

WHAT DO WE MEAN BY TELEVISION?

Television is much more than radio with pictures. It is a social cement binding together a disparate and diverse population through its constant display of myths, messages, and consumer products. It is an audiovisual opiate for a "soma" society seeking escape and distraction from the pressures of life. It is a vast agent of propaganda, a major marketing mechanism, and a constant source of both information and misinformation. The programs and pictures it broadcasts domestically and internationally shape our perceptions of ourselves and influence the way other countries and cultures perceive us. When "Dallas" developed the cliffhanger "Who Shot J.R.?" it was accorded the status of a *Time* magazine cover and attracted worldwide attention. When the surrealistic "Twin Peaks" asked, "Who killed Laura Palmer?" it generated a widely publicized cult following, and viewers held regular "Twin Peaks" parties with various accoutrements from the plot. When "Thirtysomething" featured a hostile takeover of an advertising agency, *USA Today* covered the story in its business pages, not in the entertainment section. The made-for-TV movies "The Burning Bed" and "Small Sacrifices" resulted in "copycat" crimes when adult viewers imitated the behavior they had seen on the screen. "L. A. Law's" Jimmy Smits, who merely plays a Hispanic attorney, was asked to address members of the Hispanic Bar Association. Clearly, television affects every area of our lives. The standards and values it espouses, the social behavior it models, and the stories and stereotypes it repeats say much about the culture that both produces and consumes it. At times television's vision and values can capture the nation's heart and mind. Describing "Northern Exposure," *TV Guide* called the town of Cicely and its inhabitants, "a radiant, many-layered, slightly magical place, as achingly real and yet just-out-of-reach as a dream you start to forget as soon as you wake up" (Powers 1991, 7-8).

Opponents of television have traditionally argued that it discourages children from reading, that it promotes violence, or that it makes children either passive or hyperactive. Although such claims are worth exploring, they share the common problem of being product- rather than process-centered. These claims place undue emphasis on the machine and ignore the method and manner in which we use television. The result is a climate of confrontation rather than cooperation between educators and the entertainment industry. This often leads to attempts to legislate, limit, or control both the production of particular programs and children's viewing habits. Although such measures may have validity, they emphasize legislation over education and represent a form of censorship that does nothing to help young viewers become active critical consumers capable of analyzing and interpreting media messages. Claims that television creates particular attitudes, promotes particular perceptions, or causes particular behavior also tend to ignore the whole issue of just what we mean when we use the term *television*. During the 1980s sweeping changes in technology transformed television. Today the term can be used in a variety of different ways, each of which means something completely different. Recognizing the changing nature of television technology is the beginning of acknowledging its dominant role in society and the need for schools to incorporate the medium into the curriculum.

Ten Ways to Think about TV

Agent of Socialization. Television has long been regarded as a window on the world that socializes young viewers into the views and values of the dominant culture. In a multicultural society, it is crucial that media models provide fair, accurate, and representative images of all groups in the culture. How television depicts gender roles, occupations, religious groups, races, nationalities, the elderly, the impaired, and the disadvantaged, among other groups, can in large part determine society's response to these groups. When such depictions are accurate and informative, teachers can use them to help students understand society. If the representations are biased, unrepresentative, or distorted, teachers need to put them in context and teach students to critically evaluate the images and to locate alternative sources of information.

Source of News and Information. Television has replaced the newspaper as the main source of information in our culture. That information comes in many forms, including news programs, news magazines, current affairs broadcasts, news specials, talk shows, and the widely condemned "trash" or "tabloid" TV. News specials, documentaries, and other information-oriented broadcasts now frequently make transcripts and videotape copies available, providing schools with a potentially invaluable resource. Although the evening news may cover the same stories as a newspaper or magazine, television's form and style invariably shape the way viewers receive and perceive the story. Teachers can help students understand the roles played by print, picture, visual, and verbal presentations of a story. Reading and analyzing news is covered in chapter 6 of this book.

Merchandising Mechanism. Commercial television exists because of commercials. Programs are presented to provide advertisers with the opportunity to address a vast audience. Various technological and programming developments have led to the creation of shop-at-home services, which are potentially beneficial to shut-ins but may also represent another step toward the cabled cocoon as more and more of us withdraw from society into the safety of our high-tech homes. Those who do venture forth are increasingly likely to find video vendors on elevators, escalators, store shelves, and even supermarket shopping carts. Whether these new marketing mechanisms will actually benefit shoppers or induce consumer confusion and media manipulation depends upon how prepared we are to understand the increasingly sophisticated media marketing techniques. Advertising, including television commercials, is analyzed in greater detail in chapter 5 of this book.

Political Process and Propaganda. Television technology has increasingly become an agent for patriotic propaganda and televised terrorism. The concept is hardly new. Demonstrators during the 1968 Chicago Democratic convention chanted, "The whole world's watching," and used pictures of police brutality to make their point. Many observers believe the United States lost the Vietnam War because it was the first "video," or "living room," war and people were persuaded by pictures that undermined official government statements. When the United States invaded Grenada, the military controlled media coverage of the operation. Throughout the 1980s, various governments, including those of Israel and South Africa, attempted to control the way television covered events in those countries. The massacre of civilians in Tiananmen Square during 1989 and the resulting worldwide condemnation of China again emphasized the power of the picture in the political process. The collapse of Eastern Europe's Soviet bloc can in many ways be attributed to the power of the picture as portable video cameras, VCRs, and various new technologies provided alternative media messages to those of the traditional, state-controlled media. The impact of television technology on foreign affairs and international politics was the subject of a 1989 "Nightline" broadcast called "Revolution in a Box." During the 1990 Gulf crisis, Iraq's Saddam Hussein used television as a tool of terrorism, broadcasting pictures of the women and children he held hostage in an attempt to influence public opinion. Beyond the international scene, television also remains an integral part of the democratic process. It allows the nation to watch congressional deliberations and special hearings, provides access at the local level for diverse individuals and groups to express their own ideas, broadcasts town meetings and school board meetings, and generally makes the process of government more visible to the electorate. The high cost of television and the expectations we have of the medium also make it a potentially harmful agent of the political process. Although it can promote democracy by exploring issues and giving free expression to candidates and individuals, it can also stifle debate, replace issues with images, and substitute slick slogans and advertising strategies for serious discussion and examination.

Teaching and Training. The video revolution has brought major growth in the home education market and in the application of video in teaching and training in all areas of society. Airline emergency procedures have become much more meaningful now that video is frequently used to demonstrate procedures, replacing the previous instructions from flight attendants that lacked clear visuals. Cybervision represents a new approach to training for a range of sports including tennis, golf, and skiing. Ski schools now frequently use video to help clients ascertain their own skiing ability, and video provides instant feedback for sporting enthusiasts in areas as diverse as white-water rafting, golf, and skiing. For the less active, self-help and do-it-yourself videos now address everything from potty training to plumbing. Although these applications of television technology are potentially beneficial, consumers have almost no criteria by which to effectively evaluate such products before purchase.

Educational Video. The home market is being inundated with instructional programs, and so, too, is the classroom. Cable and satellite technologies have brought the growth of educational and instructional programming, including the Arts and Entertainment Network, the Learning Channel, and the Discovery Channel. Some of these ventures, such as Whittle Communications' "Channel One" newscast, have been controversial, resulting in litigation between educators who want to use the broadcasts and educational administrators who oppose it. In many such cases, the real issue has less to do with the programs themselves than it does with the media mindsets we bring to them. The VCR is a deceptive technology. It entered the home market in the 1980s more rapidly than television did in the 1950s. The potential danger of our familiarity with the technology is that we mistake consumer convenience for instructional effectiveness. Teachers and media specialists need to be particularly wary of companies who transfer former filmstrips and slide/tape programs to video format. Although this strategy makes sense for the producers, it is potentially harmful in the classroom. Filmstrips and slide programs are designed for larger screen projection than is possible when they are reduced to video format. Filmstrips and slide programs usually produce single, still, clear pictures, which are particularly useful for objectives involving visual recognition, recall, and discrimination. These factors may all be impeded when these programs are transferred to video in the name of convenience.

Surveillance, Security, and Law Enforcement. Television technology is increasingly being used for security and surveillance purposes, from eye-in-the-sky spy satellites to video cameras mounted in banks, businesses, and homes. Recent applications of the technology have included new forms of evidence that have resulted in lower legal costs and less congested court calendars. This has been particularly effective in the case of drunk driving arrests that were videotaped by cameras mounted in the front of police vehicles. Applying television technology in this manner has obvious administrative and managerial benefits, but continued use of these techniques must be weighed carefully to protect individual privacy. The issues raised are ethical and Orwellian, and as a culture we need to understand the implications of a society in which surveillance is no longer questioned. Although video can be used by security forces as an agent of control, it can also be turned against those forces. In March 1991, the nation witnessed Los Angeles police officers beating a man who offered no resistance. That incident was captured on videotape by an amateur, which provided irrefutable evidence of the event. The spread of citizen surveillance was featured in the July 22, 1991, cover story of *Newsweek*, which announced the arrival of "video vigilantes."

Televangelism. The growth of television technology has brought religion and church services into the homes of thousands of Americans. For the infirm, shut-ins, and other groups who cannot get about easily, these broadcasts provide a potentially important service. But like so much television technology, the benefits must be considered against the potential damage. The televangelist scandals of the 1980s revealed financial corruption and fraud, often at the expense of thousands of Americans who had given generously even when they could not afford it. But the problems ran deeper than that and revealed the danger when sophisticated technology is used to address and manipulate an audience that is vulnerable because it is visually illiterate. Sophisticated mailing list techniques and a fusion of computer and television technology enabled religious broadcasters to target potential converts and contributors. Despite the doctrine of separation of church and state in this country, some of these broadcasters defined social and political agendas, registered new voters, and attempted to influence political platforms at the state and national levels. The recruiting and persuasion were often done through propaganda that played on the fears and uncertainties of the television congregation. Televangelism, perhaps more than any other development, provides evidence that any movement toward media literacy and critical viewing skills should address the adult population as well as the young people in our schools.

Family Member, Friend, and Companion. For many Americans television is and has been for some time like a member of their family. It provides a constant background presence in our homes and is often highly visible in our living rooms, kitchens, and bedrooms. Television programming often influences decisions about where we eat, when we eat, and even what we eat. Meal times are often planned around the evening's programs, and the microwave, like TV dinners of the 1950s, provides instant feeding for the fast food, instant gratification culture that television has nurtured. Studies suggest that television has contributed to a decline in family communication, and Neil Postman (1985) argues that it has eliminated serious discourse in our culture. Advances in technology have made television omnipresent in our society, so that it has become almost a constant companion. It is now so portable that it can go with us wherever we are. Campers in a pristine national park or forest can watch television, staying in touch with the very culture from which they are seeking a vacation. Spectators at a baseball or football stadium often have their eyes glued to their portable televisions, as though actually attending the event somehow is no longer real enough. There is little doubt that developments in telecommunications will continue to increase the role of video in our lives. For example, we may soon be able to see the person we are talking to when we make a phone call. Whether these developments make our culture more human and our communication more personal and meaningful will depend less on the technology than on the way we use it.

Vintage Video. Television has experienced both a "golden age" and a "vast wasteland." Today there is much evidence of broadcast television in transition, with strange but innovative programming such as "Twin Peaks" and "Cop Rock" responding to the challenges of cable and the VCR. Those not satisfied with current broadcast fare have the opportunity to return to the past by buying or renting the increasing number of vintage television programs now available on videotape. These include episodes of "Gunsmoke," "Bonanza," "The Outer Limits," "The Twilight Zone," "Star Trek," "The Honeymooners," "I Love Lucy," and "The Beverly Hillbillies." These programs serve as historical evidence of the culture that both created and consumed them. Properly used, they can be effective teaching tools to show the state of technology in the 1950s and 1960s, as well as examples of fashion, furniture, consumer appliances, and prices, and to provide extraordinary insight into the views, values, and attitudes of the characters and culture.

GETTING STARTED: Who Watches What?

America's fascination with television is well documented. Our children spend more time watching television than they do attending school, and the only thing we spend more time doing than watching television is sleeping. In 1983 Maurine Doerken, in *Classroom Combat: Teaching and Television*, observed that 9- to 12-year-olds attended school for 980 hours per year compared to 1,230 hours spent watching television. By their high school graduation, most students have had some 11,000 hours in the classroom, compared to 22,000 hours in front of the television set.

By the mid-1980s, Nielsen statistics indicated how this viewing behavior broke down over age groups. Children ages 2 to 5 watched 28 hours and 15 minutes per week. Six- to 11-year-olds watched 27 hours and 22 minutes, and 12- to 17-year-olds watched 23 hours and 20 minutes. The decline in viewing time as students get older is related to their increased freedom, greater social activities, and more time spent away from home. The fact that preschoolers watch the set almost 5 hours a day represents a major part of their waking hours and suggests how potentially powerful television is in their lives.

A 1990 report in *American Demographics* indicated that educational attainment was related to television viewing, with high school dropouts watching almost 20 hours of television a week as compared to college graduates, who watched less than 12 hours per week.

A 1988 longitudinal study conducted by the Department of Education found that eighth graders spent 21.2 hours per week watching television compared to 5.5 hours per week spent on homework.

According to Nielsen results for 1989:

- the average family watched television 7.2 hours per day.

- the United States now has 92 million TV households, double the figure for a decade ago.

- the most popular viewing time is 8:30-9:00 P.M.

- the most popular programs are sitcoms.

- the most popular night for viewing is Sunday.

- the least popular night for viewing is Friday.

In 1990, *USA Today* reported that 67 percent of U.S. homes had VCRs. In a survey of parents' attitudes about television, the paper reported that:

- 70 percent believed television broadened children's horizons.

- 70 percent said it helped develop children's vocabulary.

- 66 percent said it promoted violent behavior.

- 62 percent said it promoted sexism.

- 60 percent said it inhibited creative thinking.

These findings are useful for teachers, media specialists, and administrators as they address media literacy and its place in the curriculum. The results suggest that if the issue were raised in school board or PTA meetings, for example, there would be enough potential parental concern about television to warrant addressing the issue in the classroom. It is important to note that this study of parental attitudes about television reflects our ambiguity as a culture, recognizing both the potential benefits and the potential detriments of the medium. Harnessing these feelings by developing strategies for the classroom and the living room is the real challenge.

Positive Programs. Although it has been suggested that television programs may promote violence and sexism, it is also recognized that television can broaden children's horizons. Television can provide information about particular issues or topics or can model positive behaviors, which can be influential with young viewers, especially when such behaviors are modeled by characters they identify with. A glance at major prime-time programs quickly reveals that they frequently address issues that can help young people as they think about themselves and their role in society. This can happen more effectively when adults view with young people and put the programs in context through discussion and questioning.

- "Cagney and Lacey" dealt with contraception, abortion, and alcoholism.

- "Designing Women" has dealt with sex education, AIDS, sexism, and southern stereotypes in the media.

- "Doogie Howser, M.D." has dealt with contraception, virginity, premarital sex, AIDS, father-son relationships, and adolescent females' self-image and fear of obesity.

- "Family Ties" produced an award-winning episode in which Alex Keaton confronted the death of a teenage friend.

- "Growing Pains," like many prime-time programs, addressed the issue of teen drunk driving as an ongoing theme over several episodes.

- "Head of the Class" covered illiteracy and peer pressure, among other topics of relevance to young viewers.

- "The Hogan Family" featured a story on apartheid.

- "Life Goes On" has focused attention on Down's syndrome and addressed censorship.

- "Murphy Brown" has developed episodes on recycling and alcoholism.

- "Roseanne" dealt with a teenage girl's response to her first menstrual cycle.

- "Thirtysomething" featured ovarian cancer in several episodes.

- "The Wonder Years" continually addresses peer pressure and adolescent rites of passage.

Although no longer in production, reruns of programs such as "Head of the Class" continue to offer new viewers images of students and schooling. Producers attempted to depict learning in a positive light and offered a depiction of professions such as teacher and principal for students to examine.

Sensitive programs such as "The Wonder Years" offer young viewers a chance to empathize with characters and examine their own relationships with family and the peer group.

IS THE MESSAGE SENT THE ONE THAT IS RECEIVED?

It is not enough for television programs merely to deal with particular issues and topics. As educators, we have to understand the conditions under which our students can learn from such programs and the ways in which the strategies and activities we develop can facilitate learning. Emphasis must be placed on the process, not just the product. Teachers must function as instructional intermediaries between the programs and the students. Often this does not happen. In 1991, a study of "Channel One" conducted by the Southeastern Educational Improvement Laboratory in Research Triangle Park found that many teachers were not incorporating discussion of the news broadcasts or the advertisements into their classes. Most students who watch "Channel One" or "CNN Newsroom" "answer questions about current affairs no better than those who do not view such programs, *unless teachers reinforce the broadcasts with classroom discussions*" (*Winston Salem Journal* 1991, 8).

Exposure to a television program, like exposure to a filmstrip or a film in the classroom, does not necessarily result in acquisition, comprehension, or retention of the key concepts or ideas covered in the program. Learning may be incidental. Young viewers may give only selected attention to parts of the program, ignoring other aspects. Audiences are also capable of filtering, rejecting parts that do not correspond with their existing schema and conceptions and embracing only those that confirm their beliefs and values. In the classroom, cueing and retrieval strategies supported by effective post-screening discussion and follow-up can help students more critically process the material. In the informal environment of the living room, one of the major ways children process what they watch is through observational learning. In the real world, children learn through direct observation of other people. But the media also model behavior through symbolic representations in the form of the make-believe characters who populate the television world. Without consciously recognizing that they are learning, children often go through three stages: being exposed to a behavior, then acquiring the behavior, and finally accepting or acting upon the behavior. One striking example of television's impact on young viewers who successfully imitated modeled behavior is the case of "Rescue 911." In September 1990, "Entertainment Tonight" reported the cases of several children who had performed rescues by imitating what they had seen on the program. Six-year-old Scottie Gantt performed a water rescue; nine-year-old Kristy saved her sister from choking on a piece of candy; and nine-year-old Tyler Granlund used CPR techniques to save his brother, who was suffering an allergic reaction.

Seeing Saves

(ELEM/MID) — Tell students about the children who learned first aid techniques from watching television. Ask them to make a list of things they have learned from television programs such as these. Give them a helping hand by creating simple headings such as People, Places, and Events. If they have some misconceptions, use this as part of the lesson. Try to find out how TV shaped these ideas and then help students examine and correct them.

A Student Television Viewing Survey

(ELEM/MID/HIGH) — The "Student Television Viewing Survey" handout (see Figure 4.1) is a useful and simple data-gathering tool that can be used with individual students, single classes, or entire school populations to ascertain how much time students spend watching television and what they watch. Until we have the answer to these questions, we are ignorant about the role television plays in students' lives, and we are unable to tap into their existing viewing patterns to enable them to process their viewing more effectively. Once we are aware of what our students routinely watch, we can attempt to develop instructional tie-ins. We can find either literature and reference materials that address student preferences as expressed in the choice of programs or in-depth curriculum materials now routinely available from groups such as the Cultural Information Service.

The survey also allows us to understand viewing conditions because students record whether they view the program alone or in the company of family and friends. This information can be useful in trying to develop parental support and involve them in the concept of critical viewing at home. By modifying the survey, teachers

Fig. 4.1. Student television viewing survey.

Name _____ Age _____ Date _____

In each time slot, insert the name of the program or programs you viewed. If you did not view, leave the slot blank. Next to the program name, write the letter **A** if you watched alone, **B** with your brother/s, **S** with your sister/s, **D** with your dad, **M** with your mom, **P** if you watched with one parent and another child, **F** if you watched with friends.

Time	Monday	Tuesday	Wednesday	Thursday	Friday	Saturday	Sunday
7 A.M.-8							
8 A.M.-9							
9 A.M.-10							
10 A.M.-11							
11 A.M.-Noon							
Noon-1 P.M.							
1 P.M.-2							
2 P.M.-3							
3 P.M.-4							
4 P.M.-5							
5 P.M.-6							
6 P.M.-7							
7 P.M.-8							
8 P.M.-9							
9 P.M.-10							
11 P.M.-Midnight							
Midnight-1 A.M.							
Total per day							
Total per week							

can also attempt to find out why children watch TV. For example, do they watch for escape, entertainment, information, relaxation, or company? The survey can be taken home and kept as a journal that records viewing behavior for a week, or teachers may prefer to hand out *TV Guide* and newspaper listings of television programs so the assignment can be completed in class.

This simple instrument can be kept as part of student records. It may provide some correlation for teachers when they compare high and low academic achievers with high and low viewing profiles. It can also be a useful pre-program instrument for teachers wishing to influence both what students watch and how much they watch. A second survey completed after a critical viewing skills or media literacy unit, for example, might show some changes in these areas.

TV or Not TV

(ELEM / MID / HIGH) — TV is often blamed for the following:

making students passive

promoting violence

concentrating on the negative

stressing materialism

making children hyperactive

discouraging reading

reducing concentration span

promoting stereotypes

Ask students to develop a list of all the positive and negative things they can think of about television. Have older students consider whether these things are actually caused by television or by the way people use television. High school students could research the topic and then debate it.

No Television

(ELEM / MID) — Have students describe how their lives would be different without television. What would they do with all the extra time? Would their lives be better or worse? Some students might volunteer to go without television for a week and report all the changes that result.

IT'S NOT WHAT THEY WATCH, IT'S HOW THEY WATCH

There is no doubt that some television programs are beneficial and educationally effective. Everyone acknowledges the role the Public Broadcasting Service (PBS) and the Children's Television Workshop play in this work. Prime-time programming and other special broadcasts on network television can also be powerful instructional tools. ABC's "The Day After" was a controversial made-for-television movie that widened community discussion of nuclear power and provided teachers with materials and techniques to explore the controversy. In 1990, ABC's "Earth Day Special" brought together an all-star cast and used humor to seriously explore ecological and environmental issues. Television history was made that same year when the three networks all broadcast the same program at the same time. "Cartoon All-Stars to the Rescue" was a 30-minute antidrug animated special featuring leading cartoon characters including the Teenage Mutant Ninja Turtles, Alf, Kermit, Garfield, the Smurfs, Bugs Bunny, and the Chipmunks. Supported by the U.S. First Family, the program was broadcast over

1,000 stations in Canada, the United States, and Mexico, reaching some 20 million children and an estimated two-thirds of the under-twelve population. Animation and education also joined forces in the fall of 1990, when Turner Broadcasting introduced "Captain Planet and the Planeteers," an environmentally based cartoon series. Each episode concluded with a message telling viewers how they can help the environment. Putting its money where its mouth is, Turner Broadcasting contributed 10 percent of all royalties to environmental causes. In a different vein, both "The Wonder Years" and "Doogie Howser, M.D.," featured classroom sequences with characters speaking in French and the use of English subtitles.

Each of these programs represents a positive example of television's role as a teacher. Although we need to recognize this contribution, we must be wary of simply relying on television producers to make good programs. This response renders teachers and students little more than passive consumers dependent on the networks for educational materials. The perception also deprives teachers of the strategies necessary to transform all television viewing into a learning experience. As such it deflects our attention from two key general research findings:

1. As learning facilitators, teachers can have a major impact on what children watch and how they watch.

2. How children watch, including their expectations, attitudes, and attention, affects the way they process television. This includes their ability to recognize, recall, and comprehend information (Salomon and Leigh 1984).

To build on the implications of these findings we must break from traditional mindsets. We must let go of the idea that for children to learn from television the program must be good. That perception is product- rather than process-oriented. By developing effective cueing and retrieval strategies, teachers can turn almost any broadcast into a learning experience. The dominant media mindset to be challenged is the perception that television is somehow in conflict or competition with the classroom. This perception promotes an adversarial relationship between teachers and television, which clearly limits cooperation.

The following list provides some positive suggestions regarding the potential of television.

1. "The classroom and TV should not be in competition with each other" (Ernest Boyer, former U.S. commissioner of education, in Palmer 1988, xxiii).

2. "Rather than abolish television, we should find ways of harnessing its tremendous power in the direction of more effective education for children" (Singer, Singer, and Zuckerman 1981, 16).

3. "For many preschoolers TV may represent the only learning curriculum they have, and we must be sensitive to its vast potential for influencing their future behavior through observation and imitation" (Doerken 1983, 22).

4. "It [television] can be a powerful educational force in children's lives if we carefully select appropriate programs and make sure that children make an effort to reflect on what they watch" (Kelley 1983, ix).

TEACHERS TAKE "AIME" AT THE FRAME

If a positive outlook is a successful beginning to using television as a teaching tool, a positive strategy supported by research is even more successful. Research clearly suggests that teachers can change the level of learning from television viewing by changing children's perceptions and attitudes regarding the viewing experience. This is a potentially revolutionary approach to teaching with television for many teachers because it shifts the emphasis and onus from the program producers and the program content, replacing it with emphasis on instructional strategies and the nature and needs of young learners.

Writing in *Television, Sex Roles and Children*, Kevin Durkin acknowledged the vital role played by the viewer in any learning experience: "As much depends upon what the child brings to TV viewing as upon what it extracts" (1985, 3). Research suggests that what the child brings to television is directly related to what he or she processes from it. Gavriel Salomon and Tamar Leigh and other researchers have introduced the AIME (amount of invested mental energy) model. Essentially the theory suggests that most television viewing engages only part of the attention and participation of the audience, resulting in cognitive economy or shallow processing. To a large degree this half-hearted approach "strongly depends on their preconcepts rather than on any necessary limitations imposed by the medium" (Salomon and Leigh 1984, 122). The implications for teachers are clear: Change the way children think about television and you change the way they process television. At its most basic level, this means that teachers who provide children with cueing and retrieval strategies before any screening will potentially change what and how much a child retrieves from any screening. To do this, preview the program, make sure children expect to learn from the viewing experience, then provide them with key scenes, ideas, or contents you want them to pay attention to and remember. At a more sophisticated level, the theory implies that such viewing behavior and attitudes can be integrated into the child's total viewing experience, changing the way the student perceives and processes all visual media both in the classroom and the living room.

Thoughtful Viewing

(ELEM / MID / HIGH) — These starting exercises can be used at all levels. Select a 5- to 10-minute clip from any television program, including classic programs that are now available on video. Carefully preview the program, taking notes on what happens, the order in which it happens, camera angles, special effects, interesting vocabulary, and so on. Select several of these areas that seem appropriate for your students and then show the clip. You may decide to show the clip without any preparation (cueing and retrieval) to see how students respond to a before-and-after approach. By finding a second clip of relatively similar length and style, you could then see how cueing and retrieval influence students' processing. If you have time or if you can work with other teachers, you might actually set up a control group experiment. You could, for example, divide the class in half, showing each group the same clip but providing one group with prescreening guidelines and the other with none. The benefits of this approach are that the feedback is fairly quick and the input or material shown is exactly the same, which restricts processing differences caused by program differences and not by instructional strategies.

The various elements you might ask students to recall or comprehend will vary with the age group, but the following areas should provide some guidelines.

- Sequencing: Have students develop a list of the sequential order of events.

- Characters: Have students develop a list of the names of the characters in the clip.

- Clues and cues: Can the students find visual and verbal cues that tell them where or when the story is set? This can be something as basic as a calendar in the set; a reference to a day, month, or year; fashions; furnishings; automobiles; or weather.

- Comprehension: If the clip involves a character making a particular decision or choice, ask the students to explain the motivation, causes, or consequences of the action.

- Visual style: See if the students can remember specific techniques, camera angles, and special effects. Can they remember what techniques were used at specific moments in the clip and can they suggest why these devices might have been used?

- Verbal recall: Give students several key phrases from the clip and see if they can correctly identify the character who said the lines. If the program used words or phrases that might not be familiar to your students' vocabulary, see if they remember such words and understand what they mean.

Short exercises like this promote visual discrimination and processing, encourage students to become more critical listeners and viewers, increase their concentration spans, and change their expectations and appreciation of television as a recreational and informational tool.

TELEVISION, READING, AND LITERACY

One of the most frequent charges levelled at television is that it distracts children from print and discourages reading. In *The Plug-In Drug*, Marie Winn describes "the incontrovertible fact that children's viewing experiences influence their reading in critical ways, affecting how much they read, what they read, how they feel about reading, and, since writing skills are closely related to reading experiences, what they write and how well they write" (1977, 65). Yet, there is growing evidence that when properly used, television can foster language acquisition, general knowledge, and extend the viewer's vocabulary, and actually promote interest in reading. In *What Do Our 17 Year Olds Know?*, Diane Ravitch and Chester Finn reported that minority students were likely to gain in these areas from television viewing (1987, 151). In *Television and America's Children*, Edward Palmer argued that "television is not the antithesis of reading; on the contrary, used well it can encourage and instill a life-long love of literature" (1988, 87).

It is not difficult to find examples of television promoting reading. Project Literacy U.S. (PLUS) public service announcements feature young stars such as Neil Patrick Harris ("Doogie Howser, M.D.") and Fred Savage ("The Wonder Years") espousing the joys and benefits of reading. Programs such as "The Reading Rainbow" draw attention to books and stories and promote interest in reading among young viewers. Many students probably received their first exposure to Shakespeare when they saw "Moonlighting's" startling "Atomic Shakespeare" episode, which was based on *The Taming of the Shrew*. Often, reading and writing are addressed as themes in prime-time programs that provide good models for school-age viewers. When Fonzie ("Happy Days") took out a library card in one episode, there was a reported 500 percent increase in applications for library cards, testifying to the enormous impact television can have on the attitudes and behavior of young viewers. More recent programs have integrated the issues of literacy and reading and writing into their plots. "Head of the Class" based an episode on a black basketball star who was illiterate. Caught between the conflicting pressures of athletics and academics, the young man finally faced his problem and stayed on at school to learn to read. "Roseanne" featured an episode in which Darlene found success and self-esteem in writing a poem. An episode of "Brewster Place" entitled "The Poet" recognized the poetry of Margaret Walker and Langston Hughes. The story centered around Lewis Cross, a young black boy whose father died in the Vietnam War. Writing became a cathartic creative process that allowed the boy to express the feelings he had for the father he had lost.

How can classroom teachers utilize television and video to foster literacy? The first step is recognizing that children process different media in different ways, even when the narrative and content remain the same. *Child Development* reported studies with the well-known children's books *A Story, A Story* and *Strega Nona* that indicated that "memory and comprehension were generally better for television than text" (Pezdek et al. 1984, 2080). Video versions of stories, therefore, are a powerful instructional ally capable of strengthening children's ability to both recall and comprehend aspects of a story. Research by W. Collins et al. (1978) shows dramatic improvement in the ability of students in late elementary school years to comprehend narratives presented in movies, television, and other audiovisual formats. Appropriate instructional strategies can help children "read" such programs; the result is "continuous efforts during viewing to select, order and make inferences about the narratives" (Collins et al. 1978, 390). Remember, the emphasis is not on what they watch, but how.

Stories and the Screen

(ELEM/MID)—Marie Winn wrote that reading is "a two way process" but "television is a one way street; the viewers cannot create television images" (1977, 64). However, video technology is now available that enables students to become directors. Have the class act out a scene from one of their favorite stories and videotape it. Or have students write their own stories and videotape the one they like best. You might show students what a script looks like and have them use this writing format. If you want to keep it simple, have the students write stories that can be told visually without words or by using bold printed titles to explain the action.

(HIGH)—Students in Boston studied George Orwell's *1984* and made their own video Newspeak broadcasts, fusing traditional literature with the new visual literacy. In North Carolina, a teacher assigned her class the task of writing a current version of the *Canterbury Tales* with modern-day pilgrims snowed in at an airport.

Students came in costume and acted out the roles. The video camera often acts as an incentive, encouraging students to participate and "star" in their own interpretation of literary episodes.

Recreational viewing of television outside the classroom can also be used to develop reading skills. In their article "Using Television to Teach Specific Reading Skills," Anne Adams and Cathy Harrison said, "If we develop activities that stress the printed words on the TV screen, not only do we gain by having the student complete a specific assignment, but it will also cause the student to notice and perhaps read more of the words on TV" (1975, 48).

Television as Text

(ELEM) — Using television clips from commercials, news broadcasts, or educational programs, develop recognition and reading activities related to any of the following areas:

- consonant cluster recognition
- letter sizes
- dictionary definitions
- meaning of phrases
- alliteration
- maps, charts, and graphics

Having previewed the program, develop worksheets telling students that they will hear or see particular words and graphic devices. The class can work on all the exercises or you can divide students into groups that each focus on different elements of word and phrase usage in the broadcast. Exercises such as these may encourage more active processing of print and graphic information during recreational viewing at home.

CRITICAL VIEWING AND CRITICAL THINKING SKILLS

A growing body of research suggests that if we teach children to become critical viewers, we do more than give them the ability to analyze the construction of isolated images; we also give them the ability to think critically about the composition of the picture, enhancing their ability to read words and worlds. Although many continue to regard television viewing as a passive process, others see the potential of the video age to develop new literacies while reinforcing traditional literacy. A 1990 issue of *The Harvard Education Letter*, for example, reported: "The video screen is helping children develop a new kind of literacy—visual literacy that they will need to thrive in a technological world ... in television or film, the viewer must mentally integrate diverse camera shots of a scene to construct an image of the whole" (Greenfield 1990, 1).

Although television can be used to develop reading skills and promote traditional literacy, it is essential that educators also recognize that television is a unique medium and that to understand it fully we must be conversant with its codes, conventions, and characteristics. That means acknowledging the power of the picture and accepting the fact that seeing is not believing. Jack Solomon said, "Television images lull us into thinking that they are real, that they aren't iconic signs at all but realities. Since we see them, we trust them, often failing to realize that, like all signs, they have been constructed with a certain interest behind them" (1988, 144). Deconstructing these media representations requires relinquishing the powerful and pervasive notion in our culture that seeing is believing, that what you see is what you get. The real issue, however, is whether we "get" (i.e., understand) what we see. The process of reading television addresses some of the following elements.

1. Interpreting the internal content of the program: Essentially this involves a narrative analysis or the ability to recall and recognize what happened and why, with reference to genre codes and conventions.

2. Interpreting the internal construction of the frame: This process focuses attention on media form and style. It includes the overall design and look of the picture and involves such things as camera angles and the various shots used.

3. Recognizing the external forces and factors shaping the program: This industrial/sociological approach looks at issues such as media ownership and control in an attempt to understand how these factors shape programming. A simple example would address the relationship between media ownership and the depiction of women and minorities in the media. Can a patriarchal white industry fairly depict women and minorities?

4. Comparing and contrasting media representations with reality: This might include comparing television's depiction of the Vietnam War ("Tour of Duty," "China Beach") with documentaries or histories of the war. It might also include studying incidents of violence on television compared to national crime statistics or examining the depiction of groups, races, religions, and nationalities to detect stereotyping and bias.

5. Recognizing and responding to the potential impact of television form and content: This focuses attention on appropriate responses and viewing behavior including writing to producers and sponsors, as well as using television more selectively.

Why Bother with Critical Viewing Skills?

For many educators, the concept of interpreting and reading television is a foreign or flimsy one banished to the periphery of learning and accorded at most the status of an educational elective. Like many of our perceptions of the media, this one stems from social attitudes about television and the scant attention given television and media during teacher education.

In one study documented in *The Journal of Communication*, a critical viewing curriculum was developed for children in third through fifth grade. These children were selected because they are traditionally heavy viewers and because "their stage of mental development makes them potentially more vulnerable than children of other ages to TV's influence" (Rapaczynski, Singer, and Singer 1982, 46). Areas of particular vulnerability included the ability to distinguish reality from fantasy, confusion concerning moral judgments, and literal understanding of language. The critical viewing skills curriculum addressed these concerns as well as teaching children to recognize the purpose and power of television in areas such as advertising, stereotyping, and aggression. The study reported that students and teachers both were enthusiastic. The children "enjoyed using their newly acquired knowledge for the class and home activities," and teachers believed the lessons "not only helped to reinforce concepts related to TV, but also promoted language arts skills" (1982, 54).

The development of effective critical viewing skills can also contribute to critical thinking skills, which go beyond the ability to simply remember and understand visual information. Raphael Schneller reported a field experiment with ninth graders and concluded, "Our research has shown that it is indeed possible to change youth's credence attitudes towards mass media generally and specifically towards TV" (1982, 104). Kathy Krendl and Bruce Watkins supported these findings, concluding that "the perceptual set with which the messages are received and interpreted affect how it is processed" (1983, 211). Thus, with appropriate strategies, children can be taught to question the form and content of television. As always, teachers should focus on the context in which children view, including their attitudes and expectations.

Problem Solving from Prime Time

(ELEM/MID)—Most stories, including those on television, center around a character or group of characters confronted with a dilemma that they must resolve. Particularly in crime programs, which are so prevalent on television, the solution to the problem is physical or violent rather than intellectual or rational. These programs, therefore, are potential models of problem solving in society. By directing children's attention to such programs, we can help them develop critical thinking skills for conceptualizing problems and appropriate responses. This can be very effective with adult-oriented programs but also with programs such as "Our House," "The Cosby Show," "My Two Dads," "The Wonder Years," "Head of the Class," "Growing Pains," and "Doogie Howser, M.D.," where students can observe how people their age respond to the problems they face. Older students could battle with the pros and cons of contemporary social issues as covered on television in programs such as "Whose Side Are You On?"

Select a program that features a dilemma and a resolution. Ask students to identify the following elements of the program: conflict, causes, course of action, and consequences. Select a second program. Allow the conflict and the causes to emerge. Stop the program before the course of action and consequences have developed. Break the class down into groups and have them discuss the course of action they would take and the projected consequence. This can be used to support values education projects with strategies such as STAR (stop, think, act, review). These approaches help children think about their own behavior, placing introspection before impulse.

In the article "Problem Solving in TV Shows Popular with Children," typical plot problems or conflicts are divided into five key areas:

physical

property

authority

self-esteem

sentimental romantic (Dominick, Richman, and Wurtzel 1979).

Ask students to think about the main problems or conflicts in their own lives. Have them create a list of these items. Introduce them to the five categories identified in television programs popular with the young. Which problems that your students listed show up in television? Which problems show up in television that don't show up in your class survey? Teachers may wish to develop an anonymous survey for students to encourage them to be more honest. A student facing a physical problem with a bully, for example, will probably not want to admit that in class. The discussion of a similar event found in television may, however, help both the victim and the bully think about their behavior.

Show students an episode from a program or assign them a program to view at home. Ask them to identify conflict, causes, course of action, and consequences and to analyze the presence of particular conflict types in the program.

Encourage parents to watch such programs with their children and discuss the causes and resolutions of conflicts. This is particularly useful when the characters are children or teens or when the characters are role models for young viewers.

TELEVISION GENRES

Students who have already been exposed to literary genres and the traditional elements of folktales and fairytales can apply these concepts to the codes and conventions of dominant television genres. This analytical approach fosters their understanding of the differences and similarities among print and nonprint media. It also promotes critical thinking skills and develops their appreciation of particular genres and themes. By recognizing the conventions of primary genres, students are also more likely to incorporate such concepts into their own writing. In recent years offbeat and experimental programs such as "Cop Rock," "Twin Peaks," "Northern Exposure," and "Dream On" have begun to subvert some traditional formats and formulas.

Defining Genre

(ELEM / MID) — Introduce students to a simple definition of genre as a type of story. Drawing from literature you can introduce them to genre terms such as *fairytale, folktale, fantasy*, and *science fiction*. Have students come up with examples of movie genres such as horror films, westerns, and war movies. Now have the class come up with a list of television genres or program types. This can be done as a class discussion, or you might distribute copies of *TV Guide* or the television section of the newspaper and have the students mark different genres. Make a list with the class of all the main genres and give one specific program for each. Key genres would include cop/crime, sitcoms, westerns, war, science fiction, game shows, soaps, and drama. There are also emerging genres such as "dramedy" that fuse elements of two traditional television formats. Students in elementary school should enjoy working with the fantasy or super-hero genre. "The Flash," "Wonder Woman," and "The Incredible Hulk" are good examples of this type.

What's Your Favorite Program?

(ELEM/MID) — Ask students to make a list of their three favorite television programs. Have each student read his or her list aloud and write the programs on the board until you know the three most popular shows with your students. Then have the students write a list of the reasons they like each program. Typically their lists will include simple expressions such as "it's interesting," "lots of action," "funny," or "I like the people in it." After the students have come up with their lists, write the most common reasons on the board. Then have the students think in-depth about each expression and come up with more detailed reasons why they like the programs. For example, if students think a program is funny, try to have them analyze the source of the humor. This might include characters, situations, or the actual lines characters use. If they like a program for its action, have them describe the action in detail. This might include car chases, fights, or high-tech gadgetry and excitement. What are the most popular genres for the class?

America's Favorite Genres

(ELEM/MID) — Audience research in television comes mainly from the A. C. Nielsen ratings. These ratings provide a sense of the country's viewing preferences. Various techniques are used to develop a representative profile of the nation's favorite programs. These techniques include household diaries and guide meters with 2,000 to 4,000 viewers recording their viewing patterns. One result is the MNA (Multi-Network Area) Reports. These are detailed rating statistics drawn from approximately 70 populous cities. A rating represents a percentage of viewership based on the total number of televisions, and a share is a percentage of viewership based on the number of sets actually in use at the time. It is, therefore, possible for a program to get a low rating but a high share, such as late at night, when fewer sets are in use. Ratings are often reported in newspapers on a weekly basis or at the end of the season. *USA Today* is a good regular source for this information. Provide students with copies of the ratings over one or two weeks and ask them to analyze the list into various genres. You could break the class into groups and have each group look at a different week to develop a list of the most popular genres over two or three months. Media math exercises can also be developed to work with the percentage concepts involved in measuring ratings and shares.

Elements of the Genre

(ELEM/MID) — Each genre plays off well-developed codes and conventions that are familiar to us all. It is this familiarity that accounts for part of the success and continuity of a genre. As members of the audience we bring to the program our own expectations of what will occur. The main elements of a story can be divided into the following categories that students can use to analyze genre patterns and conventions: characters, set/locations, plot, and themes.

(MID/HIGH) — Divide the class into groups, each one responsible for a different television genre. Have each group list the types of characters, locations, plots, and themes they would expect to find in a typical example of their genre. You might facilitate the process by giving an example of this in class. If you are working with older students, you can develop this further by looking at concepts such as two- and three-dimensional characters or stereotyping.

Institutional Comedies and Cop/Crime Genres

(ELEM/MID) — Although genres conform to particular codes and conventions, there is room for interpretation in the presentation of these traditions. In *American Television Genres*, Stuart Kaminsky and Jeffrey Mahan (1985) look at these variations, providing a useful framework for any genre analysis. One interesting area they consider is the distinction between a sitcom and an institutional comedy. In the latter, the humor is based on what we know about the nature of the institution or organization. Introduce students to the term *institutional comedy* and see if they can come up with a list of programs to correspond with the following list of institutions. Have them discuss the way in which the institution influences the characters and the plots. This can also be developed as group work, with teams responsible for reporting on the main characteristics of institutional comedies based on the following settings:

school

hospital

prison

church

mass media, such as TV station, radio station, or newspaper

court

Keep in mind that institutional comedies provide a picture of how particular professions work. Have students examine how fair, accurate, or representative these pictures are.

(MID/HIGH) — The distinction between real life and television's representation of reality is clearly evident in the case of the cop or crime genre. Kaminsky and Mahan assert, "The police tale we see on television is not about real crime and never has been. In television, the overwhelming majority of crimes fall into two categories that are mythically important but exist only in very small numbers in reality" (1985, 56). In the world of television, crimes tend to be committed by organized crime families (the mob) or by lunatics and psychopaths. In television, law enforcement officers often fail to go by the book. A clear distinction exists between the institutionalized procedures of the administrators and the individual initiatives taken by those who are actually responsible for apprehending and arresting criminals. This pattern is evident in "Hill Street Blues" and "Gabriel's Fire" and is both reflected and reinforced in movies such as *The Dead Pool* and *Beverly Hills Cop*. A consistent theme in cop programs has been the buddy or team approach, whether it combines men or women ("Charlie's Angels," "Cagney and Lacey," "Miami Vice"). Perhaps the most startling variation ever tried on the theme came in 1990 when ABC premiered "Cop Rock," created by the maker of "Hill Street Blues" and "L.A. Law." This program fused all the traditional elements of the cop show with elements of MTV and rock opera. Introduce students to the following elements of the cop/crime genre and have them give examples of programs that conform to each.

- The lone hero: Program centers on a single law enforcer.

- The buddy system: Program stresses teamwork and cooperation between two law enforcers. "Starsky and Hutch" was a typical 1970s example, and "Cagney and Lacey" and "Miami Vice" were good examples from the 1980s.

- The ensemble cast: This type of program centers on a large number of key players all engaged in law enforcement. "Hill Street Blues" defined this approach.

- Do it by the book versus sometimes you gotta break the rules: This sets up the conflict between institutionalized and methodical police work versus maverick methods.

- Police officers or private investigators: Hardboiled detective stories of the 1940s created detective characters such as Sam Spade and Phillip Marlowe who have remained part of the popular imagination in television variations such as "The Rockford Files" and "Mannix." In the 1930s, the Thin Man movies introduced Nick and Nora Charles, a sophisticated husband-and-wife team involved in detective capers. Variations of this genre have found their way to television in programs such as "Hart to Hart," "McMillan and Wife," and the zany "Moonlighting." Whereas such investigators use methods reflecting their own personalities, traditional law enforcement officers want "just the facts, ma'am."

- The big city or big island: Classic crime stories evolved out of the gritty milieu of the big city represented in film noir. Television cop shows have tended to conform to this in programs such as "The Streets of San Francisco," "Wise Guy," and "Hill Street Blues." For a variation, not to mention ratings, exotic locations have sometimes been used. In the 1960s, "Surfside Six" used Miami for its exotic appeal and "Hawaiian Eye" was set in the tropics, blazing the trail to be followed by "Hawaii Five-0" and "Jake and the Fatman."

- Psychopaths and syndicates: Kaminsky and Mahan (1985) suggest that most crime on television is committed by maniacs or the mob. In testing this hypothesis, get students to focus on the crime as well as the criminals. One way to do this is to compare television crime statistics with real-world statistics.

(MID/HIGH) — Introduce students to each of these story formats and have them find examples of programs that correspond with each style.

Ask students to view episodes of cop/crime programs such as "L.A. Law" and "Equal Justice" and develop written reports comparing the themes, characters, and formats of the programs.

Historical Comparisons of Genre

(ELEM/MID/HIGH) — This exercise can be used at all levels to develop analytical skills by helping students find differences and similarities in television genres from different periods of time. Older students can extend the process to discover something about the culture in which the programs were produced and consumed. This can include the observation of fashions, furnishings, appliances, and forms of transportation. Such historical evidence can provide observant students with information about our society's values and lifestyles at different times. In addition, students can see how the types of crime have changed or remained constant, how society's sense of humor has changed or remained constant, and how the very look of television has changed. Teachers can approach this lesson by using programs commonly available in syndicated reruns or in special programs such as "Nick at Nite." The availability of vintage videos such as "Gunsmoke," "The Outer Limits," and "I Love Lucy" also provide access to classic programming. In 1991, "Honey, I'm Home" played with this process in a storyline that transported a sitcom family of the early 1960s into the 1990s. The following examples provide a few ways to approach this exercise.

- The western genre: Compare and contrast an episode of "Bonanza" or "Gunsmoke" with an episode of "The Young Riders."

- Sitcoms: Compare and contrast an episode of "I Love Lucy" with an episode of "Perfect Strangers."

- Domestic comedy: Compare and contrast an episode of "Father Knows Best" with "The Cosby Show" or "Married ... with Children."

- Institutional comedy: Compare and contrast an episode of "The Mary Tyler Moore Show" with "Murphy Brown."

- Science fiction: Compare and contrast an episode of "Lost in Space" with "Star Trek: The Next Generation."

The Name Game

(ELEM) — Develop a list of characters and a list of place names from programs you know your students watch. Have the students match the names of the people and places with the programs and locate the places on a map.

A visual variation on this game can be played by cutting out pictures of TV characters from *TV Guide*, newspapers, or magazines. Paste the pictures on cards and laminate them for protection. Assign a different genre for each area of your display board and have students match the characters with the genre. Television themes and songs are now available on record and tape. Play brief excerpts and see how quickly students can name the program and genre to match the song or theme. What moods and feelings do the students sense from the music and lyrics? How do the responses relate to each program?

FACT, FICTION, AND DOCUDRAMA ACTIVITIES

The Vietnam War on Television

(MID/HIGH) — A simple fact that many of us fail to grasp is that many things that we take for granted are simply unknown to our students. Even relatively recent events such as the Vietnam War and Watergate seem like ancient history to our students. Many of their impressions of historical periods, events, or characters have been derived from film and television. But can they understand the Korean War by watching episodes of "M*A*S*H"? Rather than reflecting the Korean conflict, "M*A*S*H" can more accurately be read and interpreted as a reflection of U.S. society in the 1970s. During the 1980s and early 1990s, the Vietnam War found its way to television in the prime-time programs "China Beach" and "Tour of Duty." At times these programs have been compelling, informative, and moving. In one episode of "China Beach," eighteen-year-old Karen set out with a video camera to research the war and her long-lost mother. "The excellent script includes realistic person-on-the-street interviews, exercises in blithe ignorance ... contrasted with moving vignettes as Karen encounters many *Beach* regulars in their new lives" (*USA Today* 1991a, 3D). Whatever the program told viewers about the war, this one episode modeled the power of student-made video projects, suggesting a new definition of the traditional term paper. Rather than just reading about Watergate, the Great Depression, or the civil rights movement, students can utilize video technology to interview those who experienced the time. The Vietnam War as depicted on television provides an excellent case study for exploring the ideas behind the images. As always, the starting point is to find out how students process the images. In what way have these programs shaped students' opinions of the war? How accurate are their impressions? A simple way to explore this is to ask students to write down whatever they know about the Vietnam War. This can include basic headings such as the following:

When was it?

What countries were involved?

What were the issues?

What was the terrain like?

What were the soldiers like on each side?

What type of conditions did they live under?

How popular was the war?

Who won?

Develop a list of the inaccuracies in your students' impressions. Ask them to think about where their impressions came from. If they refer to movies or television, make a specific list of the programs they refer to.

Remember, impressions are often based not only on what is depicted, but also on what is deleted. Are any of the students aware, for example, that Australians fought with Americans in Vietnam and were drafted like Americans? Why is this aspect of international cooperation missing from most media representations of the war? Assign the students reading that will address their misconceptions. Have them compare and contrast the impressions of the war conveyed in "China Beach" and "Tour of Duty" with the impressions made by episodes of PBS's "Vietnam: A Television History."

The Wild West on Television

(ELEM/MID/HIGH)—Although the golden days of the television western ended with "Gunsmoke" and "Bonanza," the current programs "Paradise" and "The Young Riders" continue to provide young people with potentially erroneous impressions of the past. "The Young Riders," for example, deals with the Pony Express and the young Wild Bill Hickok. But how realistic are these images?

Ask students what impressions they have of life in the Old West and where these impressions came from. Select an episode from a television western and see how it supports, reinforces, or repudiates their impressions. Assign readings to convey more accurate information about the West.

Docudramas: Dramatic License or Disinformation?

(MID/HIGH)—Television has shown a distinct proclivity to take real-life stories from recent headlines and turn them into miniseries or made-for-television movies. When they are well made, such programs can be informative and promote public debate and discussion on key issues. Properly researched, written, and produced, these docudramas can actually increase public perception and even contribute to public policy making. The real danger, however, lies in the distortion that can come from the need to utilize dramatic license to compete in the great ratings race. Is the need to get a program finished and on-air in a key ratings period compatible and consistent with authenticity and accuracy? Commenting on "The Atlanta Child Murders" program, *Time* magazine warned of the dangers inherent in the format: "If the only show on a subject is erroneous, corrective information may not sink in when conveyed in the less vivid form of print. Given what misimpressions of history a docudrama may also leave, the furor in Atlanta should provide an impetus for overdue self-restraint" (2/11/1985, 99).

Defining Documentary and Docudrama

(ELEM/MID/HIGH)—Introduce students to the term *docudrama.* Ask them if they can explain what it means. Discuss the difference between a docudrama and a documentary. Remember that although documentaries use actual footage rather than dramatizations, they still represent a particular point of view based on what the producers and the director want to document.

In docudrama, the blend of dramatization and facts has the potential to bring historical and current events and characters to life for students. It also has the ability to simplify crucial issues in the name of dramatic convenience and to reduce characters to stereotypical clichés.

Given that many students tend to think that "seeing is believing," and given the way television promotes docudrama as "true life," we deprive students of critical thinking skills if we prevent them from understanding how and why television docudramas do not conform strictly to reality. The following strategies can be used to help students judge docudramas more carefully.

- Television's time constraints: All stories tend to be told in 2 hours in the case of a made-for-television movie or 4 to 8 hours in the case of a miniseries. How does this time constraint limit television's ability to tell the whole story? What do we mean when we talk about the media's need to "collapse" or "expand" time? This essential element allows students to understand and recognize that although events may have taken place over several months, or even years, the story must be told in a matter of hours. By simply asking students if this time span represented the whole story or picture, you can draw their attention to the fact that some elements were emphasized, some elements were left out, and somebody made those decisions.

- Personal preference, perspective, and prejudice: The someone just referred to is usually the producer or director but it might also be the writer. "Entertainment Tonight" and various newspapers and magazines provide good insight into why particular docudramas are made and the personal attitudes of the creative crew. These provide "from the horse's mouth" insights into the origin of the production process and can be useful in helping students ascertain the objectivity of a program. Teachers can point out that the producers have their own perspective but they should also encourage students to recognize how the nature of the medium (time constraints, dramatic license, composite characters, etc.) compromise the authenticity of the program.

- Dramatic license: The concept of dramatic license embraces a wide range of traditional theatrical and literary devices used when telling true stories within the confines of media representations. The composite character is a simple example of this device. Actions, behaviors, and attitudes connected to several different characters are assigned and confined to a single character to make the narrative less complex.

- Promotions and disclaimers: Media publicity often hypes docudramas by claiming that they are based on true stories or real life events. The facade of factuality is used to promote and sell the program. However, disclaimers are often used at the beginning or end of a program to suggest that not everything about the story is an accurate reflection of reality. Introduce students to this aspect of production and promotion and have them discuss the concept of truth in advertising.

- Intent versus impact: Often, docudramas assert that their real aim or intention is to bring the spirit or essence of a character and story to the screen, rather than accurately recording an honest "warts and all" program. Discuss this concept with students so that they are more prepared to view docudramas as interpretations rather than accurate representations. Remember that even though the producer may intend the program to serve as a dramatization of the actual events in the same way Shakespeare's *Richard III* is a dramatization of actual events, uninformed audiences tend to take such presentations literally. In the case of *Richard III*, that image has persisted for four centuries.

- What sells?: Using *TV Guide* and various newspapers and magazines, develop a list of the type of real-life stories that become television movies or miniseries. What are the essential elements of these stories? How newsworthy are these stories? Some examples from recent times would include "The Preppy Murder" screened on ABC in 1989 and the sensational Charles Stuart Boston murder case. Although such productions seem to have little educational value, there is no reason to suggest that the genre has nothing to offer. PBS created an outstanding series based on the life of Robert Oppenheimer, the creator of the atomic bomb. "The Missiles of October" brought the 1962 Cuban missile crisis to television in dramatic terms, as did "Murder in Mississippi," NBC's treatment of slain civil rights activists, and "Blind Ambition," which was based on John Dean's account of the Watergate conspiracy. "Back Stairs at the White House" introduced U.S. audiences to their presidents in a way that made them people and personalities in addition to politicians. "The Betty Ford Story" helped audiences understand the pain and strain of being First Lady. Each and every one of these programs fused fact with fiction, telescoped time, and used composite characters. For our students to be able to distinguish between real life and television representations of actual events and real people, we must help them to understand how television constructs these images and how much of them we can believe.

Television Game Shows

(ELEM / MID) — "Square One," the educational program based on the game show format, demonstrated that learning could be presented in a lively and interesting way. Television game shows have increased in popularity in recent years so much so that "Wheel of Fortune" replaced the evening news in some markets, and in other areas news programs introduced questions and quizzes in an attempt to hold viewers. In Australia in 1990, "Sale of the Century," the most popular game show on television, included among its contestants former prime ministers of Australia and New Zealand. Although game shows are usually regarded as good clean fun, they promote a "get rich quick" fantasy and foster consumption and competitiveness.

Have students make a list of all the game shows they are familiar with. These would probably include "Wheel of Fortune," "Let's Make a Deal," "The Price Is Right," "Hollywood Squares," and "the Newlywed Game." Have the students select one game and see if they can write a list of the rules or how the game works. Which game show is most popular with your students? What do they like about it?

The Running Man is a science fiction film set in the not too distant future when television and one game show totally control society. Preview the film and select a brief clip to show students how the game works. You might like to compare it to gladiators and the games played by the Romans in the Coliseum. This could develop into a unit studying games in different cultures including the ancient Egyptian game Senat, traditional card games, Native American snow-snake games, and, of course, current games such as Monopoly, Trivial Pursuit, and Pictionary.

(ELEM/MID) — Assign students the task of developing a game show format for television. They must come up with the object of the game, the rules, the type of contestants, and the possible prizes. If you have video facilities, this could turn into a class project with some students serving as crew or set designers and others playing contestants or the program hosts.

(MID) — Break the students into groups and assign each group the task of developing a game format to teach an area of study such as history, geography, English, or math. Have the groups present their ideas to the class and pick the one that is most popular. You could even develop this quiz/game approach as a regular part of instruction if it is popular with the students.

Spot the Shot: Visual Analysis of Television

(ELEM/MID) — Introduce students to the following definitions of camera movements and shots. Then watch a brief clip from anything on television and have them find examples of each technique. Increase the level of sophistication by asking them to explain why the director chose that shot. Ask them to develop a one- to two-page script indicating what shots they would use. If you have access to a video camera, demonstrate each shot to students or break them into groups and have each group record an example of one specific shot.

- Wide shot: Entire subject and surroundings are shown. Often referred to as establishing shot, giving information about setting and location.

- Medium shot: Traditionally focuses on one or two people or objects in frame. Usually head, shoulders, and half-torso shot. Often used during conversation.

- Close-up shot: This is used for details. Often an important prop such as a gun, a phone, or a letter is shown this way to draw viewers' attention to their strategic importance to the plot. When people are shown in close-up, it is usually done to highlight facial expression and reactions.

- Extreme close-up shot: Dramatic effect, often a tight shot of an eye, a screaming mouth, or a trembling hand.

- Point-of-view: The camera is used to develop the perspective that we, as viewers, see from. Usually the camera is objective, which means we see from the perspective of an outsider looking on or in. Occasionally, the camera is subjective, assuming the position of a character. An entire episode of "M*A*S*H" was shot this way. The point-of-view technique also includes low angle (tilt up) and high angle (tilt down) camera work, each of which conveys particular meaning.

Although television uses many of the same shots as motion pictures, it is important to recognize how the different screen format affects the composition and impact. Epics such as *Lawrence of Arabia, Dr. Zhivago,* and *Reds,* all made for the big screen, suffer in the claustrophobic confines of television. Marketing strategies now mean that many movies are shot with cable or VCR in mind, as a result of which they use more close-ups than classic Hollywood cinema. Other directors feel so strongly about the difference between film and television that they insist video versions of their movies be released in letter-box format—the format of the film is the same proportion as it appeared on the movie screen; this may leave a black border around the projected image on the television screen.

(ELEM)—Show children a clip from a movie such as *Star Wars, Platoon, Lawrence of Arabia,* or *Dr. Zhivago* and ask them whether it would look better at the movies and why. Ask students if they can think of a movie they saw in a theater that lost something on television and what the difference was.

Further techniques for visual analysis can be found in chapter 7 of this book, which deals with motion pictures. Many of these analytical techniques can be applied to television.

TELEVISION AND STEREOTYPING

Television models attitudes and behaviors. These models are potentially powerful influences because (1) they enter our homes and are afforded social sanction or approval, (2) formula and format results in the repetition of these behaviors and attitudes both within programs and across programs, (3) much of the viewing that students engage in takes place without parental supervision so the programs are seldom put in context, and (4) our culture persists in the belief that television is mere entertainment that should not be taken too seriously. But television is much more than mere entertainment. In *Channeling Children,* Betty Miles wrote, "Beyond its particular plot, the program tells the child something about the way the world is: whether it is that men kill each other and women cook, or that women spend their husband's money on ludicrous hats, or that some women and men live happy single lives" (1975, 3). More important, young viewers tend to form a bond with the media models they select. Timothy Meyer said, "Favorite characters are seen as behaving quite consistently with the child's description of his own behavior, his own judgements of what is right or appropriate, and his perceptions of a friend's behavior" (1973, 3).

How television represents various groups and individuals in our society has the potential to influence how those groups feel about themselves and the way in which others see them. It is not simply a question of whom television makes visible. We must also scrutinize those that television ignores, excludes, or underrepresents. *Window Dressing on the Set,* a report of the U.S. Commission on Civil Rights, noted that "those who are made visible through television become worthy of attention and concern; those who television ignores remain invisible" (1979). Most of the time, however, studies of stereotyping center on actual representations. These representations can have national and international impact. Wendy's hamburger chain, for example, drew on Soviet stereotypes already prevalent in 1980s America, when President Ronald Reagan referred to the Soviet Union as "the evil empire." A 1987 issue of *Media and Values* identified the following key stereotypes of the Soviet Union present in U.S. thinking:

- They are unhappy with their lives and the system that controls them.
- They would leave if they could.
- They are drab and gray.
- They are fat and ugly thugs and liars.
- They are humorless, uncultured peasants with no interests or talents.
- They lack incentive to work and do nothing well.
- They are only interested in world conquest.
- Any positive foreign policy initiatives they make are propaganda ploys (Hesse 1987, 5).

Soviet Stereotypes

(ELEM/MID)—Ask students to describe Soviet citizens. How many of the stereotypes in the list in the previous section show up? Ask students where their impressions come from. Use this as a way to explore fact and fiction in media representations.

"The Cosby Show" represented a major change in the image of the Black family on television. Prime time television provides fascinating material for teachers to use in exploring the changing nature of the family in the United States. (Photograph courtesy of the National Broadcasting Co., Inc.)

Defining Stereotypes

(ELEM/MID/HIGH)—Introduce students to a definition of stereotypes. Elaborate on the definition by suggesting that the media use this mechanism for dramatic purposes knowing that audiences will recognize the characters immediately, which leaves more time for the development of the plot and action. Although the media usually do not create stereotypes, they repeat them and, therefore, reinforce them. By articulating stereotypes, television and other media affirm such attitudes in our culture. This can prevent us from thinking critically and fairly about issues and individuals because we become distracted by labels and clichés. George Bush used this technique successfully against Michael Dukakis in the 1988 campaign. The stereotype constantly invoked was "liberal," and Dukakis was placed on the defensive battling "the L word" and the charge that he was "a card-carrying member of the American Civil Liberties Union." This latter charge, of course, invoked images of being a card-carrying Communist. The presence of stereotyping on television must, therefore, be placed in the broader context of stereotypes in this culture and the way they impede the ability of our students to understand the country they live in. If the media distorts, stereotypes, or misrepresents the elderly, the impaired, the disabled, or any other group in society, it is difficult for students to understand and value these individuals.

Elements of Stereotyping

(ELEM/MID)—Introduce students to elements of stereotyping such as physical characteristics, manner of speech, beliefs and attitudes, and clothing. Provide them with a simple example such as nerds, yuppies, bikers, or jocks. Have them describe the elements of the stereotype using some of the headings developed. See if they can think of an example from television of such a stereotype. The ABC series "Coach" offers several variations on the jock stereotype. The program clearly acknowledges that not all jocks behave in one way and even explores the interaction between the jock stereotype and the feminist stereotype.

Examples of Stereotyping

(ELEM / MID) — Have the students develop a list of groups, individuals, or institutions that might be stereotyped in the media. Broad headings could include racial stereotypes, national stereotypes, gender stereotypes, religious stereotypes, regional stereotypes, occupational stereotypes, generational stereotypes, and disabled/ differently abled stereotypes. Have students break these broad headings into more specific questions. For example:

- Racial stereotypes: How are Blacks, Hispanics, Soviets, and Asians depicted on television? Name programs they appear in.

- Regional stereotypes: How is the U.S. South depicted in television programs? In what ways are Southerners represented differently from other regions? Develop a list of programs set in the South.

- Religious stereotypes: Does television show a variety of religious affiliations? How are they represented? Do we see characters observing holy days and partaking in rituals or are we simply told what their religion is? Have students develop a list of characters from television and see if they can match each character with a religion or if they can describe an episode of a program that told them something that they did not know about a religion. Middle- and high-school students may be familiar with "Father Dowling Mysteries," "Thirtysomething," and "China Beach," which give high visibility to Jewish and Catholic characters. Students who watch family-based sitcoms such as "The Cosby Show," "Growing Pains," "The Wonder Years," and "Life Goes On" might explore whether religion and church are visible in these families and how this compares to religious affiliations in the United States overall.

Content Analysis and Stereotyping

(ELEM / MID / HIGH) — Content analysis is a relatively complex process that can be modified and used at all levels of school to help students monitor the media, recognize distortion, and identify stereotypical representations. It involves observing, coding, recording, and analyzing television data; when properly developed, it fosters media literacy, critical thinking, and statistical analysis. At its most basic level, content analysis can work quantitatively to determine such things as the number of Hispanic, Catholic, or adolescent characters on television. By breaking students into groups, with each group looking at a single program, a reasonably accurate count of such elements can be made. For more involved studies, these figures could be tabulated against national statistics based on the census and other sources. A more involved form of content analysis and one more suitable for middle- and high-school students involves quantitative and qualitative analysis. This moves from simply describing the number of particular characters represented on television, focusing attention instead on how they are represented.

"L.A. Law" provided positive images of Hispanics and people with disabilities. Teachers can utilize these positive representations to explode myths and explore stereotypes. (Photograph courtesy of the National Broadcasting Company, Inc.)

IMAGES OF WOMEN ON TELEVISION

George Gerbner has suggested that disproportionate representation on television can contribute to "acceptance of minority status as natural, inevitable, right or even deserved" (1981, 4). On the surface, it seems that women have been very visible on television in recent years. Some programs that have centered on females include "Cagney and Lacey," "China Beach," "Days and Nights of Molly Dodd," "Designing Women," "Falcon Crest," "The Golden Girls," "Kate and Allie," "Murphy Brown," "Murder, She Wrote," "Roseanne," and "Trials of Rosie O'Neill."

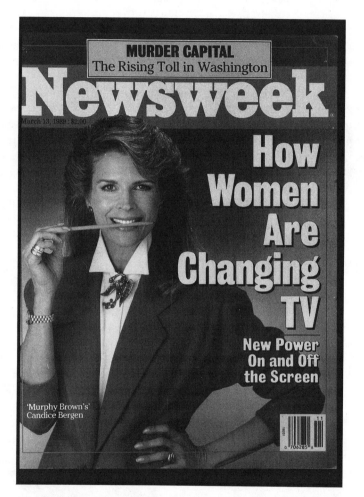

Throughout the 1980s an increasing number of women assumed creative positions behind the scenes in television. How has this development affected the depiction of women on television? (Photograph copyright © 1989 Newsweek, Inc.)

Women as Main Characters

(ELEM / MID)—Have students develop a list of television programs they watch in which women are the main characters. Do girls and boys watch these shows equally?

Female Characters in Television Cartoons

(ELEM / MID) — Although there are many shows that feature women, the real concern is not whether they are represented but how they are represented. Boston media critic Vince Canzoneri (1984) looked at the images of females in cartoons. He noted the number of cartoon programs dominated by male characters and the relatively passive role of female characters who were featured.

Have students develop a list of all the television cartoon characters they are familiar with. They should create two lists, one for males and one for females. Then have students develop a list of adjectives to describe the characteristics of each character and a list of key verbs to describe the activities the characters normally engage in. Discuss the differences between the ways female and male cartoon characters are depicted.

View a television cartoon or assign students episodes of several different cartoons to watch at home. Have students present reports saying how the program was similar to or different from the characteristics they described in class.

How Women Are Depicted on Television

(MID / HIGH) — In 1967, George Gerbner (1981) began a lengthy study of the depiction of women on television. The study looked at 5,000 major and 14,000 minor characters featured in 1,600 programs. The study found that in television men outnumbered women three to one and most women did not work outside the home. A 1987 study reported that 75 percent of television's female characters work outside the home, which was actually 20 percent higher than in real life. A 1988 study still found men outnumbering women three to one on television, which also misrepresents the actual composition of society.

Introduce students to these statistics. Ask them why they think more women on television work than they do in real life. One possible response could be the dramatic need to locate the story away from the home. Ask students why they think images of working women increased on television between 1967 and 1987. Do they see any link between this and actual social changes? Are these patterns still true on television today? Ask students to explain why males are so overrepresented on television. Some areas for discussion could include the influence of male writers, producers, and directors in a patriarchal entertainment industry and the belief that male characters offer more dramatic range than females.

Have the class conduct a statistical analysis of prime-time programs, dividing key characters into males and females. Then assign each student one or two different programs and have him or her report on the different ways the two genders are depicted. Areas to be considered could include occupation, interests, social position, income level, authority, appearance, and emotional stability. From the individual reports, compile a composite analysis of the images of men and women on television. Which program do students consider to be the most accurate, fair, and representative? Have them utilize specific incidents from episodes and storylines to justify their choice.

Creative Women in Television

(MID / HIGH) — In recent years, women have begun to make inroads into the creative side of television, and as a result the way women are represented in some programs has changed. Linda Bloodworth Thomason is the creator and producer of "Designing Women," Diane English created and produces "Murphy Brown," Esther Shapiro developed "Dynasty," and Carol Black co-created "The Wonder Years." "China Beach," on the other hand, although it dealt with women, was actually created by men and was regarded by some as a male fantasy. Assign students several different television programs and have them develop a list of the names of each program's writers and creators. Tabulate the figures to see how influential women are in the creative side of television. A 1989 report on this subject indicated that only 8 percent of directors were women and that female writers received only one-third the pay of their male counterparts. Select a female producer or writer and have the class write a letter commenting on what they like about her work. Also have students ask questions about career opportunities for women in television and the responsibility of the television industry to provide positive images of women.

THE WORLD OF WORK ON TELEVISION

If television serves as a window on the world for young children, providing them with pictures and perceptions of how their society functions, one primary presentation in almost all television fare is the world of work. What occupations and professions are most frequently depicted? What occupations and professions are ignored or underrepresented? What forces and factors influence how the work world is represented? How accurately does television depict the actual work involved in any job or profession? How do these images influence children's concept of work, and how, if at all, do they shape children's career choices? Gerbner's research of television found significant misrepresentation of the workplace. He noted the depiction of twelve doctors, thirty police, seven lawyers, and three judges per week but only one scientist or engineer (1981). There is also evidence that even when jobs are shown, the treatment is superficial and simplistic. "Designing Women," for example, is set in an interior decorating company, but the cast admits that little work is ever shown.

(ELEM) — Ask students to develop a list of all the occupations or jobs that they know. Have them write a brief description of what they think the job entails. Discuss how accurate their impressions are and where they got their impressions. Many children will describe the jobs that their parents do. Because most children do not actually observe their parents working, their impressions will be based on what they have heard and how they have interpreted it.

Next have the students develop a list of the professions and jobs they most frequently see on television, or ask them to name their favorite programs and the work the characters do in those programs. Using only television programs, have the students describe the type of work the characters do, what it involves, how long it takes, how much money they make, the work environment, and so on. Discuss how accurately television represents this work. Invite a real-life doctor, lawyer, nurse, etc., to talk to your students and discuss the work they do compared with how television represents it.

(MID) — Have the class develop a list of the jobs most commonly depicted on television. Issue the students current copies of *TV Guide* or the television section of daily newspapers and have them compile a list of programs that feature the jobs they have identified as well as programs depicting jobs they did not identify. When the lists are complete, have the class discuss some of the jobs that are seldom or never seen on television. Is Gerbner's finding that engineers and scientists are seldom seen still true? Does television depict dentists, architects, mechanics, or carpenters? If these professions and occupations are invisible on television, have the class discuss why they think this happens. Does it, for example, mean that being an architect or a dentist is boring or unimportant?

Break the students into groups, with each one studying how a different job is represented on television. Students should watch relevant programs and describe the work environment, the various tasks involved in the job, the attitudes and morale of the workers, the level of income, and how accurate they think the depiction is. In addition, they should research that job in the real world by visiting workplaces, talking to real people who hold such jobs, writing to professional associations, and finding out what it takes to enter that job or profession. Have each group report their findings to the class.

CASE STUDY ACTIVITIES

The Legal Profession

(ELEM/MID/HIGH) — One of the most frequently depicted professions on television is the legal profession. Potentially, children can learn about a range of jobs in law, including judge, prosecutor, public defendant, paralegal, and attorney. How many of your students are familiar with these terms and what do they think each type of work involves? What types of crimes do they think most commonly come before the courts, and how accurately does this reflect national crime statistics or the statistics in their own town or country? Can legal issues addressed in television programs be used to facilitate students' awareness of controversial and constitutional issues? These questions can provide a focus for studying the accuracy of the image of the legal profession and the impact that image has on the way young people perceive the law. In a March 1990 article, *TV Guide* interviewed attorneys and asked them to discuss television's depiction of the legal profession. Their comments are worth sharing with students. Jerry Spence, who successfully prosecuted Kerr-McGee in the Karen Silkwood case and successfully defended Imelda Marcos, was critical of one aspect of "L.A. Law." "Most of their lawyers are young and competent. Well, in law, you can't be both! To be a good trial lawyer takes years and years, maybe twenty of ugly hard work before you're competent to stand for an hour before a jury" (Elm 1990, 8). Alan Dershowitz, a professor of law at Harvard University, asked why 90 percent of the lawyers spent 90 percent of their time representing 1 percent of the population. "The show's cases rarely deal with the issues of social significance like whether there is a right to beg on the subways, or cases involving the homeless. If you can't resolve a case in twelve minutes, they don't do it" (Elm 1990, 5). Other complaints about "L.A. Law" suggested that "it creates a terrible impression for young lawyers. It suggests that if you go to work for a large firm like that, you'll get fun work" (Elm 1990, 5).

In exploring television images of attorneys, teachers should also direct students' attention to the distribution of power in legal firms. How many female partners are there, for example, in "L.A. Law's" McKenzie, Brackman, Chaney, Kuzak, and Becker firm? Are the female attorneys shown as being equally competent as their male counterparts? Do they receive as many major cases and the same financial bonuses as the men? If they are not treated equally, does this reflect the bias of the program producers or is it a reflection of the real workd? "L.A. Law" has been such a successful program that some law professors credit it with increased enrollments. Mike Kelly, dean of the law school at the University of Maryland, teaches an ethics course in which he uses clips from the program. Bill Simon of Stanford University Law School told *USA Today*, "Lawyers are influenced by the show and held to the high standards of *L.A. Law* because it is so plausible" (5/9/1991b, 10A). If television's depiction of occupations can influence adults, what impact would these images have on more impressionable children and adolescents?

Nursing

From the days of "Ben Casey" and "Dr. Kildare," medical shows have been a traditional staple of television. Many of today's students would be familiar with "General Hospital" or "St. Elsewhere." But other programs, particularly cop and crime shows, often feature hospital sequences that also provide an opportunity to observe the depiction of doctors and nurses. In 1989, NBC introduced "Nightingales," based on the adventures of five young nurses. The program was immediately controversial and generated debate about stereotyping and superficial images of the nursing profession. One newspaper suggested that the nursing students spent more time discussing men than medicine.

In looking at the image of nursing on television, examine factors such as the caseloads; the hours; the type of work involved; the authority, responsibility, and decision-making depicted; professional morale; and the personal qualities and characteristics associated with good nursing.

Teachers on Television

School has consistently found its way to television either for comedic purposes ("Our Miss Brooks," "Welcome Back, Kotter," "Head of the Class," and "Davis Rules") or for drama ("Mr. Novak," "Room 222," and "The White Shadow"). The consistent presence of school on the screen offers the potential to shape the public's perception of education and, therefore, influence their decisions and votes on vital bond issues. The representation of teachers also has the potential to influence the self-esteem of members of the profession and the way young people think of teaching as they formulate their career plans. George Gerbner, L. Gross, and W. Melody studied images of teachers in the media, and although the images often suggested that teachers were good and moral, "the most enduring and pervasive images of teachers in American mass culture are those that humiliate and depress them" (1973, 284). A 1989 study by Judine Mayerle and David Rarick analyzed images of school on television over a forty-year period. They concluded that the images were restricted and stereotyped but were becoming more realistic. Comparing television teaching to the real world, they wrote, "The television world of education is dominated by male teachers and administrators and as such, has a much lower proportion of students than in the real world" (1989, 45). During the forty-year period, 20.8 percent of all lead or supporting characters were administrators, 36.8 percent were teachers, 37.5 percent were students, and 4.9 percent were other staff such as counselors and coaches. Educational census data from fall 1985 shows that only 1.4 percent of participants in U.S. education at all levels were professional or administrative staff, 5.2 percent were teachers, and 93.4 percent were students.

From a statistical basis, it is therefore apparent that television does not accurately reflect the world of teaching. Have students discuss typical teaching tasks, events, and incidents depicted on television compared to their own experiences of school. In what way are television teachers different from typical teachers (dress, personality, attitudes, teaching styles)? Is there a stereotype of school administrators or principals? If so, what is the stereotype (bumbling fool, stern disciplinarian) and how does it relate to the real world?

Although the image of teachers and teaching can be inaccurate, several television programs have tried to create positive images and dismiss negative stereotypes. Jack Neuman, the creator of "Mr. Novak," worked closely with teachers and principals in developing his stories: "The school teachers that I talked to were suspicious, if not downright hostile. I couldn't blame them. Motion pictures and television have treated education as a farce comedy too many times. I said I was going to make a high school teacher the most popular hero ever seen on film."

"Head of the Class" is a more recent attempt to provide positive images of teaching and students. Charlie Moore's instructional strategies often represent a multimedia approach to teaching that his students find highly challenging. In one episode, his materials included the movie *Medium Cool*, Bob Dylan's *Bringing It All Back Home* album, and books by Eldridge Cleaver and Martin Luther King, Jr. When interviewed for this book, Michael Elias, one of the show's producers, talked about the way the program was conceptualized. Aware of traditional approaches such as "Welcome Back, Kotter" that stressed laughter over learning, the producers tried to depict an amusing but serious view of teaching and learning.

> We wanted to do a show about bright students and they're ... let me see ... they're bright but somehow insulated students who are long on study and short on life experience. Then into their lives comes a sort of freer spirit; a teacher, a substitute teacher. He's a guy who has sort of done a lot and been around; a guy who wants them, urges them to look at the world a little differently, loosen up, not be quite as dogmatic in their studies and the way they look at the world.

Although Charlie Moore does represent a positive image of teaching, the character is stereotypical to the extent that he is the hero-teacher, the loner who succeeds by being a nonteacher, by breaking the rules. As such, he deals with the principal as a buffoon (Dr. Samuels) and we seldom see other teachers or any real peer reinforcement. Responding to these suggestions, Elias accepted the stereotyping charges and said, "You've got to stay funny to stay on," thereby acknowledging the commercial and industrial constraints that control television images. Despite this, "Head of the Class" has consistently promoted a positive image of teaching and learning, including the programs it did from Moscow, which were produced in part to combat stereotyping in the miniseries "Amerika."

RACIAL MINORITIES ON TELEVISION

A 1989 report sponsored by the National Commission on Working Women and financed by the Ford Foundation studied the depiction of racial minorities in recurring roles on network television (Steenland 1989). The report noted improvements in the number and diversity of the roles but said the shows portrayed an artificial world of racial harmony in which Whites and Blacks get along with each other and no one is poor. The study said television portrays an artificial universe in which racial difficulties and realities are denied.

Analyzing the depiction of minorities, the study found that 90 percent of them were middle class or wealthy and less than 10 percent were working class. On television, minorities were more likely to be depicted as professionals or police officers than is true in real life. Although in real life many minority workers are employed as laborers or in sales and clerical positions, these were actually underrepresented on television according to the study. The depiction of minorities in the media is a sensitive and significant area that must be addressed for multicultural education to succeed. That requires addressing past, present, and future media representations of minorities. S. Melbourne Cummings has said, "Historically black people have been given roles in the media that have tended to strengthen and perpetuate the negative stereotypical images that white people have created" (1988, 75). He has also noted that television programs such as "The Cosby Show" and "227" have contributed to changing those images. Clearly, television has improved its depiction of minorities since its early days. Recent programs such as "Fresh Prince of Bel Air," "In Living Color," "In the Heat of the Night," and "Brewster Place" provide rich opportunities for students to consider the depiction of racial minorities. Educators working with young children from minority groups need to be particularly aware of the impact the media can have on their self-concept and self-actualization. *Television and the Socialization of the Minority Child* (Berry and Mitchell-Kernan, eds., 1982) is an important contribution to this realization. Discussing self-concept, Gloria Johnson Powell wrote, "A growing person's conception of his or her selfness comes into being through the reflected appraisal of others. What are the reflections of our race-conscious society that television mirrors or projects to the minority child viewer?" (Powell 1982, 124).

(ELEM/MID/HIGH) — Ask students to develop a list of all minority characters on television. Separate the list by groups, such as Hispanic, Black, Asian, and Native American. Identify the characters as minor (supporting) or major (lead) characters. Identify the types of programs the characters appear in (comedy, drama, etc.). Classify the depiction of the characters as positive or negative. Examine the incomes, occupations, and lifestyles of the characters. Now compare these media representations of minorities to real life. How fair and accurate are the images?

If the depiction of minorities seems to reflect the rosy and unrealistic image noted in the study, discuss the impact that advocacy groups, the civil rights movement, and affirmative action may have had on television producers. If the images appear to be negative or unrepresentative, discuss the racial composition of the creative community in the television industry. How is this likely to influence the depiction of minorities?

IMAGES OF THE IMPAIRED AND HANDICAPPED IN TELEVISION

For average Americans, the term *handicapped* still describes individuals who are afflicted with an illness or injury. In education, various terms such as *special, exceptional,* and *different* have been used over the years to avoid the stigma that is so often attached to the disabled. If the word *handicap* recalls the image of a beggar, cap in hand, asking for a handout, the word *disabled* too often is used to suggest unable, as though the impaired individual has no abilities or skills to offer. As a window on the world, television has the opportunity to correct many of the misperceptions our society has about the deaf, the visually impaired, paraplegics, quadraplegics, and all others who are in some way different from the rest of us. Movies such as *My Left Foot, The Miracle Worker*, and *Rain Man* have all helped in this effort. Television also has begun to address the issue more seriously. "The Facts of Life" regularly featured a character who suffered from cerebral palsy. "Life Goes On" deals with a family whose teenage son has Down's syndrome. Made-for-television movies such as "When You Remember Me" have concentrated on the dignity of the disabled. In "Ironside," Raymond Burr's wheelchair was no impediment to his sleuthing abilities. "L.A. Law" has regularly included storylines centering on the character Benny, whose mental retardation has often been depicted in a sensitive and positive manner. Every one of these programs provides teachers with the opportunity to help children see the similarities as well as the differences between themselves and individuals with disabilities.

(ELEM/MID) — Ask students to develop a list of any television characters who are somehow impaired. Movies made for television can also be included. It is likely that the list will be quite short and not very representative of the range of disabilities in our society. Are the characters presented positively or negatively? Are the portrayals stereotypical, or do they depict dignity and depth so that the character is shown to have value and abilities that are not overwhelmed by the impairment? Why are these characters not more visible on television?

IMAGES OF FAMILY LIFE ON TELEVISION

The family is the primary social unit. It is, therefore, hardly surprising to find that the family has consistently been the focus of U.S. television programs, from "The Adventures of Ozzie and Harriet" to "Father Knows Best," "The Brady Bunch," "The Cosby Show," "Roseanne," and "The Simpsons." Even if the families depicted have not always been an accurate reflection of the composition or characteristics of the U.S. family, they have often reflected the values of millions of middle Americans who tuned in. As the U.S. family has changed, it is possible to find some of those changes reflected in the way television has depicted it. In 1990, for example, National Public Radio broadcast a story on "the browning of America," describing the increase in interracial families and biracial children. The same year, the Fox Network premiered "True Colors," a situation comedy about an interracial family. Set in Baltimore, the program deals with a Black dentist with two teenage sons who marries a White kindergarten teacher with a teenage daughter. The extended family includes a cranky live-in mother.

Male bonding and the nurturing father (usually without a wife) are now also quite visible in programs such as "The Family Man" and "Davis Rules." The sensitive male is frequently addressed in such programs. In one episode of "Doogie Howser, M.D.," Doogie's father tells Vinnie, "If you feel you're not getting what you need from your father, maybe you should try asking him for it." Such programming clearly reflects current society and mirrors the success of Robert Bly's *Iron John: A Book about Men* (1990). In addition to current representations of family life, television has offered programs such as "Little House on the Prairie," "The Waltons," and "The Wonder Years" that create images of the family in the distant and not too distant past. These images often provide a yardstick by which children judge and measure their own parents and family. At times the strikingly disparate images of family life in these programs has fueled social commentary and debate. Such was the case in 1990 when two of America's favorite TV families clashed in a ratings battle, as "The Simpsons" and "The Cosby Show" went head to head. The battle was seen by many commentators as a reflection of the changing values of the U.S. population.

Although most audiences watch such programs for diversion and entertainment, sociologists believe they really can be read as indicators of the country's value system. The Huxtables in "The Cosby Show" are an idealized image of the family. Jack Solomon says (1988) this represents the dream, not the reality. *USA Today* reported, "While *Cosby* offers positive models to learn from, *The Simpsons* act as negatives. *The Simpsons* use cynical caustic humor. They teach us vicariously through bad decisions. *Cosby* raises our expectations while *The Simpsons* make us feel better about ourselves—our family will never be as bad as that" (1990, 3D). "The Cosby Show," like "Eight Is Enough," "Family," and earlier programs, has the ability to address all members of the family.

Casual viewing of these programs can result in social learning. Controlled or more structured viewing experiences can actually be used to improve parent-child communication and resolve potential sources of conflict. *Parents, Adolescents, and Television*, a Canadian study, found that such programs could facilitate communication. Such programs, they said, were learning tools for adolescents and parents. "Watching the programs together generated discussion of important topics like sexual permissiveness, the pill, drinking, and personal relationships" (Tierney 1978).

(ELEM/MID)—Have students make lists of TV families and all the members of the family. Get the class to vote for their favorite television family. The class could break into small groups with each group representing one television family and developing a presentation to the class on what they like about that family. Which family does the class think is the most realistic and which one is the least realistic? What reasons do they give?

(MID/HIGH)—This assignment can be used in English and social studies classes but also has benefits in counseling. Assign one television family to groups of three or four students until the class is studying six to ten TV families. Have them analyze the family according to the following elements:

1. members (age, sex, race)

2. occupation and income

3. neighborhood (city, suburban, or rural)

4. common conflicts or problems

5. how problems are resolved

6. authority and control in the household

7. lifestyle (clothing, cars, recreation, vacations, luxury goods, etc.)

8. functional or dysfunctional

After students have provided profiles of the families, use census and other statistical information to compare and contrast these fictional families and their lifestyles to real life.

Family Snapshots and Songs

(ELEM) — Several programs, such as "Growing Pains" and "The Wonder Years," begin with images from family photo albums or home movies. Look at the openings of such programs and discuss the moods and impressions they create of family life. How do the music and the lyrics create the mood? Create a display board featuring photographs of your students' families and television families.

(ELEM / MID) — When the class studies the customs and traditions of various cultures, study the depiction of minority families on television. Examine the number of such families that are depicted and study the accuracy of the representations. Does U.S. television provide adequate and accurate images of Hispanic or Asian-American families? If not, why not? This is an opportunity to write to the networks and ask why some groups in our culture are not visible on television.

TV Teens and Tots

(MID) — In one episode of "Doogie Howser, M.D.," the adolescent recorded the following memo in his diary: "When we're little, we want to be just like our dads. When we're teenagers we want nothing to do with them. When we're adult, we end up just like them." Like Kevin Arnold in "The Wonder Years," Doogie takes viewers on a tour of adolescence from an unusually mature perspective. Doogie's genius enables him to be wiser than his years, although the program often points out that emotionally he is just like other teenagers, with the same pleasures and fears. Kevin Arnold has the benefit of hindsight, as voiceover narration takes us through his early adolescence in the late 1960s and early 1970s. The depiction of children and teenagers on television can be both beneficial and detrimental. They offer role models to young people, and potentially they offer students the chance to recognize that other kids, even fictional kids, feel the same way that they feel. When Doogie Howser is reprimanded and grounded for underage drinking, young viewers have the opportunity to think about actions and consequences. When Alex Keaton confronts the death of a friend, adolescent viewers have the chance to reflect on their own mortality. When Janice has to accept that she's not the best cello player in the school, "Head of the Class" provides a forum for exploring self-image and self-esteem.

Statistically, Gerbner says young people are underrepresented on TV, accounting for only one-third of their true numbers in the population. As an audience, however, teenagers can be quite influential. The Fox network found success in 1991 with "Beverly Hills 90210." Beefcake, good looks, and California cool captured 50 to 60 percent of teenagers watching television, making the show number two in the time slot, second only to "Cheers." The show's creator said he devised the series because of the absence of intelligent programs for teenagers.

Provide the class with a list of the names of teenage characters on television or have them generate their own list. Discuss which characters they think are most like and least like real teenagers. The following short list represents some of the teenagers depicted on prime-time television or in reruns that students would be familiar with:

"The Cosby Show"—Theo, Denise, and Vanessa Huxtable
"Donna Reed Show"—Jeff and Mary
"Doogie Howser, M.D."—Vinnie Dalpino
"Family Ties"—Alex, Mallory, and Jennifer Keaton
"Growing Pains"—Mike, Carol, and Ben Seaver
"Happy Days"—Ritchie and Joannie Cunningham
"Leave It to Beaver"—Wally Cleaver
"Life Goes On"—Becca, Paige, and Corky Thatcher
"My Three Sons"—Mike, Robby, Chip, and Ernie Douglas
"The Patty Duke Show"—Patty and Cathy Lane
"Roseanne"—Becky and Darlene Conner
"The Wonder Years"—Kevin, Wayne, and Karen Arnold; Winnie Cooper

Have students write a character description, comparing and contrasting two teenagers on television, such as Kevin Arnold and Doogie Howser or their sidekicks, Paul and Vinnie. As an alternative, have students select one teenager from television and write a short description comparing that character to themselves.

(ELEM)—Ask students to develop a list of children who appear in television families. Which characters do your students most like and why? Have the students write a brief description of their favorite television child and then have them compare that child to themselves. Ask the children to start by listing all the ways the TV child is the same as and different from them. Develop a list of given names and surnames from television families. Mix the names up and have the class rearrange them so the right children are assigned to the right family.

(MID/HIGH)—This exercise can be used to study society in the post-World War II United States, with emphasis on the 1950s and 1960s. Rather than students simply reading about the era, students can analyze television programs from the period as historical documents that reflect lifestyles and attitudes of the time. Using programs now available on videotape or that are being shown in reruns, students can examine family life as depicted during this period. Using magazines from the period, family photograph albums, and interviews with parents and grandparents, students can begin to construct their own sense of the time. Textbooks can then be used to flesh out their histories, providing the factual background. Programs that would be suitable for this approach include "The Adventures of Ozzie and Harriet," "My Three Sons," "Father Knows Best," "Leave It to Beaver," "The Patty Duke Show," and "The Brady Bunch," among others. Guidelines in the handout (see Figure 4.2) will help students process information from the programs.

The Cosby Controversy

"The Cosby Show" dominated ratings throughout the 1980s. It was one of the most successful programs in television history, and many people were pleased to see its positive depiction of Black family life. But not everyone was pleased. Some critics argued that the show was unrealistic and that the image of family life and social life was unattainable for most Blacks. Some believed that Blacks might aspire to the lifestyle of the Huxtables but could never attain it. Some believed the program toned down color and race issues and succeeded with White television audiences by neutralizing the essence of Black life and culture. Mark Miller wrote: "as a willing advertisement for the system that pays him well, Cliff Huxtable also represents a threat contained. Although dark skinned and physically imposing, he ingratiates himself with some childlike mien and enviable lifestyle, a surrender that must offer some deep solace to a white public" (1988, 74).

(HIGH)—Such concerns suggest that intentionally or not, television can have a social and political impact. Look at "The Cosby Show" and other shows depicting racial minorities. Have students consider the following questions. Do these shows present accurate insights into minority cultures? Do they address current controversial and social issues as they would affect these cultures? Do they foster White America's understanding of minorities, or do they present minorities in such a way that the central concerns of their lives in the real world are never manifested? Is this treatment unique to the way the media represent minority families, or do the media ignore social, political, and economic issues in the way they represent all families?

Fig. 4.2. Reading the past through television.

Directions: You are analyzing television programs as a reflection of the time in which they were made. Pay attention to the plot and what is said, but also concentrate on the set, which will give you clues about the lifestyle of the characters through such things as their appliances, furniture, clothing, cars, and modes of transportation.

1. How many members are there in the family? What does the family consist of? How does this compare to the composition of your parents' or grandparents' family at that time?

2. Do the parents work? What type of jobs do they do? Compare this to your parents or grandparents at that time.

3. Describe the income level and lifestyle of the family. Are they, for example, working class, lower middle class, upper middle class? What evidence are you using for this judgment?

4. Describe the environment in which the family lives. Is it rural, urban, or suburban? Do they own their own house, live in an apartment that they own, or rent? What did your parents or grandparents live in at this time?

5. Pay careful visual attention to the family home. Make a note of the furniture and appliances. In what way are they different today? Try to find photos in your family albums that show appliances, fashions, and furniture from this period. Compare them to the ones shown in the television program.

6. Listen carefully to the interaction between adults and children in the program. Make a list of words or phrases they use that you are not familiar with. Ask your parents if they used expressions like this or if they know what the expressions mean.

7. If there are any problems or conflicts in the program, make a list of them. Are similar problems present in today's television families? Were these problems common concerns for families when the program was made?

8. Does the program contain any references (visual or verbal) to real people such as politicians or to real social and political events or issues? If it does, develop a list of them for further research.

9. Does the program refer to school in any way? If so, how is it depicted?

10. Prices will be considerably different in these old programs. Make a list of all goods and prices referred to either visually or verbally.

11. In what way is the society in this program different from the world you live in?

VIOLENCE ON TELEVISION

George Gerbner has said that "symbolic violence demonstrates power: who can get away with what against whom" (1981, 4). In *Television as a Social Issue*, Gloria Steinem noted that typically women tend to be the victims on television and that the women are "usually young, independent sexual women." What, asked Steinem, "are we being told here" (1988, 18)? It is impossible to understand crime in the United States without recognizing the role our culture plays in promoting or perpetuating violence. Although much crime stems from complex social and economic forces, there is also reason to believe that crime emerges from a culture that seems to tacitly condone violence. Rape, domestic violence, and attacks against women in general need to be studied against the constant visual backdrop provided by mass media. The repetition of violence in the media provides potential visual validation for such acts. The constant use of handguns on television provides social sanction for the presence of guns in our society, despite growing evidence that children are often victims of handguns in homes. The use of violence to resolve conflict, even when "good guys" are the ones being violent, runs the risk of endorsing violence and confrontation as a valid and socially acceptable response to human problems.

Gerbner's research indicates that five acts of violence occur during each hour in prime-time programs and a disturbing eighteen acts of violence occur each hour during children's programming. Teachers and parents need to be aware of the amount of violence on television, the victims of the violence, the context in which the violence occurs, and its potential impact on children and adolescents. To dismiss it as mere entertainment ignores social learning theory and the power of the media to model attitudes and behavior. Fredric Wertham regarded television as a school for violence: "Whether crime and violence programs arouse a lust for violence, reinforce it when it is present, show a way to carry it out, teach the best method to get away with it or merely blunt the child's (and adult's) awareness of its wrongness, television has become a school for violence" (1968).

Any discussion of violence on television requires some definition of what constitutes violence. At its most basic level, violence suggests a physical attack or assault, which may extend from a slap in the face to murder. But violence can also be verbal, and the victim of this type of attack and abuse can also be damaged. Sometimes it is also necessary to consider the context in which the violence occurs and the audience that sees the program. For example, if a character is pushed off a cliff or hit by a truck, this may clearly seem to constitute an act of violence. If, however, this character was in a Roadrunner/Wiley Coyote cartoon, many of us would tend to suggest that the act was harmless because it was clearly in the realm of fantasy. But that is an adult interpretation that ignores the context in which young children view such programs. The television industry often uses the question of context to justify its use of violence. Typically such arguments claim that violence is used to establish law and order, that it is usually used by the good guys, and that, in the end, it is shown that crime does not pay. Such claims collide with the work of Piaget and Kohlberg, which suggests that many young children do not process symbolic acts of violence according to the context or the motivations of the characters. Rather, these children tend to make their judgments based on the success of the violence. The media, therefore, potentially provide a model that tells children "might is right" and "the end justifies the means." For adults, visual violence can also have social and political implications. The constant depiction of crime on television distorts the amount of real crime in society and creates a climate in which people often respond emotionally rather than logically to law and order issues. Decisions about the death penalty, prison sentences, funding for prisons, and even the judges and politicians we elect often emerge out of this climate. The Willie Horton ad in the 1988 presidential campaign played on voters' fears of violent crime. The following questions can help focus students' examination of the issues: Is the emotionally charged climate conducive to understanding crime and violence in our society? Does this climate enable us to rationally consider how crime can grow out of poverty, hunger, and illiteracy and what can be done to prevent it? Does television violence play on our fears and emotions, escalating our predisposition to respond to violence with violence?

(ELEM)—Define the word *violence* with students. Ask them to describe acts of violence that they most often see on television. Have the students describe the type of characters who usually commit acts of violence. Do they describe criminals, law enforcement officers, superheroes, or a mixture of characters? How representative are their perceptions? Remember, research shows that children's programming contains more violence than prime-time programming.

Cartoon Violence: Fantasy and Reality

(ELEM/MID)—Young children cannot always distinguish between reality and fantasy. How do your students perceive violence in cartoons? Develop a list of all the cartoon programs your students watch and a list of the key characters in these programs. Ask students to describe the action and violence in each program. Which characters are the most violent? What type of acts do they commit? Why do they act this way? Do your students see the violence as justified and acceptable? If the students have play-action figures based on any of the cartoon characters, have them bring the figures to class. Look at the body language, clothes, and accessories of each character. Do they represent a violent nature? How do the advertisements during these cartoons reflect or reinforce violence?

What If You Acted Like That?

(ELEM)—Look at incidents of violence in cartoons or have students describe incidents that they have seen. Try to get students to describe what would happen if they acted like a cartoon character. Would their parents be pleased if they hit someone, for example? Would they feel any physical pain if they hit a person? Does cartoon violence provide an accurate picture of what it feels like to be hit, hurt, blown up, run over, etc.?

Is Violence Funny?

(ELEM/MID)—Invariably, when we talk about cartoon violence, discussion centers on adventure cartoons such as "G.I. Joe" or "Masters of the Universe." But violence has traditionally had a comedic element going back to silent movies. What funny cartoons feature acts of violence? What type of violence typically occurs? Who commits the violence? Who is the victim? Is the violence depicted realistically? If not, what is missing from it? Have any of the students ever copied something they saw in one of these cartoons? What happened? Why do we laugh at these images of violence? Is violence funny?

Sticks and Stones

(ELEM)—Remind the children of the saying, "Sticks and stones may break my bones, but words will never hurt me." Describe verbal violence. What TV programs do they watch in which characters are verbally violent to each other? Why do people act this way? In TV programs, this verbal violence is often meant to be funny. Is it funny in real life to say such things to other people?

(MID/HIGH)—Define physical and verbal violence for the class. Divide the class into groups to discuss either verbal or physical violence. Each group should develop a list of the programs most likely to contain such acts, the characters most likely to commit the violence, the typical victims, and the context in which the acts occur. This exercise can be quite involved, with the groups further dividing themselves to study violence by genre. Groups could examine violence in crime shows, westerns, war programs, cartoons, sitcoms, and even the evening nes and sporting events.

Statistical Analysis of TV Violence

(HIGH)—Assign one prime-time program to each class member. Have them record acts of violence including the age, race, nationality, gender, and socioeconomic status of the victim and the attacker. Compile the profile and compare it to actual crime statistics, discussing similarities and differences.

Women as Victims: Voyeurism and Rape

(HIGH) — Domestic violence and rape have been persistent problems in our society. Sexual attacks against women have been on the increase and date rape has become a major problem for young women, even on our college campuses. Research suggests that many rape victims never go to the police, and those who do often have to face the charge that "she asked for it" or "she really wanted it." Although rape is often depicted on television, the climate that promotes rape is often more subtle in its presence. The voyeuristic nature of television persistently packages and parades women as sex objects to fulfill male fantasies. Women are more likely than men to be shown in swimwear, underwear, or provocative and revealing clothing. Women are also more likely than men to be the objects of innuendo, double entendre, or an unwelcome touch or gaze. Every one of these images creates the cumulative climate that dehumanizes women by representing them as objects. Discuss the way television depicts men and women in terms of this argument. Ask the class to provide examples of programs and advertisements that show women in such ways. You may choose to do a separate activity focusing solely on advertising.

The Functions of Visual Violence

(MID/HIGH) — It is pointless to claim that watching violence makes people violent. If that were true, our entire society would be violent. What research does suggest, however, is that under some circumstances, watching violence will encourage some viewers to actually commit violence or to be more tolerant of violence. Other people argue that watching violence actually channels their aggression and relieves their tension. Football, boxing, and ice hockey might be good examples of the latter. Introduce students to the following concepts. Then break students into groups and have each group develop arguments and evidence to support the claim they select.

- Anesthetic: By constantly showing acts of violence, television numbs viewers to the reality of violence, making us insensitive to it. Because we are insensitive to it, we are more likely to use it ourselves or accept other people using it.

- Catharsis: Violence on television is a form of social safety valve for letting off steam. Viewing violence enables the audience to vicariously experience violence and, therefore, reduces the likelihood that they will be violent.

- Social sanction: By constantly depicting violence, television models it and endorses it as an appropriate and valid behavior.

- Social mirror: Television neither creates nor condones violence; it merely mirrors and reflects the violent nature of society.

School for Violence?

(HIGH) — Wertham has argued that television is actually a school for violence. Have students write an essay on this assertion in agreement or disagreement. Remind them to provide evidence to support their opinion.

TELEVISION AND HEALTH

The central issue of television's impact on health is addressed in the advertising section of this book (chapter 5), with emphasis on fast-food and alcohol advertisements. However, television influences several other aspects of health that are often less visible than commercials. To suggest that television is a drug and that viewing is addictive is hardly new. In her 1971 Caldecott Medal acceptance speech, author Gail Haley warned of the intoxicating effects of the medium. Marie Winn parlayed the concept into her successful book *The Plug-In Drug* (1977). In a 1990 article in *Esquire*, Pete Hamill wrote that "television works on the same imaginative and intellectual level as psychoactive drugs" (1990, 64). Interestingly, Hamill saw education as a tool for combating television and the culture of consumption. "Elementary and high schools must begin teaching television/media literacy as a subject, ... showing children how shows are made, how to distinguish between the true and the false, how to recognize cheap emotional manipulation" (64). Television's impact is so subtle and so pervasive that recognizing what it says and how it influences us remains the central challenge of the medium. In the case of human health, several areas are worth exploring.

Sedentary versus Active Lifestyle

(ELEM/MID)—If children spend several hours a day watching television, can we assume that this encourages them to be passive rather than active? Earlier in this chapter, we suggested that you survey students to discover what your students watch and how much they watch. Using this instrument enables you to ascertain the times that students watch television. If a significant portion of the viewing occurs in daylight hours, it is fair to assume that this time could be spent more actively. You could modify the earlier survey to enable students who are involved with sports to identify themselves. Do they watch television more or less than students who are not in sports? It is possible that students who are involved in sports might actually be more passive because they watch a lot of sports on television.

Obesity, Nutrition, and Television Viewing

The ABC news program "Diet of Danger" documented how fast food, TV viewing, and hectic lifestyles created dangerous eating habits for our children. This complex issue is tied into a variety of factors, including genes, diet, and school lunch programs. It also has ties to television, including the amount of exercise students get compared to the amount of time they watch television and television's ability to influence what they eat. One report analyzed the food content of eleven major network shows including "Who's the Boss?" "The Golden Girls," "Alf," "Murder, She Wrote," and "L.A. Law." The study reported that 60 percent of all food references were to low-nutrient beverages and sweets. Given that television does affect social learning, the meals it models and the images of snacking work against educators' attempts to suggest balanced meals. In addition, television characters themselves serve as models of human behavior. Tabloid and media controversy constantly centers on overweight women such as Delta Burke, Roseanne Barr, and Oprah Winfrey. The double standard seems operative because the media seldom focus on television's overweight males such as Raymond Burr and John Goodman. How does this bias influence the self-images of the television audience?

Alcohol, Tobacco, and Drug Consumption

When popular television characters consume alcohol and smoke cigarettes, they provide potential media models that may influence young people and adults alike. Jay Winsten, of the Harvard Alcohol Project and assistant dean of Harvard's School of Public Health, recognized this and attempted to change U.S. social norms related to driving and drinking by changing how the media represented driving and drinking. This cooperative endeavor between educators and the media resulted in programs integrating the "don't drive and drink" message into several prime-time shows. These programs included "Knots Landing," "Who's the Boss?" "Family Ties," and "Growing Pains." Despite the socially responsible themes of these programs, the message may be lost in the contradictory context of television's overall message to consume, to escape, or to seek instant gratification. Kathryn Montgomery has said that "television gives double messages about alcohol," and she wonders "whether a medium whose primary goal is to promote consumption can really be an effective advocate for public health" (1991, 19).

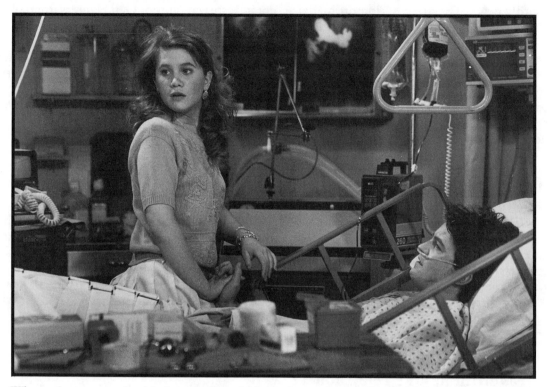

When educators work with the television industry in combating drunk driving, the result is exemplary programming that can be both educational and entertaining. One such example was "Growing Pains," which dealt with drunk driving in several episodes. (Photograph © 1991 Capital Cities/ABC, Inc. [Chic Donchin])

Public Health Awareness

Most people are familiar with public service announcements (PSAs). Perhaps the most visible is the image of frying eggs with the voice announcement, "This is your brain on drugs." Such messages attempt to address health issues in 30-second spots. But television often can integrate a message into entire programs. In 1990, "Thirtysomething," developed several programs that centered on ovarian cancer. AIDS has been addressed in the programs "Brothers" and "Designing Women." By addressing these subjects, television can help to alleviate some of the fear people harbor, and in many cases doctors and hospitals have reported an increase in people coming in for tests following the broadcast of such programs.

HUMAN SEXUALITY ON TV

The depiction of sex in the media has historically been a controversial issue. In 1990, the rap group 2 Live Crew attracted national attention when they were arrested for obscenity in their lyrics. The film industry has always been criticized for its depiction of sex. In the 1930s, the Payne Fund Studies investigated the impact of these images on adolescents. In the 1980s and 1990s, the problems caused by unwanted teen pregnancies and the AIDS crisis necessitate that those working with adolescents recognize the ways in which the media, including television, represent sexuality. In "Television and Human Sexuality," Susan Franzblau said: "Television prescribes and manipulates how we interpret subtle sexual remarks. In fact, it probably helps us to think of those remarks as sexual in the first place" (1977, 111). Stanley Baran's work on adolescent sexual self-image and television drew attention to the viewing conditions, noting that although motion pictures are more explicit, television is afforded social sanction by its persistent presence in the home. "Its impact may indeed be greater because it is constantly in the home (without apparent social restrictions), rather easily available, and it is indeed presented as enjoyable and attractive" (1976, 63). In addition to condoning sexual activity, television also models attitudes about sexuality and potentially influences learning of sex-role stereotypes.

Sex education entered U.S. classrooms in the late 1960s. Despite the fact that young people have been exposed to such information, evidence suggests that many of them do not abstain from intercourse and that many sexually active adolescents do not use contraception. According to the Alan Guttmacher Institute, 1 million teenage girls have become pregnant every year since 1973. That figure represents one out of every ten 15- to 19-year-olds, at the same time that 93 percent of high schools offer sex education. In 1990 *Newsweek* reported an increase in adolescent sexual activity. In 1979, 56 percent of 17-year-old males were having sex. By 1988, the figure had increased to 66 percent. Among females, the figures increased from 47 percent to 52 percent. Also by 1988, 50 percent of 16-year-old boys and 34 percent of girls the same age were sexually active.

Although many parents and educators would find those figures disturbing, they represent reality for our young people. Part of the drive to be sexually active is, of course, biological. Another impetus is provided by the social and cultural context, including media representations of sex. Health educators in particular need to recognize the positive and negative roles that television advertising and programs can play in depicting human sexuality. Acknowledging these messages and helping young people think critically about them should be a crucial component of any curriculum dealing with AIDS or sex education. Students arrive in these classes with a series of attitudes and perceptions about sex. These attitudes have been shaped to a large degree by media representations of human sexuality.

In *Social Learning and Personality Development*, A. Bandura and R. H. Walters (1963) acknowledge the impact of the media in shaping these perceptions. They suggest that film and television characters serve as sexual informational models in our society because of the absence of real-life observational opportunities. In essence, because sexual behavior in our culture is private, occurring behind closed doors, children and adolescents must learn about it from alternate sources. The media often are some of those sources. The media define what it means to be male or female, how couples communicate and interact, and how, when, where, and how often sex occurs. Elizabeth Roberts, in examining the image of sexuality in the media, says, "Many inconsistent and contradictory messages about sexuality and sexual pleasure are communicated to young women" (1983, 11). In terms of sexual safety and preventing unplanned pregnancy, Roberts finds that the constant presence of sex in the media provides a measure by which many young people judge themselves and that it may even push some of them toward sexual experimentation. Looking at the impact of media on adolescents' sexual satisfaction, Baran says: "The media may indeed serve as a contributing factor to an individual's picture of his or her sexual self. The virgin is not only forced to deal with peer pressure regarding his or her virginity, but apparently must also face and react to mass media pressure as well" (1976a, 473).

The problem for the adolescent is the inherent cultural contradiction in the way society provides information about sex. Two of television's most popular programs have centered on male leads intent on bedding the female leads. "Moonlighting" and "Cheers" drew enormous audiences by posing the question, "Will they or won't they?" David Addison's relationship with Maddie Hayes and Sam Malone's pursuit of first Diane Chambers and then Rebecca Howe trivialized sex and made heroes out of immature males. On "L.A. Law," Arnie Becker has been a shallow womanizer. Belatedly the program depicted Becker using contraception, and finally he got married. Those developments in themselves represented the realization that media representation of promiscuity was inappropriate in the age of AIDS.

What Is Sexy?

(MID/HIGH) — A Jovan perfume commercial called "What Is Sexy?" was censored and appeared in a different form because of its erotic images. Ask students what television ads they think stress sex appeal and sexual images to promote the product. In what way does sex have anything to do with the product? Is the sex appeal in the ad created by the people, the props, the camera angles, the music, the sound effects, or the set? Have students compare the way the characters act in these commercials and how they relate to each other compared to the behavior of people in real life.

"Cheers" has been one of the most successful sitcoms on television. What message does the program communicate about alcohol and sexuality? (Photograph courtesy of the National Broadcasting Company, Inc.)

Is Sex Funny?

(MID/HIGH)—In 1977, a study by Susan Franzblau, N. Sprafkin, and Eli Rubinstein found that sexually aggressive acts appeared in crime programs and less intimate acts such as kissing, embracing, and touching appeared in situation comedies. The dominance of sexual material in comedy programs, they reported, "supports the conventional notion that sex is a disturbing topic and is best handled humorously" (1977, 170). Situation comedies such as "Perfect Strangers," "Anything but Love," and "Growing Pains" often deal with bachelors or adolescent males constantly pursuing a female only to fail. Sex in these programs is reduced to a chase, a game with an elusive prey. The humor of the situation (which is often not very humorous) has its traditions in bedroom farce and is reinforced by canned laughter, innuendo, and double entendre. Give students copies of *TV Guide* and have them study plots of situation comedies to see how many use sex as a plot. Look at program advertising in *TV Guide*. Do words and images also stress sex as a selling point of a program? Study one or two episodes of a situation comedy, noting examples of sexual contact and humor. How are the female characters presented? Is the dumb blonde or bubble-headed bimbo stereotype present? Compare the way these characters act to the way real people behave.

In addition to sitcoms, talk shows and variety shows often feature comedians who use sex to get a laugh. In 1990, Andrew Dice Clay and Sam Kinison provoked controversy by the sexist and prejudiced nature of their comedy, which often seemed to target women and gays. If humor has a victim, can it be funny? Ask students to put themselves in the place of those who are victimized by such jokes. If we laugh at a situation, do we unwittingly accept its existence?

Sexual Dysfunction

(HIGH) — In a review of "Equal Justice," a new 1990 crime series, *USA Today* described one of the young attorneys as "a handsome stud puppy." Despite his macho good looks and sex appeal, Chris actually was shown to be less secure when the action moved from the courtroom to the bedroom. In one episode, he experiences temporary impotence and struggles to reconcile this with his own sense of masculinity. By dealing more openly and frankly with human sexuality, television offers the opportunity for an honest discussion of sexual dysfunctions including impotence, premature ejaculation, and frigidity. By using these examples, health educators can break the ice on a sensitive subject and help young people think about the causes of these problems and the available solutions.

Adolescent Sexuality

In recent years, young television characters have behaved in a more sexually open and honest way than they did when confined to "The Brady Bunch" or "My Three Sons." Teens in those programs had crushes, dated, and went to the prom and the malt shop, but it was all innocent, good clean fun, not far removed from the world of Andy Hardy and the film teens of the 1930s. By the late 1970s, television was radically reassessing its depiction of children and teens. In one episode of "Mork and Mindy" a boy referred to a girl as "a cute chick, a fox, real hot stuff." In "Eight Is Enough," Nicholas, a boy not yet in his teens, found himself chased by a girl his own age. "She's warm for my form," he announced. In an episode of "Family" eleven-year-old Annie defended herself against the football hero, who made his "first incomplete pass" and was "penalized 15 yards for illegal use of hands." "The White Shadow," "The Waltons," "Little House on the Prairie," and TV movies such as "Thin Ice," "Coach," and "Anatomy of a Seduction" all pioneered more open, if sometimes sensational, images of adolescent sexuality. One of the most controversial shows was the series "James at 15," which dealt with an adolescent losing his virginity and provoked criticism that it promoted adolescent sexuality. Richard Hawley wrote: "James's television plunge planted the anxiety producing notion in the mind of the adolescent viewer that he was sexually lagging behind not only the precocious kid down the block, but the Average American Boy character of James" (1978, 55).

But whereas James lost his virginity, several programs, particularly those dealing with female adolescents, have cautioned against early sexual activity. In "Family," Buddy faced her sixteenth birthday and increasing pressure from her boyfriend to have sex. Ultimately, she decided she was not ready for it. In "Eight Is Enough," Tommy tried to convince his girlfriend to go to bed with him only to find himself denied. In a 1984 episode of "Family Ties," sixteen-year-old Mallory was pressured by her boyfriend, Rick, to have sex. She, too, decided she was not ready.

Not all TV teens, however, are abstinent, and not all TV parents ignore the sexuality of their children. Television has provided many realistic and responsible images of sexuality. In one episode of "Cagney and Lacey," a mother told her son, "If you care enough about a girl to make love with her, you should care enough to keep safe." This episode was a recipient of the Nancy Susan Reynolds Award, given by the Center for Population Options to programs that demonstrate exemplary sexual responsibility. Other award winners included an episode of "The Bronx Zoo" that showed schools distributing contraceptives, an episode of "Valerie," the TV movie "Daddy," and an after-school special called "Teen Father." Early in the 1990 television season, viewers could watch Becky and Darlene ("Roseanne") discussing being "felt up," hear Paul tell Kevin ("The Wonder Years") that he was a virgin, or see Doogie Howser advocate the use of condoms. "Evening Shade" presented one interesting program in which a fifteen-year-old boy discussed the prospect of losing his virginity with both his father and his grandfather, who shared their own early sexual experiences. "Northern Exposure" depicted an adolescent male's loss of his virginity and his reaction to it.

(MID/HIGH) — Ask the class to develop a list of teenage characters on television. Make sure the list includes males and females. Have them discuss each character in terms of how realistically they think the character's sexuality is depicted. Becky and Darlene in "Roseanne," for example, have discussed menstruation and French kissing. But many adolescent characters are presented less openly. In "Head of the Class," Eric is the school heartthrob but there is little if any indication that he has actually had sex. A better program dealing with early adolescence is "The Wonder Years." Kevin and his girlfriend, Winnie, struggled with peer pressure in one episode when they were forced to "make out" at a party. The prospect of kissing in a dark room sent them scurrying home to the safety of family and the childhood they were not quite so anxious to leave. In "Doogie Howser, M.D.," Vinnie is anxious to lose his virginity but throws up every time he gets too close. In other episodes Doogie and his girlfriend, Wanda, almost have sex but decide they aren't ready; until a fall 1991 episode when they do.

"Doogie Howser, M.D." has actually provided a strong source of sexual information for young viewers. Doogie and his girlfriend have talked about their parents' sexual activities ("geriatric sex perverts from Mars") including the fact that they even had sex "in the afternoon." Doogie has also regularly promoted contraception. In one episode he told kids, "You wouldn't jump out of a plane without a parachute, so don't have sex without a condom." In a parody of an American Express ad, he endorsed contraception with the slogan, "The Condom: Don't Leave Your Pants without It," and the ad began with the simple acknowledgment, "You don't have to do it."

But many topics affecting teen sexuality remain taboo. These include masturbation, wet dreams, breast and penis size, and female body odor. Because the media either actively ignore them or actively promote them (for example, feminine hygiene products), many of these concerns become sources of fear and anxiety for teens. In discussing these fears, teachers should also discuss why the media ignore or inflate these topics. Other aspects of human sexuality that were once taboo are now often depicted in television. "Roseanne" featured premenstrual syndrome (PMS) as the central theme of one program. Speaking about Roseanne, one female character said, "She's a wonderful woman when her estrogen isn't whipping her into a psychotic frenzy." What impact can this type of programming have?

Initially soap operas believed their audience was mainly adults. As the AIDS crisis grew, however, they became more aware that many young people were also watching. Creators of "Santa Barbara" acknowledged that young people did get sexual information from watching soaps. As a result of cooperation between program producers and educators, many soaps such as "Days of Our Lives" and "The Young and the Restless" began to integrate more responsible themes and scenes dealing with sexuality. Use a *TV Guide* or newspaper synopsis to discuss the way sex is presented in soaps. Ask your students which soaps they watch and why. Have students compare soap opera characters to real people. When sex is presented, is it shown as a normal part of a character's life, or are the characters sex obsessed? Are there characters who could be classified as womanizers or nymphomaniacs?

An early study of pregnancy and motherhood in soap operas was called "Television's Romance with Reproduction" (Peck 1979). The study noted the pronatal tendencies in soap operas and commercials. There was, said Ellen Peck, a glorification of motherhood and the reproductive function and a parallel fear of the loss of ability to produce life. She found that commercials, by a cumulative process, idealized home and family life and conveyed the persistent and pervasive message that reproduction and large families were desirable. Look at the depiction of pregnancy and birth in today's soaps or prime-time programs such as "Roseanne," "Growing Pains," and "Married ... with Children." Are Peck's conclusions still justified? Has more honest treatment of contraception or abortion changed the way soaps depict pregnancy? If abortion is presented, is there discussion of both sides of the debate?

Fame and Shame

(MID/HIGH)—Ask students to nominate television episodes, special programs, or made-for-TV movies that they believe have provided fair and useful information about sexual issues. Make sure they develop criteria for making their decision, such as treating a topic that is seldom covered. "L.A. Law," for example, presented a program dealing with the rights and responsibilities of the mentally handicapped if they were sexually active. Gena Rowlands starred in "A Sudden Frost," a made-for-TV movie that looked at parents who discovered their son was gay and dying of AIDS. "Designing Women" has featured episodes that addressed sex education and sexual stereotyping in beauty pageants. When the class has discussed the nominees and voted for the winner, have them prepare a letter of commendation to the network and the program producers. This process can also be done in reverse: By teaching students to be aware of stereotyping and bias, you can help them recognize media misrepresentations and distortion. They can select a single episode or an entire series that they find sexually biased, offensive, or demeaning. Make sure their criteria are valid and that they do not select a program or episode because of an isolated line or incident. You might also want to draw their attention to comedy and its victims. In 1990, the comedian Andrew Dice Clay appeared on "Saturday Night Live" and provoked controversy by his sexist jokes.

SUBSTANCE ABUSE AND TELEVISION

(ELEM/MID) — Ask students to select a favorite television program that they watch regularly. Assign them the task of watching one episode and recording what each character eats and drinks. Many students can use a VCR to facilitate the accuracy of the record. Compile and tabulate the entire class record of food and drink consumption by popular television characters. Discuss the nutritional value of the food and how and when food is consumed. Do the characters snack frequently? Do they eat on the run? Is mealtime a family occasion? Do characters frequently eat in restaurants or at the office? Is the food the characters consume consistent with their lifestyle, their size, and their weight? For example, do physically active and energetic characters have a diet that would help or hinder their activities?

(ELEM/MID) — Several television characters appear to be overweight. Ask students to develop a list of programs featuring overweight people and a list of overweight characters. Which ones are men and which ones are women? Are the characters presented as healthy and happy? Does their weight seem consistent with what they eat and how frequently they eat in the programs? Are the characters dramatic or comedic? Comedy has often drawn on fat people as a source of humor. In what way (verbally or visually) is the characters' size used as a source of humor? Do the characters acknowledge that they are overweight, and do they try to do something about it? In "Roseanne," episodes have dealt with dieting and exercise, but usually the character(s) return to their old habits.

In the mid-1980s, the Caucus for Producers, Writers, and Directors developed a white paper on alcohol and television. In part the report said, "Have any of us in Hollywood unwittingly glorified the casual use of alcohol in our projects? Have we written it as macho? Directed it as cute? Produced it as an accepted way of life? In short, are we subliminally putting a label of 'perfectly okay' on alcohol related behavior?" (Caucus for TV Writers 1985, 22). If the industry has acknowledged the impact of their own image-making, health educators need to work with students, parents, and teachers so that they recognize these images and the inducements they offer.

(ELEM/MID/HIGH) — Assign students several different types of television programs to watch. Make sure the programs include situation comedies, dramas, crime programs, and soaps. Ask the students to record all incidents of smoking (cigarette, pipe, cigar) and consumption of alcohol (beer, wine, hard liquor). The record should include a description of the characters (primary or secondary, female or male, White or minority, age, religion). In addition, it should describe the context in which the smoking or drinking occurs. For example, is the drinking done in a social situation, perhaps wine during dinner at a restaurant, or is the drinking done alone? Is the drinking shown to facilitate social interaction such as a business lunch, or is it shown as a way of relaxing at the end of the working day?

Do any of the characters who drink or smoke seem to suffer from the use of the products? For example, does a character have a persistent cough from smoking or pick a fight after drinking or lose a job because of excessive drinking? Use the media modeling of smoking and drinking and compare it to the statistical impact of these products in real life.

(ELEM/MID) — Discuss the use of illegal drugs in television programs. Ask students to compile a list of drugs that they regularly see on television. Get the students to describe the types of characters usually associated with these drugs (White or minority, male or female, working class or middle class, middle-aged or elderly, urban or rural). Recent reports suggest that marijuana cultivation is increasing among law-abiding Americans in places such as rural Kentucky where the economy is in trouble. Does television reflect this reality or does it suggest that drugs are restricted to big cities and organized crime? Older students could look at this issue in terms of the existing policies and procedures of the federal government's war on drugs. Is it possible that the media's representation of the problem deflects attention from the complex causes? Do simplistic slogans such as "Just Say No" ignore the social, political, and economic aspects of addiction?

(MID/HIGH)—Several major television movies have addressed alcoholism in U.S. society. In the mid-1970s, Linda Blair starred in "Sarah T: Portrait of a Teenage Alcoholic." Later, Scott Baio starred in "The Boy Who Drank Too Much." In the late 1980s, "The Betty Ford Story" chronicled the former First Lady's chemical dependency, and "My Name Is Bill W." presented the story of the founder of Alcoholics Anonymous (AA). These programs have helped to dispel the myth that alcoholism is self-indulgence more than a disease and that it hits only skid row bums and not regular, hard-working, law-abiding Americans.

Prime-time series such as "Cagney and Lacey" addressed the issue with key characters. Viewers were not simply told that characters were alcoholics, they were shown the battle with the bottle. Christine Cagney struggled with her father's alcoholism and her own. As a police officer, she felt more guilty and responsible than most. When she felt desperate and in trouble, the program showed her attending AA meetings and introduced audiences to the role of the Twelve Steps and Twelve Traditions. Situation comedies tend to be confined by their format. "Murphy Brown" has, however, introduced in its lead character a successful professional woman who is a recovering alcoholic. At least one episode centered on whether Murphy would or would not take a drink. Unfortunately, a lot of action in the program is set in a bar, which many recovering alcoholics would steer clear of. Of course, the social setting provided by the bar is necessary to the show. It is not, however, consistent with Murphy's character or condition. The same problem is evident in "Cheers," in which Sam Malone, the recovering alcoholic, works in a bar. Compare and contrast these images of alcoholism with the literature of the field. Invite a counselor, doctor, or acknowledged member of AA to discuss alcoholism in reality compared to television's image of it.

REFERENCE LIST

Adams, Anne, and Cathy Harrison, (1975). Using Television to Teach Specific Reading Skills. *Reading Teacher*, 29:1, 45-51.

Bandura, A., and R. H. Walters, (1963). *Social Learning and Personality Development*. New York: Holt Rinehart Winston.

Baran, Stanley J., (1976a). How TV and Film Portrayals Affect Sexual Satisfaction in College Students. *Journalism Quarterly*, Autumn.

————, (1976b). Sex on TV and Adolescent Sexual Self-Image. *Journal of Broadcasting*, 20:1, 61-68.

Barton, Richard, and Robert Miller, (1977). Television Literacy: Integrating the Symbolic Worlds of Educators and Students. *International Journal of Instructional Media*, 5:3, 229-34.

Berry, Gordon, (1988). Multicultural Role Portrayals on Television as a Social Psychological Issue. In Stuart Oskamp (ed.), *Television as a Social Issue*. Newbury Park, Calif.: Sage Publications. Pp. 118-29.

Canzoneri, Vince, (1984). What Parents Should Do about TV's Feminine Mistake. *TV Guide*, January 28.

Caucus for TV Writers, Producers and Directors, (1985). Alcohol Guidelines for the Television Industry and Results. *Television and Families*, 8:3, 22.

Collins, W., et al., (1978). Age-Related Aspects of Comprehension and Inference from a Televised Dramatic Narrative. *Child Development*, 49:2, 389-99.

Cummings, S. Melbourne, (1988). The Changing Image of the Black Family on Television. *Journal of Popular Culture*, 22:2, 75-86.

Doerken, Maurine, (1983). *Classroom Combat: Teaching and Television*. Englewood Cliffs, N.J.: Educational Technology Publications.

Dominick, J., S. Richman, and A. Wurtzel, (1979). Problem-Solving in TV Shows Popular with Children. *Journalism Quarterly*, 56:3, 455-63.

Durkin, Kevin, (1985). *Television, Sex Roles and Children.* Philadelphia: Open University Press.

Fernandez-Collado, Carlos F., et al., (1978). Sexual Intimacy and Drug Use in TV Series. *Journal of Communication*, 28:3, 30-37.

Franzblau, Susan, (1977). Television and Human Sexuality. In Ben Logan (ed.), *Television Awareness Training.* New York: Media Research Center Publications.

Franzblau, Susan, N. Sprafkin, and Eli Rubinstein, (1977). Sex on TV: A Content Analysis. *Journal of Communication*, 27:2, 164-70.

Gentry, Carol, (1990). Can't Quit: Television Holds Us Fast. *Winston Salem Journal.*

Gerbner, George, (1981). Television: The American School Child's National Curriculum, Day In and Day Out. *PTA Today*, 6:7, 3-5.

_____, (1987). Television: Modern Mythmaker. *Media and Values*, no. 40-41, 8-9.

Gerbner, G., et al. (1973). Teacher Images in Mass Culture: Symbolic Functions of the Hidden Curriculum. In Gerbner, G., L. Gross, and W. Melody (eds.), *Communications Technology and Social Policy.* New York: John Wiley.

Greenfield, Patricia, (1990). Video Screens: Are They Changing the Way Children Learn? *Harvard Education Letter*, March/April.

Hamill, Pete, (1990). Crack and the Box. *Esquire*, May, 63-66.

Hawley, Richard, (1978). Television and the Adolescent: A Teacher's View. *American Film*, 4:1, 52-56.

Hesse, Petra, (1987). Stereotypes Mask Feelings of Fear. *Media and Values*, no. 39, 5-6.

Kaminsky, Stuart, and Jeffrey Mahan, (1985). *American Television Genres.* Chicago: Nelson Hall.

Kelley, Michael, (1983). *A Parent's Guide to Television.* New York: John Wiley.

Krendl, Kathy, and Bruce Watkins, (1983). Understanding Television: An Exploratory Inquiry into the Construction of Narrative Content. *Educational Communication and Technology Journal*, 31:4, 201-12.

Leifer, Aimee, (1974). Children's Television More Than Mere Entertainment. *Harvard Educational Review*, 44:2, 213-45.

McLuhan, Marshall, and Quentin Fiore, (1967). *The Medium Is the Message.* New York: Bantam.

Mander, Jerry, (1978). *Four Arguments for the Elimination of Television.* New York: Murrow Quill.

Martz, Larry, (1988). *Ministry of Greed: The Inside Story of the Televangelists and Their Holy Wars.* New York: Newsweek Books.

Mayerle, Judine, and David Rarick, (1989). The Image of Education in Prime-Time Network Television Series, 1948-1988. *Journal of Broadcasting and Electronic Media*, 33:2, 139-57.

Meyer, Timothy, (1973). Children's Perceptions of Favorite Television Characters as Behavioral Models. *Educational Broadcasting Review*, 7:1.

Miles, Betty, (1975). *Channeling Children: Sex Stereotyping on Prime-Time TV.* Princeton, N.J.: Women on Words and Images.

Miller, Mark Crispin, (1988). *Boxed In: The Culture of TV.* Evanston, Ill.: Northwestern University Prss.

Montgomery, Kathryn, (1991). Alcohol and Television: And Now for Some Mixed Messages. *Media and Values*, no. 54-55, 18-19.

Neuman, E. Jack. Correspondence and personal papers, Wisconsin State Historical Society, Madison, Wis.

Nystome, Christine, (1983). What Television Teaches about Sex. *Educational Leadership*, 40:6, 20-24.

Palmer, Edward, (1988). *Television and America's Children: A Crisis of Neglect.* New York: Oxford University Press.

Peck, Ellen, (1979). Television's Romance with Reproduction. In E. Peck and J. Senderowitz (eds.), *Pronatalism: The Myth of Mom and Apple Pie.* New York: Thomas Y. Crowell.

Pezdek, Kathy, (1985). Is Watching TV Passive, Uncreative or Addictive: Debunking Some Myths. *Television and Families*, 8:2, 41-46.

Pezdek, Kathy, Arille Lehrer, and Sara Simon, (1984). The Relationship between Reading and Cognitive Processing of Television and Radio. *Child Development*, 55:6, 2072-82.

Postman, Neil, (1985). *Amusing Ourselves to Death.* New York: Viking.

Powell, Gloria Johnson, (1982). The Impact of Television on the Self-Concept Development of Minority Children. In Gordon Berry and Claudia Mitchell-Kernan (eds.), *Television and the Socialization of the Minority Child.* New York: Academic Press.

Powers, Ron, (1991). Our Town. *TV Guide*, December 21, 4-10.

Rapaczynski, Wanda, Dorothy Singer, and Jerome Singer, (1982). Teaching Television: A Curriculum for Young Children. *Journal of Communication*, 32:2, 46-55.

Ravitch, Diane, and Chester E. Finn, Jr., (1987). *What Do Our 17 Year Olds Know?* New York: Harper & Row.

Roberts, Elizabeth, (1983). Teens, Sexuality and Sex: Our Mixed Messages. *Television and Children*, 6:4, 9-12.

Robinson, John P., (1990). I Love My TV. *American Demographics*, September, 24-27.

Salomon, Gavriel, and Tamar Leigh, (1984). Predispositions about Learning from Print and Television. *Journal of Communication*, 34:2, 119-35.

Schneller, Raphael, (1982). Training for Critical TV Viewing. *Educational Research*, 24:2, 99-106.

Silverman, Gary, (1989). TV Paints a Rosy View of Races. *San Francisco Examiner*, August 23.

Singer, Dorothy, Jerome Singer, and Diana Zuckerman, (1981). *Teaching Television: How to Use It to Your Child's Advantage.* New York: Dial.

Solomon, Jack, (1988). *The Signs of Our Times.* Los Angeles: Jeremy Tarcher.

Steenland, Sally (ed.), (1989). *Analysis of Black, Hispanic and Asian Characters on Entertainment Television.* Washington, D.C.: National Commission on Working Women.

Steinem, Gloria, (1988). Six Great Ideas That Television Is Missing. In Stuart Oskamp (ed.), *Television as a Social Issue.* Newbury Park, Calif.: Sage Publications.

Tierney, Joan, (1978). *Parents, Adolescents and Television: Culture, Learning Influence.* Canada: Canadian, Radio TV and Telecommunications.

U.S. Commission on Civil Rights, (1979). *Window Dressing on the Set.* Washington, D.C.: GPO.

USA Today, (1990). (No title available). June 12, 3D.

USA Today, (1991a). (No title available). July 9.

USA Today, (1991b). (No title available). May 9, 10a.

Wertham, Fredric, (1968). In O. N. Larsen (ed.), *Violence and Media.* New York: Harper & Row.

Winn, Marie, (1977). *The Plug-In Drug.* New York: Bantam.

———, (1987). *Unplugging the Plug-In Drug.* New York: Penguin.

Winston Salem Journal, (1991). (No title available). March 28.

Zoglin, Richard, (1989). Witness for the Defense: The Atlanta Child Murders. *Time*, February 11, 99.

RECOMMENDED READING

Barber, Susanna. When I Grow Up: Children and the Work-World of Television. *Media and Values* (1989) 47, 15-17.

Barcus, F. Earle. *Images of Life on Children's Television: Sex Roles, Minorities and Families.* New York: Praeger, 1983.

Berenstain, S., and J. Berenstain. *The Berenstain Bears and Too Much TV.* New York: Random House, 1987.

Cantor, Muriel, and Joel Cantor. Do Soaps Teach Sex? *Television and Children* (Summer/Fall, 1984) 7:3-4, 34-38.

Chesebro, James, and Caroline Hamsher. Communication, Values and Popular Television Series. *Journal of Communication* (1975) 8:3, 589-603.

Collingford, Cedric. *Children and Television.* New York: St. Martin's, 1984.

Cross, Donna Woolfolk. *Media-Speak: How Television Makes Up Your Mind.* New York: Mentor, 1983.

Dominick, Joseph. Videogames, Television Violence and Aggression in Teenagers. *Journal of Communication* (1984) 34:2, 136-47.

Fiske, John, and John Hartley. *Reading Television*. New York: Methuen, 1978.

Greenberg, Bradley, and Charles Atkins. Portrayal of Drinking on Television. *Journal of Communication* (1983) 33:2, 44-55.

Hanson, Cynthia. The Women of China Beach. *Journal of Popular Film and Television* (1990) 17:4, 154-63.

Hays, Kim. *TV Science and Kids: Teaching Our Children to Question*. Reading, Mass.: Addison-Wesley, 1984.

Hess, Dona, and Geoffrey Grant. Prime Time Television and Gender Role Behavior. *Teaching Sociology* (1983) 10:3, 371-88.

Himmelstein, Hal. *Television Myth and the American Mind*. New York: Praeger, 1984.

Kelly, Hope, and Howard Gardner. *Viewing Children through Television*. San Francisco: Jossey Bass, 1981.

Lehrer, John. The New Man: That's Entertainment. *Media and Values* (1989) no. 49, 8-11.

Leibert, Robert, John Neale, and Emily Davidson. *The Early Window: Effects of Television on Children and Youth*. New York: Pergamon, 1973.

Levinson, Richard M. From Olive Oyl to Sweet Polly Purebread: Sex Role Stereotypes and Televised Cartoons. *Journal of Popular Culture* (1975) 9:3, 561-72.

Lowry, Dennis, and David Towler. Soap Operas' Portrayal of Sex, Contraception and Sexually Transmitted Diseases. *Journal of Communication* (1989) 39:2, 76-83.

Marmorstein, Gary. TV as a Teacher of Morals. *Television and Families* (Spring 1987), 37-41.

Mayerle, Judine. "Roseanne—How Did You Get Inside My House?" A Case Study of a Hit Blue-Collar Situation Comedy. *Journal of Popular Culture* (1991) 24:4, 71-88.

Miller, Mark Crispin. Dads through the Decades: Thirty Years of TV Fathers. *Media and Values* (1989) no. 49, n.p.

Montgomery, Kathryn. *Target: Prime Time Advocacy Groups and the Struggle for Entertaining Television*. New York: Oxford University Press, 1989.

Rosenberg, Howard. TVs Work Ethic: A Prime Time Fantasy. *Media and Methods* (1989) no. 47, 17.

Schwarz, Meg. *TV and Teens: Experts Look at the Issues*. Reading, Mass.: Addison-Wesley, 1982.

Selnow, Gary. Solving Problems on Prime-Time Television. *Journal of Communication* (Spring 1986), 63-72.

Shore, Debra. TV or Not TV: Turning Teachers on to Media Literacy. *Teacher Magazine* (June/July 1990), 31-33.

Snow, Robert. Teaching Sociology through Existing Television Programs. *Teaching Sociology* (1983) 10:3, 353-60.

Spangler, Lynn. A Historical Overview of Female Friendships on Prime-Time Television. *Journal of Popular Culture* (1989) 22:4, 13-24.

Steenland, Sally. *Growing Up in Prime Time: An Analysis of Adolescent Girls on Television.* Washington, D.C.: National Commission on Working Women of Wider Opportunities for Women, 1988.

Strom, Robert, and Shirley Strom. TV Viewing and Communication in Families. *Television and Families* (1986) 9:2, 29-34.

Sunila, Joyce. The Pregnancy Cover-Up. *Television and Families* (1987) 9:4, 57-60.

Turow, Joseph, and Lisa Coe. Curing Television Ills: The Portrayal of Health Care. *Journal of Communication* (1985) 35:4, 36-51.

Verschuure, Eric Peter. Stumble, Bumble, Mumble: TV's Image of the South. *Journal of Popular Culture* (1982) 16:3, 92-96.

Zoglin, Richard. Home Is Where the Venom Is. *Time* (April 16, 1990), 85-86.

_____. Is TV Ruining Our Children? *Time* (October 15, 1990), 75-76.

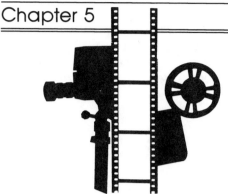

Chapter 5

Advertising: Exploring the Consumer Culture in the Classroom

WHY INTEGRATE ADVERTISING INTO INSTRUCTION?

Addressing participants in the "New Literary" conference in Canada in 1990, Scottish media educator Eddie Dick said the study of advertising was central to the study of media. Dick also asserted that the movement toward media education tends to be indicative of the health and open-mindedness of an education system. In the United States, the whole concept of advertising in education has been controversial.

The 1989-1990 dispute over Whittle Communications' "Channel One" project reflected the controversial and contradictory relationship between the mass media and education. Many educational associations around the country rejected "Channel One's" social studies broadcasts because they contained 2 minutes of advertising. The advertising was used to pay for some $50,000 of equipment for the schools that contracted with Whittle. Although other objections were made to the programming concept, much of the argument hinged on the presence of advertising in the classroom. Very little attention was directed to how the advertisements could be integrated into the instructional process. Instead, terms such as *compulsory commercialization* and *captive audience* were used to condemn the project. Given the role of advertising in our society, it would have seemed appropriate for social studies to provide a forum within which to study ads and their impact on society. Advertising plays a major role in shaping the way we think. Writing in *The Image Makers: Power and Persuasion on Madison Avenue*, William Meyers says, "Ad Alley's wizards have firmly established themselves as both the creators and controllers of our consumer culture ... they are now virtually able to dictate the food we eat, the soda or beer we drink, the cigarettes we smoke, ... the cars we drive, even the Presidents we elect" (1984, 3-4). Responding to advertising is a vital and strategic way of fostering critical thinking skills in children and adolescents. Research in the area suggests that "adolescents may have difficulty separating puffery from substantiated ad claims" and that "they appear to accept advertiser's claims as relevant criteria for their own and others' decisions" (Linn et al. 1984, 383). It has also been suggested that looking at the claims and criteria used in advertising could play a role in science education and "might foster informed decision making by helping adolescents develop procedures for selecting criteria in a variety of decision making situations" (Linn et al. 1984, 384). Recently colorization, computer-imaging, and other techniques have been used in advertising to alter reality. In 1991, for example, a Diet Coke TV spot featured Humphrey Bogart, James Cagney, and Louis Armstrong, all seemingly occupying the same scene and time. Their images were inserted into a "real-time" commercial involving other present-day actors. The implications of this form of image altering go beyond art and aesthetics and challenge our entire concept of reality. Used politically, this form of imagineering could be Orwellian.

Several key social issues have strong ties to the world of advertising. If advertising and the mass media have created some of these problems, they can also be used to combat these problems. For us to effectively work with these issues requires that we first recognize the relationship between the problems and advertising. Central to this approach is the entire concept of consumer health. A truly healthy society requires that citizens be capable of making informed choices, which means thinking critically about products, their packaging, and their promises.

Drug Education. The drug problem in this country emerged in part out of a consumer culture that pushes quick fixes and instant solutions. The consumer culture is also a chemical culture that sells highs and lows from caffeine to sleeping pills. Trying to address the problem of illegal drug use necessitates considering the socially sanctioned use of drugs, including those that we generally regard as harmless. Attention should be given to how advertising promotes socially sanctioned drugs and perceptions of them, as well as to the role that public service announcements (PSAs) play in combating the drug problem. For example, what message was sent in the Excedrin advertisement "Life got tougher, so we got stronger"? Does this form of advertising ignore the lifestyle that creates headaches and stress and offer a quick-fix chemical solution to a more complex social problem?

Alcohol Awareness. In 1989, Surgeon General C. Everett Koop called for a ban on alcohol advertising and was particularly critical of its impact on impressionable adolescents. Groups such as Mothers against Drunk Driving (M.A.D.D.), Students against Drunk Driving (S.A.D.D.), and Stop Marketing Alcohol on Radio and Television (S.M.A.R.T.) have all expressed concern about the social sanction afforded alcohol consumption in media and advertising that associates drinking with social success, athletic prowess, sex appeal, and good times. But in 1990, William Bennett said that he had been appointed drug czar, not health czar. Bennett argued that he needed to focus on illegal hard drugs and that, although alcohol was a problem, it would only confuse and cloud the issue.

Health educators seeking to address the problem of alcohol in society must explore the culture of consumption and media representations of alcohol in advertising and programming. (Photograph copyright © 1988 *Newsweek*, Inc.)

In an age of AIDS and teen pregnancy, adolescent sexual activity has increasingly negative health consequences. Research suggests media messages promote impulse and instant gratification. Health educators need to be aware of the mixed messages and cultural contradiction that confront young people as they encounter their budding sexuality. (*People Weekly* is a registered trademark of The Time Inc. Magazine Company, used with permission.)

Tobacco. In 1990 Secretary of Health Louis Sullivan launched major attacks on the tobacco industry and was particularly critical of advertising strategies targeting young women and Blacks. Tobacco and its role in our culture is more than a health issue. Attention needs to be paid not just to advertising but also to the political process, the tobacco lobby, and the role of the southern tobacco states in national politics.

Sex Education. Attempting to address complex issues such as teen pregnancy and AIDS without considering the impact of advertising and the media in these areas ignores the entire cultural context in which sexual attitudes and behavior are created. Sex sells! Advertisers have marketed sex for years and, despite the AIDS crisis, there is ample evidence that eroticism is still a major marketing strategy. Anyone who has seen magazine ads for Calvin Klein's Obsession perfume is well aware of the use of sex and nudity in advertising. It is interesting to note network television's objection to carrying advertisements for condoms, whereas their programming and ads are often sexually provocative.

Health Care. Beyond the world of tobacco, alcohol, and illegal drugs, the nation's health is strongly linked to marketing products and perceptions. This includes our physical fitness and appearance, as well as our self-esteem and self-image. Advertising has an impact on what we eat. It sells fast foods and a fast lifestyle. But do we really know what we eat and can we make informed decisions? On July 15, 1991, the cover story of *Time* was "Misleading Labels! Why Americans Don't Know What They're Eating." Advertising promotes diets and weight-loss programs for the overweight and creates an image of the ideal body for both men and women. The pursuit of "the look" keeps the consumer culture running through the marketing of everything from cosmetics to exercise equipment. Bulemia, anorexia, and other eating disorders need to be considered at least in part against this background. For athletes, the competitive edge can be chemically induced, resulting in drug scandals that taint runners such as Ben Johnson or steroid abuse by football players such as Lyle Alzado. The greatest drug of all, and perhaps the most addictive, is the illusion of the quick fix promised by so much of the media.

Ecology and Pollution. Our lifestyles contribute to the problems of pollution and ecological damage. The products we use and the materials they are packaged in are often ecologically destructive. Legislation can change business and industry, but education is more likely to change individual human behavior. That means first recognizing our own responsibility in the ecosystem and acknowledging that if we are not part of the solution, we are part of the problem. Consumer awareness can empower teachers and students in their own schools and neighborhoods where their own activities can make a difference.

Beyond health-related issues we must also recognize the role of advertising in other areas of our society.

The Political Process. U.S. schools traditionally assert that one of their functions is to prepare responsible citizens for their role in a democratic society. Given the fact that the political process is now completely infused with advertising, marketing, image-consultants, and polling, it is not possible for us to prepare students for an active role in this process without also helping them to become both critical viewers and critical thinkers.

Values, Attitudes, and Lifestyles. Good teaching requires that we know not only our subject matter, but also the nature and needs of our students. Understanding them requires that we recognize more than their IQs and aptitudes; it requires that we also be aware of the ways in which their views and values are affected by advertising and the media. Although individual commercials can be isolated and studied, we must be aware of the cumulative impact of the thousands of commercials our students are exposed to. For many students, their sense of self-worth is based not on who they are but on what they own. The materialistic culture reflected in t-shirts and bumper stickers proclaiming "He Who Dies with the Most Toys Wins" is often in conflict with the goals of U.S. education and the teachings of most U.S. religions.

The average American now sees some 32,000 commercials every year. In 1988, advertisers spent $110 billion on television and print ads. Keeping advertising out of the classroom does not protect our students from its impact. Closing the curriculum and the classroom to commercials closes the door on a powerful part of our culture and denies students the opportunity to recognize and comprehend advertising's influence. With proper planning, advertising can be integrated into many areas of the curriculum at all levels of learning to foster critical thinking and viewing skills.

Instructional Approaches

1. English and language arts: Developing thinking and viewing skills through the analysis of the verbal and visual techniques used to persuade us to purchase products. Tie-ins to literature such as *Death of a Salesman* and *1984*.

2. Art: Appreciation and application of graphic design concepts utilized in print and nonprint advertisements, as well as in the packaging of products.

3. History and social studies: Recognizing advertising's social impact through the presentation and perpetuation of social, racial, and gender stereotypes. Understanding advertising as a social artifact that can be used to study the society that produced and consumed it.

4. Business and economics: Marketing techniques and strategies. Advertising's cost to the consumer.

5. Science: Use of scientific terms and claims in the marketing of products. Also includes areas of psychology and perception.

6. Health and biology: The impact of products we use on our health and fitness, including both our physical and our mental health.

7. Geography: Advertisements in travel magazines and brochures from travel agents provide a cheap and interesting approach to exploring other countries and cultures. What pictures do students get of these countries from such ads and how accurate are those pictures?

Utilizing these broad curriculum areas to approach advertising makes it possible for the topic to be integrated into existing subjects. Cognitive, affective, and psychomotor objectives related to advertising can be established to provide students with information about commercials, an appreciation of the various design principles embodied in them, and the opportunity to create and produce their own print, audio, and video advertisements.

The Materials

Perhaps no other materials referred to in this book are so cheap and so widely available as advertisements. Utilizing newspapers and magazines that most students have at home or drawing on those housed in school library media centers provides ready access to large still images that can be more easily analyzed than television commercials. Local newspapers, telephone directories, students' notebooks, lunchboxes, even the clothes students wear can all be incorporated into lessons dealing with advertising. The following activities have been categorized by the age levels they are most suitable for. Teachers are reminded that these are broad categories and that it is often possible to modify an activity so it would be suitable for one or more levels.

ACTIVITIES AND STRATEGIES

In the summer of 1990, NBC presented a prime-time special called "Sex, Buys and Advertising." The program explored product placement and various advertising techniques and strategies. The program warned consumers of the impact of advertising but never once suggested that schools, teachers, or the curriculum should address advertising's role in society. Instead, Deborah Norville closed the program by saying, "Advertising is here to stay. It's part of our culture. It drives our economy. It's up to us as parents and consumers to make the buying decisions that make sense for us and our families." Until teachers begin to help children think about those decisions, however, we remain vulnerable to the powerful persuasion of the advertisers. As you begin this process it is important to understand that advertising is open to multiple interpretations. Encourage students to concentrate on the analytical process rather than on coming up with a "correct" answer.

An emerging area of concern related to advertising is product placement in movies. This practice is covered in the sections of this chapter that address alcohol or tobacco advertising. Motion pictures such as *Turner and Hooch* (1989) and *Mr. Destiny* (1990) abound with visual and verbal references to products.

Defining Advertising

(ELEM/MID/HIGH)—Ask the class to develop a definition of advertising. Compare it to a dictionary definition. The American Marketing Association defines advertising as "any paid form of nonpersonal presentation and promotion of ideas, goods, or services by an identified sponsor" (Mandell 1984, 3).

Older students can analyze key elements of this definition to further understand the process of advertising. For example, what type of advertising is nonpersonal? Many students tend to think that only products are advertised, but this definition also introduces the concepts of ideas and services. Have students develop a list of ideas and services they have seen advertised. Finally, examine the concept of sponsor identification. Are sponsors always named, identified, or recognized? Is the identification done in such a way that it is often ignored, overlooked, or minimized in contrast to the message itself?

Types of Advertising

(ELEM/MID/HIGH)—We have already learned that advertising promotes ideas, products, and services. These commercials are produced in many forms. Have the class develop a list of the various forms of advertising. The list should include:

- Print: Magazines and newspapers, including display and classified advertising.

- Radio: Commercial radio exists because of the presence of advertising.

- Billboards: Includes giant highway billboards as well as advertising on buses and other public transportation.

- Television advertising: This should include emerging forms of commercials, such as those that are now often in videos we rent or buy. The videos *Rain Man* and *Top Gun* both begin with this type of advertising.

Elements of Advertising

(ELEM/MID/HIGH)—A useful way to conceptualize advertising is to break it down into several key components. These include:

- The product (idea, service).

- The package as a physical object, including shape, size, and color.

- The pitch, or the persuasion by which the product is marketed.

- The position or placement. This refers to the actual strategy of placing the ad. Which magazines will feature it? What time slot and what type of programs are appropriate for it on television?

- The purchaser. Remember that advertising is essentially an act of communication that relies heavily on assumptions and attitudes about the intended audience.

These elements provide a useful introductory framework for conceptualizing advertising. It can be used to get students thinking about what is being sold, how it is being sold, and to whom it is being sold.

Associations and Appeals

(MID / HIGH) — Most of the time advertising tends to be more consumer-centered than product-centered. In other words, advertising increasingly tells us less factual information about the actual product and concentrates instead on packaging and promoting the product by associating it with attitudes and lifestyles that appeal to the target audience. An extremely simple way to demonstrate this to students of all ages is by showing them magazine advertising for Marlboro cigarettes. In most of these ads, the print and the picture of the actual cigarette, product, or packet are quite small. Emphasis is placed on the human figure or figures, the outdoor environment, and the activities the people are engaged in. Ask the students what mood is being created. Ask them how that mood is created. Ask them what type of people appear in these ads and what type of people (age, sex, etc.) they think the ads are aimed at. This process is a good way to get students to start thinking about the relationship between products and the process through which they are sold. Marlboro ads also demonstrate how advertisers use images to distract us from the truth. The ads distract consumers from thinking about tobacco's harmful effects by showing healthy, energetic people in wide open spaces and natural environments.

(ELEM / MID / HIGH) — Ask students to describe their favorite television ad and to explain why they like it. After you have heard six or seven responses, write on the board a chart showing what types of appeals work with this age group. It is likely that humor or cuteness will be mentioned a lot. Young people tend to be attracted by humor, offbeat approaches, and images of cute babies, kittens, and puppies.

(MID / HIGH) — In this country, one of the most consistent advertising associations is to link a product with broadly perceived national icons, names, or values. Insurance is packaged as "liberty," cars are sold as "the heartbeat of America," and the national flag has been successfully appropriated by political parties as their own, despite its obvious nonpartisan nature.

Various techniques of persuasion, many growing out of propaganda, have been used by advertisers in marketing their products. Introduce students to each of the following concepts and see if they can come up with an example of a magazine or television ad that works this way.

Happy Families. These often tend to use a slice-of-life approach, creating vignettes of family life to sell a product. This might include parents seeing a teenage daughter off on her first date or an older brother taking his sister out for hamburgers.

Humor. This is used constantly for many products. Joe Isuzu is a humorous advertising character whom many students would be familiar with. The Energizer battery rabbit is also a humor technique.

Exotic Places. These ads tend to blend fact and fantasy to sell a "lifestyles of the rich and famous" escape. Carnival Cruises is a simple example of such escapism.

Something for Nothing. These include standard "buy one, get one free" claims as well as all sorts of premiums and give-aways. Competitions and the chance to win something are also part of this technique. In the summer of 1990, Coca-Cola's "magic" cans promised money and prizes.

Everybody's Doing It. This sales pitch essentially uses the need to belong and peer pressure as its method of persuasion. It tends to focus on belonging to the "in" crowd. Dr. Pepper's successful "Wouldn't you like to be a Pepper, too?" campaign is a good example.

Plain Folks. Essentially, these ads operate on a populist, no-frills approach and tend to present average-looking people to convince us of the honesty and authenticity of the product. Ads for Bartles and Jaymes wine coolers, with their laid back style, demonstrate this technique quite well. So, too, does a recent McDonald's ad in which a teenage boy explains to his date that he has simple tastes. This leads into the "food, folks, and fun" McDonald's slogan.

Celebrity Endorsements. This testimonial approach uses the name recognition of the celebrity to draw attention to the product. The cola wars of the 1980s saw frequent use of stars such as Michael Jackson, Madonna, and Michael J. Fox to sell soda. Paul Hogan, better known as Crocodile Dundee, was the pitch man for Australia, promoting tourism to that country, and Bill Cosby was the pitch man for Jello.

Value and Reliability. These ads stress logic over associations, pitching both the quality of the goods and their reasonable prices.

Sex Appeal. This is probably the most widely used technique. Sometimes, an attractive or handsome body is used to attract attention. Soloflex exercise equipment did extremely well with its taut male torso and the slogan "A Hard Man Is Good to Find." Less blatant sexual appeals can be found in ads such as Close-Up toothpaste spots, which establish an association between good breath and sex appeal.

Science and Statistics. These usually are recognized through claims such as "9 out of 10 dentists surveyed" or "recommended by more people." Students need to be introduced to the ways in which such statistics and claims can be misleading. Scientific persuasion tends to include phrases such as "new and improved" or "secret ingredients" or images and phrases that promote a technological and scientific mystique that preempts critical evaluations of the claims or the product.

Health and Nature. These ads either state or imply that a product contributes to your health and well-being. Claims such as "all natural" or "no preservatives added" are typical. So, too, are suggestions that use of the product will somehow improve your performance. One example is the beer slogan "Bring Out Your Best." Sometimes the claims that a product is natural are quite the opposite. Just For Men hair color, for example, promises "the look of your *natural* color in just 5 minutes." Of course, gray is the natural color that is being disguised.

Negative and Comparison. Other appeals tend to include "tastes good," "good for you," and the promise of status or a successful career. Negative or comparison ads have dealt with everything from political mudslinging to selling cars. They are interesting because they actually name the competition. One hamburger chain featured a clown in the background, obviously to invoke the image of McDonald's, in an ad suggesting that some hamburger places packaged food in funny boxes and charged prices that were less than funny. A recent television ad for Volkswagen compared the car favorably to both Volvo and the Honda Accord. Imodium A-D disparagingly referred to its competition as "the pink stuff."

Patriotic. Patriotism is also used for profit. The U.S. flag and other national icons are often invoked to boost sales. During the Gulf War in 1990-1991, Operation Desert Storm created a bandwagon effect as companies rushed to embrace the cause. A special Coors Light can was even produced that had stars and stripes and the message "Welcome Home America's Best."

Fears and Insecurities. Slice-of-death commercials that draw on fears and insecurities are often grainy and shot with a hand-held camera to create an unsteady, cinema verité look. People in the ads appear threatened and uncomfortable. They are often sitting in boardrooms talking about the failure of a computer or telephone system and the competition they face. AT&T and Macintosh created good examples of this technique. Security is often used to sell products, which also means playing on fears. Products for urinary incontinence promote themselves with reassuring names such as Serenity and Depends.

Positive Effects. Although commercials always serve the interest of the company or product, at times they also can be educational. A McDonald's spot features Mike, who has Down's syndrome. The McJobs program and commercials such as this can help the public understand special individuals in society. Sometimes commercials also break stereotypes. An AT&T spot refers to two Detroit mechanics, but the image on the screen shows two women mechanics, a powerful departure from traditional social assumptions and occupational stereotypes. American Express suggested a new image of masculinity with its ad about a successful businessman dreaming of going to Paris and attending cooking school.

Friendly Persuasion

(MID/HIGH) — The following list is taken from actual advertisements. Give students the list and have them match the slogan with the product and identify the techniques used.

Advanced Medicine for Pain (Advil)

It's a Cooler World (Seagrams wine coolers)

The One That Won't Slow You Down (Coors Lite beer)

Just Do It (Nike athletic shoes)

The Choice of a New Generation (Pepsi)

This Is Not Your Father's Oldsmobile (Oldsmobile)

For the Moments of Your Life (Maxwell House coffee)

We Bring Good Things to You (Dow Chemical)

The Pain Reliever Hospitals Use Most (Tylenol)

The Breakfast of Champions (Wheaties)

Come Fly the Friendly Skies (United Airlines)

You Can't Top the Copper Top (Duracell batteries)

Food, Folks, and Fun (McDonald's)

Everything You Always Wanted in a Beer and Less (Miller Lite beer)

The Quality You Need at the Price You Want (K Mart)

Just for the Taste of It (Diet Coke)

The Real Thing (Coke)

Uh huh (Diet Pepsi)

Gotta Have It (Coke)

PSYCHOGRAPHICS, VALUES, AND CLUSTERS

Most of us have a basic knowledge of demographics, or the science of statistics as applied to the composition of the human population. For marketers, demographics provides useful information about the size of particular markets. This essentially means that advertisers have some sense of the number of potential purchasers. Demographics, however, provides only a broad picture of consumers, identified by quantity rather than quality.

Clustering is a process of computer-generated market research that arranges the country's 250,000 neighborhoods into 40-48 varying lifestyles. These profiles are used to predict buying preferences and purchasing decisions. One cluster system is known as PRIZM (potential rating index by zip markets). Cluster categories include such broad groups as Blue Blood Estates, Money and Brains, Pools and Patios, and New Melting Pot. Each profile lists the age group, income, and average education of its members, as well as information about the magazines they read, the television programs they watch, the cars they drive, the food they eat, and relevant national zip codes. This provides information for the targeting of very specified groups.

Psychographics is a widely used process that provides insights into the nature and needs of consumers, establishing psychological profiles. These profiles enable segmentation and fragmentation of the market, so ads can be targeted more specifically to each broad consumer group. This means the techniques used in the ads are specifically targeted at each group and run in magazines or are shown on television programs that would appeal to that group. Psychographics, developed by Stanford Research Institute, breaks the population into various values, attitudes, and lifestyle (VALS) blocks. These include Belongers, Emulators, Societally Conscious Achievers, and other categories. Emerging techniques such as emotional lexicons and benefit chains provide advertisers with even more insight into our personalities, feelings, and attitudes.

MARKETING RESEARCH

Any purchasing decision is based upon a combination of factors. Some of these are logical and rational, such as cost, quality, and relative usefulness of the product. We tend to be aware of these elements when making purchasing decisions. Part of the decision, however, depends upon less obvious factors such as the motivations and associations already discussed in this chapter. Advertisers have a clear picture of their audience. *Mirabella* magazine, for example, knows that 96 percent of its readers are women; 51 percent are married, and 49 percent are widowed. The median age is 41.4 and the median household income is $68,800. Eighty-three percent of the readers are college educated and 69 percent own their own home. In addition to these demographics and psychological factors, advertisers are also interested in the physiology of perception, particularly areas related to how the eye sees, what attracts its attention, and what factors influence recall and recognition. All of this information helps them determine how to package and display products. Some of the technological approaches they use include:

1. Eye scanner: This machine reads eye movement and helps advertisers understand where the eye looks on a page or a TV screen so they can design advertisements to match this.

2. T-Scope: This machine measures recall, including objects and brand names. Ads are tested to make sure that they draw attention to the product and that the audience can recall the product or the brand, rather than only some person, phrase, or image in the ad.

3. Analog machine: Television commercials are tested by the analog machine. This is a form of joystick measurement device. People watch commercials and indicate a score for them, ranging from very dull to very good. The results are tallied by a computer and serve as an indication of the potential success of the commercial.

Hence, by measuring consumers and their reactions, marketers are more likely to develop techniques that get us to respond positively. It must be stressed that many of these techniques influence us without our knowledge. Several examples from real life demonstrate this. When Betty Crocker put a spoon on the packet, sales increased. Packaging changes for Scotch transparent tape, K Mart film, and Bubble Yum bubble gum also resulted in increased sales. People perceived that the products were somehow better, even though only the packaging had changed.

Factors as simple as box design, shape, and color all influence the way consumers perceive a product. Pink, for example, works well for packaging cosmetics and linens. A "soft" look attracts female buyers whereas a "hard" look is more appealing to males. Cool colors promote quiet, relaxing moods, and warm colors suggest action. Billboards and neon signs used to attract customers to hotels and restaurants rely on visibility, and again color is a key variable. Blue, for example, is difficult to see from a distance, whereas yellow is very visible.

Color Counts

(ELEM / MID / HIGH)—Have students conduct a series of surveys to explore the role of color in advertising and packaging. You might want to divide the class into groups to study different aspects of this subject. Students could examine products found at home, dividing them into different categories such as food, cleaning supplies, drinks, etc. They should note what the most commonly used colors are, what products these colors are used for, and if there seems to be any difference in the colors used for products aimed at men versus women. The same assignment could be given to students during a field trip to a supermarket or a hardware store, or they might be assigned the task for homework. In the field trip, students could be assigned to specific aisles and products. Students could also be asked to determine the dominant colors used in billboards and various signs for hotels, restaurants, fast-food outlets, and businesses in their own community. Finally, students could cut advertisements from magazines and arrange a display by colors.

(ELEM / MID)—Watch a series of television ads with the color turned off. After watching the commercials in black-and-white, discuss the colors that should be used in each ad and the reasons for the choices.

HIDDEN PERSUADERS AND SUBLIMINAL SEDUCTION

The sections on VALS and market research indicate that advertisers know more about us than we know about them. They know what makes us tick, and because of that they are able to bombard us with messages that influence us without our knowledge. Sometimes what advertisers say to us is very direct and the meaning of a commercial is obvious. An ad may tell us, "Use this product and you will appear to be wealthy and sophisticated," or, "Drink this and you will be young, athletic, and socially attractive." Other times, however, the meaning of a commercial is much more subtle, with the message imbedded in the image or the text. These advertisements often appeal to us on the subconscious or unconscious level and induce responses that we are not aware of. Sometimes this occurs through the use of symbolism and other times through various subliminal images and messages imbedded in the ad in such a way that we are not consciously aware of being exposed to them. The very concept of subliminal advertising is disturbing to many individuals. It is not uncommon to find students and adults who deny flatly even the possibility of such a technique. The reasons behind such denial are crucial. One reason has to do with the fact that recognizing the existence of subliminal advertising implies that we can be manipulated and, at the same time, that we are powerless against the media. Given our basic human need for security and self-direction, the concept of subliminal advertising can be quite threatening. Another reason the subject evokes such hostility and denial has to do with the fact that these hidden messages are often sexually oriented. Bryan Wilson Key articulates some of the problems associated with this topic in his book *Subliminal Seduction.* "Any investigation of the techniques of subconscious communication involve first an investigation into one's own fantasy systems, self-images, illusions, personal vanities and secret motives. This is an investigation that might make even the toughest of us extremely uncomfortable" (1972, 1-2).

In *The Clam Plate Orgy and Other Subliminal Techniques for Manipulating Your Behavior* (1980), Key documents the widespread academic, political, and industrial opposition and denial he encountered in trying to raise consciousness about this process. Interestingly enough, *The Hidden Persuaders*, written by Vance Packard in 1957, addressed many of these concerns without provoking such opposition. One of Packard's chapters is called "The Psycho-Seduction of Children," and the opening of the book clearly recognizes the hidden forces at work in the marketplace. "This book is an attempt to explore a strange and rather exotic new area of American life. It is about the large scale efforts being made, often with impressive success, to channel our unthinking habits, our purchasing decisions, and our thought processes" (1957, 1).

Teachers who wish to introduce students to subliminal advertising must recognize some of these problems. In addition, most students go through a stage of reading too much into advertisements. This overenthusiasm needs to be tempered. It is, however, significantly better that they recognize the existence of subliminal advertising than it is for them to turn a blind eye to it. In subliminal advertising, more than in any other area, we need to acknowledge that, as consumers, not only is what we see not what we get, but also we do not "get" (i.e., understand) what we see. By the early 1990s, advertisers were beginning to spoof the idea of subliminal messages. Absolut vodka created an ad that read "Absolut Subliminal" and had a message in ice cubes. Seagram's gin created a print ad that asked, "Can You Find the Hidden Pleasure?" *Sports Illustrated* (7/15/1991) featured a similar ad that urged readers to "Find the Hidden Refreshments" by connecting the dots in the glass. A more serious essay in *U.S. News and World Report* asserted that Newport's "Alive with Pleasure" cigarette campaign has "a strong undercurrent of sexual hostility, usually directed at women" (1991, 18). Tobacco and alcohol companies, the article said, "seem to resort to subliminal themes most frequently. Despite the industry's attempt to dismiss the whole idea of subliminal techniques by lampooning it, the reality is that advertising often works covertly, by playing on social symbols and cultural codes that we are not fully aware of."

Teachers wishing to pursue this topic with students should consult the books cited in the "Recommended Reading" section in this chapter. They have excellent visual examples of symbolism and subliminal techniques. Some examples of subliminal advertising are listed below.

1. Gilbey's gin, *Time* magazine, July 5, 1971. This famous advertisement has been widely analyzed for its subliminal techniques. Among these, perhaps the best known and most discernible is the spelling of *sex* by placing one letter in each of the three ice cubes in the glass shown in the ad. Key's work also talks

about the subliminal imagery of drowning faces in liquor ads. These images supposedly appeal to the death wish of alcoholics.

2. Benetton clothing. This more recent print advertisement is likely to appear in magazines such as *Rolling Stone* and *Premier*. The ad draws upon biblical symbolism by invoking the story of Adam and Eve. In it, a teenage male and female are depicted from the waist up. The male wears blue jeans but no shirt. The female wears an open jean jacket with nothing on underneath, and the top button of her jeans is undone. She is offering the boy an apple. A snake is wrapped around her neck, and its head, its mouth open, hovers over her breast. Nothing is said at all about Benetton or their products. The entire ad operates upon a mythical and symbolic level.

3. Edge shaving cream featured a startling ad for a brief time in *Rolling Stone* magazine. The slogan of the ad is "Not Your Ordinary Shave." The top half of the page is dominated by a man's face covered with shaving cream. His eyes are closed and he has a pleasurable smile on his face. In the bottom right of the frame, a hand holds a can of shaving cream. To the left is an image of a surfer with a mountain sunset behind him, and to the surfer's left is the image of a woman's face partly obscured in shaving cream and surf. The real activity, however, is in the man's face. Although the ad was eventually airbrushed and toned down, initially it featured quite discernible sexual images. What appeared to be mountains was actually a naked woman on her back with her knees raised. The shaving cream on the man's upper lip contained several pictures of naked women and at least one penis. Perhaps this is what the ad meant when it said, "You get everything you might expect in a clean close shave and something you didn't."

HOW TO READ ADVERTISEMENTS:
In-Depth Techniques

Several visual devices can be isolated that enable us to analyze the composition and content of visual messages in still or moving form. A basic beginning might be called the "four P" approach.

- Posture: Gestures, facial expressions, and posture often convey a lot about moods, feelings, and attitudes. Students can be taught to "read" this body language and act out their own moods through posture.

- Point of view: Generally established by the placement of the camera. Tilt-ups make the subject strong, forceful, sometimes threatening, and very often masculine. Tilt-downs render the subject weak, vulnerable, sometimes frightened, and more often than not feminine.

- Position: The location of an object or person in the frame often contributes to the meaning. A person at the head of a staircase, for example, is usually in a stronger position than one at the foot of a staircase. A bottle on a table is one thing, but a bottle placed in a man's crotch, as it is in a Salem cigarette ad, says something else altogether.

- Prop: When the physical object has a symbolic or metaphysical meaning. This can be something as simple as color symbolism or as loaded as sexual symbolism invoked by images of the biblical apple and snake. (For more information, see the section on mise-en-scène in chapter 7.)

Decoding advertisements with these techniques moves through a series of stages:

1. Image: The initially constructed picture.

2. Identification: The simple process of recognizing the various objects used in constructing the composition, such as two people, a bottle of wine, a sports car, and a highway. This process is restricted to recognizing the integral elements of the frame.

3. Interpretation: In this process, we move from isolating the individual elements and their literal meanings to a consideration of their cumulative statement and their cultural context. This includes the symbolic, metaphorical, and mythical meanings of any ad. In this step we move from recognizing to reading and comprehending. It includes reading the relationships among figures and objects in the frame as well as reading their external, social, and cultural references.

4. Influence: Our ability to recognize and read the process by which advertisements and other visuals are constructed potentially empowers us. It helps to demystify the media and reveal the ideological messages imbedded in advertisements. It helps us recognize the concealed and cumulative nature of these messages and their potential social impact. Finally, we have the opportunity to utilize such visual techniques in our own creations and communication.

Sample Decoding

(MID / HIGH) — An example of this process of decoding can be seen in a print ad for Passport scotch. The key slogan of the ad is "Because You Enjoy Going First Class." This could actually be covered or cut out of the ad and students would still be able to read the visuals to see how status and sophistication were used to promote the product. At the identification stage, students would analyze the elements of the picture. These consist of a bottle of scotch, glasses, serving trays, a passport, and a building in the background. Asking the students to interpret the elements develops their analytical skills and their critical thinking, as a result of which they decode the meaning behind the ad. The bottle dominates the frame. However, the label on the bottle is deliberately designed to reiterate the message. It consists of a series of shields and insignias that suggest nobility or royalty. The glasses are expensive crystal, and they sit on silver trays. The building in the background suggests a European castle or estate. Every element in the frame, therefore, contributes to the elite message. Using this example with students, ask them to develop a profile of the consumer this ad targets and the type of magazine it might appear in.

So far, we have looked at the broad stages involved in reading advertisements. But what exactly are we reading? Applying the four P's to the broad elements of advertising helps us to translate both static (print) and dynamic (television) advertisements. These elements are:

• Graphics: The graphics consist of picture and print or text. Attention is focused on the design and composition of the frame. This might include the number of words, the size of the print, the position of the print, the shape of the package, the color of the object or text, and the sharpness or softness of the focus. Graphic design includes shape of objects and their position or place within the composition. When dealing with words, consideration should be given not just to what is said or stated, but also to how it is said (tone, mood, etc.) and to who says it. In the case of television ads, for example, one study of 1,000 commercials using voice-over found that 86 percent of the voices were male. What does this suggest about the structure of the advertising industry, the targeted consumers, and social relations as a whole?

• People: What sort of people appear in the ad? What age are they? Are age groups evenly represented in advertisements, or do they tend to represent segments of society? What gender is most evident in ads and how is that sex depicted? This element can be used to analyze the content of ads for their social implications, such as racial composition and the visibility or invisibility of various body types. Increasingly we find evidence in both print and television advertising of positive representations of the physically impaired. Target, K Mart, and other stores depict these groups that have previously been invisible. Can students find any examples of this? This method allows students to consider the ways in which advertisements construct representations of society. How truly representative are they? One study indicated that women were seven times more likely to appear in personal hygiene ads than men. Other findings found that 79 percent of ads using women were for kitchen or bathroom products, that 56 percent of women were depicted as housewives, that women were shown in 18 occupations whereas men were shown in 43 occupations, and that men tended to be depicted in business settings or outdoors. Have students try to confirm or refute these findings by their own analysis of magazine or television advertising. A simple chart (see Figure 5.1) could be used to facilitate this study.

Fig. 5.1. Advertising analysis chart.

Product	Gender	Occupation	Setting

- Social relations: So far, we have addressed the depiction of people in advertisements in quantitative terms. But what is the quality or the nature of the human relationships represented in ads? How do the posture, body language, position, and point of view used in ads convey meaning about social relationships? T. Millum (1975) provides an interesting system for categorizing the social relationships depicted in magazine advertising.

  1. Reciprocal relationships, in which each person is the focus of the other's attention.

  2. Divergent relationships, in which each person is directed to something different.

  3. Object relationships, in which the people focus on the same object.

  4. Semi-reciprocal relationships, in which one person focuses on the other, who focuses on something else.

Describe these broad categories to students and have them find examples of magazine advertisements for each group.

Advantages and Disadvantages of Advertising

(MID/HIGH) — Divide the class into two groups and have them come up with a list of the ways that advertising hurts or helps society. Teachers might want to do this as a brainstorming activity with the whole class, building ideas on the blackboard, or it might be the topic for a debate. The following list touches on some issues that might be explored.

Advantages

- Provides information about goods and services available
- Pays operating costs for television, newspapers, and magazines
- Employs thousands of people
- Reduces cost of goods by competition
- Improves the standard of living by supplying goods and materials
- Keeps the economy active

Disadvantages

- Trivializes the political process
- Promotes unhealthy products
- Encourages materialism
- Manipulates consumers
- Ruins the environment

GET THEM WHILE THEY ARE YOUNG:
Advertising, Children, and Youth

The August 1982 cover of *Advertising Age* features an article on the youth market, extolling the advantages of "getting them while they are young." Similar sentiments are expressed in a 1987 issue of *American Demographics*. "Don't be put off by the strange language, the purple hair and the one dangling earring," says the author. "In a few years, today's teenagers could be wearing three piece suits, working for an investment bank, or managing a supermarket. Make friends with teenagers now and you may have customers for life" (Guber 1987, 42). Using information drawn from Teenage Research Unlimited, a research group, the article pointed to the conservative nature of teens, indicating that boys, in particular, equate success with money and money with happiness. Two-thirds of teenagers reported getting a lot of information about new products from television. The report also noted the emphasis on macho and muscles in males and a general adolescent concern with speed, including in the food they eat and in their forms of entertainment. The peer group exerts enormous pressure on teens, and being accepted by the crowd is important to them. For advertisers, the peer group offers a powerful ally.

Adolescents are particularly susceptible to marketing strategies because of their developmental stage and their need for security. Although their clothing and appearances sometimes suggest rebellion, it tends to be a rebellion more about image or appearances than ideas, and within the confines of their cliques, individuality and deviance are not rewarded. At the very period that teens are in the process, consciously or otherwise, of defining who they are and what they want, advertisers can subvert the search for self through the marketing of prepackaged identities. This process often implies to adolescents that unless they look a particular way or can afford to wear particular labels and clothes they are not as good as those who can. Although this may not be the intent of advertisers, a very real distinction must be made between intent and impact. Willingly or not, advertisers might be suggesting to children and teens that they live in a culture in which images and appearances are more important than ideas and substance. Is it possible that we are creating a consumer culture that increasingly believes we really can judge books by their covers?

The youth market is extremely lucrative, and there is great competition among advertisers to attract young buyers. The purchasing power of teens is substantial. In 1989, they spent $71 billion. Females spent an average of $55 a week, and males spent $48 per week. Breaking the figures down further reveals the relative affluence of the young consumer. Twelve- to 15-year-olds spent $35 per week, compared to $53 per week for 16- to 17-year-olds and $78 per week for 18- to 19-year-olds. The child market is also extremely lucrative. In 1990 *American Demographics* reported that the number of 4- to 12-year-old children in the U.S. stood at 33 million and was growing. In 1989 these children represented $9 billion in sales, an 83 percent increase from 1984.

These children spend $2 billion a year on candy, soft drinks, frozen desserts, and snacks. They spend $1.9 billion on toys, games, and crafts. They spend $700 million a year on clothing, and they spend over $600 million on movies, live entertainment, and spectator sports.

Given the enormous profits the child and youth markets represent, it is no wonder that advertisers target them. Given this targeting and the purchasers' relative inexperience, it is time schools began to help these young consumers make intelligent and informed decisions. Teachers working with very young children might find *The Berenstain Bears Get the Gimmies* (Berenstain and Berenstain 1988) a simple way to start talking to children about selling.

Child or Teenage Purchasing Profile

(ELEM/MID/HIGH)—Develop a purchasing profile for your own students or use the one in Figure 5.2. Have students keep track of their purchases for three or four weeks so they become familiar with their own decisions as consumers. The exercise can be developed so they think about not only what they buy and how much they spend, but also their motivations for making those decisions and the role advertising plays in shaping the choices they make.

Fig. 5.2. Personal purchasing profile.

Personal Purchasing Profile				
Name: **Age:**			**Week #:** **Total Expenditure: $**	
Product	Type/Brand	Cost	Source of Information	Reason for Buying Brand

Modify this profile format to meet your own requirements and the nature of the students you are working with. Typical items on the list might include shoes, clothes, records (tapes, CDs), fast food, cigarettes, and, of course, entertainment expenses such as movies. In the fast-food category, they should specify not only hamburgers, pizza, etc., but also the chain they patronized and their reasons for doing so. Those reasons could include everything from convenient location to price, flavor, give-aways, etc.

(ELEM/MID/HIGH) — Research indicates that teenagers prefer reading magazines to reading books. These magazines offer advertisers an opportunity to reach consumers. Some key magazines in this group include *Teen Beat, Seventeen, YM* (*Young and Modern*), and *Teen* for females and music- and sports-oriented publications such as *Spin* and *Thrasher* for males. In 1990 *U.S. News and World Report* described the explosion in magazines aimed at children and teens. Many of these were junior versions of adult magazines trying to hook consumers while they were young and thereby attract lifetime readers. Advertising was seen as a major force behind many of the publications. "Many new entries are conspicuously ad driven, less bent on getting Johnny to read than getting him to wear Reeboks." Although many of the magazines featured advertising, others such as *P3, Challenge Plus, Hopscotch,* and *Ladybug* did not. These magazines had a tendency to "come at a price" and be "short on pizzazz." Collect some of these magazines and have students study the products advertised in them and the way those products are marketed. What images of children and youth appear in these advertisements? How realistic are they? How representative are they of society as a whole? Ask students to compare the form and content of magazines with and without ads. Develop a class profile of the magazines your students read and buy, and use these for the assignment if you do not want to buy the magazines yourself.

SLIME TIME: Pitching to Kids

John Lyons refers to television advertisements aimed at children as "slime time," suggesting that "this is the closest advertising ever comes to brainwashing" (1987, 291). Lyons is particularly critical of the violence and mayhem in Saturday morning cartoons and the products associated with them. The result of this viewing, he says, "if not brain washing is brain damaging." Peggy Charren, from Action for Children's Television, shares this opinion, calling such advertising "unique brainwashing." In Quebec, television advertising aimed at children is banned. In this country, however, our youngest citizens are seen as future consumers who are certainly capable of influencing the purchasing decisions made by their parents. As we become more aware of the impact of media in our society, targeting children is likely to become increasingly controversial. In July 1991, the American Academy of Pediatrics, for example, called for an end to low-nutrition, high-sugar advertisements aimed at children.

Concern about television advertising and child consumers hinges on four factors:

1. The developmental level of the child, which renders him or her particularly vulnerable to the claims of commercials.

2. The content, form, and style of the commercials themselves, which often make products appear more dynamic, exciting, or larger than they actually are.

3. The relationship between the program and the products, particularly in the case of animated series with a complete toy line based on them or that have actually developed out of a toy line, resulting in the charge that these are not really programs but thinly disguised 30-minute commercials.

4. The views and values implicit in both the programs and the products, especially when they represent violence and sexism.

No doubt exists that revenues and rewards can be reaped from advertising to children. The toy market alone generates some $12 billion a year. The success stories include hot new items such as Nintendo as well as old standbys such as Barbie. The Barbie Doll line, including all the accessories, was grossing in excess of $325 million annually during the 1980s, and Barbie's accessories included a designer wardrobe by fashion giant Oscar de la Renta. Other success stories include Teddy Ruxpin, an example of animated plush manufacturing, which grossed $100 million in its first year. Although Barbie and Teddy Ruxpin both have been criticized for their social implications, the real criticism has been leveled at the more visible and violent products of the toy industry. Mattel's "Masters of the Universe" program and products grossed some $1 billion in 1985, including a line of bedroom slippers for toddlers featuring the skull head of Skeletor. The war toy industry, well fueled by *Rambo* and other movies, grossed $1.3 billion by midyear for 1980 alone, causing alarm among groups and individuals who believed that such playthings afforded social sanction to the use of violence to solve problems. By Christmas 1990, with the deadline for the Iraqi withdrawal from Kuwait in the Persian Gulf approaching, the toy industry had hit the market with several games and products based on the conflict.

Of course, the concept of licensed merchandise based on cartoon, television, or movie characters is not new. Disney had great success with Mickey Mouse before the advent of television and, in the 1950s, generated a national craze with Davy Crockett merchandising. The new wave of merchandising really began with the phenomenal success of *Star Wars* in 1977. Today, thanks to corporate mergers and highly sophisticated marketing strategies, children and their parents are confronted by products pushed through films, television, and magazines. This strategy creates a toy line rather than a single product and relies upon multiple purchases within the same product category by the same child. Hence, Barbie needs Ken and a dream house, and He-Man requires Skeletor. Action figures are a staple element of this marketing strategy, and Star Wars, Batman, Beetle-juice, and other toy lines come with their own unique carrying cases. In recent years, the movies *Dick Tracy, Total Recall, Back to the Future,* and *Days of Thunder* have all been turned into video games, yet another extension of media mergers and new marketing methods. Although there is not space to address the phenomenon in this book, both teachers and parents need to think about how children are socialized by these toys. If our society is violent, is it possible that the origins of that violence lie in our sanction of explicitly aggressive action figures? If young women avoid careers in math and science or become obsessed with their appearance, are they merely responding to the cosmetic culture foisted upon them in childhood?

(ELEM/MID/HIGH)—Have students develop a list of Saturday morning or after-school programs aimed specifically at children. Develop a list of the products advertised on these programs. Which ads do the students find appealing and why?

(ELEM/MID/HIGH)—Develop a list of animated series with their own line of toys. These will probably include "Voltron," "Transformers," "He-Man," "She Ra, Princess of Power," "Go Bots," and "G.I. Joe."

Ask the students which of these programs they watch or have watched. Ask them if they have bought any toys based on these programs. Have them bring some of the toys to class and discuss whether they were satisfied or dissatisfied with the purchase.

This unit, when tackled with teenagers, provides an interesting opportunity for students to look back on themselves as children or to comment on the differences between themselves and younger or older brothers and sisters. It also can be used for an eye-opening sociological study of the differences between toys aimed at males and females.

TEACH YOUR CHILDREN WELL

The world of children's advertising offers unique opportunities to help young consumers become critical viewers and thinkers. Here are some simple suggestions to help you get started.

Food for Thought

(ELEM/MID)—Select breakfast cereal such as Barbie or Batman. Take some packets to school and ask children why these cereals have these characters on the boxes. Present price information about these cereals as compared to more traditional cereals. Try a taste test to see if the children can distinguish between character cereals and more traditional brands.

Some Assembly Required; Batteries Not Included; These Parts Sold Separately

(ELEM/MID)—Discuss the above phrases with students to see if the children know what they mean. Study toy packages and magazine or television toy ads to see if they contain such phrases, and see how much the phrases are emphasized or minimized. Consider the size of the print, the location of the print, the speed or volume with which the phrase is said, and so on.

Special Effects and Visual Techniques

(ELEM/MID)—Think about the ways toy ads are presented on television. Are there a lot of sound effects or special effects such as explosions? Does the toy seem to move by itself? Is it shot from an angle that makes it appear larger than it actually is? Is the toy shown being used by several children all having a very good time? Does the commercial feature a song, jingle, or music that creates a mood? If so, what is the mood?

TOBACCO ADVERTISING:
Where There Is Smoke ...

No product in U.S. history has been as controversial or as firmly rooted in the culture as the cigarette. Michael E. Starr's 1984 analysis, "The Marlboro Man" in *Journal of Popular Culture*, is a fascinating insight into the historical, social, and cultural evolution of tobacco in the twentieth century. Today, cigarettes have the unique distinction of being the only product that is legally available but cannot be advertised on television. The government ban on television advertising of cigarettes, which grew out of the mid-1960s report by the surgeon general linking smoking to lung cancer, remains a visible and viable demonstration that the government believes that advertising can and does influence people. In 1990, the New Jersey Supreme Court even ruled that smokers could seek damages against tobacco companies, despite the warning labels printed on packets. Discussing cigarette advertising, George Gerbner says "glowing visions of the 'good life' counter and overwhelm all other information about an addiction that kills more than 1,000 people a day, more than heroin, crack, alcohol, fire, car accidents, homicides and AIDS combined" (quoted in Pollay 1991, 13). One way these ads influence is by the attractive social settings they construct. People who smoke seem to be sexy and have fun. The response to this in Australia has been to take people out of the picture. The product has been removed from its social setting and all its concomitant suggestions. Richard Pollay refers to those suggestions as "the illusion of youth and vigor advertisers attempt to project with healthy models and pure and pristine environments" (1991, 13). Aware of the powerful impact of such visual inducements, Canada banned cigarette advertising in 1989. In the first year of the ban, cigarette sales dropped 7 percent.

In 1990 in the United States, the total cost for health care and lost productivity associated with smoking was $52 billion. Smoking contributed to some 390,000 deaths a year, or roughly 1,000 per day, compared to 50,000 deaths per year from accidental causes. Smoking cost U.S. citizens $22 per person annually. Some 50 million Americans smoked. The number of adult smokers in the country stood at 27 percent; 29 percent of Whites and 36 percent of Blacks smoked. Figures for 1988 show that children under 18 years of age spent $1.26 billion on cigarettes and smokeless tobacco products. In 1989, cigarette advertising increased 40 percent to $174 million, and in the same year sales dropped 6 percent to $524 billion. Three million children ages 11-17 smoked; 55,000 of them were 11-year-olds. The World Health Organization (WHO) estimates that some 500 million people worldwide will die as the result of smoking. In December 1991, a series of research reports in the *Journal of the American Medical Association* demonstrated the impact cigarette advertising has on children (Fischer et al.; Di Franza et al.; Pierce et al.).

Secretary of Health Louis Sullivan, in 1989 and 1990, launched major attacks on the tobacco industry and their advertising techniques, which he described as "sick" and "sinister." Sullivan was concerned about three particular issues:

1. The tobacco industry's sponsorship of sporting events. Sullivan said, "This blood money should not be used to foster a misleading impression that smoking is compatible with good health." Sullivan was referring to events such as Virginia Slims tennis tournaments. This concern was based, among other things, on the fact that lung cancer surpassed breast cancer as the main cancer in women.

2. Attempts to target young women as potential smokers. One company had developed Dakota brand cigarettes, aimed at blue-collar, 18- to 20-year-old females with a high school education or less. The planned advertisements for this new brand featured images of cruising, partying, hot-rod racing, and tractor pulls. This age group represents the only segment of the population in which cigarette smoking was increasing. The Center for Disease Control believes many females smoke to lose weight and suggest the link between smoking and being thin is stressed in advertising (Rovner 1991).

3. Attempts to target Black smokers. Sullivan was particularly critical of R. J. Reynolds's intention to market a new brand of cigarette called Uptown, which was specifically intended to attract Blacks. Part of Sullivan's concerns centered on the fact that the Black population already had a higher risk of lung cancer than Whites.

Sophisticated market research and highly skillful marketing strategies target groups through persuasive advertising techniques, often promoting potentially harmful products. Health educators can focus attention on these methods. (Copyright © 1990 Herblock in *The Washington Post.*)

(MID/HIGH) — Conduct a class survey to find out how many of the students smoke regularly. This survey can be done as a class discussion or, if it is more appropriate, as an anonymous form to be completed. Information to be provided should include sex, when they started smoking, what brand of cigarette they smoke, how much they smoke each day or week, the reason they smoke, and other members of their family who smoke. In the section related to their motivation for smoking, it is highly unlikely that any students will suggest that advertising had (or has) any influence on this. Remember, many of our motivations for buying and using products are not consciously known to us. When you have developed a profile of the smoking behavior and preferences of the class, provide the information to the students.

(MID/HIGH) — Collect a series of magazine advertisements for the cigarettes most commonly smoked by the class. Have the class study the words and images used in this selection of advertisements. What activities are depicted? What moods are created? What is the setting for these ads? List similarities and differences in locations, gender, age, occupations depicted, and socio-economic status, etc. Are the cigarettes that the female class members favor advertised differently from the ones the males prefer? What are the differences?

(MID/HIGH) — Collect a series of advertisements for cigarettes that do not show up in the class survey. Have the students look at these brands. Note that these brands represent products that the students have either actually rejected or not been attracted to. Have the class examine the ads to see if there is anything in them to suggest why people their own age and from their social background would not smoke that brand.

DOONESBURY by Garry Trudeau

There is little doubt that many young people start to smoke because they think it is cool. Study cigarette advertising with students and explore the way the people, locations, appeal, and words promote smoking. (Doonesbury copyright 1989 G. B. Trudeau. Reprinted with Permission of Universal Press Syndicate. All rights reserved.)

(MID/HIGH) — Collect a widespread sample of magazine advertisements for cigarettes. Your sample should include cigarettes that are clearly aimed at women as well as cigarettes that clearly target men. Virginia Slims and Eve cigarettes are good examples of targeting of women, and Camel and Marlboro are good examples of targeting of men. The look of the packet as well as the ad are crucial to success with men and women. In 1991, for example, Marlboro found that men considered the white filters and gold packet of Marlboro Lights "too light" and "too elegant." Women, however, responded to this packaging. The company created Marlboro Mediums for men seeking a low-tar product. Try to also select ads that seem clearly directed to different socioeconomic groups or income levels. Finally, select advertisements that use a variety of techniques such as those described earlier in this chapter (humor, sex appeal, etc.). You might want to dry mount or laminate the advertisements to protect them. You can either give the class an assignment or have instructions on the back of each ad. (Over a period of time, you can use this process to build up a series of ad boxes on different topics that students can work through at their own pace.) Have individual students or groups study single cigarette advertisements to determine (1) the sex of the target audience, (2) the age of the target audience, (3) the socioeconomic level of the target audience, (4) the type of magazine the ad is likely to appear in, and (5) the type of appeal or persuasion used to promote the product.

It might be useful to do one trial example of this with the class before having them work on their own. Camel's "Smooth Character" ad could be a useful starting point. These ads featured the dashing, smooth Camel hero in a variety of costumes and settings, including a casino, Hollywood, and as a fighter pilot. In each ad, he dominates the frame. The fact that the camel is clearly a male and that a woman (not a female camel) appears as a sex object somewhere in the frame clearly suggests the male appeal of the ads. In addition, the ads tend to combine humor and sophistication, placing the tuxedoed camel in environments significantly different from those in which Camel's male models traditionally tend to be shown. Although most teachers will no doubt choose not to mention it to their classes, it has been suggested that the camel's nose, particularly when viewed upside down, resembles a penis. The key phrase of the ads, "smooth character," seems relevant to both the texture of the penis and the sexual sophistication implicit in calling someone a smooth character or smooth operator. Given that the camel is a cartoon character, the ad also seems to target children.

SPORTS AND SMOKING

In 1929, a magazine ad for Lucky Strikes featured New York Yankee pitcher Waite Hoyt. The ad promised no throat irritation from the cigarette and urged readers to have a slender figure by reaching for a Lucky instead of a sweet. Today, the relationship between sports and tobacco advertising is increasingly controversial. In 1991, for example, the Coalition on Smoking or Health petitioned the Federal Trade Commission (FTC) to request that race cars, banners, and flags bearing cigarette logos and brand names be required to display warning labels.

(ELEM/MID) — Ask students to locate examples of cigarette advertisements that depict sporting events or activities. Make a display of these advertisements and develop a list of all the sports that are represented. Develop a list of the age groups and sexes represented in the ads and the magazines that the ads appeared in. Discuss some of the following issues with the class:

1. Why do so many cigarette ads depict healthy outdoor activities?

2. Is the process of associating harmful products with healthy lifestyles lying, deceptive, misleading, or acceptable?

3. Are any sports, such as cycling, not represented in these ads?

4. How would smoking affect the performance of runners, swimmers, or other athletes?

5. Which sporting figures endorse cigarettes, chewing tobacco, or similar products?

6. Many baseball players chew tobacco. Are students aware of this fact? Do they know that these containers now feature warning labels? What health dangers are associated with chewing tobacco?

(MID/HIGH) — Have students write a short paper or conduct a class debate with one side arguing that the tobacco industry's sponsorship of all sporting events should be banned and the other side disputing this.

(MID/HIGH) — Investigate sporting events, programs, and scholarships in your own community to see if the tobacco industry sponsors any of them.

(ELEM/MID/HIGH) — Cigarette smoking in public places in this country has been increasingly curtailed. In part this has been because of a general increased awareness about health issues. In addition, it has sprung from new medical evidence about the effects of passive smoking, rising medical and insurance costs, and industry's awareness that a healthy worker is a more productive worker. Explain the concept of passive smoking to students. Discuss smokers' right to smoke, but stress their responsibility to smoke in locations that do not intrude on the rights of nonsmokers. Have students create a list of places where smoking is either banned entirely or restricted. These would include airline flights, movie theaters, restaurants, hospitals, and many forms of public transportation. *Turning Points* suggested that schools should be smoke-free and teachers should model this (Carnegie Council 1989). Discuss this idea.

(MID/HIGH)—Investigate smoking policies in the restaurants, supermarkets, stores, and transportation systems in your own community. If your class is particularly committed to this issue, they could develop civic responsibility and awareness by attending city council meetings and even developing resolutions and smoking guidelines for the council to consider.

(MID/HIGH)—In 1990, the secretary of health recommended a ban on cigarette vending machines because of their availability to young consumers. In 1991, Iowa made it illegal for people under eighteen years of age to smoke. This represents another step toward the smoke-free society. Discuss this proposed ban with students and have them come up with points for and against the measure.

(MID/HIGH)—The decline of smoking in the United States has been accompanied by the growth of tobacco exports and the lowering of trade barriers with Taiwan, Japan, and Thailand. By 1990, some 30 percent of the U.S. tobacco crop went overseas, and overseas sales increased from $2.7 billion in 1986 to $4.9 billion. This crop entered countries where consumers were not protected in the same way that Americans are warned about the dangers of cigarette smoking. In Taiwan, for example, there are no warning labels on the packets and cigarettes are advertised on television. In 1990, the Senate Labor and Human Resources Committee held hearings on exporting tobacco to other countries. Senator Edward Kennedy said, "Because of the aggressiveness of the tobacco industry, we are acquiring a different reputation in the Third World as explorers of disease and death." The hearing indicated that U.S. cigarettes were advertised illegally in Asia, showing up on kites, the covers of children's school notebooks, and chewing gum packages. Representatives for Philip Morris International, Inc., denied that the company had a policy of marketing to children in the Third World or elsewhere. Opponents of tobacco have long argued that the companies target children. A 1991 court case in Canada involving a British company and one owned by the U.S.-based RJR Nabisco has shed light on this subject. Discussing the litigation, *The Nation* said, "the government put in evidence internal corporate documents that describe with stunning candor how the industry deliberately hooks children and markets to them" (Mintz 1991, 1). Discuss these developments with the class and have them consider what can or should be done about exporting tobacco overseas, advertising cigarettes overseas, and targeting children.

BUTT OUT!

The movement toward a smoke-free society has widespread social, medical, and political support. Representative Michael Synar (D-OK) has presented legislation to end tobacco promotion. This approach is typical of political responses that often stress legislation over education and try to make laws that dictate public behavior, rather than changing that behavior through education and example. This form of thinking tends to narrowly concentrate on one element, such as advertising, and miss the larger picture or context in which the situation is created.

(HIGH)—Seniors could examine the entire smoking controversy to study logic and critical thinking. The following guide represents some issues that seldom receive attention in the great tobacco debate.

1. Health and medical issues: Should a product that causes death and illness be allowed to be produced, and if it is produced, should it be allowed to be advertised?

2. Ethical issues: What ethical and moral issues are implicit in profiting from a product that is harmful and that is increasingly exported to Third World nations whose citizens are less aware of the dangers associated with the product?

3. Economic issues: Thousands of Americans make a living by growing or processing tobacco. If cigarettes were banned, or if advertising cut back consumption, how would these individuals survive? As tobacco is the sixth largest cash crop in the United States, it also makes a significant contribution to the national economy. Is an attack on tobacco actually an attack on the national economy and well-being? On the other hand, statistics indicate that smoking-related problems create losses in productivity and increase

the cost of health care. Finally, consideration should be given to whether alternative crops, grown in the same conditions, would be profitable if tobacco growers changed crops.

4. Political issues: Do tobacco states such as North Carolina, Virginia, and Kentucky depend so heavily on tobacco revenues that they sacrifice the national health for the financial health of their own states? What is the relationship among the half dozen southern tobacco states, presidential politics, and federal leadership in curtailing smoking in this country? How powerful are the tobacco lobby and its ties to senators such as Jesse Helms (R-NC)?

5. Cultural issues: Loss of tobacco revenues might be offset by producing alternative crops. Although that idea might be logical, it does not take into account the tradition and heritage many tobacco growers have or the long family roots behind their crop of choice. Changing the attitudes and behavior of many of these farmers would take more than simply telling them that another crop could be equally as profitable. Another major cultural consideration is the relationship between the United States and other countries and cultures. If we put warning labels on cigarettes in this country and ban tobacco advertising on television, should we require countries who buy our tobacco and cigarettes to do the same or would this be an example of cultural imperialism?

6. Constitutional issues: The idea of banning cigarette advertising, tobacco production, or even where or when people can smoke invariably invokes constitutional issues. Does a ban on cigarette advertising deny constitutional rights of free speech? Are these free speech rights more important than citizens' rights to clean air? What is the relationship between a citizen's private rights and the public good?

7. Informational issues: Because cigarette advertising generates enormous revenues that make the publication of affordable newspapers and magazines possible, would a ban on this advertising reduce our sources of news and entertainment? The May 6, 1991, cover story in *The Nation* implied that the mainstream media have not covered developments that reflect unfavorably on the tobacco industry. If the media derive income from cigarette advertising, are they likely to be critical of the industry?

Product Placement

(ELEM / MID / HIGH) — One hidden form of advertising occurs when companies pay film producers to highlight their products onscreen or in the script of a movie. Philip Morris spent $40,000 to feature Marlboro cigarettes in *Superman II* and $350,000 to feature Lark cigarettes in the James Bond movie *License to Kill*. Product placement does work. After Reese's Pieces were featured in *E.T.* (1982), sales soared 66 percent in three months. Sunglasses were promoted in *Top Gun*, Pepsi in *Back to the Future*, and Coke in *Murphy's Romance*. Legislative attempts are being made to stop this method of advertising. One group monitoring product placement is Stop Teenage Addiction to Tobacco (STAT). It publishes *Tobacco and Youth Reporter* and looks at the industry's attempt to market to teens. Have students look for examples of tobacco promotions in movies they watch.

Divestment and Consumer Action

(MID / HIGH) — In 1990, several major U.S. universities began to divest themselves of investments they had with tobacco companies. Why would they make this decision? How might the decision affect the universities? What other actions can individual consumers take to let the tobacco industry know they are unhappy with the industry's product and the way it is promoted?

ALCOHOL ADVERTISING:
Through a Glass Darkly

Unlike tobacco advertising, which was banned from television in the 1980s, alcohol continues to enjoy high visibility on the nation's television screens, as well as on radio and in billboards and magazines. Like tobacco, alcohol is a legal drug, afforded social sanction at the same time that its health costs continue to afflict individuals and the nation as a whole. The Department of Health and Human Services estimates that there are 15.1 million alcoholics in the United States, compared to 3 million cocaine or crack addicts. In 1987, the Centers for Disease Control estimated that there were some 105,000 alcohol-related deaths in the United States that year.

In 1989, nearly 2 million Americans were arrested for drunk driving. Estimates suggest that each year, drunk driving results in 23,000 road deaths, 1 million personal injuries, and $5 billion in property damage. Approximately 46 percent of homicides have been shown to be alcohol related. Fetal alcohol syndrome damages the fetus in the womb and promotes mental retardation. Possible results of fetal alcohol syndrome include escalated medical costs, increasing strain on schools to provide special education, undermined future productivity of impaired infants, and new burdens for taxpayers. A 1991 survey by the Department of Health and Human Services reported that 8 million junior and senior high school students are weekly drinkers and some 454,000 are "binge" drinkers, consuming 15 or more drinks each week. Despite the fact that all states prohibit sales of alcohol to anyone under the age of 21, the survey estimated that 6.9 million teenagers have no problem obtaining alcohol. The report said the brewing industry had confused and compounded the problem with fruit-flavored wine coolers packaged as fruit drinks. At the same time the Bush administration has proposed cutting the budget for the National Institute on Alcohol Abuse and Alcoholism (Iskoff 1991, 37).

Alcohol's grip on this society has been well documented in recent years. One of the first real breakthroughs in public awareness about alcoholism came when First Lady Betty Ford admitted to having a chemical dependency problem. The Betty Ford Center has treated show business celebrities and brought widespread publicity to the problem. This publicity has helped to change the stereotype of the alcoholic as a skid row bum. The question of alcohol abuse has been raised about leading political figures, including Senator Edward Kennedy (D-MA), and it was one of the issues that led to the defeat of John Tower as President Ronald Reagan's nominee for secretary of defense. Yet, despite growing media coverage of alcoholism and its impact on society, our culture remains confused and almost contradictory about it. A leading news magazine, for example, featured a cover story on Kitty Dukakis and her problem with alcohol, and the back cover of the same issue was a full-page ad for vodka. This contradiction pinpoints a central problem for a consumer culture and the media that serve it. That problem is the economic relationship and reliance that exists between the media and the manufacturers.

Is it, in fact, hypocritical for a newspaper, magazine, or television station to cover alcoholism as a topic at the same time that it makes money from promoting the product? Groups such as S.M.A.R.T. (Stop Marketing Alcohol on Radio and Television) are concerned about the ways advertising promotes the consumption of alcohol. In 1989, Surgeon General Koop echoed these concerns and recommended banning alcohol advertising. Koop was particularly concerned about the impact these advertisements had on impressionable adolescents.

(MID/HIGH)—Collect a series of alcohol advertisements from a variety of magazines. Have the class analyze them for the following types of information.

- What type of alcohol is promoted (beer, wine, spirits, liqueur)?

- What age group and sex are featured in each ad?

- What is the setting or location for each ad?

- What activities are the models engaged in?

- How do the body language and facial expressions suggest the mood of the scene?

- Using the list of persuasive techniques given earlier in this chapter, identify the associations and persuasions used in the ads.

- What type of magazine would we expect each ad to appear in? Remember, it is important for students to understand that advertisers target audiences and change their pitch according to what they know about that audience. Socioeconomic background will certainly affect advertising approaches. Michelob, for example, is more middle-class than Budweiser, which reflects a more blue-collar or working-class clientele.

(MID/HIGH) — Have students develop a design for a billboard or a poster to be used in your own school, library, or community to warn about the dangers of alcohol abuse or how advertisers target teens.

Warning Labels

(MID/HIGH) — In the late 1980s, federal law required warning messages on beer and other alcohol. The label specifically warns pregnant women that drinking alcohol can create birth defects. It also says consumption of alcohol impairs an individual's ability to drive a car or operate machinery. Discuss these warnings with students. Were they aware of them? Examine a can of beer. Is the warning clear and visible, or is it overwhelmed by the label and logo?

Sample Slogans and Pitches from Print Ads

(MID/HIGH) — The previous analysis of alcohol advertisements in magazines focused on the visual components. In addition to the power of the picture, some attention should be given to the pitch made in print: the slogan or phrase used to sum up the statement. The following list reflects some approaches. You might want to have a group of students concentrate on slogans used to market alcohol and have another group try to develop a slogan or pitch targeting a specific market. Are there potentially misleading or negative consequences from the slogans? For example, does the claim that a beer has more flavor and is less filling suggest that consumers can actually drink more? Why is it less filling? If it has fewer calories, does it also have lower alcohol content?

1. "America's Pop Hero" (used by Miller Lite). Picture shows close-up of can in hand, thumb opening pull top, and foam exploding. Clearly targets a young audience and would appear in something such as *Rolling Stone*.

2. "Seduce a Slice" (used by Seagrams Extra Dry Gin). Close-up of glass with slice of lemon. Clearly uses sex to sell. Placement of print on label might even rapidly be scanned and read as "sextra dry."

3. "Party Right with Bud Lite" (used by Budweiser). Features Spuds McKenzie, a dog, as party animal with a guitar around his neck. Although some might claim it supports cautious drinking, its overall appeal to the college crowd evokes the film *Animal House*.

4. "He'll Be Up Here with Us Someday" (used by Johnny Walker). This interesting line is uttered by Teddy Roosevelt to Abraham Lincoln in a depiction of the faces on Mt. Rushmore. Clearly the ad stresses success and political power, with alcohol somehow being part of that road to success.

5. "Johnny B Very Good Indeed" (used by Christian Brothers brandy). A clever association with rock legend Chuck Berry. Not only does he have the same initials as the company (C. B.), but also the ad invokes one of Berry's hit songs ("Johnny B. Goode") to promote the product. Highly likely to appear in *Rolling Stone*.

ALCOHOL ADVERTISING ON TELEVISION

Magazine and billboard advertisements for alcohol are restricted to a single frame or picture. On television, these ads come to life. The director is able to create a minimovie with a scenario, sequence, characters, setting, and even a score. These elements immediately give the advertisement power that is lacking in a magazine. They have the ability to get not only the attention of our eyes but also the attention of our ears through the use of music, voice, and sound effects. These ads can be lavish, million-dollar productions set on an estate with a large cast, an enormous banquet, and an aria from a famous opera. Or they might be less opulent but nonetheless effective, pitching light beer to armchair quarterbacks by evoking images of male bonding and buddies.

(MID/HIGH)—Have students analyze a variety of alcohol ads on television using the following guidelines.

- What type of alcohol is advertised (beer, wine, spirits, liqueur)?

- What age group, sex, and race are depicted in the ad?

- What is the setting or location of the ad?

- What socioeconomic groups are the people in the ad from? What factors in the ad lead to this conclusion (clothes, cars, language)?

- What activities are the characters in the ad engaged in?

- How do body language and facial expressions create the mood established in the scene?

- How does the use of music contribute to the atmosphere created by the ad?

- Using the list of persuasive techniques provided earlier in this chapter, identify the various associations and persuasive techniques employed in the ad.

- How realistic or true to life is the scene presented in the ad?

- What program is sponsored by the ad? What relationship is there between the product, the program, the persuasion or pitch employed, and the people likely to be viewing this program? For example, beer is more likely to be advertised during football games, whereas wine is more likely to be advertised during the news or yuppie programs such as "Thirtysomething."

(MID/HIGH)—Use the storyboard sheet (see chapter 3) to have students sketch the visual structure of an ad. Then have them use a separate sheet to develop a storyboard for their own television ad. Give them the choice of making an ad to market to a specific group or of making an ad pointing out the dangers of alcohol abuse, the need for a designated driver, or responsible drinking behavior.

If you have the facilities, you might be able to produce a public service announcement (PSA), or you might try resource sharing with your local community access television station to produce a PSA. Broadcasting provides the basis for a classroom discussion on advertising's purpose. The quote can also be applied to techniques used in marketing alcohol.

TARGETING MINORITIES

Some of the country's leading manufacturers of wine use elaborate advertisements showing sophisticated middle-class people enjoying their drinks and conversation at lavish dinner parties or intimate gatherings. There is, however, a darker side behind these glamorous images. That side is not depicted in magazine or television advertising, but it is quite clearly targeted. The target group is winos, and the product is any number of inexpensive and potentially quite harmful cheap wines. In San Francisco, opposition to this form of marketing led to withdrawal of the products from particular areas of the city. In a free enterprise economy, there is no doubt that companies have the legal right to market their product. What, however, are the ethical implications of companies creating a product that is the drug of choice for people already in need of help? This became a highly controversial issue in 1991 when the G. Heileman Brewing Company tried to introduce a malt liquor called Powermaster. The company was accused of targeting minority groups with their campaign. They were challenged by groups such as the Coalition against Billboard Advertising of Alcohol and Tobacco and the National Association of African-Americans for Positive Imagery. These groups had successfully prevented R. J. Reynolds from targeting tobacco ads at minorities in 1990. Statistics indicate that alcohol contributes to 60,000 deaths in minority communities, and 90 percent of billboards are also located in minority communities. In a stinging editorial in *USA Today* the surgeon general attacked advertising "campaigns that are designed to keep our minorities enslaved by taking away their good health, freedom and dignity" (1991). She dismissed the industry's charges that free speech was being censored, saying there is a difference between political expression and commercial expression. In a call to arms against advertisers, she urged Americans to "get informed, to get involved and to get in charge. Tell the purveyors of alcohol and their hired-gun persuaders that we have had enough disease, disability and death. Tell them that we simply will not tolerate marketing that distorts and deceives." Within days of the column, the Bureau of Alcohol, Tobacco and Firearms withdrew permission for the company to use the name Powermaster because it violated laws against marketing alcohol by "kick." The company later withdrew the product.

THE SPORTING LIFE

The National Coalition to Prevent Impaired Driving is opposed to the use of beer company logos in sporting events. In 1990, they focused attention on the race-car industry and drew attention to alcohol images at the track, on the cars, and on the clothes the drivers wear. The group believes the association between drinking and fast driving sends a potentially harmful message. Miller, Anheuser-Busch, and Coors spend some $50 million on promoting their products at race tracks. The president of the Beer Institute defends the practice, arguing that race-car drivers do not drink while they drive. He also says the opponents tend to suggest that race-car fans cannot think for themselves. The advertising industry, of course, is well aware that many people have not been taught to think about advertising or the choices they make as consumers.

(MID/HIGH) — Divide the class into groups and have each group cover a different sport such as football, baseball, soccer, ice hockey, tennis, and golf. Each group must find examples of advertising links between their sport and alcohol. They can use both magazine and television advertising and should look for elements such as:

- endorsements by sporting figures

- advertising alcohol during sporting events

- billboard or similar structural advertising at stadiums, arenas, etc.

Product Placement

(ELEM/MID/HIGH) — In *Terms of Endearment* (1983), Shirley MacLaine visits a restaurant with Jack Nicholson. Rather than simply ordering a drink, she specifies the brand, asking for Wild Turkey bourbon. Although most movie goers do not remember this moment, they were all being pitched to buy a product in the middle of a movie, which is not supposed to have advertisements. This process is known as product placement. Advertisers actually pay film companies to have their products referred to or shown. Have students develop a list of movies they have seen in which characters not only consume alcohol, but also the brand name is shown or referred to. Remember, this can happen in what appears to be a casual setting, including a street scene, a store scene, or a shot of a kitchen or a dining room.

FOOD FOR THOUGHT:
Advertising, Nutrition, and Dieting

(ELEM/MID)—The saying "You are what you eat" is a useful starting point when trying to help children and adolescents understand the relationship among their bodies, their self-image, the food they eat, and the packaging and promotion of that food. An outstanding ABC special, "Diet of Danger," looked at U.S. nutrition and the medical impact of our food choices. Among other things, the program noted:

1. By the time students are 18, they have seen 20,000 food commercials, 80 percent of which advertise food that is low in nutrition.

2. Seventy-eight percent of children influence the purchasing decisions of their parents.

3. Cereal advertisers spent $654 million in one year.

4. Fast-food advertisers spent $1 billion in one year.

5. Gum and candy advertisers spent $405 million in one year.

6. Soft-drink advertisers spent $389 million in one year.

These advertisements represent a powerful and attractive inducement to consume. The people in these advertisements are young, fit, and healthy, despite their apparently poor eating habits. Consumption is shown without consequences. Any attempts to alter patterns of consumption are challenged by the food industry. In 1991, "yielding to pressure from the meat and dairy industries, The Agriculture Department ... abandoned its plans to turn the symbol of good nutrition from the 'four wheel' showing 'The Basic Food Groups' to an 'Eating Right' pyramid that sought to deemphasize meat and dairy products in a healthful diet" (Sugarman and Gladwell 1991, 39). Nutritionists seek to provide us with one set of information while advertising consistently erodes this advice. How can we address this contradiction in the classroom? A simple starting point might be to go over the basic food groups with the class and discuss the concept of nutrition. Having established a list of the foods that are beneficial, it might then be useful to see what food is advertised most frequently on television. You might want to develop a chart listing products such as fish, beef, poultry, dairy, eggs, fruit, vegetables, and grains and bran.

How frequently is each group advertised? Which elements of a particular group are stressed? For example, is milk advertised more than eggs or cheese? How often are these foods advertised as products of fast-food chains? For example, is meat most frequently advertised in hamburgers? How are the products promoted? This can include the models used (age, race, socioeconomic situation) as well as the persuasive techniques, such as "all natural," "it's good for you," "new and improved," "happy families," etc. (Each of these techniques is treated earlier in this chapter.)

(ELEM/MID)—Have students concentrate entirely on the selling of fast foods. What types of fast foods are advertised on television: pizza, hamburgers, seafood, fried chicken, tacos, and others?

(ELEM/MID)—Divide the class into groups. Each group should study the promotion and packaging of one of the above fast foods. The assignment should include completing the chart in Figure 5.3.

Fig. 5.3. Advertising fast food on television.

STUDENT SURVEY					
FOOD Brand	Setting of Ad	Characters in Ad (age, sex, race, socioeconomic level)	Persuasion Used	Health Claims	TV Program Aired On
Burger King					
Wendy's					
Hardees					
McDonald's					
Arby's					
Kentucky Fried Chicken					
Pizza Hut					
Taco Bell					

Make sure students are familiar with the various persuasion techniques as they work on this assignment. Older students can conduct quite sophisticated analyses of each ad. The younger students, however, are quite capable of understanding how stuffed toys, character merchandise, and food specials offered for a short time are used to attract customers.

(ELEM/MID)—Conduct a class poll to see what the favorite fast food is. You might want to conduct this as an election, with one candidate speaking for each group. See if students prefer one particular chain to the others and find out why. Is it the food, the prices, the location, the give-aways, the advertising? Which of these factors seem most influential in shaping the class's preference?

(ELEM/MID)—Develop a class survey of families and food. Each student should be given a sheet and asked to list the members of their family and each person's favorite food when they eat out. The survey could include the number of times they eat fast food each week, the type of food they eat, and their reasons for selecting that food. This process not only develops a profile of the eating behavior of families in your community, but it also provides insights into the lifestyles of the parents. For example, it can provide information about how busy mothers and fathers are during the day, how much time they have for lunch, the type of area they work in, and so on. Potentially, this can open up an entire exploration of the relationship between the food we eat and the lifestyles we live. Questions about drive-in windows, or food "to go," can further develop this process. Ultimately, you can develop a picture of not just what people eat, but also why they eat it.

WHAT'S IN THIS, ANYWAY?
The Need to Read

Most students are aware that cigarettes contain warning labels, but do they know that some of the food in their kitchen cupboards also contains warnings? Sweet 'n' Low, for example, contains saccharin and carries a warning that use of the product might be hazardous to humans. Equal, on the other hand, can also be used to sweeten coffee and drinks but contains no saccharin, no sodium, and no warning. After the Food and Drug Administration (FDA) allowed advertisers to promote their products by making health claims, consumers were bombarded by statements about the benefits of all types of food. Many of these claims were misleading, because they did not provide consumers with the full picture. Campbell's Soup, for example, said it was high in fiber and stressed those benefits. The same soup, however, was also high in fat and sodium, which promote heart disease. Land-O-Lakes butter stressed the vitamin A it contained and its benefits for the skin. But the product was also high in less beneficial cholesterol. Crisco oil advertised that it had no cholesterol, but it was high in saturated fats, which can clog arteries. Pepperidge Farm pound cake said it was cholesterol free, but it was also high in fat. Lean Cuisine's chicken cacciatore was low in calories but high in sodium. The half-truths contained in this type of advertising generated complaints from the American Medical Association, the American Heart Association, and the American Cancer Society. These complaints prompted David Kessler, head of the FDA, to introduce new guidelines for labels, packaging, and advertising. In the spring of 1991, the FDA made Citrus Hill remove their orange juice from store shelves and told the manufacturers they violated regulations by calling processed juice "fresh." The problems implicit in this type of marketing necessitate that we help students become critical thinkers and consumers by reading labels, asking questions, and watching advertising carefully.

(ELEM/MID/HIGH)—A simple way of examining labels is to have each student bring one packet of food to class. In class, students should examine the box, bottle, or packet to see how it is made to look attractive. Wesson oil, for example, comes in a tall, clean, clear bottle with a bright label. The label stresses, in large letters, the fact that the oil is "100% all natural" and "Light and Natural." Many products today claim to be natural, but we seldom even ask what that means anymore. If it is processed, can it be natural? Wesson's label says it has no additives, no cholesterol, and no salt. It also says it "tastes light." Does that mean that it actually is light or that it just tastes as though it is? The expression *salt free* does not mean the same thing as *sodium free*. The term *sugar* can actually mean any number of ingredients, including glucose, dextrose, lactose, and fructose. Direct your students' attention to the small print about the contents of their packages. This is an excellent way for health, science, and biology teachers to help students understand such concepts as calories, U.S. Recommended Daily

Allowance, body fat, etc. Most packages also contain the address of the company. If your students have concerns or questions about the way a product is packaged or promoted, have them write to the company. Given the obscure phrasing on so much labeling, a simple request might include putting information on packets that the average citizen could understand. Minority students might request labeling in Hispanic or other languages. Students might also write to the Food and Drug Administration to ask for the existing guidelines concerning advertising and food and health claims. This process not only encourages students to be thoughtful consumers, but also promotes responsible participation in a democracy. This exercise develops critical thinking skills that are badly needed in this area. The secretary of health Louis Sullivan has said, for example, that to understand today's labels, consumers must be "linguists, scientists, and mind readers."

DANGEROUS DIETS

In 1990, the American Dietetic Association reported that Americans' diets reflected a desire for quick fixes to bad habits. Although Americans were taking more vitamins, using more olive oil, and eating more oat bran, for example, only 8 percent reported eating more vegetables and only 6 percent said they were consuming more fruit. In the same year, congressional hearings were held regarding the largely unregulated weight loss industry. Representative Don Wyden called the industry and its claims "a scam on the American public." Skillful advertisements used celebrities such as Tommy Lasorda and Susan St. James to promote the benefits of various weight loss programs. The congressional hearings, however, provided evidence of the potential danger of some programs, including heart attacks, brain damage, and gall bladder injury. Despite the high visibility of the diet and fitness industry, a 1991 report from the Centers for Disease Control suggested, "Americans are just as likely to be overweight today as they were in the 1960s." Twenty-four percent of men and 27 percent of women are significantly overweight. Obesity also was more prevalent among the poor and minorities. The study suggested "little progress ... in educating people about good nutrition and weight loss" (Booth 1991, 37). Spas, aerobics, jogging, Jazzercise, light beer, and Lean Cuisine have had little or no impact on "the national prevalence of fat." Several issues are involved in studying the diet industry.

1. Regulation of the industry itself: What sort of controls are necessary, and why is it possible to promote potentially harmful programs without first warning consumers? How is this related to the initial marketing of tobacco and alcohol?

2. Ideal weight: Statistics suggest that 25 percent of the nation is overweight; 65 million Americans diet, and we spent $33 billion on dieting in 1989. But how many people really planned to diet, and how many are simply trying to achieve an artificial and idealized look and image manufactured by the mass media? Isn't dissatisfaction with our looks at the very heart of the cosmetics industry, for example?

3. Physiological and psychological health: What is the relationship between self-image and our physical health? Do we live in a culture that consistently sells us excess and self-indulgence (tobacco, alcohol, fast foods) at the same time that it holds up physical ideals that cannot be achieved if we responded to those indulgences? How inadequate do we feel as people if we cannot look like models in magazines or find the self-discipline to resist the food and drink they sell us? What is the relationship between eating disorders such as anorexia nervosa and bulimia and the conspicuous consumption patterns of our culture?

(MID/HIGH)—This exercise is particularly interesting with adolescents and adults. Give each student a blank index card. They are not to write their names on it. What they have to do is write an answer to the following: If you could change your appearance, who would you most like to look like and why? Collect the cards. Read through them, and place the names on the board. Did anyone say they were happy the way they were? If not, you have just established that as a culture, we are generally dissatisfied with the way we look. The real task, however, is to think about why. Typically, most of the names you have in front of you will come from the worlds of film, music, modeling, or television. If you have sports figures, stress that these people actually look this way. The media figures, on the other hand, not only use make-up, but they also have body doubles, stand-ins, air-brushing, and a host of other techniques that make them look better onscreen or in a magazine than in real life. In essence, our culture creates idealized body images that can only be achieved by artificial means. By bringing this to the attention of our students, we begin to demystify the media and encourage students to value themselves and others for who they are, not what they look like.

(MID/HIGH)—Collect a series of magazines and have students look for examples of products related to weight loss and dieting. These might include pills, liquid diets, and clinics. Have them study the ads to see what type of people the ads are aimed at, how much weight they claim can be lost (extreme, average, etc.), the persuasive techniques they use (before and after photographs, social inferiority, etc.), and the type of magazine the advertisement appeared in. Be sure to note that statistics suggest that 75-90 percent of people who lose weight gain it back. Perhaps the most visible example of this was in the case of talk-show host Oprah Winfrey. She lost 67 pounds on a highly publicized liquid diet, but also gained a lot of it back. The public and the press's fascination with dieting was evident in the tabloids' treatment of Elizabeth Taylor and "Designing Women's" Delta Burke. Why is the media so concerned with overweight women, whereas it ignores men such as William Conrad, Raymond Burr, and John Goodman? Is this a double standard, or does it address the role of women as sex objects in a media industry that is controlled by men and caters to male fantasies? This question can be tackled by older students in a content analysis of images of obesity in the media.

(HIGH)—Doctors are reporting an increase in the number of teens seeking plastic surgery because they are unhappy with their looks. Discuss this trend with your students. What do they think of it?

CONDOMNATION: Selling Safe Sex

In the mid-1980s, as the severity of the AIDS crisis really became known, government and health officials around the world turned to advertising to alert the public to the need for sexual safety and responsibility. At times, the ads were highly successful. Perhaps the best example were Scandinavian ads that utilized humor to get the message across. Sometimes scare tactics were used. One Australian ad featured a figure of death bowling and knocking down pins that were people. A highly controversial Australian poster depicted two young men kissing and the words, "When you say yes ... say yes to safe sex." In England, some of the ads were so obscure that people mistook them for gardening commercials.

In the United States, the real controversy has centered on getting condom advertisements on television. The American College of Obstetricians and Gynecologists had to delete reference to the word *contraception* in an ad they submitted. NBC helped them re-create the ad in a blander format, saying that they did not want "to put off people who were concerned about a pitch for contraception." The advertising campaign for Lifestyle condoms also ran into objections, and all three networks blocked it. An ABC vice-president said the ad was "contrary to our policy of accepting products which related to controversial issues." The condom ads were rejected because they dealt with birth control, which the networks regard as a moral and religious issue. The ads did begin to appear on about 30 of 1,200 local television stations, usually late at night.

When congressional hearings were held on the issue, Representative Henry Waxman of the Health and Environment Subcommittee accused the networks of hypocrisy, saying that they would not depict sexual responsibility but they regularly depicted scenes of sexual titillation and seduction. Surgeon General Koop testified at the hearings that advertising was a necessary weapon in the fight against AIDS. Koop said television advertising was particularly necessary because high-risk groups such as Blacks and Hispanics relied heavily on television as a source of information. The Fox Network responded in November 1991 that they would run condom commercials after Magic Johnson, the professional basketball player, announced he had AIDS. CBS and NBC said they would review their opposition to such commercials.

(MID/HIGH)—The controversy over condom commercials could be explored in sex education classes, as well as in English and social studies classes. The essence of the dispute hinges on the public's right to receive information during a health crisis and the right of the networks to determine what they do or do not broadcast. Today, groups such as Musicians for Life advertise condoms on MTV. Where else do our young people get their information about AIDS prevention? Isn't it ironic that potentially harmful products such as alcohol and tobacco can be advertised but potentially life-saving products such as condoms are restricted? What does this say about our culture's contradictory messages about sex?

SEX-ROLE STEREOTYPES AND ADVERTISING

In the mid-1980s, television advertising began to feature a series of images of men in unusual circumstances. In each case, the men appeared to be losers, jerks, wimps, or hapless individuals, particularly when compared to the women in the ads. In one spot for Kellogg's Bran Flakes, a husband and wife play doubles tennis. His main contribution is to return the ball when it bounces off his head. Midas, Drano, Nutri-Grain, and Rice Chex spots all featured men who acted more like children in need of guidance and discipline. The images of men in these commercials is clearly transitional and also clearly a response to the way women have been depicted for years. A magazine ad for Charlie perfume reversed the traditional image of women as sex object and featured a woman with her hand on a man's backside. The *New York Times* refused to carry the ad, but *Ms.* magazine ran it.

The feminist movement has contributed much to our awareness of media representations of sex roles. In 1963, Betty Friedan's *Feminine Mystique* drew attention to the restrictive roles presented to women by the media and manufacturers. In the movie *Killing Us Softly: Advertising Images of Women*, Jean Kilbourne documents these roles and perceptions.

Although these images may be changing slowly, the media and women themselves actually often deny the existence of the problem. In the summer of 1991 for example, "20/20" featured a story called "The Beauty Myth," only to have Barbara Walters dismiss Naomi Wolf's ideas as "a crock." Attention is also now being focused on male stereotypes in advertising. Men Organized against Sexism and Institutionalized Stereotypes (OASIS) has created a fascinating program called "Stale Roles and Tight Buns."

(ELEM/MID) — Ask students to find out who makes the purchases in their family. This can be broken down into individual family members, as well as individual goods, such as food, gasoline, furniture, clothes, etc. Try to find out why the dominant buyer in the family has that job. Is it because one parent works and the other does not? Is it a question of preference? Is it a matter of tradition?

(MID/HIGH) — Select a series of magazines and have students look for the ways that men and women are depicted. They can create columns and divide the ads into traditional and nontraditional roles. Typical traditional roles would include:

Men	Women
sportsman	housewife
father	mother
businessman	sex object/femme fatale
authority figure	

Typically, ads assign males an aura of competence and control, either physically or financially. Are there ads in which the woman appears to be assertive and involved in decision making? What sorts of things do the women make decisions about? Are there ads in which men appear to be in a nurturing or supportive parental role?

(MID/HIGH) — Use the above exercise for television advertisements. It might be useful to keep a list of what programs the ads appear in. Is there such a thing, for example, as women's programs? How are women depicted in the ads during these programs? Is this different from the ways women are depicted in ads during other programs? Progressive and liberal programs such as "Thirtysomething" and "Designing Women" feature characters who are not content with old stereotypes. Is this reflected in the commercials screened during these programs?

Back-Handed Compliments

(MID / HIGH) — Sometimes advertisers assert or advocate one thing, but contradict themselves in the process. Virginia Slims cigarettes, for example, developed the slogan "You've Come a Long Way, Baby." On the one hand, the ad seemed to congratulate women on the strides they had made, but on the other hand, the use of the word *baby* infantilizes women and diminishes their prestige and power. The ad also stresses an idealized body image. Show students one of these ads and ask them to find the back-handed compliment. Can they identify other examples?

Pieces-Parts

(MID / HIGH) — Advertisements for lingerie, perfume, lipstick, stockings, shoes, and a range of other products are consistently presented by showing only pieces of the female body. The process robs the woman of her identity and reduces her to a collection of prime parts displayed in a meat market. Can students find examples of the male body treated in the manner described above? Using magazine advertising, have students find examples of this technique, for both sexes if possible.

There are likely to be significantly more examples of body-part female models. Discuss with the class the social and cultural factors that lead to this different depiction of the sexes. How does it show up, for example, in movies, television, and art? The entire concept of nudity also might be addressed here. Why are there so many female nudes in the world of art and so few male nudes? How does this tie in to the gender of the artists, cultural convention, and patronage of the arts in a patriarchal society?

Body Billboards

It is not uncommon to find women's bodies used as billboards adorned with slogans, logos, and graffiti. Tanqueray sells alcohol by displaying a beautiful woman in a bikini with the words "Imported Tanqueray Special Dry" on her torso. Budweiser turns three women into a giant label for their product. Have students find other examples of body billboards. Are men ever depicted this way?

Androgynous Advertising: Gender Blenders

(MID / HIGH) — The pop world has created images of adrogyny in the various persona assumed by David Bowie and in performers such as Boy George, Michael Jackson, Mick Jagger, Sinead O'Connor, and kd lang. Each of these performers emerged at a time when the sexual revolution of the 1960s and the women's movement of the 1970s and 1980s were redefining traditional gender notions. As pop icons, they influenced fashion, style, and appearance. Today, advertising shows signs of sexual ambiguity and uncertainty. This is most evident in magazine advertising, where it is often difficult to tell whether the models are male or female.

Show some examples of such androgyny to students, or have them find their own examples. What products are advertised this way? What magazines do the ads appear in? What type of consumer are they aimed at? Do your students find the ads interesting, attractive, offensive, etc.?

Women in Advertising: Female Executives

(MID / HIGH) — Have students research the advertising industry to see how many women hold executive positions in advertising agencies or run their own agencies. Have the students track down some of the products the women promote and the way they promote them. Is there any evidence that ads produced by women are less stereotypical than those produced by men?

MARKETING MINORITIES:
Demographics Is Destiny

Advertising reflects the society that it serves. In the process, it also helps to perpetuate the views and values of that society by repeating and, therefore, reinforcing social stereotypes. As society changes, the way it changes will be reflected in advertising. The transitional images of men and women that appeared in some commercials in the 1970s and 1980s are examples of this. We can also expect that the changing composition of the population will be reflected in advertisers' responses to Asians and Hispanics. Sometimes marketers themselves fall victim to the stereotypes: "Sensational headlines about black poverty have frightened many marketers away from black publications ... but blacks are a lucrative market" (Waldrup 1990, 30). Census figures suggest that Asian Americans are the fastest growing section of the population, increasing from 3.8 million in 1980 to 6.9 million in 1989. Hispanics are expected to account for one-fifth to one-half of the nation's population by 2010. By the same year, Black, Hispanic, and Asian children will be in the majority in seven states, including the big three: Florida, Texas, and California. By that time, 38 percent of Americans under the age of 18 will be minorities. Companies such as Benneton already stress the multiracial composition of the country. Have students find their own examples of this in advertising.

Pictures of Pluralism

(ELEM/MID/HIGH) — One of the leading models of the late 1980s was Vietnamese-born Mary Xinh Nguyen. Estée Lauder introduced the exotic looks of a Czech model to promote their products. In a global economy, the blonde-haired, blue-eyed, all-American look is increasingly likely to be replaced by more cosmopolitan and international images. Have students look at magazine or television advertisements to find examples of this new look. What products do such models represent? What programs or magazines do they appear in?

National Stereotypes

(ELEM/MID/HIGH) — A Wendy's commercial made fun of the lack of choices available to citizens in the Soviet Union. A Kentucky Fried Chicken ad featured an image of a wise old Chinese man and a group of children calculating on an abacus. An ad for Kaopectate featured a Mexican family promoting an anti-diarrhea formula. Several contemporary ads featured unflattering images of the Japanese. Find examples of ads that draw on stereotypes of national characteristics and discuss these ads with students. Discuss the problems associated with stereotyping and the promotion of images of national groups.

THE GRAYING OF AMERICA

The number of Americans who are sixty-five or over is increasing and will continue to increase for many years now as Baby Boomers move beyond middle age. Just as the youth market dominated the 1960s, when Baby Boomers were in their teens, the gray market will exert a dominant influence throughout the 1990s and into the twenty-first century. Ask students to identify products and services that are likely to increase as a result of this development.

(MID/HIGH) — Magazine and television advertising are not only beginning to market products for senior citizens, but also increasingly feature older people in ads. McDonald's created an ad called "New Kid." Shot in sepia tones, it featured an elderly man going off to his first day on the job at McDonald's, where he impresses the younger workers. "Don't know how they got along without me," he tells his wife at the end of the day. Geritol-Extend uses the slogan, "50's Nifty" to promote its product, adding, "Because you're as young as you feel." Have students look for examples of ads aimed at consumers who are fifty or older. What type of products are advertised, what pitches do they use, and what magazines or TV programs have the commercials?

(MID/HIGH)—Look at a program such as "The Golden Girls" that is clearly aimed at an older audience. What type of products are advertised during this program? How do they differ from commercials aired during "Thirtysomething" or similar programs targeted to a younger audience?

(ELEM/MID)—Have students interview their grandparents to get their opinions of advertising. Some students might want to shop with their grandparents to compare what their grandparents buy with what their immediate family buys. Are there any goods and services that their grandparents need that they find difficult to locate?

ADS AS HISTORICAL ARTIFACTS

The American Advertising Museum in Portland, Oregon, has an outstanding collection of print and television advertising in addition to an extensive display of packaging and premiums. The museum is currently developing plans to expand, including the prospect of arranging travelling exhibits. The existence of the museum serves to demonstrate and document the social and historical significance of advertising. History and social studies teachers who recognize the relevance of advertising to the curriculum can draw upon magazines and newspapers from the twentieth century and teach students how to uncover the past by analyzing the advertisements. A recent example demonstrates just how clearly advertising is tied into political and economic developments. When the Berlin Wall fell in 1989, several leading U.S. companies were quick to send production crews to Berlin in time to have ads running on U.S. television before the Christmas shopping rush. During the Vietnam War, Kodak created a spot featuring a soldier returning home to his family and fiancée. By fusing images of the grain belt, middle America, farmland, soldier, and the lyrics of "The Green, Green Grass of Home," the commercial created an indelible record of the national mood at a particular moment in time. In *Advertising the American Dream*, Roland Marchand addresses the historical evidence that advertising affords us. "Once we have placed the advertisements in the same category as many traditional historical documents, it may be possible to argue that ads actually surpass most other recorded communications as a basis for plausible inference about popular attitudes and values" (1985, xix). Marchand believes ads reveal social values, the state of technology, fashions, styles, and insights into the economy.

Most communities today have one or more flea markets or antique and collectible fairs. Often, these travel to various malls once or twice a year. It is quite common for dealers to have dated copies of *Life, Look, Saturday Evening Post*, and other magazines rich in advertising. University and public libraries can also be good sources for such magazines. In addition, your students may have parents or grandparents who collected some of the magazines, and you might be able to draw on them. Country craft and collectible stores are now also quite common, and they often feature antique advertising for wall display. These can be particularly good examples of racial stereotyping in advertising. Finally, old tins, boxes, cans, and packets also provide good historical materials, and if the originals are not available, many of them are now sold as reproductions.

(ELEM/MID/HIGH)—Before starting the study of a historical period with students, provide them with magazines, newspapers, or other advertising from the time. Their assignment is to find out about the period by looking at the pictures. If you like, you can divide the class into groups and have each group make a class presentation on one of the following topics:

- fashion and clothes (men, women, children)
- food (prices, packaging)
- appliances and furnishings
- recreation and leisure (movies, sports, theater, etc.)
- transportation and communication (cars, trains, planes, telephones, etc.)

- occupations (shown in display ads, positions vacant in classifieds; wages)
- family life (size of family, number of children, type of home)
- views and values (how were social ideals reflected?)

(HIGH)—Older students might extend the above process by investigating whether these materials provide an accurate or representative picture of that period and society. Might it not reflect the middle-class society of the advertisers or magazine subscribers, but ignore other levels of society? Might it not reflect social aspirations and fantasy, rather than social reality? These questions are crucial to the consideration of popular culture as historical evidence, and exploring these issues promotes critical thinking skills, which have applications in all areas of the curriculum.

MISCELLANEOUS STRATEGIES AND ACTIVITIES

Most of the instructional activities suggested in this chapter have been arranged around themes. The following activities represent single-concept lessons that can be used without a thematic approach.

And the Winner Is ... Advertising and "Badvertising"

(ELEM/MID)—The advertising industry presents many awards for outstanding commercials, including awards for television commercials and print and billboard ads. The CLIO awards recognize high achievement in advertising. Other awards such as the Baddies and the Trumpet are given to ads that were not well received by the industry. Have students discuss their favorite and least favorite ads. Develop critical criteria for voting for and evaluating ads. Conduct a class poll for best and worst ad. Have students create their own award certificates for best and worst ad. Send the winning and losing certificates to the relevant companies, along with a letter from the class saying what they liked and disliked about each ad.

Clean Dreams

(ELEM/MID/HIGH)—An enormous number of ads that appear on U.S. television emphasize the need for cleanliness. Have students develop a list of the number of products that are advertised by emphasizing cleanliness. What type of people appear in these ads? What are the rewards of cleanliness? Younger students will be likely to concentrate on household cleaners. Older students, however, might discuss how the "clean dreams" approach is applied to people, as well as to sinks and dishes. Teeth must be whiter than white, armpits must be heavily deodorized, and any number of feminine hygiene products marketed as "natural," actually disguise a woman's natural odor.

Green Consumerism

(ELEM/MID/HIGH)—In recent years, consumer activism has led to protests against commercials and companies and has often resulted in organized efforts to boycott products. This movement suggests that consumers are beginning to think more critically about marketing and its impact. One example has been the emergence of "green" consumerism. Exxon found itself in trouble with the way the public perceived the company following the *Valdez*, Alaska, oil spill of 1989. Various tuna distributors have been attacked because traditional methods of catching tuna resulted in killing or hurting dolphins. By 1990, the tuna industry had begun to produce ads addressing these concerns. McDonald's was criticized for the use of polystyrene food containers, and Coca-Cola was criticized for its ties to South Africa and that country's policy of apartheid. AT&T was criticized for contributions to Planned Parenthood.

Sometimes putting pressure on a company has no impact on sales or productivity. Companies are merely forced to address a public relations problem. Nonetheless, critical consumers tend to be active citizens exercising the rights afforded them in a democratic society. Until we begin to see a relationship among the products we purchase, the way they are packaged and promoted, and the way we dispose of them, we cannot hope to solve national and international problems such as pollution, acid rain, and the greenhouse effect. Teachers might want to talk to students about their own behavior and the choices they make as consumers. What do they do with their soft drink cans? Do they buy fast food in polystyrene packages? What is the impact on the environment? Which companies can they write to about packaging and the ecological consequences? Can they set up recycling at home, at school, or in their neighborhood? Teachers should also help students question the claims made by advertisers and manufacturers that their products are environmentally safe. Are the claims true or just another sales pitch?

Advertising and the Telephone Directory

(ELEM / MID) — The phone directory offers a cheap, readily available source of advertising for classroom use. Utilizing it in the classroom not only helps students understand advertising, but it also provides them with practical, day-to-day skills necessary to live in this culture. For students from different cultures, understanding the icons and information in a phone book can serve as useful survival skills.

Depending on the age level you are working with, you can introduce students to the organization and alphabetical format of the directory. What logos, images, and icons are used to represent different businesses, industries, and professions? Photocopy some of the various corporate logos. Cut the name of the companies out of the ads and see which ones students can identify. The front of the directory also uses logos and icons for emergency numbers. Familiarize the students with the images that represent services such as doctors, firefighters, ambulances, and police.

Looking at Logos

(ELEM / MID) — Many major companies and corporations are instantly identified by the images or logos they use. Shell Oil, McDonald's, Paramount Pictures, and Arm & Hammer detergent are all examples of high name recognition. Cut logos from various ads, packets, or boxes. Make sure there are no names on the ads, and see which images the students recognize. You might create a mismatch game, giving labels the wrong names and asking the students to reclassify them. Have students design and draw logos for various companies and products you make up, such as Sunshine cereal, Bluewave detergent, Knight car polish, and Crown carpeting. In each case, ask the students to explain why they chose the logo they did. You can reverse this exercise by having each student show his or her logo to the class and asking the class to correctly identify the concept of the logo.

Selling Seasons

(ELEM) — Most elementary school teachers develop materials, activities, and displays to observe Thanksgiving, Halloween, Valentine's Day, and other holidays, celebrations, and special days. Almost all holidays and observances, including Presidents Day, Memorial Day, and Labor Day, are used by retailers and advertisers for special sales. Older students might explore how commercialization affects the true spirit of these holidays. Younger children can collect and study advertisements from local and state newspapers to see how the holiday is linked to selling. Have the students make a list or a display board of the key words and pictures advertisers use to promote their products. At Christmas, for example, we commonly see images of Santa Claus and reindeer. At other times of the year, we see images of Abraham Lincoln and George Washington, witches, the U.S. flag, and so on. For Memorial Day 1990, McDonald's promoted a red, white, and blue special for those who had served their country, and the special included free apple pie.

"Shelf-Help"

(MID) — In 1990, a study by the Center for Science in the Public Interest reported that the organization and display of products on supermarket shelves was designed to attract the attention of children. The report concentrated on sugar-heavy breakfast cereals. It indicated that brands such as Fruit Loops and Cocoa Puffs tended to be placed on shelves at children's eye level. More nutritious brands such as Total and All Bran were placed on the higher shelves. Is this a manipulation of shoppers, or is it simply an effective sales technique? Have students study the organization of cereal on shelves in their own supermarkets to see if this pattern is repeated. A more advanced study could include observations and interviews to determine what cereals people buy, why people buy them, how children influence the choice of cereal, and the sugar content of cereals. Finally, the exercise can be extended to introduce students to the ways that display influences purchases. How, for example, are weekly specials highlighted in local supermarkets? Why is impulse buying, and why are candy, magazines, and cigarettes so consistently arranged near the cash registers in supermarkets?

Songs That Sell

(ELEM/MID/HIGH) — A major marketing device to draw our attention to products is the use of a song or a jingle. The first jingle used for marketing was developed in 1923 for the Happiness Candy Company. Today, an enormous number of songs are used to promote a wide range of products. One of the most successful campaigns to use this technique was the California Raisins spot that featured "I Heard It through the Grapevine." Many of today's ads feature yesterday's songs, particularly those from the 1960s and 1970s. But why? One reason is that some of these songs are old and are often relatively cheap to use. A more significant reason, however, is that the songs are instantly recognized by a generation that now has major spending power; they are, in fact, the songs this generation grew up with. The widespread use of pop music has included some of the following:

"Revolution," The Beatles — sports shoes
"Mack the Knife," Bobby Darren — McDonald's
"Splish Splash," Bobby Darren — Drano
"The Twist," Chubby Checker — Oreo Cookies
"I Am Woman," Helen Reddy — tampons
"Satisfaction," The Rolling Stones — Snickers

In 1990, rap music found its way into advertising. Rapper Young M.C. did a pitch for Pepsi, Miller Lite beer used Run D.M.C., McDonald's "Fries Surprise" campaign used rap music, and Jovan perfume sponsored a "Write Your Own" rap tune contest. Compile a list of songs that are used to promote products. Mismatch the list and have students match the correct product to its song. Have students make their own list of all the pop songs and jingles they know that are used to promote products. Have the students select a song they are familiar with and write new lyrics to make their own jingle. Give students a current list of Top 40 songs. Look at the titles. Discuss which current songs might be used to promote particular types of products. Select "oldies" that could be turned into product pitches. For example, Roy Orbison's "Only the Lonely" might become an Oscar Mayer theme, sung as "Only Bologna."

Strike a Pose

(ELEM/MID/HIGH) — This is a simple exercise that young children, teens, and adults can benefit from. The purpose is to promote awareness of body language and the ways that advertisers structure social and human tableaus that express gender attitudes and relationships. Collect a series of magazine ads aimed at both men and women. Look for striking differences in facial expression, gesture, stance, and posture. These will not be hard to find. The "male" look tends to be closed, stern, sullen, hands on hips, arms folded. The "female" look tends to be open, provocative: arms, legs, and mouth open, the body often reclining. Break the class into groups of two or three. Give each group a picture and have them mimic the postures in the picture. Then have them change gender roles, so the boys strike the pose of the females and the girls strike the pose of the males. A variation on this is to keep the pictures with you at the front of the room and call upon individual students to come forward and mimic the pose in one of the pictures. The rest of the class has to guess whether the pose belongs to a male or a female.

What's in a Name?

(MID/HIGH)—The choice of a name for a product often involves as much decision making as naming a child. The name must be memorable, simple, and communicate something about the individual nature of the product. Sanitary napkins, for example, promise women that they will not be restricted by the problems associated with menstruation, so the names chosen include such words as Freedom, Stayfree, and Security. The dirt associated with dishes is handled by selecting names that invoke freshness and cleanliness, such as Dawn, Sunlight, Cascade, and Ivory. Shampoo promises a better appearance and greater social acceptability, so it is marketed as Finesse, Style, and Agree. Select a series of products and have the class develop a list of all the different names used to sell those products. Discuss the reason each name was selected. Divide the class into small groups and assign each one a specific type of product. The group must come up with a name for the product and justify their choice. Finally, older students might discuss what happens when human values and emotions such as love, joy, passion, and liberty are turned into promotional vehicles and brand names. Does this process trivialize these values and feelings?

THE PACKAGED PRESIDENT:
Advertising and the Political Process

During the 1984 presidential campaign, a member of the Reagan team told a television commentator, "It's the images we care about most, the balloons, the flags, the symbols." By the time of the 1990 election, pollsters reported widespread voter apathy and low turnout. Many people, they said, were turned off by the process. Although voters became increasingly disenchanted with the political process, they also had dramatic, even historic choices to make. In 1989, Virginia elected Douglas Wilder as the state's first Black governor, and a Black was elected mayor of New York City. The following year, North Carolina Democrats selected Harvey Gantt, a Black, to challenge conservative senator Jesse Helms. Women were becoming increasingly visible, both at the voting booth and as candidates, highlighted by the campaigns of Ann Richards and Diane Feinstein for the governor's office in the key states of Texas and California. Controversial issues, including abortion and flag burning, also provided the opportunity for voter involvement. Yet, despite strong personalities and sharply different policies, there is substantial evidence that the U.S. political process itself fails to attract the interest or active involvement of millions of citizens who stay home on election day. To begin to understand the reasons behind this apathy, we have to take a new look at how the business of politics is conducted in this country. Presidential historian Theodore White has noted, "American politics and television are now so completely locked together that it is impossible to tell the story of one without the other" (1982, 165). White describes the U.S. electorate as a vast television audience divided into major television markets known as ADIs (areas of dominant influence). These markets provide national hubs for the focus and flow of images and information about the candidates. At the center of this process we find advertising, which provides the bread and butter for network television and now dominates U.S. politics. Kathleen Jamieson says:

> Political advertising is now the major means by which candidates for the presidency communicate their messages to voters. As a conduit of this advertising, television attracts more candidate dollars and more audience attention than radio or print. Unsurprisingly, the spot ad is the most used and the most viewed (1984, 446).

If White and Jamieson are correct in their description of the political process, voter indifference and apathy may actually be consistent with viewer attitudes and behavior about both television and advertising. In one case, that of advertising, viewers have traditionally disliked the format, embracing remote control devices that allow

"...ON THE OTHER HAND, WITH THE PROPER VISUALS, BACKDROPS AND SOUND BITES YOU CAN FOOL ALL THE PEOPLE ALL THE TIME!"

To make informed political decisions voters must be able to analyze the form and content of political advertising which often stresses the negative or replaces serious issues with simplistic images and slogans. (Cartoon reprinted with permission of Doug Marlette and Creators Syndicate.)

them to turn the sound off from the comfort of their armchairs and sofas. In the other case, that of television, viewers long ago learned to change the channel or turn off the TV if they didn't like the program. If we apply a Nielsen rating to the political process in this country, we see viewer/voters tuning in less and turning off more.

But what is it about the nature of the process that turns these viewer/voters off? Two potential responses are worth exploring. One suggests that political ads are dishonest or deceptive and that viewers are inherently suspicious of them. George Bush, for example, campaigned in 1988 by saying, "Read my lips. No new taxes." Although Bush was elected, polls suggested that many Americans did not believe he would keep the promise. More generically, political ads tend to promise and promote slogans, clichés, slick solutions, and quick cures to problems such as the national deficit that do not go away and often are even ignored after elections are over. The result is cynicism and a widespread suspicion that what you see is not what you get or that it really doesn't matter whom you vote for anyway. A second concern expressed by viewer/voters centers on the nature of the ads themselves, specifically the tendency toward "negative" advertising. At its simplest level, the negative ad concentrates on attacking an opponent rather than on extolling the abilities and policies of the candidate. In worst scenarios, the election degenerates into name calling, smears, and mudslinging. In the 1989 gubernatorial contest in New Jersey, both Democratic and Republican candidates used images of Pinocchio to accuse each other of lying. The vicious 1990 Texas gubernatorial primary also was waged with negative ads.

When candidates do not attack each other, their campaigns and strategies are often based on creating fear and polarization, distracting voters from the exploration of real issues, and avoiding solving key problems through devices such as wrapping themselves in the flag. The flag-burning issue was widely criticized in the national press as a cynical and manipulative exercise exploited for partisan purposes. The use of fear to intimidate voters is not new. The Lyndon Johnson campaign of 1964 gave birth to the negative commercial with the notorious "daisy" spot. The ad showed a young girl picking petals from a daisy, while an ominous voice counted down from 10 to 1, culminating in an atomic explosion. The Republican candidate, Barry Goldwater, was thereby associated with the atomic apocalypse and lost in landslide proportions. In 1988, the Republican party candidate, George Bush, used the Willie Horton spot and images of Black inmates and a revolving prison door to play on voters' fear of crime. By 1990, the issue was being tapped in Florida and Texas, with death penalty ads that one newspaper called electric chair one-upmanship.

In addition to overt advertising, consideration must also be given to the ways that staged news, photo opportunities, and media events increasingly allow politicians, particularly incumbents, to receive favorable coverage. In this chapter, the concept of product placement has been discussed as it applies to cigarette and alcohol advertising. It is now necessary for us to consider this concept in terms of how it is used in the political process. In the Reagan White House, Michael Deaver was extremely effective in making sure that the president appeared frequently on national television and in the most favorable light. Central to this was the framing of presidential appearances against symbolic backdrops such as the flag and the Statue of Liberty. The composition of the picture was deliberately constructed to eliminate from the frame any sense of opposition or discord. During coverage of the 1984 presidential campaign, for example, television cameras were consistently placed where they could not show hecklers or demonstrators. The networks, eager for good footage, were unknowingly coopted into consistently presenting orchestrated images of the president, thus compromising their neutrality and objectivity. At the time, reporters such as Lesley Stahl believed that strong, critical commentary would get through to viewers. Later, as reported in both Martin Schram's *The Great American Video Game* (1987) and the outstanding PBS series "The Public Mind," Stahl realized she was wrong. In the television age, a picture is worth a thousand words, and with the White House controlling the pictures, the reporters' words were overwhelmed. Richard Cohen, senior political producer at CBS, came to realize that Reagan's right-hand man was really an executive producer of network news. "He suckered us," Cohen admitted.

This is the backdrop against which the U.S. political process and advertising's role in it must be considered. As the last decade of the twentieth century began, discon-

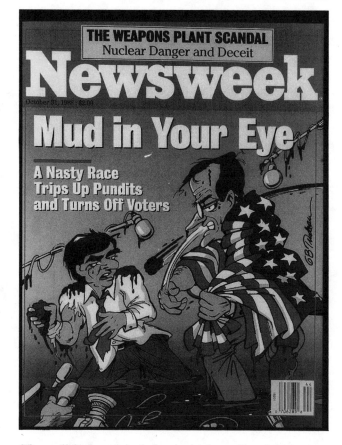

The political process is increasingly a pictorial process. Can schools really claim to prepare students to be responsible citizens in a democracy without teaching them to evaluate how TV and other media affect the public's perception of candidates and issues? (Photograph courtesy of *Newsweek* copyright © 1988 and G. B. Trudeau.)

tent with the process was evident in voter apathy and in media scrutiny promoted by watchdog groups intent on finding a better way. The *Long Beach Press and Telegram* had created a hotline in 1984 for readers to report on unfair or untrue campaign tactics. By 1990, the *New York Times*, the *Washington Post*, the *Philadelphia Inquirer*, and Cable News Network, among other groups, had established a critical approach to campaign tactics. The Center for National Independence in Politics focused on negative, issueless campaigns, and the same theme became the focus for forums at the Annenberg School of Communication and the Harvard Kennedy School. PBS announced plans to provide air time to candidates in 1992 as an antidote to commercials that avoided issues, stifled debate, and marred campaigns. In politics, the national debate has clearly begun to address the very process itself. It is important in teaching about the political process in this country that educators focus not only on the structure of the legislature, but also on the very process by which those legislators are elected. In looking at presidential campaigns, attention should be given not only to who ran and won, but also to how the campaign was conducted and the role of television, advertising, and the media in the process. New technologies now promise the cassette candidate in VHS or Beta, direct-mailed to a letter box near you. This trend, perhaps more than any other development, fuses the content and competencies of the traditional curriculum with the emerging curriculum and provides an opportunity for developing both critical thinking skills and critical viewing skills. By studying campaigns from the past, we can trace the growth of advertising in the political process and help students recognize various tactics and strategies used in packaging the president and all our politicians.

THE CAMPAIGN TRAILS:
Teacher's Overview of Selected Case Studies

1960: Kennedy vs. Nixon

Historian Theodore White won the Pulitzer Prize for his book *The Making of the President 1960* (1962). Interestingly enough, the book's index makes no mention of media or advertising. The term *television*, however, is used and is central to any understanding of the election and the result.

Between 1950 and 1960, the number of television sets in U.S. homes had grown from 4 million to nearly 40 million, or 88 percent of the population. The presidential debates were the first televised debates in history and immediately gave the underdog, John Kennedy, national visibility.

On paper and in print, Richard Nixon, a two-term vice-president in a popular Republican administration (that of Dwight Eisenhower) had more experience, was better known, and was favored to win. Kennedy had several negatives to contend with. He was Catholic, and no Catholic had ever been elected president. He would have been the youngest president ever elected, and this reinforced the claim that he was inexperienced. Finally, he came from East Coast money and privilege, which contrasted sharply with Nixon's middle-class background.

The impact of the televised debates has been well documented. Research suggests that those who heard the debates on radio thought Nixon won, whereas those who saw the debates on television believed Kennedy won. Looking at the debates today, it is easy to see why Kennedy's ratings went up rapidly. Despite his youth and his relative inexperience, he appeared calm, cool, and controlled, whereas Nixon, recently released from the hospital after an illness, looked awkward, tense, uncomfortable, and sweaty.

Addressing the style of the debates, White suggests that Nixon used television less effectively than Kennedy. "Nixon was addressing himself to Kennedy, but Kennedy addressed himself to the audience that was the nation.... It was the sight of the two men side by side that carried the punch" (1961, 287-88). White also acknowledges the powerful role television had begun to play in the U.S. political process and the emergence of being "telegenic" as a criterion for high office.

Kennedy campaigned under a simple slogan: "Kennedy: Leadership for the 60s." It was a progressive, forward-focused theme that addressed a nation entering a new decade and facing the space age. By implication, it suggested that Nixon was yesterday's man. His tired television image reinforced that. The Republican slogan, "Nixon-Lodge: They Understand What Peace Means," promised security and strong leadership and implied that Kennedy's inexperience in foreign affairs was dangerous. Yet, in a country buoyed by the Baby Boom, Kennedy's attractive wife and his father image were in keeping with the times and promised a new look after the aging image of Dwight and Mamie Eisenhower.

The popular vote was very close and not decided until well into the early hours of the following morning. In terms of electoral votes, Kennedy won 303 to 219. In terms of the popular vote, however, Nixon missed becoming president in 1960 by just 112,000 votes. Kennedy received 49.7 percent of the popular vote over Nixon's 49.5 percent. Looking at Nixon's campaign, White says it had neither philosophy nor structure, offering no whole picture either of the man or of the future he represented. Kennedy's people promised optimism, epitomized in their use of the song "High Hopes," which was frequently associated with the campaign.

1964: Johnson vs. Goldwater

Taking place so soon after the assassination of Kennedy, the 1964 election gave voters the chance to both commemorate and consolidate. The country needed security and was in no mood for a change. A vote for Lyndon Johnson represented a continuation of the Kennedy program. That choice was made easier when the Republicans selected conservative Barry Goldwater as their standard-bearer. Goldwater's off-the-cuff remarks and strong statements alarmed many people and set him up as a prime target for negative advertising. His statement that "extremism in the defense of liberty is no vice" continued to feed the critics.

Johnson liked the commercials for Avis and Volkswagen that had been created by the Doyle, Dane, Bernbach firm, and they were given charge of getting the unelected president elected. The campaign's advertising is most notable for two spots. The "daisy spot" developed by Tony Schwartz was an exercise in fear. The picture showed a small girl playing with the petals on a daisy. At the end, the picture changed to a nuclear explosion. Behind the images, Johnson's voice said, "These are the stakes—to make a world in which all of God's children can live, or to go into the dark. We must either love each other, or we must die." The other spot used Goldwater's words against him and showed a saw slicing off the eastern seaboard and the region floating away from the rest of the country. When the nation needed calming, the images of holocaust and fragmentation frightened the electorate and doomed the Goldwater campaign.

Goldwater's campaign slogan was, "In your heart you know he's right." Many responded with the saying, "In your guts you know he's nuts." Relying on scare tactics, Democrats used the slogan, "The stakes are too high for you to stay at home." Goldwater carried only six states—his home state of Arizona, as well as Louisiana, Mississippi, Georgia, Alabama, and South Carolina. In the electoral college, Johnson piled up 486 votes to 52. The Democrats got 61 percent of the popular vote and the Republications, 38 percent.

During the campaign, Johnson had said he would not send American boys to Vietnam. It was a pledge he would not keep, and that decision would stop him from seeking office again.

1968: Nixon vs. Humphrey

By 1968, advertising and the political process had become increasingly fused. The rebirth of Nixon and the role of advertising in that process were documented in *The Selling of the President 1968*. Among other things, Nixon's creative people were told, "Voters are basically lazy, basically uninterested in making an effort to find out what we're talking about" (McGinnis 1970, 36).

Nixon had lost to Kennedy in 1960 and was subsequently defeated in the California governor's race. He had turned bitterly on the media, saying they would not have him to kick around anymore. He was widely referred to as "Tricky Dick," and yet here he was running again for the highest office in the land. He had been unable to successfully sell himself in the past. If he was to get his message across this time, something would have to change. In *The Selling of the President 1968*, Joe McGinnis reported the thinking of Nixon's people as they pondered this: "The response is to the image not the man.... It's not what's there that counts, it's what's projected ... it's not what he projects but rather what the viewer receives. It's not the man we have to change, but rather the received impression" (1970, 38). This account by McGinnis has been challenged by Jamieson. But however accurate or inaccurate the report, there is no doubt that the 1968 campaign saw a growth of the use of both advertising and television. The campaign also was the first presidential campaign in which Roger Ailes, an advertising and media specialist, played a major role. Ailes was in charge of Nixon's television appearance. He would also be a major player in the media campaigns of Reagan (1980, 1984) and Bush (1988). But in 1968 Nixon was his client and his problem. Ailes said: "Let's face it. A lot of people think Nixon's dull. Think he's a bore, a pain in the ass. They look at him as the kind of kid who always carried a bookbag.... That's why these shows are important. To make them forget all that" (McGinnis 1970, 103).

If Nixon's image was a problem, the Democrats were in worse shape. Johnson had deepened the country's involvement in Vietnam, "the living room war." The draft had sharply divided the country. On the domestic front, Johnson's vision of the Great Society and the War on Poverty had taken second place to the Vietnam War. Riots in Watts, a Los Angeles suburb, in 1965 escalated racial unrest, which had exploded again in major rioting in April 1968, following the assassination of Martin Luther King, Jr. Facing humiliation at the polls and challenges from within his own party, Johnson announced in March that he would not seek reelection. The Tet offensive that January and Walter Cronkite's critical broadcast about Vietnam further eroded public confidence in Johnson and the Democrats. Attention shifted to Robert Kennedy's bid for the White House. When he was assassinated in June 1968, the country seemed to be plunging deeper into chaos and violence. By the time the Democratic convention assembled in Chicago, the national theater of the absurd played out nightly on the nation's television screens.

Overzealous police attacked, clubbed, and gassed demonstrators in the Chicago streets. Tear gas found its way into the convention and the hotels. Dan Rather was roughed up on the air by Democratic party workers. Hubert Humphrey's nomination for the presidency was marred by the images that flooded into America's living rooms while demonstrators in the streets chanted "the whole world's watching." There was little doubt that the country was in turmoil and that Richard Nixon offered some promise of unity. The key issues of the campaign were Vietnam and crime and lawlessness. Nixon's theme was simple: "This Time Vote Like Your Whole World Depended on It." The Democratic slogan was "Humphrey: There Is No Alternative."

Advertising and the media played a major role in the campaign. Nixon outspent the Democrats two to one on television. He also outspent them four to one on radio and two to one in print. The television spots were strong, bold, and controversial. Nixon's words hammered with these themes on television:

> We see Americans dying on distant battlefields abroad. We see Americans hating each other; fighting each other; killing each other at home. We see cities enveloped in smoke and flame. We hear sirens in the night. As we see and hear these things, millions of Americans cry out in anguish. Did we come all this way for this?

Against the background music of "Hot Time in the Old Town Tonight," viewers saw Republican ads with montages skillfully juxtaposing the Democratic convention and candidate with images of rioting, violence, and the Vietnam War. A shot of Vietnam carnage followed by the smiling face of Humphrey led to protests by the Democratic National Committee. Despite Nixon's media blitz, his numbers in the polls remained constant between May and November, staying at around 42 percent.

The Democratic campaign is probably best remembered for two spots, both created by Tony Schwartz and both centering, interestingly enough, on Nixon's choice of Spiro Agnew as running mate. Given Agnew's future fate and the role he took on, attacking the media as "nabobs of negativism," the Schwartz strategy was interesting. One spot called "Heartbeat" asked voters to consider whether they wanted Agnew to be that close to the presidency. The other, generally referred to as "Laughtrack," showed Agnew's face as raucous laughter grew louder, only to terminate with the voiceover, "this would be funny if it weren't so serious." The strategy of attacking a popular candidate through his choice of running mate would again be used in 1976 to question Gerald Ford's choice of Robert Dole and in 1988 in the attacks on Dan Quayle as George Bush's running mate.

Despite an early wide lead, Nixon saw his advantage dwindle. Many believe a media overkill by the Republicans energized sluggish Democrats into voting. President Johnson announced a bombing halt late in the campaign that further helped Humphrey's standing. On November 2, both the Harris and Gallup polls gave Nixon a slim 42 percent to 40 percent lead. Considering his financial advantages and the Democratic disarray, Nixon had come close to blowing a commanding and irreversible lead. In the final outcome, Nixon received 31,770,237 votes (43.40 percent) and Humphrey got 31,270,333 votes (42.72 percent). In electoral votes, Nixon received 302, Humphrey 191, and George Wallace 45. The Wallace campaign had succeeded in carrying Arkansas, Louisiana, Mississippi, Alabama, and Georgia.

1976: Ford vs. Carter

The most important point to note about the 1976 campaign is that the winner, Jimmy Carter, began with 3 percent recognition in the polls and that he ran against the power of the incumbency. It has often been said in parliamentary democracies that oppositions do not win elections; rather, governments lose them. The U.S. Republican administration of 1976 was tainted. Gerald Ford was the unelected president who had taken office when Nixon resigned. At the time he addressed himself to what he called "the long national nightmare." Ford thought it was over. In pardoning Nixon, however, he angered many and reminded others of a time they would rather forget.

Nineteen seventy-six was also the nation's bicentennial. Americans wanted to believe in their system. They wanted their faith, hope, and optimism renewed. The Oscar for best picture that year would go to *Rocky*. Although its cinematic merit may be questionable, its values were in keeping with the time. The cinematic fantasy that reenergized the American dream was the story of an outsider, an underdog who triumphed. It is an important social barometer to read when viewing Jimmy Carter's emergence from obscurity to become president of the United States.

But good timing and the national mood alone would not have gotten Carter elected. First and foremost he needed visibility, and television offered it. Writing in *America in Search of Itself*, Theodore White noted, "There could have been no Carter presidency without television" (1982, 195). In 1976, the television set made Jimmy Carter a household name and gave him what he needed. But four years later, it would also destroy him.

Jamieson (1984) describes 1976 as "a watershed year in campaign advertising." The campaigns stressed personal appeals and person-in-the-street testimony. Utilizing the polling strategies of Patrick Caddell and the media skills of Gerald Rafshoon, Carter was able to develop spots and strategies that contrasted his plusses to Ford's negatives. He campaigned as an outsider, against Washington corruption. He invoked images of small-town, rural, populist U.S. sentiment against the cynicism and greed of the city and the corporations. The Carter campaign had the flavor of Frank Capra's *Mr. Smith Goes to Washington*. But if Carter was country and a peanut farmer, he was neither redneck, cracker, nor hayseed. He was a born-again Baptist, a theme that was to emerge more strongly as the New Right grew in the 1980s. He was educated. He had been in the armed services and he had been governor of Georgia. If southern stereotypes were still present in the media (*Deliverance* [1972] and *Macon County Line* [1974]), Carter's candidacy addressed the New South and comforted northern fears.

In the 1976 campaign, federal financing laws awarded the candidates $21.8 million each. Both Ford and Carter spent more than 50 percent on paid media, including 30- and 60-second spots. Ford's spots often asserted, "He's making us proud again." Unfortunately, the slogan invoked a time voters did not want to remember. In addition, many Americans got their impression of the president from television, and the cameras were not kind to Ford. He was shown falling down airplane steps, hitting spectators when he played golf, and as the butt of jokes in comedian Chevy Chase's parodies on "Saturday Night Live."

He also had to face a challenge from within his own party in the person of Ronald Reagan. It was a bruising, damaging process that Ford narrowly won, racking up 992 delegates compared to Reagan's 886. The power of the incumbency redistributed uncommitted delegates in Ford's favor, but nonetheless he remained damaged goods.

Carter's ads addressed the broad themes of his campaign. His slogan was simple: "Leadership for a Change." The man from Plains, Georgia, delivered "plain folks" ads. They talked of "a president who is not isolated from our people but who feels your pain and shares your dreams and takes his strength and wisdom and courage from you." So Carter wore his heart on his sleeve. He told *Playboy* magazine he had lusted in his heart. He assured the nation, "I'll never lie to you." He delivered a major speech from the porch of Franklin Roosevelt's home in Warm Springs, Georgia, symbolically fusing the New South with the New Deal and the popularity of the Roosevelt legacy. But the campaign was not all positive. Ads questioned Ford's choice of Dole as a running mate, and polls showed that the choice did influence some voters. Carter was also able to forcefully articulate the failures of the Ford administration in television spots:

> We have been a nation adrift too long. We have been without leadership too long. We have had divided deadlocked government for too long. We have been governed by veto too long. We have suffered enough at the hands of a tired, worn-out administration without new ideas, without youth or vitality, without vision and without the confidence of the American people.

When the votes had been cast and counted, Carter had 297 electoral votes to Ford's 241. The South had fallen in line solidly behind Carter, disrupting a major voting block that had gone for Republicans Nixon and Goldwater. With the exception of Texas, the West went solidly Republican, and Texas, of course, could well be counted as part of Johnson's and Kennedy's southern strategy.

1980: Carter vs. Reagan

Theodore White notes television's role in making the Carter presidency; he also sees its role in Carter's destruction. "He who comes to power by television must be prepared to be destroyed by television ... though he [Carter] might control camera attention, he could not control events" (1982, 195).

Jimmy Carter's presidency was in trouble well before 1979, when Iranian radicals seized the U.S. Embassy in Tehran and took U.S. citizens hostage. For a moment, it even seemed as though the crisis might help the embattled president by unifying the nation behind him in his attempts to free the prisoners. Certainly Carter needed a distraction. The country was beset with an 18 percent interest rate and 18 percent inflation. The national mood was sour, variously described as a malaise, and Carter himself in a televised address to the nation described a "crisis in confidence." Compounding problems, the Soviets had invaded Afghanistan. Carter boycotted the 1980 Olympic Games and imposed a grain embargo in retaliation. Meanwhile, just as Ford had had to battle Reagan before facing Carter, Carter now found himself fighting off a challenge inside his own party in the person of Edward Kennedy.

But the real attrition in the Carter campaign came from the nightly news as it covered the hostage crisis. Night after night for more than 300 nights, national attention was focused on U.S. impotence. "Day 222 of the hostage crisis," Frank Reynolds would intone as he anchored ABC nightly news. Day after day, week after week, little changed but the number of days. It was April 25, 1980, when the last real chance of the Carter administration died on the desert floor in Iran. The president was forced to go on television and admit that the rescue mission had failed; the technology had malfunctioned and the most powerful nation in the world could do little to free its own people from foreign captors. Still stinging from the loss of the Vietnam War, many Americans raised on John Wayne movies questioned what on earth had gone wrong with the country's leadership. When Carter's secretary of state, Cyrus Vance, resigned in protest at the attempted rescue mission, the administration's credibility was further eroded.

Against this background Ronald Reagan appeared. For Reagan, his time had come. There would be challengers such as George Bush, who called Reagan's financial views "voodoo economics," but Reagan was an old war-horse with a strong, well-financed organization. In addition, Carter and the times had handed him the issue to run on. Whereas Carter seemed weak, Reagan had always seemed strong. Carter's inexperience was balanced against Reagan's record as governor of the major state of California.

Reagan had been an actor and president of the Screen Actors Guild. He knew how to work a crowd and how to face a camera. His presidency consistently used television to bypass the Congress and appeal directly to the American people. Like Roosevelt's use of radio and his famous "fireside chats," Reagan entered U.S. living rooms and invoked key elements of U.S. mythology. "Win one for the Gipper" recalled the legendary Notre Dame football player and became a standard tool in Reagan's repertoire. When he debated Carter during the 1980 campaign, he was able to brush the incumbent aside and score points with one-liners such as "There you go again." Reagan looked and sounded secure and in charge throughout the campaign. Although the Democrats tried to depict Reagan as an extremist with a dangerous foreign policy, the electorate was more concerned about inflation, interest rates, and the declining prestige of the United States. The widespread public perception was that Carter was incompetent. Although many Americans liked Jimmy Carter as a person, they did not want him to be president. Late in the campaign, when his attacks on Reagan became more strident, many people even began disliking Carter as a man and the Democrats' own polls began to record the dive. Carter and Mondale won only their home states of Georgia and Minnesota, plus West Virginia. In electoral votes, the Reagan-Bush ticket won 489 votes to 49.

One footnote on the 1980 campaign should acknowledge the role the media played in first launching and then linking the Kennedy challenge to Carter. Media polls, pundits, predictions, and projections created the climate for Kennedy to challenge Carter. But once Kennedy announced his candidacy, the same media that had seemed to favor him turned against him. Kennedy's campaign was not helped when he could not explain to Roger Mudd why he wanted to be president. In media circles, the interview became known as the "Muddslide." Finally, it must be noted that only 53.9 percent of Americans voted in the 1980 election.

1984: Reagan vs. Mondale

In many ways, the record Reagan landslide in 1984 merely reaffirmed the judgment the electorate had made in 1980. Walter Mondale had been Carter's liberal vice-president, and he was perceived as being a rehash of old views that the "Reagan revolution" and the New Right had wiped out.

In looking back at the 1984 campaign, three points need mentioning. The campaign was historic because Mondale selected a woman, Geraldine Ferraro, for his running mate, which was a major breakthrough. A second noteworthy point was the way the media looked for conflict and competition to make even the primary process seem interesting. Mondale's election was a foregone conclusion in the primaries, and that would not generate ratings or newspaper sales. The media were attracted to Gary Hart, and the sudden surge in Hart's campaign can be traced in large degree to this. Hart's debate with Mondale gave the former vice-president his best line for the campaign, when he asked "Where's the beef?" thus invoking a hamburger slogan to undermine Hart's credibility. The third point was the fact that the morning after the election defeat, in a televised speech, Mondale acknowledged that television had not warmed to him and he had not warmed to television. He lamented the growing tendency for the U.S. political process to be controlled by sound bites, photo opportunities, and "hooks." The next election, in 1988, would be described as the most negative in presidential history. At the end of the 1984 campaign, the Democrats won only Minnesota and the District of Columbia, accumulating 13 electoral votes to 525. Mondale-Ferraro got 40 percent of the popular vote, compared to 58 percent for Reagan-Bush.

This brief history of campaign advertising and the media's role in the political process provides a background to the study of current elections. It helps students conceptualize the election process in a fundamentally different way. Rather than simply knowing who ran and who won, students now have an opportunity to conceptualize the increasing roles that advertising, television, and technology play in U.S. politics. They have an opportunity to study the personalities, the policies, and the process. Until voters become aware of the ways the process influences the outcome, including the very decision as to who will run in the first place, elections in this country are likely to continue to be more image than issue and more style than substance, governed by impulse and emotion rather than by logic and rational decision making. These authors do not believe that the complex domestic and global issues of today or the twenty-first century can best be addressed by such a political process.

Activities

(HIGH) — Discuss the political process in your school. What offices can students run for and vote for? What is the level of student interest or apathy in these elections? What qualities does a typical candidate have? Are the looks of the candidates important? Do candidates actually campaign, make speeches, and use publicity?

Study a recent political television advertisement. You might actually show the class an ad from a current campaign or you might have access to ads from older campaigns. Remember, even if you can't get an actual ad, several slogans and actual ads are quoted in this chapter.

If you are working with a videotape of an ad, show it to the class without the sound. Have them concentrate on the images, including both the content and the form. What type of camera angles are used? Look at the posture, facial expression, and body language of the candidate. How do these affect our impressions of the politician? Does the spot use montage and rapid editing to juxtapose the candidate with themes and issues he or she wants to be associated with? Are there any strong graphics, props, or backdrops such as stars and stripes, the U.S. flag, or the Statue of Liberty? Do we see images of a multiracial society and the young as well as the old? What target audience do students think the ad is aiming at?

When they have developed strong responses to these questions, show them the ad with the sound. How does the sound contribute to the message? Direct their attention to music, words, sound effects, and the tone of the narrator's voice. Could the soundtrack be successfully used as a radio spot; that is, can it stand independently from the images?

Locate a negative or adversarial commercial. Aristotle Industries is one source for such advertisements (see the "Resources" section at the end of this chapter). Introduce students to the concept by describing the "daisy" spot and several other negative ads referred to in this chapter. Have them analyze the new commercial to determine what makes it negative. Issues that should be discussed include the difference between truth and fairness and the relationship among distortion, deception, and dishonesty. For example, the 1988 Bush campaign hit Michael Dukakis for not cleaning up Boston harbor, but the ad did not tell us what role the federal government played (or didn't play) in funding the cleanup. In another example, the controversial Willie Horton spot painted Dukakis as soft on crime but ignored the fact that when Ronald Reagan was governor of California he also had a furlough policy and that, in fact, Dukakis merely followed a common practice. Neither of the ads lied—they simply did not provide all the information. It should be noted that for all that is written about them, negative ads are not always successful. Despite Roger Ailes's successful campaigns for Nixon and Bush, his 1989 candidates for mayor of New York City and for governor of New Jersey both lost.

Break your class into groups, each representing an advertising agency. Each group has to come up with the best strategy, slogan, radio spot, TV spot, and print ad for the 1996 or 2000 presidential election. Have them conceptualize the work in terms of personality; policy, slogan, and themes; and process. They should attempt to use the turn of the century to sell their candidate. What type of candidate do they believe will be successful at this time? How will the changing composition of the U.S. population shape the choice of candidates and issues? Will new technologies allow new forms of advertising?

Will they run a positive or a negative campaign? Look over some of the slogans from past campaigns that were not successful, such as Ford's "He's Making Us Proud Again." What are the potential pros and cons of using a slogan such as "The Dream Team"? It sounds good and it's catchy, but do people want to believe in the dream? Doesn't it leave the campaign wide open to negative attacks suggesting the candidate and the party are asleep or even are creating a nightmare? As students develop their own spots, have them use the storyboard format from this chapter.

If you have the facilities, the class could actually record a radio spot or a television spot. Footage from old campaigns could be cut and re-edited with new voiceover to remarket a candidate.

Have the class debate the advantages and disadvantages of political advertising. Use the following lists as idea generators. They can actually have the debate or you might want them to develop a paper on this topic.

Advantages

- Encourage voters to vote.

- Bring the issues directly to the people.

- Are cost-effective in that TV ads reach more people for a lower price than direct mail or newspaper.

- Don't change voters minds but simply confirm their existing beliefs and attitudes (see the previous section on Nixon's 1968 campaign).

- Are quick and simple.

Disadvantages

- Create apathy and alienation.

- Substitute images for issues.

- Make campaigns so expensive that only the rich can run.

- Make campaigns so expensive that political action committees (PACs) and special-interest groups influence the candidate.

- Rely on emotion, not logic.

- Manipulate a visually illiterate electorate.

- Require candidates to be "telegenic" or attractive, thus disadvantaging average-looking candidates who are otherwise well qualified. Could Lincoln or Franklin Roosevelt be elected in a TV age?

- Rely increasingly on negative techniques.

Movie Tie-Ins

The Candidate (1972). Oscar nominations: Best screenplay (Winner); best sound

(HIGH) — This is a very interesting film for any study of the relationship between advertising and the electoral process. It is the story of Bill McKay, a young idealist who is talked into running for a Senate seat against a three-term incumbent. He is lured by the promise and prospect of being his own man, able to run his own campaign without interference from media or machine.

This is one of those rare occasions where using an entire film in class can be justified. The message of the film links historically to the media's role in repackaging Richard Nixon in 1968 and 1972 and their continued role in today's political process. Additionally, the issues of the McKay campaign (ecology, energy, crime, abortion) remain crucial issues twenty years after the making of the film.

Teachers wishing to save time can fast-forward past the opening scene and credits until Robert Redford appears as Bill McKay. Here is a rundown of key scenes and issues.

The Offer: The initial encounter between McKay and Marvin Lucas establishes the promise and perception of politics. McKay needs convincing to run; Lucas promises the contacts and the resources. McKay's wife and the political consultant define what the candidate has going for him: credibility, a name, looks, and power. Note that there is no mention of issues or beliefs. In fact, McKay is not even a registered voter. Nonetheless, because he is not expected to win, he is told he can "say what you want."

The Announcement: The press conference to announce McKay's candidacy for the Democratic primary produces some surprises. What is surprising about the candidate's answers to some of the questions? How do the reporters respond?

The Opposition: McKay is introduced to the way his opponent, Crocker Jarmon, used the media to promote himself. Draw students' attention to the use of image and to the strategies McKay's people develop to counter Crocker's incumbency.

Banquets and Ballrooms: The Big Time: The campaign propels McKay into the heady world of Democratic politics. Vice-president Hubert Humphrey is shown arriving at a gala. This is McKay's first major address. His introduction belittles the entire process by calling him "a man who shoots from the hip and who's hip when he shoots." This is the second opportunity to see the candidate fumbling with issues, trying to distinguish between policies and the process. In the end, he tells the party faithful, "Maybe people aren't ready to listen." Given low voter turnout in the United States this issue remains relevant today and can be applied to current elections.

Media Montage: Packaging the Candidate: Three quick scenes show the erosion of McKay's individuality as he is rehearsed and prepared for his campaign. The candidate is seen making ads at the beach with young people and walking through Watts. Why are the two photo opportunities selected? How relaxed and comfortable does the candidate seem?

Post Primary: The New Spots: McKay wins the primary. A string of new commercials are developed for the main assault on Jarmon. The slogan adopted is "For a Better Way, Bill McKay." Some of these ads are strong and appealing. McKay is concerned that the health care issue is not used in his ads. Why did they drop it? Who is really in charge?

The entire process of getting McKay elected now struggles for a balance between the individual, the image, and the issue. McKay is disgruntled: "This TV stuff isn't working. I'm not talking to anyone. I'm not saying anything." His media advisor's response is crucial for any understanding of the process. "The point is you're showing your face. That's what we have to sell first."

Putting Out Fires: A Malibu fire provides a great photo opportunity for McKay to address the ecology and the watershed issue. He cancels one plan and heads to the fire to meet the media and address the issues. The scene is a crucial indication of the power of the incumbent. McKay arrives by car; Jarmon arrives by helicopter. Jarmon announces he has spoken to the president and the area will be declared a disaster and be eligible for funding. Finally, he subverts McKay's issues by announcing his intention of introducing new legislation. In the 1988 campaign, Michael Dukakis used the Yellowstone fires as a dramatic photo opportunity. Draw your students' attention to disasters and the way politicians use them to their own advantage.

Fear and Loathing on the Campaign Trail: Three quick scenes in the shopping mall, the bus, and the school gymnasium demonstrate the downside of the campaign and how planning, staff, and proper venues are crucial to the process. The Making of the President series by Theodore White and Hunter Thompson's *Fear and Loathing on the Campaign Trail* (1973) provide excellent reading on this subject. The film has run about 50 minutes by this time and the key issues have been framed, so it could be stopped here, which would allow it to fit into one period.

The campaign trail continues to dominate the film with several scenes dealing with the candidate's family, the intrusion of the media into the family home, and a scene at a rally when the candidate is punched.

Howard K. Smith and the Packaging of the Candidate: Television commentator Howard K. Smith criticizes McKay for selling out and packaging his candidacy like detergent and underarm deodorant.

The Debate: McKay picks up 14 points in the polls, which forces Jarmon to take him on in a debate. This is an interesting scene and can be useful during any presidential debate. The first thing McKay is told is to forget everything he learned about debate in high school. Why is he told he has to be sitting? In the 1988 campaign, Michael Dukakis used an elevated lectern to counter the impression that he was short. Candidates have used chiller vents to blow cold air across their faces so they did not sweat and therefore appear to be uneasy. The Kennedy-Nixon debates of 1960 are well worth looking at in relation to this scene. Perhaps the most telling comment is when McKay is told, "You can't say too much on TV." Observant viewers might note that the panel that questions the candidates does not include a woman. Compare that to the composition of panels during recent major political debates.

The Eyes of Jarmon Are upon You: Toward the end of the film, Crocker Jarmon makes a major speech. The visuals are worth some consideration. He is shot from below in an exaggerated tilt-up to stress his power and authority. Behind him looms an enormous poster of his own head with two eyes staring out at the audience.

Cynicism and Seduction: As the campaign proceeds, McKay is seduced by a young worker and big unions. By the end of the campaign, his integrity and individuality have been consumed by media and machine. When he wins the Senate seat, he is left asking his advisors, "What do we do now?"

Power (1985).

(MID/HIGH)—Directed by Sidney Lumet, starring Richard Gere, Gene Hackman, Denzel Washington, and Julie Christie, *Power* is a fascinating look at the impact of advertising on the political process. The film centers on the work of Pete St. John, a media consultant for the political Left, Right, and Center. Several key scenes in the film provide opportunities to look at the way television spots are designed and developed to create particular perceptions about candidates.

Keep Your Bloody Shirt On: The opening scene takes place in a Latin American country during a rally for the presidential election. St. John's camera crew is on hand to make ads for their client. During the speech, there is an explosion and the candidate pushes through the crowd to embrace an injured bystander. All the time, the cameras keep rolling. Later, in a car, St. John tells the candidate to use the attack to his advantage and to appear for the rest of the campaign in the bloodied shirt. The film implies that the bomb and the bloodshed may have actually been media events engineered for political purposes.

I'm Running for Governor of New Mexico: Back in the United States, St. John meets Wallace Furman, a mild-mannered, lackluster millionaire who is running for governor of New Mexico. St. John immediately begins to control the campaign and the candidate, making recommendations about the clothes he wears, his diet, his appearance, and his need to work out. When Furman complains, "You're trying to run my life here," St. John responds, "My job is to get you in. Once you're there, you do whatever your conscience tells you to do."

The Family Issue: One of St. John's clients is Andrea Stannard, the incumbent governor of Washington State. Her campaign is in trouble because she ran on family issues, but has recently left her husband and children and married her campaign manager. To be reelected, she needs to change the public's perception, and St. John has to create a successful media strategy to do this.

Selling the Candidate in Santa Fe: This is a brief but very important scene that shows St. John working with Furman and a team of advisors on the New Mexico strategy. It provides specific reference to some of the concepts discussed in this chapter, including clusters and the "pools and patios" voters.

Back in the Saddle Again: The Making of a Spot: About 45 minutes into the movie, a desert scene provides the backdrop for the making of a commercial to promote Wallace Furman. It is an elaborate ad with horses, wagons, and riders poised against the panoramic scenery of New Mexico. It gives students a sense of how words, music, editing, and props are used to create an impression of a candidate. When Furman falls off his horse, it also shows how editing can be used to alter reality and create false impressions.

A New Vision for New Mexico: Furman's opposition begins to produce a series of commercials attacking him as an outsider because he is not a native New Mexican. St. John watches the ads and knows he has to counter-attack with a series of rebuttal commercials. It might be interesting to stop the film and have students devise their own strategies for responding to such an attack. St. John's approach includes the slogan, "He Didn't Have to Come Here, He Wanted To."

Here's Mud in Your Eye: In Washington, Andrea Stannard's campaign is in trouble. St. John has to develop ads to accentuate her positive side. The slogan promises, "Courage—Compassion, Now More Than Ever." The scene shows St. John using paint-box techniques to create an ad that responds to mudslinging and negative advertising. How do the images, words, and techniques he utilizes defuse the issue? Again, before showing this scene to your students, you might want to set up the scenario and ask them how they would respond if they were the advertising agency handling the Stannard account.

KEY DEVELOPMENTS IN THE HISTORY OF ADVERTISING

1704   First paid ad in a newspaper, the *Boston News Letter*.

1741   First magazine ad in the American Colonies, in *General Magazine*.

1768   Paul Revere writes advertising copy.

      Volmey Palmer of Philadelphia becomes the first advertising agent.

1850   First transit ads: Lord and Taylor on horse-drawn streetcars in New York City.

1868   First full-page newspaper ad appears in *New York Daily Tribune* for druggist.

1880   John Powers becomes first full-time copywriter.

1881   Advertising messages on burlap school bags represent start of special ad industry.

1883   Cyrus Curtis starts *Ladies Home Journal*. Curtis pioneers modern magazine circulation, promotion, distribution, and market research.

1886   Celebrity endorsement for Pears Soap by Lillie Langtry, actress.

1900   Quaker Oats becomes first food processor to utilize distinct four-color package.

      U.S. businesses spending $540 million on advertising.

1902   Pioneering in market research and the concepts of placement and position put Campbell's soup in a designated place in the *Saturday Evening Post*.

1904   Creation of Campbell's Kids.

1908   Sunkist created by California Fruit Growers Exchange, the first advertising co-op.

1917-1918   War themes in advertising.

1919   Total advertising expenditures up to $2.5 billion per year.

1923   Happiness Candy Company creates first radio advertising jingle.

Eveready sponsors first radio series, "The Eveready Hour."

1930s   Growth of supermarkets. First celebrity endorsements for Coca-Cola.

1930   *Advertising Age* starts as a weekly publication and is still being published.

1932   George Gallup joins Young and Rubican Agency and pioneers opinion polls.

1933   Proctor and Gamble starts soap operas.

1939   Gillette sponsors World Series on radio and sells 2.5 million razors.

1942   Creation of War Advertising Council.

1946   The novel *Hucksters* is critical of the advertising industry.

1949   Advertisers sponsor television programs, including "Voice of Firestone," "Texaco Star Theater," "Kraft Television Theater," and "Goodyear TV Playhouse."

Animated Lucky Strike cigarettes square dance on television in new advertising promotion.

1950   4.4 million U.S. homes have television.

1951   Coaxial cable links East and West coasts for television broadcasts.

1952   Citizens for Eisenhower run the first television ad for a political candidate. Richard Nixon saves his spot on the ticket by using television to make his famous Checkers speech. Model Betty Furness upstages the nominating conventions and becomes an overnight celebrity by promoting Westinghouse refrigerators on television during the convention.

1960   45 million U.S. homes have television.

Kennedy-Nixon televised debates.

1963   Three days that shook the world: Kennedy assassination and funeral seen by millions all over the world.

Evening news goes from 15 to 30 minutes.

1964   Doyle-Dane-Bernbach's "daisy" spot, used by Lyndon Johnson against Barry Goldwater, marks the beginning of the negative commercial.

1965   Passage of the Cigarette Labeling and Advertising Act.

All networks convert to color.

1970   Cigarette ads banned from U.S. television.

1976   Carter-Ford presidential debates, the first presidential debates held in sixteen years.

1980   80 million U.S. homes have television.

REFERENCE LIST

Berenstain, Stan, and Jan Berenstain, (1988). *The Berenstain Bears Get the Gimmies.* New York: Random House.

Booth, William, (1991). Quit Nagging and Pass the Cookies. *Washington Post*, weekly edition, July 22-28, 37.

Carnegie Council on Adolescent Development, (1989). *Turning Points: Preparing American Youth for the 21st Century.* New York: Carnegie Council on Adolescent Development.

Christian, George, (1990). *Washington Post*, weekly edition, April 23-29, 23.

Di Franza, Joseph, et al. (1991). RJR Nabisco's Cartoon Camel Promotes Camel Cigarettes to Children. *Journal of the American Medical Association*, 266:22, 3149-54.

Fischer, P. M., et al. (1991). Brand Logo Recognition by Children Age 3 to 6: Mickey Mouse and Old Joe the Camel. *Journal of the American Medical Association*, 266:22, 3145-48.

Germond, Jack, and Jules Witcover, (1989). *Whose Broad Stripes and Bright Stars: The Trivial Pursuit of the Presidency 1988.* New York: Warner Books.

Guber, Selina, (1987). The Teenage Mind. *American Demographics*, 9:8, 42-44.

Iskoff, Michael, (1991). Just Say Alcohol. *Washington Post*, weekly edition, June 17-23, 37.

Jamieson, Kathleen, (1984). *Packaging the Presidency: A History and Criticism of Presidential Campaign Advertising.* New York: Oxford University Press.

Key, Bryan Wilson, (1972). *Subliminal Seduction.* New York: Signet Books.

_____, (1980). *The Clam Plate Orgy and Other Subliminal Techniques for Manipulating Your Behavior.* New York: Signet Books.

Kilbourne, Jean, (1991). Deadly Persuasion: 7 Myths Alcohol Advertisers Want You to Believe. *Media and Values*, no. 54/55, 10-12.

Leo, John, (1991). Hostility among the Ice Cubes. *U.S. News and World Report*, July 15, 18.

Linn, Marcia, et al., (1984). Adolescent Reasoning about Advertisements: Relevance about Product Claims. *Journal of Early Adolescence*, 4:4, 371-85.

Lyons, John, (1987). *Guts: Advertising from the Inside Out.* New York: American Management Association.

Mandell, Maurice, (1984). *Advertising.* Englewood Cliffs, N.J.: Prentice-Hall.

McGinnis, Joe, (1970). *The Selling of the President 1968.* London: Andre Deutsch.

McNeal, James, (1990). Children as Customers. *American Demographics*, 12:9, 36-39.

Marchand, Roland, (1985). *Advertising the American Dream.* Berkeley and Los Angeles: University of California Press.

Meyers, William, (1984). *The Image Makers: Power and Persuasion on Madison Avenue.* New York: Time Books.

Millum, T., (1975). *Images of Women: Advertising in Women's Magazines*. London: Chatto and Windos.

Mintz, Morton, (1991). Marketing Tobacco to Children. *Nation*, May 6, 577, 591-96.

Monk, John, (1990). Tobacco Ads Aimed at Women, Blasted. *Charlotte Observer* (October 4), 1, 10a.

Moog, Carol, (1991). The Selling of Addiction to Women. *Media and Values*, no. 54/55, 20-22.

Novello, Antonia, (1991). Liquor Industry Must Stop Targeting Minorities with Alcohol Ads. *U.S.A. Today*, July 1.

Packard, Vance, (1957). *The Hidden Persuaders*. New York: Pocket Books.

Pierce, John, et al. (1991). Does Tobacco Advertising Target Young People to Start Smoking? *Journal of the American Medical Association*, 266:22, 3154-58.

Pollay, Richard, (1991). Cigarettes under Fire: Blowing Away the PR Screen. *Media and Values*, no. 54/55, 13-16.

Rovner, Sandy, (1991). Up in Smoke: Why Do So Many Kids Ignore All the Evidence Condemning Cigarettes? *Washington Post Weekly*, December 16-22, 11.

Schram, Martin, (1987). *The Great American Video Game: Presidential Politics in the Television Age*. New York: William Morrow.

Sugarman, Carole, and Malcolm Gladwell, (1991). Once Again the Foxes Set Policy in the Henhouse. *Washington Post*, weekly edition, May 6-12, 39.

Thompson, Hunter, (1973). *Fear and Loathing on the Campaign Trail*. New York: Fawcett Popular Library.

Waldrup, Judith, (1990). Shades of Black. *American Demographics*, September, 30-34.

White, Theodore, (1961). *The Making of the President 1960*. London: Jonathan Cape.

———, (1982). *America in Search of Itself: The Making of the President 1956-80*. New York: Harper & Row.

U.S.A. Today, (1991). n.t., September.

U.S. News and World Report, (1991). n.t., n.d., 18.

RECOMMENDED READING

Altman, David, et al. How an Unhealthy Product Is Sold: Cigarette Advertising in Magazines 1960-85. *Journal of Communication* (Autumn 1989) 37:95-106.

Atkins, Charles, et al. Teenage Drinking: Does Advertising Make a Difference? *Journal of Communication* (1984) 39:2, 46-54.

Baran, J., and Jin Ja Mok. You Are What You Buy: Mass Mediated Judgements of People's Worth. *Journal of Communication* (1989) 39:2, 46-54.

Curry, Timothy, and Alfred Clarke. Developing Visual Literacy: Use of Magazine Advertisements Depicting Gender Roles. *Teaching Sociology* (1983) 10:3, 361-70.

Diamond, Edwin, and Stephen Bates. *The Spot: The Rise of Political Advertising on Television*. Boston: MIT Press, 1984.

Dyer, Gillian. *Advertising as Communication*. London: Methuen, 1982.

Ewen, S. *Captains of Consciousness: Advertising—The Social Roots of the Consumer Culture*. New York: McGraw-Hill, 1976.

Ewen, Stuart, and Elizabeth Stuart. *Channels of Desire: Mass Images and the Shaping of American Consciousness*. New York: McGraw-Hill, 1982.

Fine, Gary Alan. The Psychology of Cigarette Advertising: Professional Puffery. *Journal of Popular Culture* (1974) 8:3, 513-22.

Gabler, William. The Evolution of American Advertising in the 19th Century. *Journal of Popular Culture* (1978) 11:4, 763-71.

Goldberg, Marvin, and Gerald Gorn. Increasing the Involvement of Teenage Cigarette Smokers in Anti-Smoking Campaigns. *Journal of Communication* (1982) 32:1, 75-86.

Gorman, Christine. The Fight over Food Labels. *Time*, July 15, 1991, 52-56.

Hecker, S., and D. W. Stewart. *Nonverbal Communication in Advertising*. Lexington, Mass.: Lexington Books, 1988.

Himmelstein, Hal. *Television, Myth and the American Mind*. New York: Praeger, 1984.

Horst, Stipp. Children as Consumers. *American Demographics* (1988) 10:2, 26-32.

Kilbourne, Jean. Beauty and the Beast of Advertising. *Media and Values* (1989) no. 49, 8-10.

Mieder, Barbara, and Wolfgang Mieder. Tradition and Innovation: Proverbs in Advertising. *Journal of Popular Culture* (1977) 11:2, 308-19.

Miller, Mark Crispin. Hollywood, the Ad: How TV Ad Techniques Are Reshaping the Movies. *Atlantic* (1990) 265:4, 41-68.

Moriarty, Sandra E. Global Advertising and Visual Communication. *Journal of Visual Literacy* (1989) 9:1, 58-69.

Mullen, Chris. *Cigarette Pack Act*. New York: St. Martin's, 1979.

O'Hare, Willis. A New Look at Asian Americans. *American Demographics* (1990) 12:10, 26-31.

Piirto, Rebecca. Measuring Minds. *American Demographics* (1990) 12:12, 30-35.

Riche, Martha Farnsworth. Psychographics for the 90s. *American Demographics* (1990) 11:7, 24-31.

Schlosberg, Jeremy. The Demographics of Dieting. *American Demographics* (1987) 9:7, 34-37.

Schudson, Michael. *Advertising: The Uneasy Persuasion*. New York: Basic Books, 1990.

Skelly, Gerald, and William Lundstrom. Male Sex Roles in Magazine Advertising, 1959-1979. *Journal of Communication* (1981) 34:4, 52-57.

Starr, Michael E. The Marlboro Man: Cigarette Smoking and Masculinity in America. *Journal of Popular Culture* (1984) 17:4, 45-57.

Tankard, James, Jr. The Effects of Advertising on Language: Making the Sacred Profane. *Journal of Popular Culture* (1975) 9:2, 325-30.

RESOURCES

Resources for use in the study of advertising are abundant. Almost any magazine or newspaper in a school library or at home contains some form of advertising. On their way to school any morning, many children pass billboards, displays, and other forms of advertising. Many students arrive at school carrying or wearing some form of advertising, often character merchandising. We have referred to many articles from *The Journal of Communication*, which is a very good resource for high school teachers. A good file of clippings can also be developed just by reading the business and entertainment sections of *USA Today*.

Videotapes

Campaign Advertising. Aristotle Industries has a large collection of political ads from various campaigns including 1984, 1986, and 1988. Tapes are usually $75 a copy. Write or call Aristotle Industries, 205 Pennsylvania Ave., SE, Washington, DC 20003, (202) 543-8345 or (800) 243-4401.

"Consuming Images," from the series "The Public Mind" with Bill Moyers. An excellent look at the advertising ethic and its impact on U.S. society. PBS Video, 1320 Braddock Pl., Alexandria, VA 22314-1698.

Crazy People. A 1990 Dudley Moore comedy that looks at the consequences when an advertising creator decides to make ads that tell the truth. Airlines, laxatives, automobiles, and everything else come in for his scrutiny. An interesting companion piece for *Beer* (1985).

The Hucksters. This 1947 movie looks at the world of radio and advertising. Features Clark Gable and Ava Gardner. Usually available from Blockbuster Video stores.

Mr. Blandings Builds His Dream House. This 1948 Cary Grant comedy includes a subplot of an advertising executive trying to develop a campaign to sell ham.

Publications

AdBusters
The Media Foundation
1243 W. 7th Ave.
Vancouver, B.C.
V6H 1B7 Canada
    A magazine of media and environmental issues.

Advertising Age
220 E. 42nd St.
New York, NY 10017
    An insider look at the business.

Adweek
ASM Communications
820 Second Ave.
New York, NY 10017
   Inside the industry.

American Demographics
108 N. Cayuga St.
Ithaca, NY 14850
   Not just useful for advertising and consumer developments but also a real guide to the changing composition, character, and tastes of the U.S. public, with uses in everything from math and economics to social studies.

Zillions (previously *Penny Power*)
Box 2878
Boulder, CO 80322
   Here's a great one for teachers and students in elementary school. Shows real ads, how they are put together, who they are aimed at, and how they work.

Chapter 6

Reading the News:
Interpreting Form and Content

WHY STUDY THE NEWS?

In 1982, John Naisbitt wrote in *Megatrends* that the United States had moved from an industrial society to an information society. One of the key characteristics of that society, says Naisbitt, is "the collapsing of the information float" (1982, 19). What he refers to is both the proliferation of information and the increased speed at which information is transmitted from one point to another. But producing more information is meaningless and potentially dangerous unless it is accompanied by a corresponding growth in our ability as a culture to process and interpret that information. From Naisbitt's perspective, "we are drowning in information but starved for knowledge" (24).

Five years after the publication of *Megatrends*, Chester Finn (the assistant secretary of education) and Diane Ravitch published *What Do Our 17 Year Olds Know?* a report of the first national assessment of history and literature. In the chapter "A Generation at Risk," the authors conclude that the younger generation "is ignorant of important things it should know" (1987, 201). Looking at the knowledge gap they discovered in high school students, Ravitch and Finn ask, "Can they make sense of what they see and hear?... Can they interpret the significance of the day's news" (202)?

In the preface to *Manufacturing Consent*, the authors recognize the need for all members of a democratic society (not just students) to understand the form and content of the information they receive from the news media. "If ... the powerful are able to fix the premises of discourse, to decide what the general public is allowed to see, hear and think about and to manage public opinion ... the standard view of how the system works is at odds with reality" (Herman and Chomsky 1988, xi). The way the news media work requires an exploration not merely of form and content but also of ownership. Ben Bagdikian warns, "When the central interests of the controlling corporations are at stake, mainstream news becomes heavily weighted by whatever serves the economic and political interests of the corporations that own the media" (1990, x).

Recognizing what news is and how it is constructed requires discipline and intellectual rigor. The news media often discourage this form of thinking. An editorial in *The Catholic Register* suggested that "TV news is an adult pacifier. Just as what calms the baby is not mother's milk but the act of sucking, what reassures the viewer of TV news is not information received, but the watching ritual." The ritual trivializes the function it claims to be serving. "What are said to be the important stories ... are boiled down to a few words and pictures.... A picture is not worth a thousand words but a picture can render a thousand words useless. We allow pictures to make up our minds for us" (Trueman 1990, 8). At times the news media adopt a self-defensive mode and belittle any attempt to analyze or scrutinize them. In an extraordinarily shallow and sarcastic 1991 article, *Time* belittled what it called "the media's wacky watchdogs" (Queenan 1991, 54). The article purported to examine various media watchdog groups but was little more than a two-page putdown of the very concept that the media might need watching at all. The author dismissed organizations of "unapologetic leftists" as well as right-wing publications. It questioned "jeremiads by professors from obscure universities" and the credentials and respectability of small or independent publishers. With weighted words and a total unwillingness to explore the serious media research going on in this country or the media studies curriculum overseas, the *Time* article represented a perfect example of why the news media need watching. But do our students watch, and if they do, can they understand what they see and hear?

As we entered the last decade of the twentieth century, evidence indicated that our students tune out the news and the world depicted in it. A report from the Times Mirror Center for the People and the Press suggested that what theoretically should have been the best educated generation in our history had actually managed to grow up ignorant in the "information age." The study reported that only 24 percent of the under-35 population had read a newspaper the day before, compared to 67 percent 25 years earlier. Only 41 percent had watched television news the day before, compared to 52 percent 25 years earlier (Morin 1990, 35).

As the amount of information continues to grow, the integrity of that information has come under increasing scrutiny. In April 1990, *New Dimensions* ran a cover story depicting what they called "America's Biased and Abusive News Media." Although the report clearly reflected right-wing attitudes, it also provided important insights into the liberal bias and confrontational stance of many in the news industry. Sam Donaldson, for example, was quoted as saying, "You'd better be glad I'm leaving the White House beat in November, because if Bush gets elected, I'd savage him" (26). In the early 1980s CBS found itself tied up in a major suit brought by General William Westmoreland following a broadcast entitled "The Uncounted Enemy: A Vietnam Deception" in which they accused him of conspiracy to misinform the American people during the Vietnam War. That suit was one factor in attempts by Senator Jesse Helms to take over the network. During the Reagan administration senior State Department spokesperson Bernard Kalb resigned, protesting a government policy of misleading the press on the subject of Libya. Later, White House spokesperson Larry Speakes admitted he had invented statements attributed to the president and reported them as news. In the early months of the Persian Gulf crisis in 1990, media correspondents were accused of bias, boosterism, and a lack of balance in their reporting. In 1991 a Denver television journalist went to trial charged with organizing a dog fight to stage a news report. The visual violence, it was suggested, was an important ingredient in the ratings race. While journalists are often criticized for aggressive tactics, they can also be too easy. The press was criticized in the controversial 1991 Louisiana gubnatorial election for not dealing firmly enough with the candidacy of former Nazi and Ku Klux Klan member, David Duke (Berry 1991). This is the backdrop against which teachers, principals, media specialists, and parents must consider the need to teach students to critically evaluate news in all its forms. As the amount of information continues to grow and as evidence accumulates that news coverage often represents personal prejudice rather than an objective reflection of reality, responsible citizens in a democracy must be capable of analyzing and evaluating the form, content, and origin of their news.

Throughout the 1980s controversy surrounded the fairness and accuracy of news reports. If students are to understand the world they live in, they must be taught to critically evaluate the form and content of news coverage. (Cover reprinted with permission of *New Dimensions* magazine, P.O. Box 811, Grants Pass, Oregon 97526.)

If our students cannot think about what news is, how it is constructed, who owns it, and how accurately and fairly it represents reality, they lack basic thinking and viewing skills, which makes them extremely vulnerable in an information age. There is no doubt that the news media are powerful. In 1990, shortly after ABC's "American Agenda" segment characterized the secretary of education as ineffectual, he was replaced. Other factors contributed to his replacement as well, but the power of the media was evident here. Shortly after "Prime Time Live" reported on the shocking conditions of a Cleveland Veterans Administration hospital, Senator Howard Metzenbaum (D-OH) was onsite. But the same network that ran both stories also ran a 1990 interview with former child star "Buckwheat," despite the fact that the real actor had been dead for ten years. Journalists are capable of mistakes! The ratings race often rewards speed rather than accuracy, which places the onus on us as consumers to analyze the news. In the case of television news, this need for analysis cuts across all our cultural assumptions about television. Of course, the news is not a program to be watched like a sitcom or a drama. It is our primary source of information, and for that reason we must gain the tools to critically look at it and listen to it. Until students are given these tools, they remain in danger of becoming what Richard Morin called "the Doofus generation whose values are lightly held and whose opinions remain ripe for manipulation" (7/9-15/1990, 37).

The Nature of News

What is news? There is no better way to begin a study of the news media than to ask this question. The question leads to a series of other questions:

1. Is news new?

2. To whom is it news?

3. Who determines what is newsworthy?

4. Is it *all* the news?

For students, particularly those in middle school and high school, these questions are crucial if they are to begin to understand the communication process and the way the media operate as gatekeepers, filtering information before passing it on to society.

Where Do We Get Our News?

- newspapers
- newsmagazines
- radio
- television

Newspapers

Have students bring in an example of each one of these types of newspapers: national, morning, evening, weekly, local, tabloid and special interest. Divide the class into groups and have each group study a different type of paper. Compare and contrast the papers for:

- size (number of pages and size of pages)
- color/black-and-white
- cost
- front page (content—stories covered, types of headlines, etc.)
- back page (of whole paper or of sections)
- editorials
- features
- cartoons/comic strips
- photographs (size, content)
- advertising
- classifieds
- circulation
- sports

In what way do the differences in these elements suggest something about the community and consumer group that each paper is intended for?

Have students research life in their own community based on the elements they find in their local newspaper. Remember that they are looking at all of the newspaper, not just the stories. What, for example, do they learn about their community from display advertising and help-wanted ads and other classifieds?

Have students examine the Sunday edition of one of the larger newspapers in the state. In what way is it different from the regular weekday edition? Why is it different? Make a display board that compares the Sunday edition to the daily paper.

Obviously, the Sunday paper will be larger in size and it will cost more, but why is it larger? Is there more news every weekend? If that's the case, why is there actually less television news coverage in a weekend? These questions provide a useful framework for considering how the definition of news changes on a weekend and how the consumer influences news.

The fact that many Americans do not work on Sunday means we have more time to read. Because we have more time to read, the newspaper creates a bigger edition, which includes not only weekend sports but also features designed for different members of the family.

Sensationalism and Ethnocentricity

(MID/HIGH)—Quite obviously, the news in a newspaper is not all the news that happened in the world on any given day. Rather, it is the news that the publishers and editors think will be of interest to their readers. The news is ethnocentric because rather than dealing with all countries and cultures equally, it presents stories that are of interest to people with similar cultures, backgrounds, and value systems. Although this makes good marketing sense, it might also limit the scope of the news, and in the process, by ignoring certain stories, it may prevent consumer/citizens from more fully understanding other cultures or may limit them to just one perspective.

An article in the *Charlotte Observer* criticized the media's obsession with Charleston in the wake of Hurricane Hugo. Charlotte suffered terribly from the hurricane, as well, but the national media ignored it, and most of the country had no idea that it had been affected. But the invisibility factor sometimes has much greater consequences. A 1991 issue of *Extra* examined Africa and the U.S. press. In particular it suggested that the press ignored the growing famine that afflicted Ethiopia, Somalia, and Sudan throughout 1990. By failing to fully cover the crisis as described by the United Nations and the U.S. Agency for International Development, the press actually exacerbated the crisis. "The blame for inadequate coverage," said the report, "does not lie primarily with the few reporters covering Africa for the U.S., but with editors, publishers and news directors who make Africa their lowest priority" (Hunter and Askin 1991, 10).

Sometimes the victims of news media are not those who are ignored, but those who are shown in a distorted way. An article in the *San Jose Mercury News* asserted that "TV coverage cheapens Arab lives" and gave examples of how words and pictures distorted Iraqi and Arab life (Husseini 1991). A 1989 article in *TV Guide* asked "Is TV news guilty of Japan bashing?" The article reported studies that "found stereotypes everywhere. Japan as a closed society, at once hostile and indifferent; the clannish driven Japanese; the anthill lifestyle" (Diamond and O'Neill 1989, 25). Given Japan's increasing economic power in the world and its trade relationship with

Ask students to compare and contrast the way stories are covered in newspapers and television. (Cover design copyright © Ken Condon. Used with permission.)

the United States, it is important that Americans have much more than a simplistic and stereotypical image of the people and the culture.

On the domestic front press coverage also creates victims. A 1991 publication of Fairness and Accuracy in Reporting complained about press reaction to the disabled and the disability rights movement.

> The U.S. media have studiously avoided covering disability rights issues for years in favor of the soft but ever-popular story of the courageous individual.... For the press, disabled people are either tragic, hopeless cases constantly bemoaning their fate, or incredibly brave, courageous and inspiring (Johnson 1991, 15).

Research studies suggest that the percentage of stories dealing with foreign or international issues and events has declined. In 1971, 10 percent of editorial space in the nation's 10 leading newspapers was dedicated to foreign news. By 1986 the figure had dropped to 2.6 percent. Writing in *The Humanist* in 1990, Dan Rather said this trend had occurred at "the very time it has become indisputably clear that America's future depends upon our having a better understanding of that great big world beyond our shores" (1990, 6). In the case of television news, although we often see stories about events in Japan, Poland, El Salvador, and the Soviet Union, they are often filtered through a U.S. prism, as a result of which we always look at other countries and cultures from our own perspective. This raises the issue of the ways the news media represent and construct reality and how this affects public perception and the political process. This topic is addressed in more detail in the section on television news.

Have students conduct a content analysis of a large city or national newspaper to determine what types of people are most often featured in stories. Are they, for example, White, middle class, male, professional?

Over a period of a week have students develop a table that shows the number of stories, location of the stories, size of the stories, and photographs that appear about various groups. Figure 6.1 (page 160) might be a useful guideline.

At this point the exercise is merely a quantitative analysis rather than a qualitative analysis. Students are measuring the frequency of stories. They are not yet evaluating the objectivity of stories.

Once the students have developed a picture of what type of groups are most frequently covered, move their attention to considering how these groups are covered. Are there more positive or negative stories about certain groups? Are some groups more or less visible than others? What types of stories are there, for example, about children, the elderly, and teenagers?

Do factors such as violence, sensationalism, and scandal seem to be prominent in all or some of these stories? How many of the stories could be classified as good news? Is it true that no news is good news?

Women in News

(MID/HIGH) — The presence of women in the news industry has enormous implications for our society. As a growing industry, news offers career opportunities for young women. Communication research suggests that the presence of women in the industry would increase the likelihood that stories might be presented from a female perspective which is often lacking in an industry that is largely owned by men and in which men make most of the decisions. The question of women and the news involves a discussion of both visibility and viability. The absence of women from the news is often explained in terms of their low profile in national politics and in the policy-making process. "Women's absence from the public sphere as well as their lack of status as authority figures or experts gives the news media a ready made justification for women's absence from news programs" (Rakow and Kranich 1991, 13). This is essentially a chicken-and-egg argument that claims women are not covered because they are not powerful enough. Obviously, it could conversely be argued that women's viability as authority figures is minimized by the amount of coverage they receive. But the question of coverage must address quality as well as quantity and explore how women are covered. When Pat Schroeder chose not to run for the presidency in 1988 the media made much of her tearful announcement. Her femininity was covered by men as though it were a political handicap and liability. It might equally have been argued that a nurturing, emotionally honest candidate could have been refreshing. So often women are seen through male eyes and perspectives. One report suggests that when women do appear on the news they do so as examples of uninformed public opinion, consumers, housewives, spouses to the men in the news, or as victims of crime or political decisions or

Fig. 6.1. Frequency and form of newspaper coverage.

Group Featured in Story	Sex	No. Stories per Issue	Average Page Location	Average Size of Story	No. & Size of Photos
White, middle class					
Black, middle class					
White, working class					
Black, working class					
Hispanic American					
Native American					
Asian American					
Elderly					
Teenagers					
Children					

disasters. "Thus not only do they speak less frequently, but they tend to speak as passive reactors and witnesses to public events, rather than as participants in those events" (Holland 1987, 139). Students can test their findings as they monitor and analyze news broadcasts. For most of them, the issue of how women are represented in the news media will be something they have never considered.

How aware are students of women in the news industry? Is the most famous female journalist they can name Lois Lane or Murphy Brown? Although women appear to be well represented in television news, visibility does not necessarily indicate power. A 1990 report in the *New York Times* suggested an increasing number of female anchors were becoming "evening stars," particularly in news magazines. But journalist Linda Ellerbee told the newspaper that the trend was not necessarily a positive one. "They put the star before the show. All they really want people to watch is the person ... this trend does no good for women and it doesn't matter if the show's good or not. It's all based on the person. Then if the show fails, the woman gets blamed" (Carter 1990, H-27).

Ask students to develop a list of all the female journalists they can think of. Which of the following names appear?

Linda Ellerbee	Carole Simpson
Jane Pauley	Lesley Stahl
Diane Sawyer	Barbara Walters
Maria Shriver	

What other local or national journalists do they list? What formats (newspaper, radio, television) do the women report for?

Just Another Pretty Face?

Sometimes the way female journalists are treated reflects the deep-seated bias of a male-dominated industry and society. One female sports reporter was subjected to insult and abuse by players and management for the New England Patriots, resulting in a heavy fine for the club. In January 1991 *TV Guide* ran a cover story with a picture of Jane Pauley. The heading asked "Is She Tough Enough to Make It in Prime Time?" The cover recalled the August 1989 cover of *Time*, which featured Diane Sawyer and the heading "Is She Worth It?" Both women's credentials were implicitly challenged by even asking the questions. When Peter Jennings, Tom Brokaw, or Dan Rather gets a raise, one seldom finds cover stories questioning their value or contribution.

In U.S. society women constitute approximately 50 percent of the workforce, 45 percent of the labor force, and 50 percent of newspaper readership. Does the press provide an objective reflection of women in society? A 1989 study concluded that:

- Female journalists contribute only 27 percent of front-page bylines

- Only 24 percent of front-page photographs featured females

- The average percentage of references to women on the front page is only 11 percent (Bridge 1989, 11-13).

Break students into groups and assign each group one copy of various large city and national newspapers. The students should select an area of interest, such as bylines, photographs, or story content, and tabulate the proportion of each that are contributed by men or deal exclusively or largely with men. This concept can also be applied to analyzing television news.

Identify a series of issues that would be of particular concern to females, such as child care, contraception, abortion, and the ERA. Are women's issues well represented in the news media? Are they presented by women or by men? Are there issues for which the gender of a reporter would limit his or her ability to accurately present a story?

Weighted Words and Prejudiced Pictures

Many people usually assume that because it is news, it is real and, therefore, true. They also assume that the story consists of a series of facts that are reported neutrally for viewers' consideration. Often, however, stories are presented in such a way that viewers are actually led to draw a particular conclusion. We are being encouraged to adopt the perspective and point of view of the writer, reporter, or anchor rather than to draw our own conclusions.

Have students read editorials on several key issues to try to develop a sense of the views and values of the newspaper editor. Are these views and values reinforced throughout other sections of the paper written by other journalists?

See whether the newspaper regularly features two opposing points of view on important issues. Such columns usually appear on the editorial page. In *USA Today* this section is called "Face Off."

Cut out a series of photographs from newspaper articles and give them to students. Make sure to keep a record of the article, the accompanying photographs, and whether it was a positive or a negative story.

Have the students look at the photos and indicate what they think the story was about and whether they think the person pictured was presented positively or negatively in the story. Then ask them to explain how they reached their answer. Facial expression and body language can be read and interpreted as clues in this process. Props can also play a part. For example, was there a gun in the picture, or perhaps a police car or a sheriff's badge? What about the camera angle? Is it objective, or does it impose a point of view and perspective? Does it, for example, tilt down or up at the subject? More information on reading visuals can be found in chapter 5, "How to Read Advertisements," page 106, and "The Four Ps" in chapter 7, page 207, of this book.

How often are the pictures truly neutral, needing words to establish a context, and how often do they speak for themselves? Is the role of the photograph to decorate or elaborate? Does it contain and convey meaning independently of the story?

(ELEM/MID) — Give students a list of stories and ask them to decide where they would place the stories in a newspaper and to explain their choices. Some possible stories might include:

- Death of a senator

- Plane crash

- Coal miners' strike in England

- United States loses America's Cup

- Coup in Soviet Union

- President visits flag factory

- Former president has surgery

- Stock market closes down

- Baseball star arrested in drug raid

- Storm damages wheat crop

- Animals saved from forest fire

Now give students a series of stories and pictures that you have cut out of several newspapers. Make sure you have removed any evidence of what pages the stories came from, but keep a record of the pages for yourself. Have the students arrange the stories in the order that they think they would have appeared in the paper, and compare the students' arrangement to the actual positions you have recorded. Students must be able to explain their decisions.

Do students make the same decisions as editors and publishers? Some of the films discussed later in this chapter provide an insight into this decision-making process. They might offer useful clips to use during this exercise.

Writing Headlines

(ELEM/MID) —Journalists typically use catchy headlines to grab our attention. These headlines often involve literary devices such as metaphor, simile, or alliteration. A newspaper report of an unstable vehicle in the solar car race across Australia read, "Sun Setting on U.S. Car." When a student's automobile engine design won a scholarship, the story was headed, "Engine Design Drives Student to Success." During the Iraqi invasion of Kuwait in 1990, one headline declared Saddam Hussein the "Bully of Baghdad." Later headlines read, "Butcher of Baghdad."

Share these examples with the class and discuss why the headings were selected. Look for examples of similar headings in newspapers. Collect the headings and separate them from the stories. Present the stories to the students and ask them to come up with their own headlines.

The McPapering of the United States

(MID / HIGH) — In *Unreliable Sources* (1990), Martin Lee and Norman Solomon write, "stuffed with celebrity gossip and other bite-sized light items, the innards of many newspapers largely resemble fluffy bonbons" (1990, 14). *USA Today*, which started in 1982, is often cited as an example of this type of newspaper. How much news do these papers contain? In what way have they influenced the form, content, look, and coverage of other newspapers? Are these papers more useful or less useful than television as a source of news?

INTEGRATING MOTION PICTURES INTO STUDYING NEWSPAPERS

"All the President's Men" (1976)

(MID / HIGH) — Oscar nominations: Best picture; best director, Alan J. Pakula; best supporting actor, Jason Robards (winner); best screenplay from another medium, William Goldman (winner); best art / set decoration (winner); best sound (winner); best film editing.

This powerful film is worth viewing in its entirety, either for a study of Watergate in U.S. history and social studies classes or for a behind-the-scenes examination of investigative journalism and the ethical issues it raises about the press and the public. The language is strong at times, but it must be kept in mind that the Watergate tapes revealed that President Nixon used such language.

Character Analysis. Divide students into groups and have them analyze the various characters in the film. This is very useful when considering the day-to-day operations of the *Washington Post*. Students can make notes on the roles of the reporters, the editor, the sources, etc. It might be useful to begin by finding out what students know about newspapers and journalism in general and then see how this contrasts and compares to the film's image of a big-city newspaper.

Tracking the Story. Compare and contrast the techniques used by Bob Woodward (Robert Redford) and Carl Bernstein (Dustin Hoffman). What strategies and methods do they use? How ethical, valid, legitimate, or honest are their approaches? Do they manipulate people? Whom do they call? How important is the telephone to them? Draw students' attention to Woodward's behavior on the telephone. Note that when he calls someone, he identifies himself by name; he says where he works and what story he is investigating.

Power Struggles and the Press. The behind-the-scenes struggle to get the newspaper out provides an interesting insight into how stories are assigned to individual reporters; differences of opinion between reporters and editors; and the significance and space assigned to different stories. There are several useful scenes that highlight this. Direct students' attention to some of the following scenes and have them describe the operations of the press from the perspective of story significance and space allotted in the paper.

1. Bernstein rewrites Woodward's material.

2. The reporters give Ben Bradlee "a good solid piece of American journalism."

3. The meeting between the various newspaper department heads (Foreign, National, State, Metropolitan).

Distrust of the Press. Various characters throughout the film express suspicion of the press and media. Have students discuss some of these issues or debate the credibility of various sources of news such as radio, television, and newspapers. Cite recent examples of this controversy, such as CBS ("60 Minutes") versus General William Westmoreland. Consider the following statements.

"I can't do the reporting for my reporters, which means I have to trust them, and I hate trusting anybody," Ben Bradlee, editor of the *Washington Post*.

"I don't like newspapers. I don't care for inexactitude and shallowness," Deep Throat, Woodward's source from the Executive Office.

"Absence of Malice" (1981)

(MID / HIGH) — Oscar nominations: Best actor, Paul Newman; best supporting actress, Melinda Dillon; best writing.

This useful film deals with the right of the public to know and the role of the press to responsibly inform them. Sally Field plays the reporter who is unwittingly duped by police into running a story that is not true. The film centers on the consequences her story has and its impact on those whom she wrote about. The essence of the film centers around this observation: "I know how to print what's true. I know how not to hurt people. I don't know how to do both at the same time." For students in middle school or high school, this film and scenes from it can provide an interesting starting point for a discussion on the role of a free press in a democratic society.

First amendment issues could be discussed, including the issue of whether reporters should be jailed for refusing to reveal their sources. The public's right to know could be balanced against the individual's right to privacy. Does the individual who seeks public office, for example, forfeit his or her right to privacy? What are the likely consequences of this? Would it, for example, deter qualified men and women from seeking public office? Have students investigate some of the following people to see how press coverage affected their lives:

Geraldine Ferraro	Thomas Foley
Gary Hart	Jimmy Swaggart
Jim Wright	Pete Rose
Barney Frank	Donald Trump
Jim Bakker	

In the film, the reporter initially does not feel that her story has caused any harm. Her attitude is that she presents the information and people react to it. It is the reaction rather than the reporting that is at fault. "That's not the paper's fault. It's people. People believe whatever they want to believe." That statement might be valid if everything that was reported was true, objective, and unbiased. Often, however, stories are quite slanted toward one point of view or another. Sometimes this is in the overall tone or in particular words and phrases. Sometimes it is even in the pictures, which may be suggestive or particularly unflattering. Have students search through newspaper stories and build up a file of prejudicial reporting in both pictures and words. When appropriate, tabloid coverage of celebrities and law suits might be used to facilitate this study.

NEWS MAGAZINES

(MID / HIGH) — Give students a selection of news magazines such as *Time, Newsweek,* and *U.S. News and World Report.* Have the students analyze the form and content of the magazines, including the following criteria:

- size of pages
- number of pages
- price
- type of advertising

Using issues of the three magazines from the same week, have students compare and contrast:

- the cover story
- the editorial
- international stories
- national stories
- coverage of business
- coverage of education
- coverage of sports
- coverage of entertainment

Which magazines do students believe provides a better and more informative view of the week and why?

Based on the type of advertisements appearing in each magazine, ask the students to develop a profile of the primary readers of each magazine. Would the readers, for example, be more likely to be male or female, working class or middle class, college-educated or with no college? These questions help students understand the concept of targeting audiences. In looking at the advertisements they are actually looking at the audience. How do the products, pictures, and form of persuasion reflect the audience for the news magazine? (See chapter 5 of this book for more information.)

TELEVISION NEWS

(ELEM/MID/HIGH)—When we talk about "television news" we are referring to news on television, and most of the time we think about network evening news. Actually the term *television news* refers to many different types of programs broadcast at many different times. Give students copies of *TV Guide* or the television listings in daily newspapers and have them compile a list of all programs that would be classified as news oriented. These programs should include:

- Morning news programs from networks, such as "Good Morning America"
- Evening news programs from networks
- Late-night network news programs, such as "Nightline"
- Lunchtime news programs
- Weekly news programs/news magazines, such as "Hard Copy," "20/20," and "60 Minutes"
- Weeknight news forums and discussions
- Local news, A.M. and P.M.

(ELEM/MID)—Have students conduct a survey of their parents, relatives, and other adults to find out which news programs the adults regularly watch and why. Compile the results and display a chart showing the news viewing preferences in your area. Compare your results to Nielsen ratings for these programs. (Ratings appear regularly in *USA Today*.)

(ELEM/MID/HIGH)—Break the students into groups and assign each group the task of viewing and analyzing one of the types of programs listed above. Things to look for include:

- Broadcast time
- Length of broadcast

"...AND FILLING IN FOR PETER JENNINGS ON 'WORLD NEWS SIMULATION TONIGHT'..."

If citizens are to become media literate, they must be able to distinguish between authentic footage and simulated dramatizations of events. In 1989 ABC showed simulated events without telling viewers. (Cartoon used with permission of Doug Marlette and Creators Syndicate.)

- Number of presenters, such as anchors, reporters, sports, film reviewer, meteorologist, etc.
- Gender balance of presenters
- Types of stories covered, such as international, national, regional, state, local
- Format, such as interviews in the studio, on-locating footage, anchors' and other reporters' commentaries, etc.

News Anchors

(MID/HIGH)—What is a news anchor? What does the term imply? Look at national network news on ABC, CBS, NBC, and CNN. Who anchors the evening news on a weeknight for each network? What do these anchors all have in common? Do the same people who anchor the evening news on a weeknight anchor it on a weekend? Who anchors the weekend evening news? How are these people similar to and different from the weeknight anchors? In *Television, Myth and the American Mind*, Hal Himmelstein says: "He [a news anchor] does more than read us the news—he guides us through the world as his news organization has defined it. Anchors become arbiters of correct reactions to the news. The anchor is detached one moment, cynical, amused, folksy or self-righteous the next" (1984, 205).

Compare Himmelstein's impression of the anchor to various network news anchors. It is important to note that Himmelstein thinks that the actor/anchor's mannerisms actually influence the way we perceive and process the news. Draw the attention of your students to elements such as facial expression, tone, gesture, and body language, and see if they can develop a sense of how the anchor feels about a story or a series of stories through these clues.

Anchors Away!

(ELEM/MID/HIGH)—Frequently the network anchor is not located in the studio but in some far-off location that usually provides a dramatic and visually interesting backdrop. In the early days of the Persian Gulf crisis in 1990, Dan Rather could be seen with the pyramids behind him. Red Square in Moscow is also a favorite location. These backdrops are used to catch our eyes and to convey the impression that the anchors are at the center of the story.

Travel became an increasingly important part of network news anchoring after local affiliates began to get more and more international footage for their local broadcasts during the mid-1980s. For the national network news to survive, they had to have the international picture, presence, and prestige that the locals could not afford. Ask students to develop a list of the places where leading network news anchors report from. What events typically force anchors to leave the studio? Are there times when one network sends an anchor to a location and the others do not, or are there times when different anchors actually go to different locations? Is this trend apparent only in the evening news, or is it also reflected in morning news broadcasts?

Visual Analysis of News

(MID/HIGH) — The outstanding PBS program "Illusions of News" examines the impact images had on the flow of information during the Reagan administration. Bill Moyers interviews Michael Deaver, Reagan advisor, who ran operations at the White House. Deaver discusses in detail how simple objects such as jelly beans and flags were deliberately used as props to create a positive public perception of Ronald Reagan. CBS's reporter Lesley Stahl discusses how network news programs unwittingly became propagandists for the president by using footage the White House gave them. What Stahl and other journalists did not realize at the time, and what Deaver fully understood, was the fact that on television, the image always overwhelms the words. The result was that even when network news stories were critical of Reagan, the images were often supportive and contradicted the report. The old adage "A picture is worth a thousand words" was demonstrated time and time again during the Reagan administration, and this provides evidence of the need to teach students to be critical viewers as well as critical listeners. Film studies offer one useful approach.

The concept of mise-en-scène, which emerges from French film theory, suggests that the total meaning of a film can best be understood by looking at the composition of the frame. We are conditioned to follow the plot through the dialogue and narrative, but mise-en-scène suggests that visual elements, whether we are conscious of them or not, actually contribute to the full impact. These elements include point of view or camera angle; posture or body language; position or placement within the frame; and props, including their symbolic meaning.

Analyzing the evening news by applying some or all of these concepts provides us with an opportunity to further understand meaning and manipulation in the news media. It is important to note that this process can be applied to all visual media and can be taught to children and adults alike, whether they are studying film, television, or advertising. Further information on visual analysis can be found in chapters 4, 5, and 7 of this book.

The Opening. The beginning of the evening news is prepackaged to convey a sense of importance and authority. Some of this occurs visually and some of it occurs aurally. Compare the opening of the news on two or more networks.

- What type of music is used? What does it suggest?

- Is there a voiceover introduction to the news? What does it say? What is the tone? Is it a male or female voice?

- Does the introduction begin with a logo or some form of graphics? If so, what is it?

- Does the program start with the formal introduction of the top story, or does it use a "hook" and quickly preview the top two or three stories to grab our attention?

- When the anchor first appears, how do we first see him or her? Is the anchor in the studio or on location? Is the anchor sitting or standing? What is the anchor wearing? Is it a long shot, a close-up, or a medium shot?

The Studio Set. Often we pay little attention to the studio in which the anchor is located. We think of it as the background, so it is seen as neutral and as having little to do with the story. Actually, the set can very effectively confer status and authority upon both the anchor and the news organization. This is usually done by surrounding the anchor with telephones, computers, even people moving back and forth, busily in the process of gathering news.

Study the background and the whole set. Does it conform to this approach? Do we always see the studio from the same angle or camera position? At what times do we see more of it? At what times do we see less of it? When do these changes occur and why?

News Boxes. "News boxes" are simply the graphic inserts that are usually placed behind the anchor's head as a new story begins. They are meant to be title slides, almost like chapters in a book. They need to be strong and simple, so they usually combine a graphic or visual with one or two words. To be successful they must be legible, which means their meaning must be clear to most of the audience. One simple way of testing this is to run a story without sound and ask students what the graphic at the top of the story represents.

A strong and simple news box was used by ABC during the televangelist scandals of the late 1980s. It consisted of a cross made out of television screens. Without words they successfully fused symbols of Christianity and television. Not all news boxes, however, are so successful. Give students several storylines and have them construct their own news box to serve as the lead-in to each story.

Framing and Point of View. The question of framing is crucial to any understanding of the authenticity of television news. As we know, the evening news is not actually all of the news for that day; it represents the network's construction of the news. They edit out what they do not think is newsworthy. But another editing function that we are less aware of occurs when the camera position or placement establishes the frame. Often the most dramatic image is used. It might be a raging storm or a political demonstration or an erupting volcano. The point is, the moment producers place people and objects within the frame, they also place others outside of the frame. If we do not ask what was going on to the left or right of the camera, or what was happening behind the camera, we tend to assume that what we see is the whole picture, or reality, and therefore is representative. The question of framing is a mental and visual exercise for students that says: "Imagine you are to the left or right of the camera or behind it. What might you see that is not in the frame? Why was it left out?"

This same exercise can be applied to illustrations in children's books, by asking children to extend, complete, or enlarge the frame. Framing also is a useful starting point for the discussion of camera angles and types of shots. Long shots, medium shots, and close-up shots are not used randomly. Like parts of speech, they have a function and contribute to the overall meaning. A long shot might be used to establish the scene or general setting of a news story, such as the mountain in Afghanistan where rebel soldiers are hiding. Because the story is going to concentrate on the soldiers, we would expect that the camera would fairly quickly move in to a medium shot of a group of soldiers on one hillside and finally a close-up interview with one or two soldiers. The shot is determined by the message to be sent. Another way of saying this is that the image is determined by the information carried and conveyed by it. If the camera tilts down on a person, that person tends to appear weak and vulnerable. If the camera tilts up on a person, that figure appears to have power, prestige, and authority. If the camera is objective, the presentation is neutral and imposes no visual perspective or point of view on the subject.

Have students study segments from the evening news for examples of close-ups, long shots, and medium shots. Have them describe how and when such shots are utilized in a single story. Remember, they must be able not simply to recognize the different shots, but also to see how each shot supports the story.

Have students look for examples of camera angles in segments of the evening news. Do they note a difference between camera angles for sequences in the studio compared to camera angles used during on-location shooting? What other factors might influence the way the camera is placed? Aerial shots, for example, must tilt down on the subject, but is this done to suggest vulnerability, or is it forced by problems such as the fact that it was too dangerous on the ground to shoot the footage?

Have students write a brief script for a story to run on the evening news in which they designate what type of shots they are going to use and how they will structure elements within their frame. Lesley Stahl says reporters like to "wallpaper" their stories, or have good images behind them. Does the wallpaper or style sometimes contradict or overwhelm the content of the story? Have students look for examples of this.

BALANCE, BIAS, AND BOOSTERISM:
How Objective Is the News?

In 1990 Lee and Solomon made a major contribution to news analysis with the publication of their book *Unreliable Sources: A Guide to Detecting Bias in News Media* (1990). The authors describe what they call "a lexicon of media buzzwords" and assert that "what we hear over and over again shapes our language and guides our thoughts" (10). Consuming the news, they suggest, "is to partake of a steady offering of buzzwords and catchphrases that range from the vaguely factual to the questionable to the ridiculous" (11). Other recent contributions also offer teachers the opportunity to help students become critical consumers of news media. The Center for Defense Information has produced an outstanding videotape called "The Language of War." The program looks at the way language can be used to mislead and manipulate. There was, the program suggests, an enormous psychological advantage in changing the name of the Department of War to the Defense Department. Recent military operations have taken on code names such as "Just Cause" or "Desert Shield," and the very use of these phrases injects nonneutral language into news reports, as a result of which the reports essentially endorse the administration line. The invasion of Grenada was actually described as "a pre-dawn vertical insertion."

The increasing use of such terms and the tendency of the news media to repeat them creates a form of doublespeak or "technotalk" that prevents the public from understanding what is actually going on. Phrases such as "target-rich environment" and "arbitrary deprivation of life" are used by government officials not simply as a form of insider jargon, but also as a way to prevent outsiders from fully comprehending what is being said. So the words that reporters use or repeat can actually mislead the public they are meant to inform. English teachers might wish to contact the Doublespeak Committee of the National Council of Teachers of English. Official language used by government officials also can be compared to the language of George Orwell's *1984*.

In recent years, the National Opinion Research Center reported that the number of people saying they had a great deal of confidence in the press declined from 29 percent in 1976 to 13.7 percent in 1983. The 1980s provided several examples of bias and distortion in the presentation of news that may have affected public confidence. One of the most controversial examples was the 1982 CBS broadcast "The Uncounted Enemy: A Vietnam Deception." With a title like that, viewers hardly needed to wait to see the program to understand its point of view. The result was a $120 million libel action against CBS by General William Westmoreland and attempts by Senator Jesse Helms and others to take over the network. During the 1988 presidential campaign, the same network again found itself at the center of a storm of protest when Dan Rather aggressively challenged George Bush about Iran-Contra on the air. In a cover story called "Journalism under Fire," *Time* wrote: "They are rude and accusatory, cynical and almost unpatriotic. They twist facts to suit their not-so-hidden liberal agenda. They meddle in politics, harass business, invade people's privacy and then walk off without regard to the pain and chaos they leave behind" (*Time* 1983, 76).

Although some reporters are obviously aggressive in their pursuit of a story and others zealously slant stories to their own agenda and perspective, sometimes the journalists are actually restricted by the medium. In the case of television news, Dan Rather has said, "Television has difficulty with depth.... We have troubles with stories of complexity.... I think CBS is very good at covering news stories. I'm not sure that we're all that good at covering the issues" (Weisman 1984, 4). Rather's comments were reported in a *TV Guide* study of 661 television news stories about Central America. The study suggested that after all the images and stories, "one ends up knowing almost as little about Central America, and why the United States is involved there, as one knew before" (4). Similar complaints were made about the often simplistic coverage of the Iranian hostage crisis in 1979-1980. After six months of coverage of the Persian Gulf crisis in 1990-1991, network news had done little to convey the vastly different cultures and value systems of the forces that confronted each other. The differences that were highlighted were often simplistic, easily conveyed elements such as the fact that the soldiers wanted beer but could not get any in Saudi society.

Coverage of the Persian Gulf crisis was particularly controversial. One columnist complained: "There is no question that war is a possibility; but possibility has been hyped into probability in the telling. All reserve has been stripped away and the need for caution disregarded in the race for coverage and the drive to inform" (Collins 1990).

The American Arab Anti-Discrimination Committee accused the news media of failing to weigh the country's involvement in the crisis. Sam Donaldson, however, actually introduced a "Prime Time Live" report on the crisis by saying they intended to ask the questions the media had not asked soon enough about the Vietnam

War. *Newsweek* raised concerns about both Barbara Walters and Ted Koppel using "the national we" when questioning the Iraqi ambassador. "American reporters," wrote *Newsweek*, "cannot or at least should not write their reports as agents of American policy, or as propagandists or government spokesmen" (Greenfield 1990, 76).

As a visual medium, television needs movement, and conflict often generates that movement. The stories that are selected, the images that are shown, and the words that are used to present stories often stress conflict. For example, Tom Browkaw described abortion as "a national trauma," and Dan Rather said it was "tearing at the social fabric of the nation." "CBS News" insisted on calling a special 1990 meeting of the Soviet congress "Showdown in the Kremlin." In the early days of 1991, as the United Nations deadline for Iraq to get out of Kuwait approached, "CBS News" consistently billed the story as "The Gulf Crisis: Countdown to Confrontation."

The drug war is another issue that has often been covered in less than objective terms. CBS ran a special called "48 Hours on Crack Street." A cover story of *The New Republic* was "Confessions of a Drug Hype Junkie" and *Village Voice* featured a cover that declared "Drugs Are Us." In October 1986 *Time* warned about this type of reporting: "What we have done by the sheer quantity of stories is to imply that a very serious problem has become a pressing domestic crisis ... we have helped to create an atmosphere in which hysterical legislation is more likely to pass" (Henry 1986, 73). Questioning the news media's penchant for sensationalism, the *Washington Post* wrote, "To an unsettling degree, we distort the larger picture by training our blinding spotlight on an assortment of kooks and crazies and crackpots whose mission is to divide and polarize" (1990, 24).

Television's treatment of disasters and crises has been extremely well documented in *Nightly Horrors* by Dan Nimmo and James Combs (1985). The authors studied the way the network news responded to major crises including the mass suicides in Jonestown, the nuclear accident at Three Mile Island, the Iranian hostage crisis, and the Tylenol poisonings. The book provides an outstanding content analysis of this coverage and an excellent framework for teachers and students to use in their own studies.

COVERING THE 1991 WAR IN THE PERSIAN GULF: Case Study

In May 1991, the Association for Media Literacy in Canada published *Media and the Gulf War: A Case Study*. In the preface the authors said that although the war was over, "all the pop culture hoopla and patriotic fervor ... will continue for some time" (1). The study guide acknowledged that "our students like ourselves were confused about this war. Powerful images flashed across our television screens—whole groups of people became good or bad guys. Fact, rumor and propaganda became indistinguishable as life and death images were packaged—constructed into news" (1). Writing in *TV Guide*, television critic Jeff Greenfield expressed concern about "the most significant, most troublesome aspect of television's first real time war—the uneasy blend of instant, immediate, round the world, round the clock access to information that is inherently incomplete, fragmentary or downright wrong" (Greenfield 1991, 5). By the summer of 1991, when the war was still being used to promote everything from preseason ball games to car sales, the press was starting to question the value of the war that they had seemingly enthusiastically endorsed. On August 5, 1991, *Time* ran a cover story asking "Was It Worth It?"

Edward Herman and Noam Chomsky have written that the mass media "serve as a system for communicating messages and symbols to the general populace" (1988, 1). In the case of the news media, although they "serve the ends of a dominant elite," this fact is often difficult to see because they "periodically attack and expose corporate and governmental malfeasance" (1). Although the news media may be critical of the establishment, they are part of it, deriving income and profits from it. The Persian Gulf War was a crisis that promised profit or prestige through special bulletins, 24-hour coverage, and information saturation. For Ted Turner's Cable News Network (CNN), it provided a spectacular international showcase. CNN, said *The Nation*, "represents a new dimension of an emerging global culture that is already heavily Americanized" (Rosen 1991, 622-25). Whereas politicians and average citizens were impressed by CNN's coverage, *The Nation* cautioned against the impact of "dramatic visuals deployed for their oomph value rather than their importance in any exploratory scheme" (623). Such coverage, the magazine suggested, would promote international competition in which news coverage on the global level could be reduced to the triumph of the image over the issue. As a result, "political deeds that lack a visual dimension may tend to escape world notice because they bore the image hungry producers" (623).

In attempting to reflect on coverage of the war, it is therefore necessary to consider the form as well as the content of the stories.

As a backdrop to these elements, one must raise the crucial question of ownership, or what we have called the origin of media messages. Understanding the ownership and origin of the news provides some context for understanding why particular stories are ignored and others are stressed and the forces and factors affecting the coverage. *Manufacturing Consent* addresses what it calls "news filters" that shape coverage (Herman and Chomsky 1988). These filters include:

- Size and ownership: As part of the corporate United States, the mass media, including the news media, have ties to big business. That relationship must affect how stories are selected. What, for example, are some likely effects of the fact that General Electric owns ABC?

- Advertising: It keeps programming on the air. At its most basic level, however, it could be argued that he who pays the piper calls the tune. How would the profit motive and the needs of the consumer culture influence coverage?

- Reliance on government perspectives: Unnamed sources and official government representatives feed news bureaus points of view, values, and policies that are often uncritically reported as fact. When coverage is censored and controlled as it was in Grenada or the Persian Gulf, reporting is invariably slanted.

- Flak: Simply refers to an institutionalized form of discrediting alternative perspectives. Spiro Agnew served as a hit man who constantly condemned media coverage. President Reagan criticized the media's role in affecting public opinion. By using flak, government officials can create a climate that induces a more positive form of coverage. The result, of course, is to stifle alternative points of view. What range of perspectives was provided about the Persian Gulf War?

These filters affected the coverage of the war in the Persian Gulf and continue to affect the way news is presented on a daily basis. At times the bias is evident, but often it is much more subtle. Throughout the war and the events leading up to it, President Bush continually referred to a "new world order." According to one source, he used the phrase 42 times in public statements. It was a vague, undefined reference that the media seldom questioned, despite Bush's earlier vagaries evident in phrases such as "a thousand points of light." By not challenging the expression, the news media followed the administration line and allowed the president to project himself as an international visionary. By July 1991, *U.S. News and World Report* said, "The president has almost entirely dropped the words ["new world order"] from his lexicon, indicating another turn in U.S. foreign policy" (21). The news media did more than simply report the war. They presented it from a particular perspective that contributed to the climate of acceptance. In covering the war with such intensity, they also distracted the public from pressing domestic problems. On April 7, 1991, Peter Jennings on the "ABC Nightly News" almost acknowledged this when he asked, "Remember the way it was before the war?" But even if the media seemed ready to shift tack, move on to a fresh agenda, or think more critically about the war, the consequences and impact of that coverage were coming under greater scrutiny from outside the media. In May, the New School for Social Research conducted a forum called "Media Mirage: Coverage of the Gulf Crisis." A study by Fairness and Accuracy in Reporting (FAIR) found that "of 878 on air sources, only one was a representative of a national peace organization—Bill Monning of Physicians against Nuclear War. By contrast, 7 players from the Super Bowl were brought on to comment on the war" (Naurekas 1991, 5).

FAIR also reported the impact of coverage of dissenters. "Relying, as network TV did, on random protesters to present a movement's view is to deny that movement its most articulate and knowledgeable spokespeople" (5). Turning its attention to the media coverage of death and casualties, the FAIR report said, "When ... more than three times as much attention is given to victims in Israel, where four people were killed by missiles, than to civilians in Iraq and Kuwait, where thousands died, such coverage ceases to be sympathy and becomes exploitation" (78). Research also began to focus on just how the public processed and perceived news accounts. A study from the University of Massachusetts Center for Studies in Communication concluded that "the news media have failed quite dramatically in their role as information providers. Despite months of coverage, most people do not know basic facts about the political situation in the Middle East" (Jhally et al. 1991). The study suggested that support for the war was "built on a body of knowledge that was incorrect or incomplete" and that "the more people know the less likely they are to support the war."

If a country can go to war claiming a popular mandate and widespread support, it is crucial that such support be based on facts well presented and judiciously considered. Increasing evidence supports the contention that in the case of the Persian Gulf War, neither the presentation nor the processing were balanced. A combination of hoopla and hysteria created a climate conducive to waging war. Although it would be comforting to regard this as an aberration, the phenomenon is more systemically tied to the nature of the news media itself. In May 1991, *The Nation*, in an editorial, said the failures of coverage "were not one time lapses of judgement or moments of inappropriate obedience, but rather the result of their [the media's] integration into the political, economic and ideological establishments they are supposed to be covering" (687-88). As classroom teachers we have little opportunity to change the control of the news media in this country. We may, however, affect coverage of future crises by providing our students with the analytical skills necessary to question what they see and hear. We must also nurture in them the emotional strength and personal courage to stand alone, knowing that sometimes questioning and disagreeing is the most patriotic course of action.

LOADED LANGUAGE AND NATIONAL PERSONIFICATION

Sometimes the very words that an anchor or a reporter uses are designed to catch our ears, hold our attention, and even shape our impression of a story. When Hurricane Hugo hit the Carolinas in September 1989, CBS opened the evening news with these three words: "Huge Hurricane Hugo." Certainly, it grabbed the attention of those watching. It was clear and direct and employed alliteration for emphasis. This technique is specifically criticized in the movie *Broadcast News*. Later in the night, as the hurricane drew closer to shore, Dan Rather, appearing on the news program "48 Hours," told viewers in the path of the storm, "We care about you. We're thinking about you." Is this an acceptable way for an anchor or reporter to present the news? How do you draw the line between objectively reporting a story and becoming involved in it? Is loaded language conducive to good reporting?

When the space shuttle program got back into space after the long delay caused by the blow-up of the *Challenger*, many news broadcasts seemed to abandon objectivity and function instead as national cheerleaders, in the process actually serving to create the mood and response that they were at the same time reporting. Some journalists tend to identify themselves and their reports with the nation, personifying the country, as a result of which they speak for the country and establish themselves as the arbiters of national opinion. ABC's "American Agenda" nightly news segment often provides excellent coverage of important social issues, but the packaging should really read "ABC's Agenda." ABC and the United States are not synonymous. In April 1990, when U.S. hostages were released, Peter Jennings opened the news by saying, "Good evening, there's nothing Americans would like more than to see it [release of hostages] become a trend."

Whether an anchor correctly or incorrectly gauges the national mood is not the point. The issue is whether network news should seek to speak for the nation. When the stock market fell dramatically in the late 1980s, the news media presented the story with a sense of gloom and doom that may have actually made people more pessimistic than the event merited. By early 1991, media coverage of the recession and the Persian Gulf crisis was being blamed for an increase in reported cases of anxiety and depression.

FROM INFORMATION TO "INFOTAINMENT": "Soft" News vs. "Hard" News

Crisis and conflict form a staple of the evening news. Ask students to divide any network news into its key components, and they are likely to come up with the following categories:

- International
- National
- The White House
- The Pentagon
- Wall Street and the economy

- The Supreme Court
- Weather
- Regional coverage
- Human interest

As we have seen, crises, disasters, or stories that can be presented in terms of conflict often dominate the news. In recent years, however, there has been a trend toward "soft" news stories. This trend has resulted in what some call "infotainment," or news being presented with more and more emphasis on its appeal as entertainment and less on its accuracy and importance. In his book *Happy Talk* (1990), Fred Graham talks about these changes at CBS News in the post-Cronkite era. According to Graham, that period saw CBS News capitulate to the ratings race, searching for "magic moments" to capture viewers' hearts and make the news look entertaining. The news, he said, shifted from being driven to provide the public with information and became concerned instead with the need to increase the ratings. Sometimes this goal involves human interest or "feel-good" stories. They might deal with a small child who is lost or trapped in a dangerous situation. Often we get nightly updates on the child's welfare punctuated by tearful interviews with family and friends. Or the stories might deal with the plight of whales marooned on a beach or frisky sea lions invading a tourist resort in San Francisco. On other occasions the stories center on celebrity scandals: a senator's affair or the trial of a millionaire for tax evasion. One of the most publicized stories of recent years involved the separation and divorce of Donald and Ivana Trump. CBS even reported on how the media reported the story. Liz Smith, who broke the story, said, "This has been a media circus; I have been one of its performers." Although many people are no doubt interested in some of these stories, and many of the stories are genuinely moving, other people wonder about giving valuable time and space to this coverage when the plight of the poor, the impaired, the homeless, and others could instead be getting more national attention.

(MID/HIGH) — Introduce students to the concept of euphemisms, jargon, and doublespeak. View a segment of evening news or assign them an evening news broadcast to watch, asking them to list examples of euphemism, jargon, or doublespeak. Have students write to the station with a list of terms and phrases they think need clarification.

Surveys suggest that public confidence in the news media is declining. Have members of the class conduct a survey with their parents and neighbors to see how much these adults trust the news media. This could be group work, with one group studying newspapers and another studying television news. Alternatively, you could break the study into various news broadcasts, such as ABC, CBS, NBC, and CNN.

Select an example of crisis coverage for analysis with the class. In what way do the tone and presentation of the report suggest that this is a crisis? What is the relationship between the words and the pictures? How much time is the story given? Does the anchor leave the studio to report from the scene of the crisis? Does the story run over several nights? If so, how much time is devoted to it each night? How does its position in the 30-minute broadcast vary? When the story is no longer covered, has the crisis been resolved? Compare and contrast television coverage of the crisis with newspaper reports.

Dan Rather has suggested that television is not good at covering issues. Surely that assessment is based on an assumption about what television news is rather than on what it might be. Clearly, there are occasions when television does in-depth investigative reporting that does look at issues. Select an important social, political, or economic issue and have students monitor television coverage of it. What do they learn from the coverage? What questions or aspects of the issue are not covered? Do newspapers and news magazines do a better job when dealing with the same issue?

Television news often tends to thrive on conflict, matching one side or point of view against the other. The more prominent matchups include Democrats vs. Republicans, management vs. labor, conservatives vs. liberals, pro-life vs. pro-choice, and Palestinians vs. Israelis. Ask the class to develop a list of other stories in which the networks frame the issue as conflict between or among groups. How is the conflict conveyed: in words, images, or words and images? Is this concept of conflict equally evident in newspaper accounts?

The concepts of balance, bias, boosterism, and national personification are addressed in this chapter. Explain these concepts to students and ask them to document examples of each in television news. Write to the

The ratings race has forced news coverage to become dramatic. "Infotainment" replaces information. How does the location for the news and the behavior of the anchor influence the public's perception of a story? (Cartoon copyright © 1990 Wayne Stayskal. Reprinted with permission.)

networks, providing specific examples of each, including dates and comments made by reporters or anchors. The letters should request more balanced reporting and ask why these pieces were produced this way.

Introduce students to the concepts of "hard" news, "soft" news, and "infotainment." Have them monitor the evening news for examples of "puff pieces," or soft news. How much of a given 30-minute broadcast is devoted to such stories? Are the stories always at the end of the broadcast?

Taking viewers on a tour of the White House, Diane Sawyer on "Prime Time Live" said "Time, turbulence and tastes have all changed the presidential home." Alliteration, metaphor, and simile are among literary techniques employed in scripting the news. Introduce students to these concepts and have them find examples of each technique in news broadcasts.

Occasionally news items run without any footage, and the anchor simply tells us what happened. Ask students to spot such examples and explain why no film was used.

Dan Rather wrote in a 1990 issue of *The Humanist* that "a journalist's job isn't always to make America feel good about itself" (Rather 1990, 5). Former vice-president Spiro Agnew called the news media "nabobs of negativism." Perhaps the adage "No news is good news" now applies to the gloom and doom approach of many broadcasts, or, conversely, is Graham's (1990) description of "happy talk" correct? Ask students to monitor news broadcasts and rate the mood of the stories as positive or negative, upbeat or downbeat. Is there a balance, or does one mood tend to prevail?

The ratings race has been blamed for a lot of problems in the evening news. Dan Rather said, "Too many of us are becoming known as news packagers, not news gatherers" (1990, 42). In what sense is the news packaged?

The ratings race also results in a race to get the "scoop," or be the first to break the story. In the 1990 Gainesville serial killings, parents and family members sometimes heard of the murder of a loved one from the media, not the authorities. Discuss the ethical issues involved in this situation. Is the public's right to know more important than the privacy of the family and victims?

BROUGHT TO YOU BUY ...: Advertising and the News

A discussion of the function of television news will probably result in a lot of answers that suggest that the function of news is to inform the public of the day's events or even to educate them about the world and important issues. Other topics in this chapter suggest, however, that the news does not really report the entire news but only someone or some group's concept of what is newsworthy. In addition, we have seen that networks and newspapers do not agree on what news is and even differ on interpretations of the same event. If we stop thinking of the news as somehow unique and regard it instead as merely another in a whole series of television programs, we are able to see that the real function of the news, like all TV programming, is to deliver to sponsors a large audience so that the sponsors can promote their products through advertising.

This view, of course, subjects the news to a ratings race like all other programs and may explain some of the recent trends toward soft news or infotainment. The simple fact is that news programs are coming under increasing pressure to be entertaining in order to gain and maintain large audiences. The following activities can be used with students of various ages to help them understand something about advertising and the relationship between the program and the viewer. Teachers wishing further information about advertising are referred to chapter 5 in this book.

Types of Advertisements

(ELEM/MID/HIGH) — Keep a list of all the types of advertisements that appear during the evening news. These will include products, services, and promotions (such as ads for other programs on the network).

Number of Advertisements

Keep a list of how many advertisements appear during the news. Compare this number to other networks. How many minutes of the news are actually used for news?

Curing the News Blues

Communication theory asserts that media messages cannot be read in isolation from their audience. In part this suggests that both programs and advertisements can be seen as reflections of the audience, including their hopes, dreams, and fears. Look at the advertisements that appear consistently during news programs. What products or types of products tend to be commonly represented on all networks? Why would advertisements for such products be run at this time? A simple way to establish this context with students is to ask what type of advertisements run during Saturday morning cartoons. Most students will say toys, and others will be aware of cereal and other sugar-heavy products. They will also understand intuitively that these advertisements are aimed at children, so they are shown when children are viewing. Older students will be able to suggest that one is most likely to see beer or truck commercials during sports programs.

Over the years several products have regularly been featured during evening news programs. These include alcohol, headache relief medicine, bladder control products, and various ointments and suppositories. The following products were among some advertised on a single broadcast of ABC evening news in 1991:

Just for Men shampoo and hair color	Anusol suppositories
Maalox antacid	Crest toothpaste
Carnival Cruises	Chloraseptic Lozenges
Efferdent denture cleaner	Lens Crafters eyeglass stores

The one thing these all have in common is what we can call a message "flow." Roughly translated, the message suggests to the adult audience that life at the office has been tough. But that's okay, the message goes, because now you are home and there are all these wonderful products to kill the pain and make you feel better. That message not only is consistent with the vulnerability of the adult audience after a hard day at the office, but it is also in keeping with the news content, which is more than likely to deal with international and national problems and trouble spots. The other great panacea is the idea of a cruise or a vacation to some exotic location, which also offers a promise of relief.

The consistent message of both the consumer and chemical culture is one of pain, stress, and vulnerability that can be either cured, alleviated, or escaped from with drugs or distraction. Even seemingly harmless products such as eyeglass stores, toothpaste, or hair color all play on a sense of inadequacy and the need to change our image. A block of ads such as these is seldom so concentrated as in the evening news. Although the products may show up in advertisements during other programs, their cumulative message suggests that the news in and of itself is a "Maalox moment." Anyone with an interest in drug and alcohol problems in this society must recognize the way the chemical culture is enforced by advertisers during TV news. Of course, not all products center on this message. Quite often there are a lot of high-tech advertisements for automobiles, computers, and various communication systems. What can we deduce about the nature of the audience from these advertisements?

Finally, it is suggested that each network has its own loyal viewing public and that those who watch one network are somehow different from viewers who watch another. Develop a list of all the products advertised on each network in one week during the evening news and see what sort of audience profile can be generated from this list.

Media Events and Photo Opportunities:
Staging the News

(HIGH) — Sam Donaldson's *Hold On, Mr. President* (1987) provides a valuable inside look at the news industry. He tells of one incident when Larry Speakes, the Reagan White House's principal deputy press secretary, told reporters, "You don't tell us how to stage the news, and we won't tell you how to cover it" (1987, 123). Speakes would later admit that he had gone before the national press and made up what had transpired during presidential meetings. In effect, Speakes admitted that he had put words into President Reagan's mouth and passed them off to the press and the nation as being authentic.

The Reagan administration also brought the resignation of State Department spokesman Bernard Kalb because of a controversy over disinformation. It was suggested that Kalb was unhappy that the press had been deliberately misled in regard to the United States' approach to Libya. These events raise serious questions about the validity of the news and invite some comparison to George Orwell's *1984*, in which the author notes that "there is truth and there is untruth." Although it is possible that the public is sometimes manipulated by the news, it is also possible that the news media themselves are manipulated by politicians, public relations people, and other groups who seek to create "media events" or "photo opportunities" that will attract media attention and therefore get coverage for their candidate, client, corporation, or issue. "Illusions of News," a PBS video, documents this process.

Positive coverage can be conveyed by something as simple as the background. It might be the Statue of Liberty or perhaps Niagara Falls. In a natural disaster a good politician will always want to be seen in the middle of the storm. After major fires in Yellowstone National Park, for example, candidates went to inspect the damage. In the process, of course, they virtually guaranteed getting themselves on the evening news. Sometimes the attention-getter is not the background or the location, but rather the conflict. Martin Luther King, Jr., for example, is said to have selected certain southern cities for his civil rights marches because he knew the anticipated conflict and confrontation would attract media coverage and therefore focus attention on the issues with which he and his followers were concerned. During the 1968 Democratic convention in Chicago, the young, media-aware demonstrators chanted, "The whole world's watching." They, too, understood the old advertising slogan that "Unseen is unsold." One problem with both media events and photo opportunities is that the backdrop or conflict may actually distract from the idea or issue that is really meant to be covered. The other is that the audience simply becomes immune to constantly being bombarded with these types of images.

Have students watch the evening news and select a story that they believe was really a media event or photo opportunity. Discuss the significance of the story. Was it really worth covering, or was it covered simply because it was visually interesting? Some examples of the latter might be the president's visit to a flag factory or the birth of puppies at the White House.

Have students write a brief 3- or 4-minute script for a media event or a photo opportunity. Make sure their script clearly details how the event is going to be presented. Remember, this can include elements such as backdrop, setting, conflict, and music. These elements are all part of the packaging of the news.

Network News Analysis

(HIGH) — This is a complex assignment that should be tackled only by students who have considered other areas of this chapter such as bias, balance, and the relationship between the form and content of the evening news. A chart is provided to assist in logging the sequence of the stories; their running time; and key elements related to the use of sight and sound, anchor, and reporter in conveying the story. Teachers are encouraged to enlarge or modify the chart to suit their students. The chart is not intended as the only source of information. It is a simple way of logging and summarizing key elements, which can then be recorded in lengthier notes. Concepts that are included in this chapter but not included in the chart might also be added. Some of these concepts are news boxes, graphics, studio sets, and the way the news is introduced and concluded, such as "Where More Americans Get Their News Than Any Other Source" (ABC) and "And That's Part of Our World Tonight" (CBS). The assignment increases in importance if students are broken into groups, with each group monitoring a different network broadcast on the same evening so that the form, content, and advertising can be compared and contrasted. Although there are often many similarities in what is covered and how it is covered, there are also many occasions when the news is strikingly different. These differences reflect each network's values and priorities in selecting, ordering, and structuring news. Several simple examples illustrate this point.

1. May 1990: ABC opened with the deaths of puppeteer Jim Henson and Sammy Davis, Jr. These stories ran ahead of both a confrontation between President Bush and the Congress and a visit to Moscow by the secretary of state, Jim Baker. CBS opened with Dan Rather in Moscow.

2. June 1990: ABC led with the opening of an international AIDS conference in San Francisco. Peter Jennings reported from that city. CBS opened with Nelson Mandela's visit to New York City, and the AIDS conference was not among their top three stories.

3. Summer 1991: ABC began its top story by declaring "alarm bells are ringing" in northern Iraq. They chronicled a threat to the Kurds. CBS did not cover the story at all.

The selection, omission, and sequencing of stories can be used to develop critical thinking skills. On Earth Day 1990, for example, would the lead story be Earth Day or the release of a hostage from the Middle East? How many people would be directly affected or influenced by Earth Day? How many people would be directly affected or influenced by the release of Robert Polhill? Which story was most likely to produce the best pictures, the greatest conflict, and the highest emotional response? Although Earth Day had ecological significance to the world, the Polhill release was more dramatic, and that story was elevated to the lead that evening. Posing questions such as these is the real purpose of the exercise. Students are not meant simply to record what was presented and how it was presented, but also to think in depth about the decisions behind those presentations (see Figure 6.2, page 178). For a more in-depth study, the television logs can be compared to newspapers from the same day or next morning.

Science and Medical News

(ELEM / MID / HIGH) — Most networks have correspondents who specialize in particular areas. Viewers are familiar with the ones who cover the White House, the Supreme Court, or the Pentagon. In the background, however, are correspondents who specialize in scientific or medical news. Despite the enormous impact of medicine and science on all our lives, these stories are seldom covered in depth and they are nowhere near as numerous as stories about politics or the economy. Because scientific research is comparatively slow and a medical laboratory is not visually exciting to most people, these stories tend to rate low in the priorities of network executives who make decisions about what to show on a visual medium. Yet the impact of the near invisibility of these stories could potentially be quite significant. The United States lacks scientists and engineers. Our schools do not turn out enough students skilled in science and math. Many students are not motivated to enter these areas. How does the public perception of science shape our society, and how do the media contribute to this perception? How is medical news constructed? Most news originates in publications such as *The New England Journal of Medicine* and *The Journal of the American Medical Association* (*JAMA*). They provide copies to science reporters on Tuesdays, embargoed for release on Thursdays. In essence the journals control what the press has access to and when. One result of this is episodic reporting. The journals try to limit journalistic speculation and exaggeration. The editor of *JAMA* has said, "There's a tendency on the part of some journalists to be cheerleaders, to hype advances that might not be as big as they seem" (Kurtz 1991, 38).

Break the class into groups, with each group responsible for monitoring TV news coverage of medicine and science. If there are 7 students per group, each student could watch the news just one evening per week. Over a month, a fairly good analysis should be possible. Students could document the stories by covering elements such as:

- topic of story
- position of story in news (first, last, etc.)
- running time of story
- anchor's lead-in
- reporters' comments
- visuals
- positive or negative depiction of science or medicine

Fig. 6.2. Network news analysis.

Story #	Topic	Anchor's Intro. & Location	Film Footage: Content/Form	Voiceover/Tone	Bias	Length

The *Wall Street Journal* and *Forbes* dominate economic and business reporting. The medical world also has major sources. What is *The New England Journal of Medicine* and why is it so consistently cited in medical news? What other medical or scientific sources are consistently cited?

INTEGRATING MOTION PICTURES INTO STUDYING TELEVISION NEWS

"Broadcast News" (1987)

Oscar nominations: Best picture; best actor, William Hurt; best actress, Holly Hunter; best screenplay; best cinematography; best editing.

(MID/HIGH) — This very interesting and useful film has strong applications in any lessons that deal with news and its impact on society. As this film specifically examines television news, it can be very usefully contrasted to films such as *All the President's Men* and *Absence of Malice* that look at newspapers. Although the film can be viewed in its entirety, the top 30-45 minutes are more than sufficient and provide numerous incidents, topics, and issues to explore with students.

The Softening of News. Shortly after the credits, Jane (Holly Hunter) is seen presenting a lecture to a group of journalists. "Our profession is in danger," she warns them. She points out how all the news media ignored a major change in SALT II, but showed a domino contest. How do the journalists react to her warning? Have students discuss the concept of what is newsworthy and examine newspapers and television news for examples of what gets covered and what does not get covered.

Behind the Scenes. Break students into groups and have them study the behavior, attitudes, and activities of various people in the news department:

- Tom (William Hurt), the local anchor
- Jane, the journalist and sometimes executive producer
- Aaron, the writer and aspiring anchor
- The national network anchor (Jack Nicholson)

Assembling the News. Several key scenes provide fascinating insights into the pressure and politics of getting a story to air. Study each scene with the students:

1. When Tom first arrives at the station, he watches as a news story called "The Homecoming" is assembled. How is it put together? How many different people are involved? What decisions are made? Why do they decide at the last minute to use the Norman Rockwell painting? Was it worth it? From whose perspective?

2. Aaron and Jane are sent to Nicaragua to cover a story. An incident occurs concerning the soldiers' boots. "We are not here to stage the news," Jane declares. Why is she so concerned about this issue? Why is the image of the boot more than a simple question of soldiers with or without shoes?

3. Tom presents a story about faulty military weapons. His presentation is well received. One journalist notes, "I like it. He's not afraid of being human." Aaron, however, is concerned about the impact Tom's style and personality have on the story. "Let's never forget, we're the real story, not them," he says bitterly.
   This scene is very important for drawing the attention of your students to the ways that television form and style influence our reactions. Tom's fake tear late in the film is a good example of audience

manipulation. This clip can also be used in conjunction with the chart that helps students analyze the form and content of the evening news (Figure 6.2).

4. The scene about the Libyan crisis provides an interesting insight into a late-breaking story, as Tom is forced to anchor a news bulletin with little notice or preparation. How does Jane respond? Aaron is more informed on the topic. Why do they give the anchor job to Tom rather than to Aaron, who knows more about the story? What role does Jane play in helping Tom present the story?

5. The date-rape story once again raises the issue of impartiality in presentation of the news. Aaron again rejects these techniques, commenting sarcastically, "Sex, tears, this must be the news." What camera technique or editing choice in this news story is considered unusual and why?

The Anchor. Aaron gets an opportunity to anchor the news and Tom agrees to coach him. Have students study this scene and develop a list of presentation techniques that show the importance of the image, the picture, and personality in presenting the news.

Tom's advice to Aaron on this subject is worth discussing: "Just remember that you're not just reading the news, you're narrating it. Everybody has to sell a little. You're selling them this idea of you, you know. You're sort of saying, 'trust me, I'm credible....' So when you feel yourself just reading, *stop* and sell a little."

What does Aaron's on-camera appearance suggest about the difference between writing and gathering news compared to actually presenting news? A useful exercise here would be to have students research and write a story and then videotape it. It is extremely likely that those with the best on-camera presence will not be the best researchers and writers.

"Network" (1976)

Oscar nominations: Best picture; best actor, Peter Finch (winner); best actress, Faye Dunaway (winner); best supporting actor, Ned Beatty; best supporting actress, Beatrice Straight (winner); best writing, Paddy Chayefsky (winner); best director, Sidney Lumet; best cinematography; best editing.

(MID/HIGH)—This outstanding film has become more rather than less relevant since it was made. The emergence of "trash" or "tabloid" television, corporate takeovers of networks, firings at television news bureaus, and the softening of news all provide current contexts for studying this film and, through it, the nature of television news. The film can be viewed in its entirety or selected scenes could be used to explore particular issues. Language is strong.

Wheeling and Dealing in the Newsroom. Break students into groups and have them study individual characters in the film in terms of their roles at the network:

- Howard Beale, the news anchor
- Max, president of the news division
- Edward Ruddy, chairman of the board
- Diana, head of programming/producer
- Nelson, president of the network
- Frank Hackett, CCA management

You might want to have students compare and contrast these power struggles with those in *All the President's Men* or *Broadcast News.*

Ratings and the U.S. Audience. Two key issues in this film are the integrity of information and whether network news should be judged by the same standards that are set for entertainment programs. Max clearly thinks the news should be objective and impartial even if it loses $33 million a year. Diana thinks news is like any other show and would do anything to get ratings.

Have students discuss and debate this issue from their own perspective and that of various characters in the film. Diana would justify many of her decisions by saying she is just giving people what they want. "The American people are turning sullen. They've been clobbered on all sides by Vietnam, Watergate, the inflation, the depression. They've turned off ... shot up ... nothing helps.... The American people want someone to articulate their rage for them."

Use this concept to discuss the notion of television programs as products to meet a consumer demand or need. Ultimately this is a chicken-and-egg argument. It might be useful to explore the often quoted notion that television is a "vast wasteland" or to look at Neil Postman's *Amusing Ourselves to Death.* What can we tell about the U.S. public from the programs they watch? Is it true that television is a mirror of society?

Ethics and Electronic Journalism. Diana is involved in two major programming changes in this film.

1. She ultimately takes over the news bureau and restructures the news, allowing "a manifestly irresponsible man" to anchor the evening news. Why is Howard Beale allowed to continue to anchor the news even after he has threatened to commit suicide on the air? In what other ways does Diana restructure the format of the evening news? Look at the scene that begins in the control booth and has the announcer saying, "The Network News Hour with Sybil the Soothsayer." What other characters are now featured as a regular part of the news team? Notice the set behind Howard Beale. What does it suggest?

2. Diana develops the Mao Tse Tung Hour using raw footage from revolutionary groups such as the Ecumenical Liberation Army. Is she merely using materials that the groups supply her, or does the fact that the network wants the material encourage the revolutionaries to commit further antisocial acts? This issue involves an ethical matter about the neutrality of the media. Does the presence of the camera merely record reality, or does it shape and influence reality? Why were television cameras not allowed to record the U.S. invasion of Grenada? Why have Israel and South Africa limited news coverage of events in their countries? How did television images influence events in Tiananmen Square in China in the spring of 1989?

The Soma Society. Howard Beale sees a sick society of couch potatoes, gullible and manipulated by the media. In the end he manipulates them himself. Have students write a paper discussing one of Howard Beale's following claims:

1. "The American people don't want to know the truth."

2. "Television is not the truth.... Television is a goddamn amusement park."

3. "We're in the boredom-killing business."

4. "The only truth you know is the truth you get out of this tube.... This tube is the gospel, the ultimate revelation. This tube can make or break presidents, popes or prime ministers."

"The China Syndrome" (1979)

Oscar nominations: Best actor, Jack Lemmon; best actress, Jane Fonda; best screenplay; best art director/ set decoration.

(MID/HIGH) — Although the film is usually regarded as an antinuclear statement, the subtheme of the film is the nature of news coverage. The movie raises ethical questions about the public's right to know and the responsibility and honesty of news organizations. It also provides an interesting commentary on the male-dominated media and the role of women in television news. Several key scenes can be utilized to generate thinking on some of these issues, or the film could be viewed in its entirety. One warning: If the film is used in its entirety, the students are likely to be distracted by the nuclear issue, so they will need to be given clear cueing and retrieval strategies that will help them focus on the news aspect of the film.

Opening Scene: Kimberly Wells. The scene takes place before the title or the credits. It is crucial for establishing the role of the reporter and the way the males at Channel 3 perceive her. A voiceover is heard while the screen is blank: "On camera 2.... Come on, we need to clear bars." These are standard directions as a program is preparing to go to air. Then we hear behind-the-scenes banter between two as-of-yet unknown men:

"Red hair was a good idea. We talked about cutting it."

"What did she say?"

"We haven't talked to her about it yet, but she'll do what we tell her."

Meanwhile, Kimberly is trying to set up for a live minicam report for "Live at Noon," and she cannot get anybody in the studio to pay attention to her. "Hey, fellas, anybody listening to me?" The talking males continue to discuss her role at the station. Since she joined the program the ratings are up, confirming research's report that she would do well in the Los Angeles market. When her report on singing telegrams is over, they suddenly change the schedule on her and she heads off for Ventana as the title and credits begin. These scenes run about 5 or 6 minutes and can be used to stimulate discussion about soft versus hard news, male control of media, on-camera control versus off-camera chaos, and marketing research and media.

On Location. After the credits, Kimberly and her crew visit Ventana Nuclear Power Plant to film part of a series on energy in California for the six o'clock news. They are given a guided tour of the facility by William Gibson, the plant public relations officer. In the process they witness a problem in the radiation containment area. This scene sets up several possibilities to explore with students:

1. The news crew consists of three different people. Who are they and what job is each one responsible for? Are they all employed by the station (Channel 3)?

2. Kimberly worked with Richard and Hector before she went into news. What work did the three of them do in the past?

3. Several production problems occur that show how difficult it can be to get a piece of film to air. Have students watch and listen for flubbed lines, swearing, and technical problems with sound and light.

4. Sometimes viewers think that what they see on the news was shot in continuity. In fact, editing using inserts and outtakes gives an illusion of continuity and actually telescopes time. A good example of this is the sequence in which Mr. Gibson uses a chart to explain the operation of the plant. Kimberly's reactions to his explanation are all shot after the event. In essence, her reactions are faked. This raises ethical questions and ties in very well with the faked tear in *Broadcast News.*

5. Perhaps the central ethical question raised in this scene occurs when Richard shoots footage of the accident despite the fact that he has been told not to. Why does he do this? Are his motives personal or does he have the public interest at heart? What evidence can students find to support their answer?

The Scoop. This scene can be run independently of the earlier scenes if the teacher provides the background of the plot.

1. Kimberly arrives back at the television station excited by the scoop she has witnessed and Richard has recorded on film. "I got the lead story," she tells her boss and prepares to write it up to go to air.

2. The station manager refuses to run the piece. Why would a television news broadcast refuse to run a scoop that would get strong ratings?

3. There's a transitional scene at the board of the energy company, and then it cuts back to the next morning at the television station. Several different perspectives are provided before the station seizes the film and determines not to use it. What are the reactions of management, Richard, and Kimberly? Notice management's attitude toward Kimberly: "This is none of her business. She doesn't make policy. She's a performer." In what ways are reporters and news anchors performers? Kimberly goes from a potentially significant hard news scoop to covering a tiger's birthday party at the zoo.

It's a Man's World. This scene takes place at a cocktail party and is used to further develop male management's control over Kimberly as a performer and a reporter. Although she finds stories such as the tiger's party trivial and demeaning, management assures her that "it was brilliant" and says the station got a lot of calls about it. Kimberly expresses a desire to become involved in more serious reporting. Management responds with, "Let's face it, you didn't get this job because of your investigative abilities." Why do you think Kimberly got the job?

Management seems absolutely obsessed with Kimberly's appearance and almost unaware that she has a mind of her own. What evidence is there of these attitudes in this scene? Older students might explore the issue of sexism in media management in conjunction with this theme. One useful book would be *Too Old, Too Ugly and Not Deferential to Men* by Christine Craft (1988). Craft was fired from her position on television news and sued the station in one of the most controversial and widely covered cases of the 1980s.

Other Useful Films on Video

All the King's Men (1949). Academy Award-winning film based on Pulitzer Prize-winning novel by Robert Penn Warren. Deals with the rise of a southern politician generally regarded as resembling Huey Long. Examines the role of the press in covering, promoting, and observing the political process.

Citizen Kane (1939). Widely regarded by film critics as the best film ever made. Only part of it deals with the role of the press, but it does provide an interesting insight in the newspaper business of the early twentieth century. Kane himself is probably based on William Randolph Hearst of the Hearst newspaper chain.

Cry Freedom (1987). This interesting film about apartheid in South Africa focuses on the relationship between Black activist Steven Biko and White liberal newspaper editor Donald Woods.

The Image (1990). Albert Finney plays James Cromwell, a nationally respected television journalist who hosts the investigative program "Here and Now." Cromwell's ethics and journalistic techniques are called into question when a banker kills himself after the program reports on a savings and loan scandal. Strong and interesting inside look at television news.

The Killing Fields (1984). Winner of several Academy Awards, this film is based on the memoirs of *New York Times* reporter Sidney Schanberg. Provides an interesting insight into a reporter's role in covering war, in this case Vietnam and Cambodia.

"Max Headroom." The ill-fated television series (from the mid-1980s) about television, technology, and truth in a not too distant future. Now available on videotape, it is an interesting program, particularly when used with Orwell's *1984*.

Mr. Smith Goes to Washington (1939). Academy Award-winning film directed by Frank Capra and starring Jimmy Stewart. Worth watching for the filibuster sequence alone and Smith's attempt to win popular support against the might of the communication networks controlled by crooked politicians and businessmen.

Newsfront (1978). This interesting Australian movie looks at the pre-television era and the newsreel photographers. Includes actual footage from the 1940s and 1950s and would be very interesting compared to "The March of Time" series produced in the 1930s and 1940s.

Riders of the Storm (1986). Not worth watching in its entirety, but like "Max Headroom" it raises questions about the validity of television news. In this case Vietnam vets create pirate news and interrupt regular network broadcasts to bring the truth to the American people.

Salvador (1986). A companion piece for *The Killing Fields*, this film also deals with the role of the correspondent in a war, in this case the experiences of Richard Boyle in El Salvador in the early 1980s.

Special Bulletin (1986). A very interesting program that looks like crisis news coverage. Story centers on how a television news team deals with a terrorist threat in Charleston, South Carolina, and what happens when the city is actually destroyed by a nuclear explosion. Some viewers thought they were watching actual news coverage.

Talk Radio (1988). Has some interesting scenes that deal with a radio announcer's involvement with and impact on his audience. Given the popularity of talk radio in this country and the murder of Denver talk-radio announcer Alan Berg in 1984, it has relevance to the role of radio in this video age. Compare to *Pump Up the Volume* (1990).

WUSA (1970). Paul Newman and Joanne Woodward in a story about a drifter who becomes a deejay only to discover the radio station's right-wing agenda.

The Year of Living Dangerously (1983). An Academy Award-winning film that follows the role of the press in a foreign country. In this case the film deals with Indonesia in the mid-1960s and the impending fall of the Sukarno government. Is the role of the press to simply report events or to take part in them?

RESOURCES

Accuracy in Media
1275 K St., NW
Suite 1150
Washington, DC 20005
Organization to promote fair and accurate journalism.

American Newspaper Publishers Association
Foundation
Newspaper Center, Box 17407
Dulles Airport
Washington, DC 20041
Includes Newspapers in Education (NIE).

The Center for Defense Information
1500 Massachusetts Ave., NW
Washington, DC 20005
"The Language of War" and other videos available.

The Center for Media and Public Affairs
2101 L St., Suite 505
Washington, DC 20037

CNN Newsroom
c/o Turner Cable Network
One CNN Center
Atlanta, GA 30348-5366

The Committee on Public Doublespeak
c/o National Council of Teachers of English
1111 Kenyon Rd.
Urbana, IL 61801

Fairness and Accuracy in Reporting (FAIR)
130 W. 25th St.
New York, NY 10001
Publishes *Extra*, which provides excellent accounts of media coverage of significant national and international topics. Back issues available.

Networks

ABC
7 Lincoln Square
New York, NY 10023
(212) 887-7777

CBS
524 W. 57th St.
New York, NY 10019
(212) 975-4321

NBC
30 Rockefeller Plaza
New York, NY 10112
(212) 664-4444

Newspower: Using Newspapers in the Classroom
P.O. Box 203
Northfield, MA 03160
Write for catalog.

Whittle Communications ("Channel One")
Whittle Communications Educational Network
706 Walnut St.
Knoxville, TN 37902

REFERENCE LIST

Association for Media Literacy in Canada, (1991). *Media and the Gulf War: A Case Study*. Weston, Ontario: Association for Media Literacy in Canada.

Bagdikian, Ben, (1983). *The Information Machine*. New York: Harper & Row.

_____, (1990). *The Media Monopoly*. Boston: Beacon Press.

Bennett, Lance, (1983). *News: The Politics of Illusion*. New York: Longman.

Berry, Jason, (1991). "Louisiana Hateride," *The Nation*, December 9, 727-29.

Bridge, Junior, (1989). No News Is Women's News. *Media and Values*, Winter, 11-13.

Broder, David S., (1987). *Behind the Front Page: A Candid Look at How the News Is Made.* New York: Simon and Schuster.

Carter, Bill, (1990). Women Anchors Are on the Rise as Evening Stars. *New York Times*, August 12, H-27.

Collins, Thomas, (1990). Frenzied Media Correspondents become Cheerleaders for War. *Charlotte Observer*, August 28.

Cooper, Marc, and Lawrence Soley, (1990). All the Right Sources. *Mother Jones*, February/March, 20-27.

Craft, Christine, (1988). *Too Old, Too Ugly and Not Deferential to Men.* New York: Dell.

Diamond, Edwin, and Katryna O'Neill, (1989). Is TV News Guilty of Japan Bashing? *TV Guide*, May 20, 24-27.

Dionne, E. J., (1990). Mainstream Reports and Middle East Extremities: What Is Fair to Report When It Comes to Saddam? *Washington Post*, September 1.

Donaldson, Sam, (1987). *Hold On, Mr. President.* New York: Random House.

Ellerbee, Linda, (1986). *And So It Goes.* New York: G. P. Putnam.

Fong-Torres, Ben, (1989). Why Are There No Asian Male News Anchors? *Media and Values*, no. 48, 14-16.

Gergen, David, (1991). Bye Bye to the New World Order. *U.S. News and World Report*, July 8, 21.

Getler, Michael, (1991). The Gulf War Good News Policy Is a Dangerous Precedent. *Washington Post*, weekly edition, March 25-31, 24-25.

Graham, Fred, (1990). *Happy Talk: Confessions of a TV Newsman.* New York: Norton.

Greenfield, Jeff, (1991). America Rallies 'Round the TV Set. *TV Guide*, February 16, 4-7.

Greenfield, Meg, (1990). Whose Side Are We On? *Newsweek*, September 3, 76.

Halberstam, David, (1979). *The Powers That Be.* New York: Knopf.

Henry, William A., (1986). Reporting the Drug Problem. *Time*, October 6, 73.

Herman, Edward, and Noam Chomsky, (1988). *Manufacturing Consent.* New York: Pantheon.

Himmelstein, Hal, (1984). Television News and the Television Documentary. In *Television, Myth and the American Mind.* New York: Praeger.

Holland, P., (1987). When a Woman Reads the News. In H. Baehr and A. Dyer (eds.), *Boxed In: Women and Television.* New York: Pandora. Pp. 133-50.

Hunter, Jane, and Steve Askin, (1991). Hunger in Africa: A Story Untold Until Too Late. *Extra* 4:5, 8-10.

Husseini, Osama, (1991). TV Coverage Cheapens Arab Lives. *San Jose Mercury News*, February 27.

Jhally, Sut, Justin Lewis, and Michael Morgon, (1991). *The Gulf War: A Study of the Media, Public Opinion and Public Knowledge.* Summary Report by the Center for Studies in Communication, University of Massachusetts, February.

Johnson, Mary, (1991). Media Miss the Disabled Rights Issue: Courageous Cripples Instead of Access Activists. *Extra*, 4:4, 15.

Kenworthy, Tom, (1990). Jive at Five: How Incumbents Get to Be Newsmakers. *Washington Post*, weekly edition, October 22-28, 7.

Kurtz, Howard, (1990). A Note to Fellow Newsies: How about Some Self-Restraint. *Washington Post*, weekly edition, May 28-June 3.

————, (1991). Calling the Shots on Health News. *Washington Post*, weekly edition, July 1-7, 38.

Lee, Martin A., and Norman Solomon, (1990). *Unreliable Sources: A Guide to Detecting Bias in News Media.* Secaucus, N.J.: Carol Publisher.

McCabe, Peter, (1987). *Bad News at Blackrock: The Sell-Out of CBS News.* New York: Arbor House.

Media and Values, (1990). News for the 90s: A Question of Values. Spring, whole issue.

Morin, Richard, (1990). Waiting in the Wings: The Doofus Generation. *Washington Post*, weekly edition, July 9-15, 37.

Naisbitt, John, (1982). *Megatrends.* New York: Warner Books.

Nation, (1991). Media Engulfed. May 27, 687-88.

Naurekas, Jim, (1991). Gulf War Coverage: The Worst Censorship Was at Home. *Extra*, 4:3, 3-10.

Nimmo, Dan, and James E. Combs, (1985). *Nightly Horrors: Crisis Coverage in Television Network News.* Knoxville: University of Tennessee Press.

Postman, Neil, (1984). *Amusing Ourselves to Death*. New York: Viking.

Powell, Jody, (1984). *The Other Side of the Story*. New York: William Morrow.

Queenan, Joe, (1991). The Media's Wacky Watchdogs. *Time*, August 5, 54-55.

Rakow, Lana, and Kimberlie Kranich, (1991). Women as Sign in Television News. *Journal of Communication*, 41:1, 8-23.

Randolph, Eleanor, (1990). Are Daily Papers Old News? *Washington Post*, weekly edition, April 8-15.

Rather, Dan, (1990). Journalism and the Public Trust. *Humanist*, 50:6, 5-7, 42.

Rather, Dan, with Mickey Herskowitz, (1977). *The Camera Never Blinks: Adventures of a TV Journalist.* New York: William Morrow.

Ravitch, Diane, and Chester E. Finn, Jr., (1987). *What Do Our 17 Year Olds Know?* New York: Harper & Row.

Reasoner, Harry, (1983). *Before the Color Fades*. New York: Quill.

Rosen, Jay, (1991). The Whole World Is Watching CNN. *Nation*, May 13, 622, 625.

Sabato, Larry, (1991). *Feeding Frenzy: How Attack Journalism Has Transformed American Politics.* New York: Free Press.

Trueman, Peter, (1990). Pictures Offer Hazy Reality. *Catholic Register*, March 10, 8.

Wallace, Mike, and Gary Paul Gates, (1985). *Close Encounters*. New York: Berkley.

Washington Post, (1990). n.t., May 28-June 3, 24.

Weisman, John, (1984). Why TV Is Missing the Picture in Central America. *TV Guide*, September 15, 2-7.

White, Theodore, (1969). *The Making of the President 1968*. London: Jonathan Cape.

U.S. News and World Report, (1991). n.t., July, 21.

Chapter 7

Movies as Mentors: *Teaching with Motion Pictures*

INTRODUCTION

The film-going experience is firmly rooted in U.S. society. From the inception of "talkies" in the 1920s through the development of color, cinemascope, 3-D, and other technologies the motion picture industry has fascinated the U.S. public and foreign audiences alike. In 1990, nearly 3 million Americans a day attended a movie, spending a total of $5 billion annually. Nearly 6.5 million people rented a video that year. Worldwide, some 187 million households had a VCR, one-third the number that had TV sets. The development of the videocassette recorder, large-screen television, and cable TV has made more movies available to us than at any time in the past. Whether in a theater or in the privacy of our own homes, we now have more opportunity to look at films than ever before.

August 24, 1991, was the 100th anniversary of Thomas Edison's patent for the kinetoscope. Movies have changed a great deal in that time. But do we really see and understand movies, or are they just another distraction for a soma society? Do we recognize the relationship between film form and content? Do we understand codes and conventions in film genres? Can we distinguish between historical fact and dramatic license? Do we recognize product placement and understand that references to Bacardi or Whiskas (*A View to a Kill*) are actually disguised advertisements? Can we develop strategies that will enable us to integrate motion pictures into the curriculum, to develop critical viewing skills and critical thinking skills, and to capitalize on the recreational viewing behavior of our students?

Whether in theaters, on video, or broadcast on our television sets, motion pictures convey ideas and impressions about individuals, issues, and institutions that are studied as part of the traditional curriculum. As such they can contradict or confirm the way these topics are covered in the classroom.

In addition to educating cognitively, movies are a powerful affective agency, capable of influencing students' moods and feelings. Reading about the Sand Creek massacre or the Vietnam War in a book is one thing; actually encountering these episodes on the screen is another experience altogether. If movies are capable of profoundly affecting our moods and feelings, we should utilize this to enliven instruction while making sure that logic and clear thinking are not overwhelmed by sentiment and emotion.

Movies also are capable of bringing the past to life by re-creating historical events, eras, and characters. Students studying *Murder in the Cathedral* would find the twelfth century brought to life in *Becket* and *The Lion in Winter*, for example. If we ignore motion pictures, it is possible that they will more memorably, and less accurately, influence the way students think about historical periods and personalities. When Oliver Stone released *JFK* in December 1991, many journalists attacked the film as a distortion of history. Will today's young people believe the official version of the Kennedy assassination or Hollywood's version? Movies are also capable of bringing distant lands and different cultures to the classroom to enliven and enrich the study of other cultures. If a culture is stereotyped and misrepresented in a film, it is necessary for teachers to challenge these inaccuracies. Teachers can also look at films from other countries to see how they depict their own culture and the United States.

As a dramatic medium with a limited time to develop a story, movies traditionally rely upon clichés, conventions, and stereotypes. By repeating and reinforcing stereotypes (racial, occupational, religious, national, gender, etc.), movies potentially impede the way children see the society they live in and the diverse groups and individuals they must live with. School systems dedicated to promoting cooperation in a multicultural society cannot afford to ignore media representations of those cultures.

Motion pictures also can be a powerful ally in promoting literacy and the enjoyment of literature. Film versions of books and plays can bring the characters to life and help students recognize universal themes and the human condition. Comparisons between various versions of a film can also help students see the role individual interpretation plays in literature. Mel Gibson's Hamlet could be compared to Sir Laurence Olivier's or Kevin Kline's. Roman Polanski's stunning treatment of *Macbeth* could be contrasted to the Orson Welles version. Dustin Hoffman's 1985 characterization of Willy Loman (*Death of a Salesman*) could be compared to the 1951 Fredric March version. The 1990 U.S. version of *Lord of the Flies* is an interesting contrast to the less stylish but more accurate 1963 British version. When students are excited by a film they often express interest in reading the book. Movies such as *The Neverending Story* encourage reading and can be explored as fantasy during genre studies in literature. Brief clips from films can also be used to motivate students to write.

Motion pictures can also be used to promote visual literacy. Students can be taught to interpret information conveyed in iconic form. The openings of both *Turner and Hooch* and *Born on the 4th of July*, for example, convey an enormous amount of information about the characters and locations before the story has really gotten underway. If we draw students' attention to sequences such as these we can help them recognize and utilize nonverbal communication. On a more sophisticated level, film form and style also contribute to the message. Religious symbolism abounds in *On the Waterfront*. Water symbolism dominates *Psycho* and *Splendor in the Grass*. *Lost Weekend* offers many possibilities for visual analysis, including various camera angles and a striking sequence of dancing overcoats in the opera scene. *The Grifters* opens with an unusual split-screen sequence.

Because it is a visual medium, the study of film can also be integrated into art classes. Film noir and German expressionism are strongly linked. The set decorations for *The Wizard of Oz*, particularly the early black-and white sequences, have more than a passing similarity to regionalism and paintings by Grant Wood and others. The lives of artists such as Michelangelo, Vincent van Gogh, Paul Gaugin, and Henri de Toulouse-Lautrec can also be studied by looking at films such as *The Agony and the Ecstasy, Lust for Life,* and *Wolf at the Door*.

Although we think of film as primarily a visual medium, sound also plays a significant part. Music teachers can explore motion picture scores to see how they evoke particular moods and emotions. Biographies of classical and current composers can also be useful in bringing the individuals and the creative process to life. Some examples include *Amadeus* (Wolfgang Amadeus Mozart), *Lisztomania* (Franz Liszt), *A Song to Remember* (Frédéric Chopin), *Words and Music* (Richard Rodgers and Lorenz Hart), *Deep in My Heart* (Sigmund Romberg), and *Night and Day* (Cole Porter).

Finally, movies are a very youth-oriented medium. Adolph Zukor once said, "The average movie goer's intelligence is that of a fourteen-year-old child." If movies target young audiences, then parents, teachers, librarians, and media specialists need to monitor films and help students understand the views and values expressed in them. Social learning theory suggests that movies can model behavior and attitudes that children and adolescents may identify with or imitate. The repetitive nature of film, enhanced by the multiple screenings made possible by cable and VCR, increases the potential impact of these media models and messages. In 1990, a fourteen-year-old Washington girl allegedly copied the movie *Heathers* and poisoned two eleven-year-old playmates. Although such instances are rare, they demonstrate how impressionable young people can be. Adults who are trying to help young people deal with the pressures and problems associated with substance abuse, sexual experimentation, self-image, and other issues cannot afford to ignore the allure and social sanction often afforded by the silver screen. *Porky's, Animal House, The Last American Virgin,* and numerous other films are all potentially suspect in this area. On the other hand, *Zelly and Me, The Breakfast Club, Member of the Wedding, Empire of the Sun, The Diary of Anne Frank, Hud, Stand by Me,* and *Bless the Beasts and Children* are among many memorable films that can be used to help children and adolescents think about their own lives and the process of growing up.

Of course, like all instructional materials utilized in education, movies must be examined before use. Only by previewing a film for content, form, and language can teachers determine the suitability of the film and effectively integrate it into instruction. Prescreening and postscreening strategies can provide students with cueing and retrieval skills that will enhance their recall and comprehension. Although the screening of an entire film is sometimes appropriate, students usually get more from a movie when it is shown in shorter segments with preparation and discussion that clearly link the film to the objectives and the topic being studied.

There are four ways to read a film that are useful in the classroom. Typically found in the English and language arts area, the first approach considers film as celluloid literature. Instruction usually hinges on comparing and contrasting the play or novel with the film version. Examples of this would include *To Kill a Mockingbird, The Great Gatsby,* and *A Separate Peace.* A visual medium, film also can be analyzed as art, including the French concept of mise-en-scène, which considers the impact of lighting, camera angle, symbolism, editing, and other factors in creating the whole meaning of the film. Viewing film as archaeological and historical evidence, a potentially powerful approach, has so far not found widespread use in the classroom despite the presence of a growing body of literature to support the approach. In this case, movies are essentially regarded as cultural artifacts that can be decoded and studied as reflections of the time in which they were produced and consumed. *Rocky,* for example, won the Academy Award for Best Picture in 1976. The story and form of the film and the public's response can be read as reflections of the national mood in the bicentennial year. Rocky's emergence from obscurity to triumph also parallels the election that year of Jimmy Carter.

The fourth method, film as sociology, looks at image and influence and studies the ways that motion pictures can affect society or particular groups in society. For those of us who work with young people, this important approach raises the issue of media role models. Regarding current problems such as substance abuse and teen pregnancy, this approach examines the role film might play in sanctioning such behavior. In addition, a sociological approach provides an opportunity to study stereotyping and the role film might play in promoting and perpetuating stereotypes. In our increasingly multicultural society movies can hurt or help the way we see others. *Welcome to Paradise, Do the Right Thing,* and *Dances with Wolves* are three recent examples of films that explore Japanese Americans, Blacks, and Native Americans. A sociological interpretation of motion pictures examines the way movies represent society and construct culture. It requires an analysis of how groups are represented and why these images are repeated. In a discussion of race-issue films, *USA Today* suggested that Hollywood assumes that "white audiences are interested in stories about racial injustice only if the stars—and viewpoint—are white" (*USA Today* 7/27/1988, 4D). Recently these stories have been shown through the eyes of Black directors such as Spike Lee who offer a different perspective. Reviewing *Do the Right Thing, The Christian Century* wrote: "Lee renders with considerable accuracy the black experience from within.... Popular entertainment in this country seldom provides such experience" (*Christian Century* 1989, 739). Such comments focus our attention not just on the message but also on the messenger.

FILM AS LITERATURE

Young students are so fascinated with the image on the screen that it never occurs to many of them that before the picture ever got on the screen, it first appeared in print, on paper, in the form of a script. Many of these students understand that a film or television program is made, or shot, but they are not really aware that it is written. Actually, as all English teachers know, novels and motion pictures share many similarities including character, plot, conflict, and resolution. Some of our greatest writers have, at one time or another, also written for the movies. They include Nathaniel West, F. Scott Fitzgerald, and William Faulkner.

Chain of Events, Sequencing, and Narrative Structure

(MID/HIGH) — Meaning in motion picture is derived from the way we interpret the chain of events. We are conditioned from our early experiences with movies to intuitively understand that not all things are shown. If we see the hero leave his office and head for the subway, we do not, for example, have to watch his subway journey. When we next see him opening his front door, we mentally fill in the blanks and know how he got there. Sometimes, however, when a film cuts from one scene to another, there is a disruption to the continuity that leaves us wondering what has occurred between the scenes. Two highly acclaimed 1989 movies, *Driving Miss Daisy* and *Born on the 4th of July*, have moments like this. In the first film, Miss Daisy attends a banquet for Martin Luther King, Jr. The next time we see her she is ill and has regressed into her youth, thinking she is still a teacher. It is difficult to know how much time has elapsed between the King dinner and this scene. Often this is clearly the intention; on other occasions, the disruption seems less intentional. *Born on the 4th of July* has a similar problem when Ron Kovic (Tom Cruise) arrives at the railway station and is met by his high school sweetheart. The jump from one moment in the film to this is abrupt, and consequently it is difficult to read this scene.

Because film is merely an illusion of reality, its time frame is not accurate. Dramatic conventions as well as technology enable the filmmaker to "telescope" time. In the movies, time can be compressed or expanded. Flashbacks and flash-forwards are two methods by which this occurs. Explain these two terms (*flashback* and *flash-forward*) to students and have them come up with examples of films that employ these techniques. Some important examples include *Casualties of War, Citizen Kane, D.O.A., Double Indemnity, Home of the Brave, Lost Weekend, Mildred Pierce, Once Upon a Time in America,* and *Sunset Boulevard.*

In the space of about 2 hours, a film can deal with a day in the life of one character, a character's entire life, or the lives of several generations. *The Breakfast Club* takes place on one day when a group of high school students find themselves in detention on a Saturday. *Ferris Bueller's Day Off* takes place in one 24-hour period, chronicling the adventures of a high school student who cuts class. *Same Time Next Year, The Color Purple, Gandhi,* and *When Harry Met Sally* are examples of films that occur over several years. Divide the class into three groups and have each group create a list of films that occur (1) in a single day, (2) over a brief period of time, and (3) over several years.

What sort of problems have to be considered when dealing with films that take place in one day or over several years? Stories that operate on the "day in the life of" format tend to require either a very special individual, a special set of circumstances, or a willing suspension of disbelief. *Ferris Bueller's Day Off*, for example, is fun but hardly believable. On the other hand, an epic such as *The Color Purple* requires more time to tell the story and needs make-up, sets, and costumes that convey the different times in which the film is set. *Same Time Next Year* achieved this transition from one period to the next through music and a series of still images highlighting key events in each era.

Excellence in Editing

(ELEM/MID/HIGH) — As we have seen, editing represents decisions about what to leave out, what to put in, and the transitions inbetween. Sometimes the cuts are from one location to another, from one group of characters to another, or from one moment in time to another. At other times, the editing represents rapid cutting to build pace, tension, and excitement centering around one moment. The threat of the attacking shark in *Jaws*, for example, is enhanced by the editing. Examine the selected list (below) of films that have won Academy Awards for editing and have students discuss the type of films that tend to win this award. Show students one or two example scenes from these films and have them discuss the editing and what impact it had on the scene. Interesting examples include the shark attack in *Jaws*, the chariot race in *Ben Hur*, the dock fight at the end of *On the Waterfront*, the showdown sequence from *High Noon*, the final attack sequence in *Star Wars*, and the opening sequence of *West Side Story*.

(MID/HIGH) — After the class has examined a scene closely and discussed it, have them write the scene as though it were in a novel. In follow-up discussion, talk about problems involved in the process. What can the camera and editing do that words cannot?

Partial List of Academy Award Winners for Film Editing

National Velvet (1945)
The Best Years of Our Lives (1946)
High Noon (1952)
On the Waterfront (1954)
Around the World in 80 Days (1956)
Bridge on the River Kwai (1957)
Ben Hur (1959)
West Side Story (1961)
Lawrence of Arabia (1962)

How the West Was Won (1963)
Mary Poppins (1964)
Sound of Music (1965)
In the Heat of the Night (1967)
Patton (1970)
The French Connection (1971)
Cabaret (1972)
The Sting (1973)
The Towering Inferno (1974)

Jaws (1975)
Rocky (1976)
Star Wars (1977)
The Deer Hunter (1978)
All That Jazz (1979)
Raging Bull (1980)
Raiders of the Lost Ark (1981)
Gandhi (1982)

The Right Stuff (1983)
The Killing Fields (1984)
Witness (1985)
Platoon (1986)
The Last Emperor (1987)
Born on the 4th of July (1989)
Dances with Wolves (1990)

And Then What Happened: Movies as Motivators

(ELEM/MID)—When writer's block sets in and students stare blankly at an empty page, motion pictures can inspire and jump-start those sluggish minds. A simple strategy for this is to take a dramatic moment from a film, show it to the class, and turn off the set just at the climactic moment. After the class has finished groaning and complaining, ask them, "And then what happened?" Their job is to complete the scene. An alternative approach is to have them write a story that ends where the clip began. The clip you show should be 5-10 minutes long, no more. It is better if the students are not familiar with the film; remember, you are using the images to inspire them and to stimulate their imaginations. They should not write an end they already know.

Rebel without a Cause has a very good scene that has been successfully used this way. The clip, generally known as "the chickie run" scene, centers on two teenage males caught up in a game of chicken. The boys take their cars to a cliff over the ocean. The object of the dare is for the boys to drive rapidly to the edge of the cliff; the first one to jump out of his car is a chicken. The scene appeals to students because it has action, fast cars, young people, a peer group theme, and a sense of danger. Make sure you are thoroughly familiar with the scene before using it, so you can stop it before one of the boys goes over the cliff. Before showing the clip, you might tell the class they are going to see a story about four young people—Judy, Jim, Buzz, and Plato. Depending on the level of your class, you might also introduce them to concepts such as conflict and resolution. This same scene has very good applications in social studies and in any discussion about peer pressure.

Director as Author

Whereas an author or playwright usually works alone, movies require many specialists, so films are always collective projects or creative collaborations. Someone first writes a screenplay, which goes through revisions, and often a different writer is even hired. A director then contributes to the overall look and feel of the film. Occasionally a director even writes the script. This was true with Spike Lee's *Do the Right Thing*, Barbra Streisand's *Yentl*, Woody Allen's *Hannah and Her Sisters*, Oliver Stone's *Salvador*, and Peter Weir's *Green Card*.

French film theory and criticism has created the auteur theory, which suggests that the director has artistic control over the film and that a body of films by any such director has a particular style, form, and continuity. The theory works with some directors and is a useful approach to classic U.S. films made during the heyday of the studio system. Today, however, few directors have the power to control their films entirely. *Skywalking*, a biography about George Lucas, provides an informative look at the conflicts involved in the production and distribution of *American Graffiti* and *Star Wars*. The following directors are among those usually mentioned in auteur theory: Frank Capra, John Ford, Howard Hawks, Alfred Hitchcock, Fritz Lang, Sam Peckinpah, and Billy Wilder.

(MID/HIGH)—Divide the class into groups and have each group select one auteur director to research. They should develop a list of the films he made, the types of films he made, themes that appeared in the films, and awards and honors received by the director and the films. Each group should plan to make a brief class presentation on their findings, including showing one or two clips that they think best demonstrate the director's work. After each group has presented their report, conduct a poll to see which current director(s) students think might qualify as auteur directors. Have a discussion to justify their opinions.

Some Important Academy Award-Winning Directors

Below is a partial list of directors who have won the Academy Award. If you look at the brief list (above) of auteur directors, you will note that the names of Howard Hawks, Alfred Hitchcock, Fritz Lang, and Sam Peckinpah are missing from the list of Academy Award winners. Students should be made aware of this and reminded that, although George Lucas and Steven Spielberg have directed some of the most successful movies in history, as of yet neither has received an Oscar for an individual picture. Both directors might, however, qualify as auteurs. Many students will be familiar with the films of Lucas and Spielberg. Have them compile a list of films by each director and explore recurring themes, plots, and motifs. Can they find any similarities, for example, between *Close Encounters of the Third Kind* and *Poltergeist*? Where do *Jaws* and *The Color Purple* fit in to Spielberg's body of work? Advanced students might enjoy exploring thematic links in the two seemingly different Lucas movies *American Graffiti* and *Star Wars*. One other current director, Oliver Stone, has also produced a body of work that might be studied in its entirety from an auteur perspective. His films include *Salvador, Platoon, Born on the 4th of July, Wall Street, The Doors,* and *JFK*. Can the students detect continuity in theme and style in these movies?

The following list also contains the names of actors who have become directors and won an Academy Award for directing. Four of them are Warren Beatty, Robert Redford, Woody Allen, and Kevin Costner.

Woody Allen (*Annie Hall*)
Warren Beatty (*Reds*)
Robert Benton (*Kramer vs. Kramer*)
Bernardo Bertolucci (*The Last Emperor*)
James L. Brooks (*Terms of Endearment*)
Frank Capra (*You Can't Take It with You*; *Mr. Deeds Goes to Town*; *It Happened One Night*)
Michael Cimino (*The Deer Hunter*)
Francis Ford Coppola (*The Godfather II*)
Kevin Costner (*Dances with Wolves*)
John Ford (*The Quiet Man*; *How Green Was My Valley*; *Grapes of Wrath*; *The Informer*)
Milos Forman (*Amadeus*; *One Flew over the Cuckoo's Nest*)
George Roy Hill (*The Sting*)

Elia Kazan (*On the Waterfront*; *Gentleman's Agreement*)
David Lean (*Lawrence of Arabia*; *Bridge on the River Kwai*)
Joseph L. Mankiewicz (*Letter to 3 Wives*; *All about Eve*)
Mike Nichols (*The Graduate*)
Sydney Pollack (*Out of Africa*)
Robert Redford (*Ordinary People*)
George Stevens (*Place in the Sun*; *Giant*)
Oliver Stone (*Platoon*; *Born on the 4th of July*)
Billy Wilder (*The Apartment*; *The Lost Weekend*)
William Wyler (*The Best Years of Our Lives*; *Ben Hur*; *Mrs. Miniver*)
Fred Zinnemann (*From Here to Eternity*; *Man for All Seasons*)

The Common Elements of a Novel and Film

(ELEM/MID/HIGH)—Novels and films have several common elements, including characters, conflict/dilemma, setting, resolution, plot, and theme. Introduce each of these terms to the students. With younger students, a "three P" approach can be successful: people, place, and plot.

Characters. Have students pick their favorite film and, using the elements of a novel or silm, analyze the film into its component parts. Younger students can deal with characters in broad terms as heroes and villains, whereas older students could consider aspects such as antagonist, protagonist, or anti-hero. Literary tradition and the theater have provided other staple roles that can still be found in films. These include the "everyman" character, who often has the privileged position of being able to directly address the audience. Robert Bolt's *Man for All Seasons* has an interesting example of this. Many of William Shakespeare's plays feature a fool or clown who, although appearing foolish, often sees more than any other characters. Spike Lee's controversial production *Do the Right Thing* (1989) provides a fascinating group of characters to consider from this perspective. (The film features strong language and some sexual situations and would be suitable only for high school seniors or for selected clips.) In addition to the central characters, students should consider the functions of Mother Sister, Mr. Mayor, Smiley, and Radio Rahine.

Dilemma. The characters usually find themselves faced with a dilemma that is worked through in the unfolding of the plot or the events and action of the film. Sometimes characters are faced with dilemmas not unlike those that face average people. At other times ordinary people find themselves faced with extraordinary dilemmas. Consider the dilemmas in the films below. As an alternative, give students a list of dilemmas faced by characters in books and movies they should be familiar with, and see if they can correctly identify each book or movie.

- A young boy finds an alien in his back yard. (*E.T.*)

- A sheriff risks having his wife leave him if he faces a man who has come to kill him. (*High Noon*)

- A small boy is forgotten by his parents when they go on vacation and he has to single-handedly stop burglars from breaking in. (*Home Alone*)

- A young girl suddenly finds herself and her dog transported to another world. (*The Wizard of Oz*)

- A teenage girl finds herself attracted to a strange autistic boy who thinks he can fly. (*The Boy Who Could Fly*)

- A young boy wakes up one day and discovers his hair has turned green. (*The Boy with Green Hair*)

- A young man buys a robot only to discover that it contains a mysterious message from a young woman asking for help. (*Star Wars*)

- A wounded soldier, crippled for life, returns home and tries to cope. (*Born on the 4th of July*)

- A farmer hears mysterious voices in his cornfield telling him, "If you build it, he will come." (*Field of Dreams*)

- An Italian pizzeria owner in a Black neighborhood faces violence and hostility because he is not like them. (*Do the Right Thing*)

- A woman discovers that being a wife and mother is not enough to make her happy. (*Kramer vs. Kramer*)

- A loner from the Australian outback finds himself in New York City, where he struggles to fit in. (*Crocodile Dundee*)

- A boy meets two cyborgs from the future who return to Earth in the 1990s and battle for its future. (*Terminator II*)

- An inventor accidentally shrinks his children. (*Honey, I Shrunk the Kids!*)

- A young man falls in love with a beautiful girl, only to discover she's a mermaid. (*Splash*)

- A young man must choose between the honor of running for his country in the Olympic Games or observing his religious beliefs by refusing to run on a holy day. (*Chariots of Fire*)

You might also develop your own list of dilemmas based on films you think your students will be familiar with.

Screenwriters

Most film discussion centers on the look of the film. Attention can also be focused on the language, writing, dialogue, and speeches by selecting scenes from films that have been honored for their writing. Show clips and discuss the quality of the writing with students. The following is a partial list of writers who have won an Academy Award for Best Screenplay.

Tom Schulman (*Dead Poets Society*, 1989)
John Patrick Shanley (*Moonstruck*, 1987)
Woody Allen (*Hannah and Her Sisters*, 1986)
William Kelley (*Witness*, 1985)
Robert Benton (*Places in the Heart*, 1984)
Horton Foote (*Tender Mercies*, 1983)
John Briley (*Gandhi*, 1982)
Colin Welland (*Chariots of Fire*, 1981)
Bo Goldman (*Melvin and Howard*, 1980)
Steve Tesich (*Breaking Away*, 1979)
Nancy Dowd and Waldo Salt (*Coming Home*, 1978)
Marshall Brickman (*Annie Hall*, 1977)
Paddy Chayefsky (*Network*, 1976)
Robert Evans (*Chinatown*, 1974)
Jeremy Larner (*The Candidate*, 1972)
Francis Ford Coppola and Edmond North (*Patton*, 1970)

William Rose (*Guess Who's Coming to Dinner*, 1967)
James Webb (*How the West Was Won*, 1963)
William Inge (*Splendor in the Grass*, 1961)
Nathan Douglas and Harold Jacob Smith (*The Defiant Ones*, 1958)
Paddy Chayefsky (*Marty*, 1955)
Budd Schulberg (*On the Waterfront*, 1954)
Billy Wilder (*Sunset Boulevard*, 1950)
Robert Sherwood (*The Best Years of Our Lives*, 1946)
Billy Wilder and Charles Brackett (*The Lost Weekend*, 1945)
Julius G. Epstein, Philip Epstein, and Howard Koch (*Casablanca*, 1943)
Herman Mankiewicz and Orson Welles (*Citizen Kane*, 1941)

Genre Studies

The concept of film genre suggests that motion picture story types can be analyzed into identifiable groups with their own codes, characteristics, and conventions. Genre studies can provide an analytical tool for comparing and contrasting individual films. For students in English, this approach enables them to understand broad themes as well as the ways that the story types have evolved and developed. Stuart Kaminsky points out in *American Film Genres*: "the roots of genre are not solely in the literary tradition, but in the fabric of existence itself. Genre films deal just as surely and deeply with social issues, considerations of life and death and the unknown as do art films" (1974, 5). This approach to genre is examined in this chapter in the areas of both film as history and film as sociology.

(ELEM / MID / HIGH)—Essentially, genre refers to a story type or a category of story types. Introduce students to the term and give them one example, perhaps the western. The western is an easy place to begin genre studies. It is the most American of genre forms, and all students have some sense of what happens in a western.

Break the class into groups and assign each group one of the following topics: (1) typical names / people / characters, (2) typical names / places / location / setting, and (3) plot / events / incidents. Each group has to develop a descriptive list of the characters, environment, and incidents we can expect to encounter in a western. They will have some background in this area simply from having watched television. The research can, however, be supplemented with various readings listed in this chapter and a TV movies viewing guide. The groups can divide work among members so that one member might develop a list of western film titles and another might compile a list of stars or directors who are best known for westerns. Each group should make a presentation to the class, and there should be discussion and classification of the information.

The simple process of defining what a western is can prove to be a thought-provoking exercise. Is it, for example, set in the American West? Is it set in the West during a particular period of time? In *Go West*, the Marx Brothers were clearly in the American West at a particular point in time; nonetheless, this comedy is not a western in the true sense of the genre. Similar problems arise with *Blazing Saddles*, which is clearly a comedy set in the West. In terms of the iconography of the western, horses are a dominant feature. Westerns have sometimes been called "horse operas." But will your students accept technology in their westerns? *The Wild Bunch*, a classic western of the late 1960s, features automobiles, and *Butch Cassidy and the Sundance Kid* features a bicycle. Another interesting aberration is *Westworld*, which looks like a western but is actually science fiction. *Zachariah* had classic elements of the western, including black hats and white hats, but this "electronic western," with Country Joe and The Fish, is certainly not what we mean by a typical western. Finally, Sergio Leone developed an important series of westerns. Because they were Italian, they became known as "spaghetti westerns." Select a series of clips from important westerns to demonstrate the form and format of the genre. Compare the clips to the students' reports. These short categories might help in formulating research on the western and serve as a model for approaching other genres.

Elements of Westerns

Characters

Doctor (sometimes alcoholic)
Newspaper editor
Sheriff/deputy
Saloon keeper/barman
Dancehall girl (sometimes prostitute)
Female schoolteacher
Banker
Gambler
Indians
Cavalry
Scout
Preacher/missionary
Gunslinger
Hero/loner

Locations

Town
Fort
Plains
Indian village
Jail
Ranch

Plots

Showdown/shootout
Cattle rustling
Jail break
Cleaning up corrupt town
Gold Rush
Indian attack
Journey of wagon train
Struggle between farmers and ranchers

In the Beginning ...

(MID/HIGH) — A useful way to approach genre studies is to select a group of films from one genre and watch the first 5-10 minutes of each. In the case of westerns, films such as *Johnny Guitar, The Wild Bunch*, and *Dances with Wolves* provide strong, contrasting openings. Students can be assigned various tasks as they watch. One group might study the landscape, environment, and setting. Another group might make notes on the music and the mood it creates. Other areas for analysis would include a list of the key characters and the way the plot begins. Using four or five clips, each of about six minutes, would occupy only one lesson. The students could write up their reports overnight and class discussions and presentations could occur the next day. Listed below are a group of westerns that provide interesting material for contrast and comparison using the opening sequences. Remember, this exercise can be used with any genre.

1. *The Plainsman:* An interesting beginning. The titles will look familiar to anyone who has seen *Star Wars*. The prologue is important and demonstrates the use of dramatic license, compressing characters and events to suit the dramatic format. Clip can be stopped after the Lincoln assassination.

2. *Stagecoach:* Often regarded as the quintessential western. It has John Ford's familiar milieu of Monument Valley and a cast of characters that defined the human elements of a western. Clip can be stopped when Doc and Dallas board the coach.

3. *She Wore a Yellow Ribbon:* One of the classic cavalry films. The opening establishes the characters, conflict, and tone. Clip can be stopped when John Wayne says, "Six more days and I retire."

4. *The Searchers:* The arrival of the hero and the landscape are classic elements of this western. Stop clip after the supper sequence.

5. *Soldier Blue:* A very interesting contrast, particularly in terms of the music, prologue, and the treatment of women. Stop clip when the payroll is attacked.

For another activity, ask the class to come up with a list of other genres, such as gangster/crime, horror, science fiction, fantasy, musicals, war, and love stories. The approach used with the western can be applied with any of these genres, with students working individually or in groups.

And They All Lived Happily Ever After

The successful resolution of the conflict usually brings closure to the story. Sometimes order is restored when the lone gunfighter or hero defeats the villain and cleans up the town or village. At other times the man gets the woman and they find true love. Sometimes, however, the conclusion is much grimmer. At the end of *Magic*, the dummy has finally destroyed its ventriloquist master and the camera provides closure as it pulls back from inside the cabin, distancing us from the victim and the frame. *Psycho* concludes with a similar cinematic technique, with Norman's crimes explained, the loose ends tied up, and two personalities merged in the image of Mother's skull superimposed over Norman's face. The camera pulls back as the car emerges from the lake and the curtain closes on our voyeurism.

Sometimes students might find that the end of a movie seems unsatisfactory. Discuss this with them. What end would they have preferred? Why do they think the director closed the film the way he or she did? Advanced students may think that the conclusion is inconsistent with the character. These issues can also be connected to classic conflict and characters in literature. The closure of *Hamlet*, for example, leaves much room for discussion, which could even be conducted in the form of a post-mortem or coroner's inquest. Whereas Shakespeare's plays often end tragically, Hollywood, particularly in the 1950s, seemed intent on providing a happy ending, no matter how unrealistic or inconsistent it might be. Often that closure asserted control by restoring the patriarchy or asserting the dominance of a male figure. *Rebel without a Cause* closes by banishing the mother to the periphery of the frame and action as Jim reconciles with his father. Nicholas Ray did the same thing at the end of *Johnny Guitar*, which finds Vienna washed clean of her sins and literally crawling on her hands and knees to Johnny. *Mildred Pierce* closes with the male detective shedding light on the murder and a new day as the once dominant Mildred symbolically steps into the light and returns to her former husband.

Even recent films such as *Kramer vs. Kramer* and *Ordinary People* establish closure through male bonding and banishing the female. But current films are much less likely to have a happy ending. Sure, the guy still gets the girl (*Top Gun*), but in cleaning up the world the hero may be killed (*Terminator II*). Mature motion pictures such as *Presumed Innocent* also close with a much stronger sense of moral ambiguity and uncertainty. For the story to succeed the end must do more than make us feel good. It must be plausible and consistent with the characters and context. Teachers can explore this element of movies to help students think about literature and their own writing.

The Fantasy Genre: A Case Study. Some of the most enduring classics of children's literature are fantasies. *Peter Pan, The Wizard of Oz, Alice in Wonderland,* and *Charlotte's Web* are just a few examples. Picture books by Chris Van Allsburg and novels by Susan Cooper, Russell Hoban, Natalie Babbitt, and Lloyd Alexander, to name just a few, provide current examples of the fantasy genre in children's literature. These books stimulate children's imagination, and they can also be used to develop analytical skills as children consider the elements of the genre, compare and contrast film and book versions of the same story, and explore examples of the genre in the field of motion pictures. The most basic rule of thumb in a fantasy is to expect the unexpected. The everyday laws of nature do not apply. Everyday worlds are replaced by encounters with strange environments. Dorothy visits Oz, Peter Pan and the Darlings go to Never-Never Land, and Alice falls down a rabbit hole and winds up in Wonderland. Many recent movies give children the opportunity to follow heroes and heroines on quests to strange lands where they encounter exotic creatures, magical spells, and the trials and tests that confront such travellers. *Labyrinth* and *Legend* are two good examples. One of the most enjoyable modern film fantasies is *The Neverending Story* (1984).

The Neverending Story offers students a chance to explore the fantasy genre in literature and film. (Photograph used with permission of Museum of Modern Art Film Stills Archive, Noah Hathaway, and © 1984 Neue Constantin Film Produktion GmVH. All Rights Reserved.)

The film opens in the modern world, where the central character, ten-year-old Bastian, feels alone and frightened. His mother has died. He is afraid of the school bullies who beat him up, and his father does not understand him. The boy is troubled at school and bothered by dreams about his mother. When he tries to confide in his father he is told, "We each have responsibilities and we can't let Mom's death become an excuse for not getting the old job done … you're old enough to get your head out of the clouds and start keeping both feet on the ground." When Bastian leaves for school, both feet are rather quickly off the ground as the bullies pursue him and throw him in a dumpster.

These two incidents at the start of the film clearly create a sense of Bastian's alienation at school and at home. Before moving into the fantasy, both episodes should be explored with students so they understand the boy's circumstances. His only real joy in life comes from reading. In a mysterious bookstore he excitedly tells the equally mysterious owner all the titles he has read. This scene also provides an opportunity to talk to children about the value of reading. The bookstore owner initially doesn't even want to talk to Bastian. Because he's a modern child, the bookstore owner is sure Bastian is not interested in books: "The video arcade is down the street. Here we just sell small rectangular objects called books and they require a little effort on your part." The book that Bastian leaves the store with is the beginning of his journey as he enters the land of Fantasia and shares the quest of Atreyu.

The following questions and activities are designed to help teachers explore part or all of the film with students.

1. The initial fantasy sequences introduce us to a common element of the genre in the form of the fantastic creatures the Rock Eater, the Racing Snail, and the Night Hob riding the giant bat. Have students make a list of the characters. Others are seen shortly as the adventurers arrive at the Ivory Tower. Compare these exotic characters to those found in the cantina sequence of *Star Wars*. Ask students to compare and contrast the Emerald City with the Ivory Tower.

2. At the Ivory Tower we learn the dilemma facing the kingdom of Fantasia. What is it? How can Atreyu help Fantasia and how do the people at court initially react to him? What is the primary quest he is given and what conditions are established?

3. Another key element of the fantasy genre is fantastic lands, places, and environments. In this movie some are just referred to and others, such as the Swamp of Sadness, are featured. Make sure students keep a list of places such as the Silver Mountains, the Desert of Shattered Hopes, and the Sea of Possibilities.

4. Atreyu's quest actually takes him on a series of secondary missions and trials. In one adventure he has to find the Morla. Why? In what way is the Morla like Yoda in *Star Wars*? How is he different? Another mission sends Atreyu to the southern oracle. Why does he go there and what tests does he have to endure? Ultimately, Atreyu must find a new name for the empress. How does this involve Bastian?

5. *The Neverending Story* features a rich cast of heroes and villains. Students should make a list of each group and describe the characteristics of each individual. Villains would include the Nothing, Gmork, and some students may even put the bullies in this group. The heroic characters would include Atrax the pony, Falkor the flying luckdragon, the empress, Urgle the gnome, and her husband, the scientist Engywook. Some of these characters are more helpful than heroic. Use this distinction to have students explore each character's role in the story.

6. In *Star Wars* the great evil is the Empire and the dark forces of Lord Darth Vader. In this story the evil is the Nothing. Is the Nothing a character or a presence and force? *Star Wars* referred constantly to the power of the Force. In this film such a force is also implied. Just as Luke Skywalker must blind himself with the helmet and go inside himself to master the Force, Bastian must conquer his own fears. Those fears actually feed the force. We are told that Fantasia is dying "because people have begun to lose their hopes and forget their dreams." The film takes on almost a political tone with the statement, "People who have no hopes are easy to control, and whoever has the control has the power." This concept could be explored with more advanced students.

7. Throughout the film action constantly shifts from the world of Fantasia to Bastian's hideout at school where he reads books. A series of incidents begins to suggest that he is part of the world of the story and that its characters are aware of his presence. What incidents begin to suggest this? In what way can we say that Bastian goes on a quest as well as Atreyu?

8. If Luke Skywalker learns the power of the Force and Dorothy learns there's no place like home, what does Bastian learn about life? In what way is his growth from his journey similar to the knowledge gained by the Scarecrow, the Cowardly Lion, and the Tin Man?

The Young Adult Novel and the Teen Screen: A Case Study. English teachers and their students will be familiar with the young adult novel and authors such as Judy Blume and S. E. Hinton. Several novels dealing with adolescents have achieved prominence. These include *Catcher in the Rye, A Separate Peace, Red Sky at Morning, Bless the Beasts and Children, The Heart Is a Lonely Hunter,* and *Last Summer.* Many of S. E. Hinton's novels have found their way to the screen, including *Tex, Rumblefish,* and *That Was Then, This Is Now. The Outsiders* is an interesting example of the genre for a number of reasons, including its Academy Award-winning director and the ensemble cast. At the time the film was made the young cast members were relatively unknown. Now most of them are household names. Ralph Macchio, who plays Johnny Cade, had success with *The Karate Kid* series. Patrick Swayze went on to find success in *Dirty Dancing* and *Ghost.* Tom Cruise, who had a minor role in the movie, had major hits with *Rainman, Top Gun,* and *Born on the 4th of July,* among others. The rest of the cast, including Rob Lowe and Emilio Estevez, became part of the "brat pack" and made a number of movies aimed at adolescents. But the film does not necessarily work. It is highly stylized, and audiences have quite different reactions to it. In New York City, a young audience laughed at it, and in rural North Carolina a young audience cried. It is certainly an interesting film to discuss with young people whether they have read the book or not. Like most young adult novels it explores alienation, peer pressure, rites of passage, and the search for self. The questions and activities on page 202 are suggested approaches for exploring *The Outsiders.*

The Outsiders was one of many S. E. Hinton novels brought to the screen in the 1980s. Explore elements of the young adult novel, comparing and contrasting film and book versions. (Photograph used with permission of Warner Bros., Inc.)

1. In what way is the start of the film *The Outsiders* reminiscent of *Gone with the Wind*, and why did Coppola choose to do this?

2. *The Outsiders* starts and ends the same way, with Ponyboy's composition book and his voiceover, "When I stepped out into the sunlight from the darkness of the movie theater...." Later in the movie we see other examples of his journal, such as "One morning I woke up earlier than usual. The church was colder than ever." Use these examples to discuss creative writing techniques and vocabulary with students. Encourage your students to keep their own journals. Discuss *The Diary of Anne Frank* with them as an important record of adolescent experiences in difficult times.

3. The cast is introduced at the start according to the two cliques, or gangs, they belong to—the Greasers and the Socs. Most schools have various cliques. Movies such as *Pretty in Pink* and *The Breakfast Club* explore this, and the feuding families of Romeo and Juliet are another example. Have a class discussion about what makes people divide up into groups and the positive and negative results of this process.

4. Cherry is a Soc but she can still talk to some of the Greasers, and she likes Ponyboy. But she tells him, "If I see you at school and I don't say hi, please don't take it personal." Like Molly Ringwald's character in *The Breakfast Club*, she finds it hard to break from peer pressure. Discuss the idea of peer pressure and the "in" crowd with your students. What makes someone "in"?

5. Have students make a list of all the characters in the movie, dividing them into Greasers and Socs. Are there any fence sitters who don't really belong to any group? Now have the students describe the attitudes, appearance, clothes, and characteristics of each group. The groups see each other as quite different. Are any examples given to suggest that they are actually very similar in some ways?

6. There is an age difference between Ponyboy and Johnny, but they are best friends. Compare and contrast the two boys and describe what their friendship is based on.

7. One common element of the teen screen and the young adult novel is the absent or negative parents. Johnny's father beats him, but the boy still says, "I think I like it better when the old man's hitting me. At least he knows I'm there." Ask students to describe the parents in this movie. How many examples do we see in this story? Ask students to name other books or films in which the parents are either absent or negatively depicted. Why does this happen in so many stories and how realistic is it?

8. There is only one girl in this story, Cherry Valance. Most of the film deals with male issues, rites of passage, and bonding. There seem to be no female Greasers. Ask students if the story needed more females. Have them create a list of teen movies that center on girls. It won't be a long list. Some of them will know *Heathers* and *Pretty in Pink*. Other examples include *Sixteen Candles*, *Puberty Blues*, *Effects of Gamma Rays on Man in the Moon Marigolds*, and *Member of the Wedding*. Have a discussion with your class about why there are so many male "coming-of-age" stories compared to those dealing with females. How would the structure of the publishing or film industry influence this? Remind them that S. E. Hinton is a female writer and her novels deal mainly with males.

9. The movies at the drive-in, the cars, and the music all provide evidence of the time in which the movie is set. See if students can ascertain when the story takes place. There are a few clues as to where the story is set. What evidence can they find in the film to indicate what state the story is set in?

10. When Bob is stabbed by Johnny, the director chose not to directly show the killing. Instead the incident is depicted subjectively from Ponyboy's position as his head is held under water and the water turns red. When he wakes up, the camera is also used subjectively and we see an angled image of Johnny as Ponyboy turns over. Introduce students to the concept of subjective camerawork (seeing from the point of view of a character). Ask them why the director chose not to show Johnny stabbing Bob.

11. On several occasions throughout the film, reference is made to the importance of appearances, such as, "Gee, this really makes me look tough," and "It's our looks or us." Why are appearances so important to the characters in this story? In what way are these concerns typical of the way teenagers feel today?

12. One of the most interesting sequences in the film begins when Ponyboy and Johnny run away from the city and hide in an old church in the country. One morning they wake early and watch the sunrise. "I never noticed colors or clouds or stuff until you started reminding me," Johnny tells his friend. Ponyboy recites words from a Robert Frost poem. How does your class react to this rather sensitive and tender moment between the two boys? We have seen an earlier moment with the same emotion between them as they huddle by a fire, afraid to go home to their families. Are these moments regarded by your students as evidence of weakness, honesty, loneliness, homosexuality, or do they think they are just corny? Discuss the range of their reactions and talk about the way characters in the media model socially acceptable behavior. *City Slickers* is an interesting 1991 comedy that stresses the need for males to be open and honest. That theme is clearly evident in *The Outsiders*. Like Buzz in *Rebel without a Cause*, Dallas Winston dies because he is locked into being tough. *Mr. Mom*, "Who's the Boss?" and other recent examples can be used to explore the image of sensitive males presented by both Ponyboy and Johnny Cade. Adolescent males concerned about their budding sexuality may benefit from thinking about these issues.

13. After the boys have rescued the children from the fire, they return to the city, where they are hailed as heroes by the press. Randy, the new leader of the Socs, tells Ponyboy, "I just would never have believed a Greaser could have pulled something like that." Randy is a prisoner of his perceptions. He knows the Greasers are not as bad as he thought, but he cannot break from the ritual of the rumble or the expectations of the peer groups. Like the chicken-run sequence in *Rebel without a Cause*, the rumble is something the gangs do ritualistically and mindlessly. Compare and contrast this rumble to the one between the Jets and the Sharks in *West Side Story*. Discuss the idea of heroism with the class after they have heard Randy's discussion with Ponyboy. What characteristics or circumstances do they think create heroic behavior? In what sense is Cherry Valance heroic in this story?

14. The gang behavior is rather primitive, seeking to settle everything by violence. *Lord of the Flies* is an interesting companion piece, with the struggle between Ralph and Jack and their groups. Use the conflict and the consequences as a way of discussing the role of violence in our culture. Some students could study gangs in society and cinema in movies such as *Walk Proud, The Warriors*, and *Boyz 'n' the Hood*. Other groups might explore violence in sports or the media. What evidence is there of female membership in gangs or female violence?

15. There is an important sequence after Ponyboy and Two-Bit visit Johnny in the hospital. Walking home they see small children playing noisily and say they are future Greasers. Just then Cherry Valance arrives. She and Ponyboy quarrel during this scene but they also communicate. What do they learn from each other? What function does this scene have in terms of suggesting anything about breaking the cycle of gang violence?

16. In a review of *The Outsiders*, *Time* wrote, "You can do good or do bad—but everybody dies" (*Time* 1983, 78). This, said the reviewer, was the moral of the film. Ask students what they think of this conclusion. Have them write their own review and/or moral. For more in-depth information on adolescent movies, see *The Cinema of Adolescence* (Considine 1985).

A Selection of Key Films from Various Genres

Westerns

The Plainsman (1936)
Stagecoach (1939)
My Darling Clementine (1946)
She Wore a Yellow Ribbon (1949)
The Gunfighter (1950)
Broken Arrow (1950)
High Noon (1952)
Shane (1953)
Johnny Guitar (1954)
The Searchers (1956)
The Left-Handed Gun (1958)
Rio Bravo (1959)
The Magnificent Seven (1960)
How the West Was Won (1962)
The Man Who Shot Liberty Valance (1962)
Cheyenne Autumn (1964)
Hombre (1967)
The Good, the Bad and the Ugly (1967)

Butch Cassidy and the Sundance Kid (1969)
The Wild Bunch (1969)
Once upon a Time in the West (1969)
True Grit (1969)
Little Big Man (1970)
The Missouri Breaks (1970)
Soldier Blue (1970)
A Man Called Horse (1970)
McCabe and Mrs. Miller (1971)
The Cowboys (1971)
Pat Garrett and Billy the Kid (1973)
The Outlaw Josey Wales (1976)
The Shootist (1976)
Windwalker (1980)
Heaven's Gate (1980)
Silverado (1985)
Young Guns (1988)
Dances with Wolves (1990)

Science Fiction

The Day the Earth Stood Still (1951)
The Thing (1951, 1982)
War of the Worlds (1953)
Them (1954)
Tarantula (1955)
1984 (1956, 1984)
Forbidden Planet (1956)
The Fly (1958, 1986)
The Time Machine (1960)
Fantastic Voyage (1966)
2001: A Space Odyssey (1968)
Silent Running (1971)
A Clockwork Orange (1971)
Soylent Green (1973)
Zardoz (1974)

Rollerball (1975)
Man Who Fell to Earth (1976)
Logan's Run (1976)
Star Wars (1977) (science fantasy)
Close Encounters of the Third Kind (1977)
Alien (1979)
Black Hole (1979)
E.T. (1982)
Tron (1982)
Dune (1984)
Starman (1984)
Running Man (1987)
Total Recall (1990)
Terminator II (1991)

Fantasy

The Wizard of Oz (1939)
Thief of Baghdad (1940)
Cabin in the Sky (1943)
The Secret Life of Walter Mitty (1947)
5000 Fingers of Dr. T. (1953)
20,000 Leagues under the Sea (1954)
Seven Faces of Dr. Lao (1964)
Willy Wonka and the Chocolate Factory (1971)

Bedknobs and Broomsticks (1971)
The Little Prince (1974)
Lord of the Rings (1978)
Watership Down (1978)
Heaven Can Wait (1978)
Dragonslayer (1981)
Excalibur (1981)
The Neverending Story (1984)

Fantasy *(continued)*

Legend (1985)
Cocoon (1985)
Labyrinth (1986)

Willow (1988)
Big (1988)
Field of Dreams (1989)

Horror

Dracula (1931)
Frankenstein (1931)
Dr. Jekyll and Mr. Hyde (1932, 1941)
King Kong (1933)
The Wolfman (1941)
Cat People (1942, 1982)
Invasion of the Body Snatchers (1956, 1978)
Psycho (1960)
Whatever Happened to Baby Jane? (1962)
Rosemary's Baby (1968)

Night of the Living Dead (1968)
Play Misty for Me (1971)
The Exorcist (1973)
Carrie (1976)
Halloween (1978)
The Shining (1980)
The Howling (1981)
An American Werewolf in London (1981)
Nightmare on Elm St. (1984)
Silence of the Lambs (1991)

Gangster / Crime

The Public Enemy (1930)
Little Caesar (1930)
Scarface (1932, 1983)
Dead End (1937)
Angels with Dirty Faces (1938)
The Roaring Twenties (1939)
Dillinger (1945)
They Live by Night (1947)
White Heat (1949)
Joe Macbeth (1955)
The Rise and Fall of Legs Diamond (1960)

Pretty Boy Floyd (1960)
Al Capone (1959)
Bonnie and Clyde (1967)
The St. Valentine's Day Massacre (1967)
The Godfather (1972)
Once upon a Time in America (1984)
The Untouchables (1987)
Miller's Crossing (1990)
Goodfellas (1990)
Mobsters (1991)
Bugsy (1991)

FILM AS ART

The idea that we need to be taught to "read" film or television seems strange in a society that often asserts that "seeing is believing" and "what you see is what you get." Using all the elements available, filmmakers encode their story with various cinematic techniques (camera angle, shot, lighting, etc.). Our ability to interpret these messages depends upon our familiarity with these codes and conventions and with the cultural conventions, connotations, and contexts associated with them. Essentially, then, film audiences can either perceive and process film on a shallow level or have a richer and deeper understanding of it, depending upon how visually literate they are.

When we ask students about films they have seen and films they like, they almost invariably talk about the narrative or action, with little sense of how the visual composition conveyed the story. In teaching them to "read" film, we have to draw their attention to the various elements of film language.

Types of Shots

Types of shots include the following:

1. Establishing or long shot. Usually used to establish the primary location at the beginning of a film or to designate a change to a major new location. *Psycho, The Lost Weekend,* and *West Side Story* open with excellent examples of establishing shots.

2. Close-up shot, in which the character or object fills most of the frame. When used with props, symbolism is almost always implied. *Ordinary People*, for example, uses close-ups of the napkins and napkin rings to symbolize Beth's need for order, control, and neatness.

3. Medium shot. Sometimes designated as medium close-up (MCU). If a close-up shows a character's head and shoulders, the MCU would show a waist-up view.

4. Extreme close-up. Camera comes in very tight, concentrating on a hand, eye, etc. The end of the shower sequence in *Psycho*, for example, fills the screen with just one eye of the murdered woman.

5. Dolly shot. Camera is mounted on a dolly and moving.

6. Tracking shot. The movements of the character are tracked, or followed, by a moving camera.

7. Pan shot. Abbreviated term for panoramic. The camera swivels in a horizontal plane to scan the scene.

(ELEM / MID / HIGH) — Introduce students to the above key terms and ask them for a definition and a purpose or context in which each would be used. Look at brief clips from motion pictures to get some examples of these shots. Lavish musicals are often good sources for dolly, pan, and tracking shots.

Following are two brief plot descriptions. Give these outlines to students and have them indicate what type of shot they would use for each action. Discuss the reasons for the decisions they make.

Scene 1

A platoon of soldiers marches across the desert.

Some of the soldiers worry about the mission they are on.

The enemy opens fire.

One of the platoon is hit.

His friend is shocked.

Scene 2

The story opens in San Francisco.

Three young women walk along a crowded street.

They stop for a traffic light.

The light turns green.

As they cross the street a car lunges at them.

One woman is hit.

The car speeds away.

The two friends offer assistance.

Mise-en-Scène

In *Understanding Movies*, Louis Giannetti says that mise-en-scène "refers to the arrangement of all the visual elements of a theatrical production within a given space—the stage" (1976, 48). The concept of mise-en-scène enables us to analyze the composition of the frame. It looks at visual elements such as shots, camera angles, lighting, costume, props, and sets to ascertain the mood and meaning that they cumulatively create. The mood and meaning created by the visual composition of the frame can then be considered in conjunction with the narrative.

Mise-en-scène: The meaning in this image is created cumulatively through the use of prop, posture, point of view, and position. The claustrophobic frame and the tilt down, combined with the use of stairs as symbolic prison and cage, stress Norman's vulnerability in this image from *Psycho*. (Photograph used with permission. Copyright © by Universal Pictures, a Division of Universal City Studios, Inc. Courtesy of MCA Publishing Rights, a Division of MCA Inc.)

The Four P's

(MID/HIGH) — Initial mise-en-scène analysis can be facilitated by the application of the "four P" approach used throughout this book. Introduce students to these terms and use short film clips to give them practice in recognizing the presence and function of these elements.

1. Point of View (POV): POV generally refers to the camera position approximating the position of the character, so the audience is placed in the position or perspective of the performer. POV, however, can also be understood as the perspective the camera and director give us on a character, location, or object. Two common camera angles are the tilt-up and the tilt-down. Neither perspective is neutral, and both carry cultural codes that convey meaning. A tilt-down invariably means vulnerability and a loss of power. The expression "looking down on someone" suggests this. The tilt-up, on the other hand, empowers and creates a sense of authority and control, such as the expression "to look up to someone." *Superman II* contains good simple examples of tilt-up and tilt-down in the sequence when Lois Lane discovers that Clark Kent is Superman.

2. Posture: Posture or body language are key clues in reading a character's mood and reaction. No one can watch James Dean in *East of Eden* or *Rebel without a Cause* without becoming aware of how the actor used his body to convey his inner conflict. Also watch Conrad's rapidly changing body language in the family photograph sequence of *Ordinary People*.

3. Props: Analyzing the function of props in a frame or scene promotes awareness of metaphor and symbolism. On the most basic level, this can be handled through the western convention of white hats for good guys and black hats for bad guys. On a more sophisticated level, it can be used to consider the function of the baseball bat in *The Natural*, the stuffed birds in *Psycho*, the dinner plate in *Ordinary People*, and the milk bottle in *Rebel without a Cause*.

4. Position: Position refers to placement within the frame and is usually considered in conjunction with other elements. Placing a character at the top of the stairs, for example, usually involves a tilt-up and promotes a different response than placing the character at the bottom of the stairs. Excellent symbolic use of staircases can be seen in *Johnny Guitar* and *Rebel without a Cause*.

Film Analysis: Teacher's Guides

(MID/HIGH)—*All Quiet on the Western Front* (1930). An interesting black-and-white film to study along with the novel or in conjunction with any topic dealing with war. The opening scene provides a brief sequence for mise-en-scène analysis.

- Doorways, arches, and gates are major motifs in this film. The movie begins with a shot of a doorknob being cleaned and then the door opening onto a village scene as troops parade through the street.

- A storekeeper and the postman stand in a doorway talking. Their position in the frame is claustrophobic, because the door hems them in. Their conversation makes reference to the war that is also closing in on them.

- Women throw flowers in praise as the troops pass. Later, the flowers will be placed without celebration.

- Troops are seen marching beneath another arch.

- The camera pulls back from the street scene and leads us into a classroom, but the structure of the frame clearly shows how the outside world impinges on the school. The teacher is flanked on each side by massive arched windows that look out onto the troops.

- A key prop continues to force the world upon the students. As the teacher talks to the boys, a globe of the world is in front of him. When the camera shows the boys at their desks, the globe dominates the left-hand side of the frame.

- Close-ups on individual faces of the boys are used frequently as they imagine themselves going off to war.

- Once they have made the decision to enlist, a tilt-down is used, ironically depriving the boys of power and prestige at the very moment they think they have assumed it. This is consistent with the illusion many of them have of war, as well as their teacher's illusion that it will be a short war.

- The scene ends as it began, with another door opening as the boys leave the classroom for the reality of the soldiers in the street. Stop film here.

(MID/HIGH) — *Ordinary People* (1980). This film belongs in every high school media center. It won multiple Academy Awards, including best picture and best director. The novel is popular in English classes and the subject matter of adolescent suicide and dysfunctional families has applications in the areas of health and counseling. Many sequences lend themselves to analysis of the mise-en-scène. The one selected here centers around taking a family photograph. Fast-forward the videotape until you find this sequence. Posture, position, and props are highly active in this scene. Mention this to the students before you show the clip. After they have seen it, ask them questions based on the guidelines set out below. Some visual variations might be useful here because many students may be inhibited from answering verbally. Some students might be more comfortable doing stick figure drawings in their books or on the board to show the positions of key characters at different points in the scene. You might also select several students to play key characters and ask them to re-enact the postures and positions of the characters. Role play is very useful in understanding body language and how movies use it.

- The scene opens with Beth, the grandfather, Conrad the teenage son, and the husband/father (Calvin) arranged left to right across the frame while the grandmother takes a photograph.

- The next picture to be taken is of "the young people," so the grandfather joins his wife. The characters are now arranged left to right: Beth, Calvin, and Conrad.

- Conrad's grandfather tells him to change places, "over in the middle between your mother and your father." There is a progressive change in the boy's body language. Watch his hands and arms.

- In the photo when Calvin kisses his wife, watch his own posture. "Come on, you can do better than that."

- Calvin wants to take a photograph of Conrad and Beth. Look at the expression and posture of mother and son throughout this, as Calvin tries to get the picture he wants.

- A very angry Conrad screams, "Give her the goddamn camera!" and walks away. What does he do and how do his posture, his position, and the point of view convey his feelings?

- What is Beth's reaction to the incident? What two props does she use as a form of displacement activity?

- Watch the camera angle and the position of the camera in the kitchen sequence with Beth and her mother.

- The motif of the broken home is repeated several times in the film. What is ironic about Beth's comment, "You know I think this can be saved. It's a nice clean break"? Stop film here.

(MID/HIGH) — *Rebel without a Cause* (1955). Sociologically this is one of the most important films of its decade because it reveals the fragmentation of the family in the post–World War II United States and shifts juvenile delinquency to white middle-class families. The entire film lends itself to mise-en-scène analysis, from the very beginning, when Jim (James Dean) is seen in a fetal position playing with a toy monkey, until the conclusion, when his father finally stands up for him and his mother is banished to the edge of the frame.

This is a complex but exciting scene to analyze and should only be attempted after students have had practice exercises with some of the shorter scenes recommended in this chapter. Fast-forward the video after the car crash. The scene begins just as an extreme close-up of Judy's compact fades out. The scene commences with Jim arriving home and getting a drink.

- The milk bottle is a major prop. Note how the director centers attention on it and how Jim uses it to soothe and cool himself. The bottle and its color invoke both purity and a maternal bond.

- Jim enters the living room and curls upon the couch in a fetal position. The posture recalls the opening of the film and further invokes the mother-milk metaphor.

- In a startling point-of-view shot, Jim's mother comes down the stairs and enters the living room. The shot, of course, is subjective, reflecting the boy's perspective, but it also symbolizes the sexual imbalance in the family, because Mother wears the pants in the Stark household. In Jim's world, everything is upside down because his father offers no real male role model. He is henpecked and even wears an apron.

- Jim confesses that he was in an accident in which a boy was killed. Two pivotal elements are active in this sequence. The stairway clearly functions as a power base, and the shifting positions and postures of the mother, father, and son on the stairway reinforce this function. Sketching the movement of the characters at key points helps us understand the symbolic role of these elements. When the son confesses his behavior to his parents, he sits at the bottom of the stairs, and his parents stand. When he begins to assume moral responsibility, he rises and is now head and shoulders above his parents, who want him to cover up the crime. At times in this sequence, the staircase railing seems to suggest a prison, and the father even seems to resemble a prisoner in the dock of a court. At times Jim turns his back on his parents, and a window further fragments the frame. When the mother moves above Jim on the stairs, the power structure of the family is evoked with the son clearly trapped between his mother and his weak father. Unable to assert himself, the father sits at the bottom of the stairs. The scene now features a series of tilt-ups and tilt-downs that empower the mother and depower the father.

- There is a constant interaction between the visual devices and the verbal content. The son finally pleads, "Dad, stand up for me," and drags his father from the chair.

- When the boy finally runs from the house in frustration, he kicks in a portrait of his grandmother, symbolically turning his anger on the matriarchal structure of the family.

- Finally, Jim's clothes in this sequence symbolize his all-American nature. He wears a white t-shirt, blue jeans, and a red jacket. The red jacket ties in with his name (Stark) and symbolizes that he wears his heart on his sleeve. This is in marked contrast to the tough, unfeeling gang members in their black leather jackets. In an earlier scene, it is a black leather jacket that traps one teenager in a car and leads to his death. After James Dean's death, shortly before the release of this film, the red nylon jacket became an icon to thousands of American kids who identified with Dean's rebel without a cause.

(ELEM)—Teachers wishing to use some of these concepts with younger children might select films with less serious themes. *Honey, I Shrunk the Kids!* has very good use of perspective or point of view, as does *Superman II.*

Color Versus Black-and-White

(MID/HIGH)—One of the most basic choices in designing the look of a film is deciding whether to shoot it in black-and-white or color. Many students typically assume that if a film is made in black-and-white, it is old. Others assume that it is low budget. Although both are sometimes true, often the decision to shoot in black-and-white is an artistic one based on the mood and feeling to be created. Occasionally, a film is shot in both formats. *Rebel without a Cause* began as a black-and-white project but ended up in color. *The Wizard of Oz* starts in black-and-white and changes to color. Lindsay Anderson's *If* uses both color and black-and-white.

Select one or two scenes from some of the following films and discuss the ways that mood and feeling are enhanced through black-and-white cinematography.

Grapes of Wrath (1940)
My Darling Clementine (1946)
On the Waterfront (1954)
The Defiant Ones (1958)
On the Beach (1959)
Psycho (1960)
Raisin in the Sun (1961)

To Kill a Mockingbird (1962)
Dr. Strangelove, or How I Learned to Stop Worrying and Love the Bomb (1964)
The Pawnbroker (1965)
Who's Afraid of Virginia Woolf? (1966)
The Last Picture Show (1971)

Film Noir

(HIGH) — In the 1940s, a whole style of film emerged based on black-and-white cinematography and bleak, brooding human themes. The psychological mood of these films reflected a peculiar mixture of neurosis, psychosis, and paranoia that could not have been created if the films had been shot in color. Shadows dominate the look of these films and much of the action occurs at night. An episode of the popular 1980s TV series "Moonlighting" was shot in film noir style. Foster Hirsch (1981) compares the brooding tension of these films to the city paintings of Reginald Marsh. Key films from this style include:

The Maltese Falcon (1941)	*Kiss of Death* (1947)
Double Indemnity (1944)	*Lady in the Lake* (1947)
Mildred Pierce (1945)	*The Big Clock* (1948)
Scarlet Street (1945)	*Key Largo* (1948)
The Blue Dahlia (1946)	*Sorry, Wrong Number* (1948)
The Big Sleep (1946)	*Lady from Shanghai* (1948)
Gilda (1946)	*The Naked City* (1948)
The Postman Always Rings Twice (1946)	*Sunset Boulevard* (1950)
The Killers (1946)	

Art teachers may want older students to look at some of these films to study the ways the visual elements convey the mood and tone of the film. English teachers might want to trace the literary origins of the films by looking at novels and short stories by Dashiell Hammett, Raymond Chandler, and James M. Cain.

German Expressionism

(HIGH) — Study of film noir can be connected to a study of German expressionist cinema and to expressionist painting in Germany. This is a fascinating movement to study because it can be integrated into art, social studies, and history. The films emerge most strongly in the period after World War I, when Germany's defeat leaves the country in psychological and social turmoil. This period is depicted in literature by the Berlin stories of Christopher Isherwood and in recent motion pictures such as *Cabaret* and *The Damned*.

Expressionist art represented a radical departure from the past. Lotte Eisner calls it "the apocalyptic doctrine of Expressionism" (1969, 9). She notes that as early as 1910, "the movement had tended to sweep aside all the principles which had formed the basis of art until then" (10). Expressionist art manifested itself in the look of German cinema. The sets, architecture, props, and lighting conspire to create the brooding, mystical, satanic landscapes that convey the national nightmare represented in this disturbing body of films. Art teachers can provide students with examples of these films to view or clips from several of them. In addition to drawing students' attention to chiaroscuro and other visual effects, teachers may wish to integrate history into these lessons by looking at the role of the artist in times of social, political, and economic turmoil.

Key films of the era that are now widely available include:

The Golem (1920)	*The Cabinet of Caligari* (1924)
The Threepenny Opera (1920)	*Metropolis* (1926)
Dr. Mabuse the Gambler (1922)	*M* (1931)
Nosferatu (1922)	

Among the German directors of these films are Fritz Lang, who left Germany and settled in the United States. His German expressionist background merged into U.S. film noir in movies such as *The Big Heat*, *Ministry of Fear*, and *Scarlet Street*.

Art Deco

(HIGH) — If German expressionism says something about the nature of German society after World War I, art deco can certainly be read as a reflection of the United States at the same time. Howard Mandelbaum and Eric Myers write that "art deco was closely allied to the fantasies of wealth and elegance prevalent in America between the wars" (1985, 1). The term "encompasses everything from the ornate zigzags of the movement's infancy in the 20s, through the stripped down, streamlined geometric form of 30s Moderne" (1). Hollywood's use of art deco can be seen in various ways in films of the period, and students can look at the overall effect or the specific designs of art directors such as Cedric Gibbons and Van Nest Polglase. Areas to look for include everything from the studio logo at the start of the film to furnishings, sets, and lighting. The worlds created in these films are opulent and lush. Their fantasies reverse the nightmare of expressionism. The action occurs in grand hotels, enormous ballrooms, expensive nightclubs, lavish penthouses, and ocean liners. They fuse technology and the good life. By creating such images, Hollywood reinforced and promoted their presence in U.S. architecture and styles of the times. Perhaps the most obvious example is the movie palaces where the products of the "dream factory" were shown. Major buildings in New York City also emerged as part of the deco movement. Advertising, graphic art, and design also showed the strong influence of art deco.

Teachers looking for brief film clips to present the period might want to look at the extravagant sets and geometric choreography of Busby Berkeley (*Footlight Parade, Gold Diggers of 33*) or the elaborate sets and dance numbers in Fred Astaire and Ginger Rogers movies (*Gay Divorcée, Top Hat*).

Key films of the period include:

Trouble in Paradise (1932)
Footlight Parade (1933)
Gold Diggers of 33 (1933)
The Gay Divorcée (1934)

Top Hat (1935)
Swing Time (1936)
Shall We Dance (1937)

Cinematography, Art Direction, Costumes, and Effects

(ELEM/MID/HIGH) — Costumes, sets, photography, lighting, and visual effects all contribute to the look of a film. Sometimes the effects bring to life something beyond our imagination. Sometimes the sets and costumes lavishly and perhaps accurately create a bygone era. Gotham City comes to life as a brooding presence in *Batman* (1989) largely due to the art direction. Comic-book style and color were skillfully recreated in 1990's *Dick Tracy*. The battle sequence set on the beach in *Glory* (1989) shows the power of cinematography to evoke emotion and paint a portrait of epic grandeur. By selecting examples from films that have won awards in these areas, teachers can draw students' attention to the role of these elements in creating the overall look of the film. This process can be facilitated if the sound is turned off when students look at the clips. Older students can analyze these compositions in depth, and younger students can be asked to describe the mood and feeling the images create. In the case of *Batman*, they should have strong reactions to Gotham City.

Partial Lists of Academy Award Winners

Cinematography

Dances with Wolves (1990)
Glory (1989)
The Last Emperor (1987)
The Mission (1986)
Out of Africa (1985)
The Killing Fields (1984)
Fanny and Alexander (1983)
Gandhi (1982)
Reds (1981)
Tess (1980)

Apocalypse Now (1979)
Days of Heaven (1978)
Close Encounters of the Third Kind (1977)
Bound for Glory (1976)
Barry Lyndon (1975)
The Towering Inferno (1974)
Cries and Whispers (1973)
Cabaret (1972)
Fiddler on the Roof (1971)
Ryan's Daughter (1970)
Butch Cassidy and the Sundance Kid (1969)

Cinematography *(continued)*

Romeo and Juliet (1968)
Bonnie and Clyde (1967)
Who's Afraid of Virginia Woolf? (1966, black-and-white)

Art Direction/Set Decoration

Dick Tracy (1990)
Batman (1989)
The Last Emperor (1987)
Room with a View (1986)
Out of Africa (1985)
Amadeus (1984)
Fanny and Alexander (1983)
Gandhi (1982)
Raiders of the Lost Ark (1981)
Tess (1980)
All That Jazz (1979)
Heaven Can Wait (1978)
Star Wars (1977)
All the President's Men (1976)

Man for All Seasons (1966, color)
Ship of Fools (1965, black-and-white)
Dr. Zhivago (1965, color)

Barry Lyndon (1975)
The Godfather II (1974)
The Sting (1973)
Cabaret (1972)
Nicholas and Alexandra (1971)
Patton (1970)
Hello, Dolly! (1969)
Oliver (1968)
Camelot (1967)
Who's Afraid of Virginia Woolf? (1966, black-and-white)
Fantastic Voyage (1966, color)
Ship of Fools (1965, black-and-white)
Dr. Zhivago (1965, color)

Artists on Film

Biographical accounts of Van Gogh, Michelangelo, and other artists have been turned into major motion pictures (see page 214). In addition, several films look at artistic temperament, the artistic process, and the artistic personality. Brief clips from these films can be used to help students understand the creative process and the personalities behind the paintings.

Rembrandt (1936)
Moulin Rouge (1952, Toulouse-Lautrec)
Lust for Life (1956, van Gogh)
The Horses Mouth (1958)
The Naked Maja (1959, Goya)

The Agony and the Ecstasy (1965, Michelangelo)
El Greco (1966)
Hannah and Her Sisters (1986)
The Wolf at the Door (1987, Gaugin)
New York Stories (1988)

Film as art: *Lust for Life* brought Van Gogh to life and won an Oscar for Anthony Quinn's portrayal of Paul Gaugin. (Photograph used with permission. Copyright © 1956 Turner Entertainment Co. All Rights Reserved.)

REELING IN THE YEARS:
History and Film

The emergence of the VCR during the 1980s made available to teachers an enormous amount of previously hard to get motion pictures. Not only did the lucrative home market for video free up these movies, but also the new technology made using motion pictures in the classroom considerably easier. The fast-forward, rewind, scan, and freeze frame mechanisms permit techers to locate specific scenes, which was difficult and time-consuming with a 16mm film projector. The declining price of videotapes continues to make many Hollywood movies affordable for schools and offers the possibility that school library media centers can develop significant collections of important motion pictures. Because of their library science background and their formal training with "educational media," media specialists are likely to bypass many films with applications in history/social studies in favor of film versions of great novels or traditional documentaries. This problem occurs because after a century of filmmaking, we have yet to raise a generation of public school educators who comprehend the ways that entertainment films can be integrated into history and social studies. Writing in *American History/American Film*, Arthur Schlesinger notes this problem: "Social and intellectual historians draw freely on fiction, drama, painting, hardly ever on movies. Yet the very nature of film as a supremely popular art form guarantees that it is the carrier of deep enigmatic truth" (1979, ix).

Schlesinger argues that, when properly studied, motion pictures provide significant clues about the inner and outer natures of the society that both produced and consumed the movies. A proper reading of movies as more than mere entertainment "offers the social and intellectual historian significant clues to the tastes, apprehensions, myths, inner vibrations of the age" (x).

This notion is hardly a new one. Writing in *From Caligari to Hitler* in 1947, Siegfried Kracauer argued that "the films of a nation reflect its mentality in a more direct way than any other artistic media" (1947, 5). Kracauer believed that, because movies were made collectively and consumed by the masses, they represented a form of social barometer that could reveal "the psychological patterns of a people at a particular time" (5). In his study of the depression through film, Andrew Bergman took a similar approach. "Every movie is a cultural artifact — deadly as the phrase may sound, associated with pottery shards, stone utensils, and so on — and as such reflects the values, fears, myths and assumptions of the culture that produces it" (1971, xii).

There is a strong and growing body of literature to help history and social studies teachers integrate this concept into their classes. These materials present students with the opportunity to analyze movies as historical evidence in the same way that we expect them to be able to interpret a written document or a speech from another age. In addition to the fact that movies can be utilized this way, there are other reasons for wanting to work with them in history. The first of these is the simple fact that for many of our students, their perceptions of the past come from the pictures they have seen. Right or wrong, Hollywood has a clear impact. If we ignore that, we deprive ourselves of a potentially powerful instructional ally and allow Hollywood to dominate the way our students think about historical personalities, characters, events, and places. If a movie does a poor job of re-creating the past, we can expose its anachronisms and mistakes and thereby provide our students with research activities and analytical skills. If the film does a good job of capturing the past, we can use it to gain and maintain the attention of our students and to bring the past to life in a way that a textbook cannot.

> Pictures as history are exceptionally effective because it is difficult to miss messages carried in a motion picture as it explains a historical period or event — the historical message, the background, the setting, language and incidental details.... The aesthetic power of a motion picture, historically correct or incorrect, is difficult to resist" (Browne 1983, ix).

Kracauer's belief that films can be read as reflections of the society that makes them offers teachers the opportunity to teach students to read documents that they are predisposed to be interested in. The cold war suddenly becomes much more engaging if it is studied through movies such as *On the Beach* or *Invasion of the Body Snatchers*. But how do we go about teaching students to "read" films as historical evidence, and what are the movies evidence of?

Historical Authenticity

(**MID/HIGH**) — The real process here is to develop students' ability to analyze and read films for historical accuracy. By comparing a movie version with historical accounts, students develop analytical skills. Areas in which they can concentrate include the chronology of events; the depiction of historical figures (see page 229 for a listing of historical figures and films in which they are depicted); the visual validity of the sets, environment, and costumes; and the accuracy of the language. The language provides an interesting and often amusing approach because so often it reflects the vocabulary and slang of the audience rather than reflecting the period in which it was set. When the soothsayer warns Julius Caesar to "beware the Ides of March," is it unlikely, for example, that Caesar's response was, "One day's as good as another"? In *Becket*, which is set in the twelfth century, the bishop of London refers to King Henry II as an "adolescent," despite the fact that the term was not coined until the twentieth century.

Bonnie and Clyde (1967) is a useful film to consider from the perspective of historical evidence. Certainly the real Clyde Barrow and Bonnie Parker looked nothing like the glamorous screen versions played by Warren Beatty and Faye Dunaway. Although the physical resemblance may not be accurate, the circumstances under which the characters died and the impact of the depression on average Americans are much more authentic. Several scenes in the film can be usefully compared to photographs from the Dust Bowl era. The Farm Security Administration (FSA) photographs in *In This Proud Land* (Stryker and Wood 1973) are particularly suitable. Given the role the still camera plays in *Bonnie and Clyde*, the thematic link is also important.

Cultural Values

(HIGH)—Some of the distortion and glamorization in *Bonnie and Clyde* can be understood if we realize that films must appeal to an audience. The function of film is not to provide a historically accurate record, but to create an entertaining vehicle that will attract audiences and make money. The nature of this attraction, however, actually provides historians with a second approach to movies as historical evidence. This approach argues, as did Kracauer, that films reflect the views and values of those who pay to see them. In the case of *Bonnie and Clyde*, director Arthur Penn made this perfectly clear when he said, "We wanted to make a modern film whose action takes place in the past" (Hillier 1973, 11). Penn was also interested in the role of myth in U.S. history. He said when Bonnie and Clyde were killed, they were regarded as folk heroes by many people. Interestingly enough, the youthful audience of the 1960s found something appealing about the 1930s gangsters—the film was a commercial success. A fashion line based on the period developed, and Faye Dunaway appeared on the January 12, 1968, cover of *Life* in an article on film and fashion. English singer Georgie Fame had a hit record with "The Ballad of Bonnie and Clyde," which featured the sound of machine guns echoing the bloody conclusion of the film.

Bonnie and Clyde can, therefore, be seen as an interesting case study of film as historical evidence. Its violence and hipness mirror something of the generation gap of the 1960s and Americans' reaction to the Vietnam War and President Kennedy's assassination. A year after the film was released, the Tet offensive and the assassinations of Robert Kennedy and Martin Luther King, Jr., provided further evidence of the violent nature of U.S. society.

Two other films by Arthur Penn are worth noting. *The Left-Handed Gun* (1958) is an interesting story of Billy the Kid that examines another U.S. myth but also be read as an extension of 1950s juvenile delinquency. In this version, Billy is a kind of crazy mixed-up kid in the mold of James Dean's *Rebel without a Cause*. Another film, *Little Big Man* (1970), was an Indian/cavalry story, but Penn saw it as much more than that. The movie, he said, addressed "what was really the fate of the Red Indians at the time of Custer. Obviously the analogy with the Negroes is great" (Hillier 1973, 11).

Primary and Secondary Evidence

(MID/HIGH)—The twentieth century is the only period in history during which the motion picture has been present. The motion picture camera recorded the past as it actually happened, and Hollywood has reinvented the past by continuing to set stories in it. For historians, this means we have an opportunity to compare and contrast a period as it saw itself to the way we have seen it with hindsight. Changes in historical characters, for example, reflect the changing nature of society. Billy the Kid and General George Custer have undergone major transformations over the years. Teachers wishing to utilize this approach could select a topic or period from the chart below and study the difference between films made at the time (primary documents) and those made after the event (secondary documents). Magazines, photographs, books, and newspapers can all be used to supplement this approach. Decade by decade suggestions are provided in upcoming sections.

Period	Primary	Secondary
1930s	*The Public Enemy* (1931)	*Grapes of Wrath* (1940)
	Little Caesar (1931)	*Bonnie and Clyde* (1967)
	Wild Boys of the Road (1933)	*They Shoot Horses, Don't They?* (1969)
	Footlight Parade (1933)	*Lady Sings the Blues* (1972)
	Gold Diggers of '33 (1933)	*Sounder* (1972)
	Top Hat (1935)	*The Way We Were* (1973)
	Swing Time (1936)	*Paper Moon* (1973)
	Mr. Smith Goes to Washington (1939)	*Bound for Glory* (1976)
		Honky Tonk Man (1982)
		The Journey of Natty Gann (1985)

Period	Primary	Secondary
1940s	*Meet John Doe* (1941) *Mrs. Miniver* (1942) *Casablanca* (1942) *Double Indemnity* (1944) *The Lost Weekend* (1945) *Spellbound* (1945) *Mildred Pierce* (1945) *The Best Years of Our Lives* (1946) *Gentleman's Agreement* (1947) *The Boy with Green Hair* (1948) *Home of the Brave* (1948) *Mr. Blandings Builds His Dream Home* (1948) *The Snakepit* (1948) *Pinky* (1949) *Knock on Any Door* (1949)	*The Longest Day* (1962) *Red Sky at Morning* (1970) *Summer of '42* (1971) *The Way We Were* (1973) *New York, New York* (1977) *Yanks* (1979) *Raging Bull* (1980) *Swing Shift* (1982)
1950s	*I Married a Communist* (1950) *The Day the Earth Stood Still* (1951) *On the Waterfront* (1954) *Executive Suite* (1954) *The Caine Mutiny* (1954) *The Blackboard Jungle* (1955) *Rebel without a Cause* (1955) *Marty* (1955) *Invasion of the Body Snatchers* (1956) *The Man in the Grey Flannel Suit* (1956) *I Want to Live* (1958) *The Defiant Ones* (1958) *Blue Denim* (1959) *On the Beach* (1959)	*The Last Picture Show* (1971) *Grease* (1978) *September 30, 1955* (1978) *The Atomic Cafe* (1982) *Daniel* (1983) *Desert Bloom* (1986)
1960s	*The Apartment* (1960) *The Ugly American* (1963) *A Hard Day's Night* (1964) *Failsafe* (1964) *Dr. Strangelove* (1964) *The Pawnbroker* (1965) *Who's Afraid of Virginia Woolf?* (1966) *Bonnie and Clyde* (1967) *The Graduate* (1967) *In the Heat of the Night* (1967) *Wild in the Streets* (1968) *Bob and Carol and Ted and Alice* (1969) *Easy Rider* (1969) *The Green Berets* (1969) *The Midnight Cowboy* (1969) *The Wild Bunch* (1969)	*American Graffiti* (1973) *Coming Home* (1978) *Purple Haze* (1982) *The Right Stuff* (1983) *1968* (1968) *1969* (1988) *Mississippi Burning* (1988)

In working with films from this list, teachers should keep in mind that these represent only a handful of films made in any given period. Although many of the films are worth viewing in their entirety, teachers are again encouraged to select brief, 5- to 10-minute clips for analysis and comparison. This guideline to the decades is, by nature, a generalization. The links made between film and society should be taken as suggestions rather than conclusions. Teachers and students should have the opportunity to investigate and test these associations. Remember, these connections are based on the concept that films can be read as a reflection of society. How we read them and what we read into them needs to be balanced against other historical evidence. This evidence would include textbooks, journals, and magazines. In addition, the video revolution continues to make new materials available for teachers. Two useful sources here are *The Video Encyclopedia of the Twentieth Century* and "The March of Time" newsreels.

The 1930s: Overview. The single most dominant factor of the 1930s was the Great Depression. Its presence is visible in many of the films of the era, either overtly or latently. The gangster films clearly reflect the little man's struggle to succeed. A populist series of films by Frank Capra reflect rural, middle-American values versus big-city corruption. *Mr. Smith Goes to Washington* is an excellent example. The Andy Hardy series that started in 1937 is another good example of small-town American values in the tradition of Booth Tarkington's Penrod stories. The musicals, however, remain one of the most important and least understood reflections of the era. *Top Hat* and other musicals with Fred Astaire and Ginger Rogers are pure escapism. They provided a cathartic release and extravagance for movie audiences of the depression. The Warner Brothers musicals are almost social commentaries. The Shanghai Lil sequence at the very end of *Footlight Parade* features images of FDR and is consistent with the studio's support for Roosevelt and the New Deal. *Gold Diggers of '33* offers two outstanding depression era songs, "We're in the Money" and "Forgotten Man." This era is captured particularly well in a compilation documentary called *Brother, Can You Spare a Dime?* (1975). Propaganda films such as Germany's *Triumph of the Will* and the U.S. films *The River* and *The Plough That Broke the Plains* can be used by teachers to show society in the 1930s as well as the growing power of the motion picture.

The 1940s: Overview. World War II is the dominant aspect of films of the early 1940s. The classic example would be *Casablanca*. The war also saw the first sophisticated use of motion pictures as propaganda and training vehicles. Frank Capra's *Why We Fight* series, available on video, gives students an interesting insight into Hollywood's role in the war. As a lighter approach, teachers might want to use cartoons from the era. The *Private Snafu* series is available, as are several of the Daffy Duck cartoons that pushed the war effort for civilians and soldiers. For understanding U.S. society after the war, there is no better film than *The Best Years of Our Lives*, which deals with social adjustment. Maladjustment is reflected in many of the so-called social problem or issue-oriented films. Film noir, which is covered elsewhere in this chapter, also reflects the darker side of the United States after the war. Of interest for war's impact on society are the number of movies dealing with trauma, psychosis, and alienation. *Spellbound* and *The Snakepit* both examined mental illness. *The Lost Weekend* took on alcoholism. *Pinky* and *The Gentleman's Agreement* addressed racism, prejudice, and anti-Semitism. On a much lighter note, *Mr. Blandings Builds His Dream Home* is a comedy about the growth of both the suburbs and advertising in U.S. life.

The 1950s: Overview. The period between 1946 and 1964 in U.S. society was dominated by the Baby Boom. It is not surprising when we look at films from the era that we see evidence of the presence and power of teens. It was the age that gave us James Dean, Gidget, and rock and roll. It also reflected a growing tension between young people and their parents. Juvenile delinquency moved to white, middle-class suburbs (*Rebel without a Cause*). Teens clashed with their teachers in movies such as *The Blackboard Jungle*. Sex was often a cause of conflict, which is evident in *Blue Denim, A Summer Place* (1959), and *Peyton Place* (1957). For adults, the era seems to suggest the continual struggle to get ahead and achieve power, money, and prestige (*The Man in the Grey Flannel Suit, Executive Suite*). The atomic jitters of the cold war era, so well documented in 1982's *The Atomic Cafe*, show up in science fiction fare from the period. *On the Beach*, set in Australia, dealt with the end of the world after an atomic war. It would be an interesting companion piece for 1983's *The Day After*. *The Day the Earth Stood Still* preaches the need for cooperation in a nuclear era. Cooperation is also stressed on a racial level in *The Defiant Ones*, which clearly reflects the United States after the court order to desegregate public schools. The various mutants and monsters of movies such as *Them* and *Tarantula* (1955) are also allegories. They represent either fear of science that has endangered humanity or fear of communism. One other major trend throughout the era was the epic or biblical film. These included *The Robe* (1953), *The Ten Commandments* (1956), and *Ben Hur* (1959). In part they reflect an escape from the present to the safety of the past. Technologically, they also reflect Hollywood's struggle to attract adult audiences away from television through the development of cinemascope and film spectacle.

The 1960s: Overview. The 1960s remain one of the most talked about and least understood eras, often due to the media's emphasis on certain highly visible but not necessarily representative elements of the period. The 1960s were actually more like two decades, with the election of Lyndon Johnson in 1964 marking the beginning of the second stage. Undoubtedly the period between 1960 and 1969 was turbulent and traumatic. The Vietnam War and the civil rights movement were the most visible evidence of this disturbance. *The Ugly American*, made in the year of President Kennedy's assassination, is a useful glimpse at U.S. involvement in Southeast Asia and its consequences. The nuclear nightmare fed by the Cuban missile crisis of 1962 was highly visible in films such as *Failsafe* and *Dr. Strangelove, Or How I Stopped Worrying and Learned to Love the Bomb.*

The youth revolution and the generation gap show up in *Easy Rider, The Graduate*, and *Wild in the Streets.* Changing sexual attitudes in the wake of the birth-control pill are evident in many films of the era, including *Bob and Carol and Ted and Alice, The Midnight Cowboy, The Sterile Cuckoo,* and *Who's Afraid of Virginia Woolf?* These films represented major changes in motion picture censorship and ratings and reflect the liberalization of U.S. society in the 1960s. In part this liberation was manifested in new themes and in part through stronger language. It was also evident in the more graphic depiction of violence, whether in westerns such as *The Wild Bunch* or gangster films such as *Bonnie and Clyde.* The civil rights films are dealt with in more detail later in this chapter. Finally, we have to remember that alongside all of this turmoil, there were many extremely successful family films during this decade. These included *Mary Poppins* (1964), *My Fair Lady* (1964), *The Sound of Music* (1965), *Camelot* (1967), and *Oliver!* (1968).

Exploring the 1970s and 1980s

The 1970s are perhaps still a little too close for us to see clearly. Nonetheless, some patterns seem evident in films of the era, and these patterns might prove useful for examination. The Vietnam War is indirectly addressed in both *Patton* and *M*A*S*H*, which provide strikingly different images of war. George Patton's speech early in the film, as he is dwarfed by the U.S. flag, is well worth looking at. *Catch-22*, made the same year, clearly indicates the visibility of war in the national consciousness. Westerns such as *Little Big Man* (1970) and *Soldier Blue* can also be read as allegories of the Vietnam War. *Boys in the Band* (1970) and *Carnal Knowledge* (1971) are two of many films of the era to provide evidence of changing sexual attitudes. The women's movement changed attitudes about women and, as a result, notions of masculinity also changed. Films such as *Alice Doesn't Live Here Anymore* (1975), *An Unmarried Woman* (1978), *Norma Rae* (1979), and *Kramer vs. Kramer* (1979) all showed women rethinking their roles. *The Great Santini* (1979) and *Kramer vs. Kramer* also reflected the need for men to be nurturing and giving rather than simply providers and punishers. The generation gap that had begun in the 1950s and exploded in the 1960s took on a new element in the 1970s. *The Exorcist* (1973) stunned audiences around the world with its images of a demonically possessed child. The child or teen as a monster out of control seemed a popular motif in the 1970s, as evidenced by *Carrie* (1976), *The Omen* (1976), and *Halloween* (1978). President Gerald Ford called Watergate the "national nightmare," and films of the 1970s might suggest that a nightmare had replaced the American dream. At times this appears allegorically in the so-called disaster films. *The Poseidon Adventure* (1972), the *Airport* series, and *The Towering Inferno* (1974) all imply that we cannot trust leaders or technology. Something is wrong in the system and it threatens us all. One need only look at Jack Lemmon's Oscar-winning performance in *Save the Tiger* (1973) to understand images of corporate corruption and despair. If the White House is tainted (*All the President's Men*, 1976), so, too, are the television stations (*Network*, 1976) and the nuclear power plants (*The China Syndrome*, 1979). It is not surprising that the era that experienced the energy crisis, oil embargoes, acid rain, pollution, and the Love Canal also warned us about our water. "Just when you thought it was safe to go back in the water," *Jaws* (1975) observed, there is something else lurking just below the surface waiting to get you. Is it any wonder so many Americans joined George Lucas in outer space (*Star Wars*, 1977) and wished "may the Force be with you"? Escapism from Watergate and the Vietnam War fed a nostalgia wave evident in *The Way We Were* (1973), *The Summer of '42* (1971), *American*

Grafitti (1973), *Grease* (1978), and others. Those who stayed earthbound contemplated the fall of Saigon and the cost of the war (*Coming Home*, 1978; *The Deer Hunter*, 1978) or disappeared into the disco phenomenon of *Saturday Night Fever* (1979).

Looking back to an era that is still very close, several trends do seem evident in films of the 1980s. The family was still being redefined. *Ordinary People* (1980), *On Golden Pond* (1981), and others explored family relationships. As more and more Americans got older, so-called gray power began to exert an influence on the box office. *The Trip to Bountiful* (1985), *The Whales of August* (1987), *Cocoon* (1985), and *Driving Miss Daisy* (1989) were some of the numerous films that provided rich images of the elderly. The impaired and disabled also attracted new attention in films such as *Children of a Lesser God* (1986), *Rain Man* (1988), and *Born on the 4th of July* (1989). United States foreign policy in the Reagan era, with its stridently anti-Soviet tone, is evident in films such as *Missing in Action* (1984), *Rambo: First Blood, Part II* (1984), *Red Dawn* (1984), and *Rocky IV* (1985). The Vietnam War's continued impact on the U.S. consciousness is seen in several important films, including *Platoon* (1986) and *Born on the 4th of July*. Materialism, corporate takeovers, and the cost of a booming economy show up in *Wall Street* (1987) and *Working Girl* (1988).

Throughout the 1980s, reflecting the drug crisis in U.S. society, the film industry also changed its depiction of alcohol and drug use. The casual consumption evident in *Annie Hall* (1977) and *The Big Chill* (1983) gave way to much more serious depictions of alcoholism and addiction in movies such as *Less Than Zero* (1987) and *Bright Lights, Big City* (1988). In *10* (1979) and *Arthur* (1981) Dudley Moore had played a loveable drunk, but as the truth emerged about Betty Ford, Liza Minnelli, Elizabeth Taylor, John Belushi, and others, Hollywood decided it was time to get *Clean and Sober* (1988). Finally, several interesting films dealt with the Black experience in the United States. These included *The Color Purple* (1985), *Native Son* (1986), *A Soldier's Story* (1984), and *Glory* (1989). Perhaps the most controversial of these films was one made by independent Black producer Spike Lee. *Do the Right Thing* (1989) created enormous debate, and Lee was nominated for an Academy Award for his screenplay. Interestingly enough, the main story of the 1980s, AIDS, was almost totally ignored by the film industry.

Pictures of the Past

> There is a popular belief that wherever history is concerned, Hollywood always gets it wrong. What is overlooked, however, is the astonishing amount of history Hollywood has got right and the immense unacknowledged debt which we owe to the commercial cinema as an illuminator of the story of mankind (Fraser 1988, xi-xii).

(ELEM / MID) — When beginning a new topic about some historical period, character, or event, start by asking the children what they know about the subject. Use the board to compile a list of their entry-level knowledge. Alongside it, build up a source list, indicating where the students may have gotten their ideas and impressions. This source list might include other classes, books, word of mouth, and, of course, the media, including film and television. If they have misconceptions about the topic you are covering, and if these came from the media, take the time to discuss misconceptions. You might want to make a distinction between deliberate lying and dramatic license. The important thing is to use the opportunity to get students to realize that history did not always happen the way Hollywood shows it.

When studying a particular historical period, character, or event, use the resources listed in this chapter to locate a film on that subject. Select a brief 5- to 10-minute clip from the film to bring to life some aspect the class is studying. This might include the lifestyle of people at a given time, making note of their clothes, housing, furniture, occupations, modes of transportation, and speech. If you select a historical figure, have the students talk or write about the way they imagined the person and compare it to the film depiction.

(ELEM / MID) — This exercise can concentrate on one character from a single film or you might want to select several characters from several different films. The objective is to develop students' visual literacy and critical thinking skills by having them note differences and similarities between primary documents of historical figures and the secondary documents represented by Hollywood's depiction of these figures.

The primary documents can include statues, paintings, and photographs of famous people. They must all have been made at the time the individual lived. Advanced classes or groups might investigate the authenticity of these documents. Would a painter or photographer, for example, flatter a patron or client and leave out some physical defect or imperfection? The following list gives some examples for this exercise.

- Bonnie and Clyde (photographs compared to film *Bonnie and Clyde*, 1967)

- Cleopatra (statue, bust, etc., compared to movie *Cleopatra*, 1963)

- Julius Caesar (statue or coin compared to movie *Julius Caesar*, 1953)

- Michelangelo (statues, self-portraits compared to movie *The Agony and the Ecstasy*, 1965)

- Henry VIII (portraits by Hans Holbein compared to films such as *Man for All Seasons*, 1966, and *Anne of a Thousand Days*, 1969)

- Saint Thomas More (portrait by Hans Holbein compared to *Man for All Seasons*)

- Charles I (portraits by Anthony Van Dyck compared to movie *Cromwell*, 1970)

- Napoleon (portraits by Jacques Louis David compared to films such as *Desiree*, 1954, and *Waterloo*, 1971)

- Franklin Roosevelt (photographs compared to the film *Sunrise at Compobello*, 1960)

The exercise can concentrate simply on physical features, with students discussing similarities and differences between the actors and the people they portray. Teachers might also focus attention on clothes, jewelry, furnishings, and other elements present in the primary documents. The primary documents can be located in most encyclopedias and in various art histories. Students can be given the task of tracking the pictures down as research. Postcards found at various major museums traditionally feature important historical portraits, and these can be laminated and labeled to build up a pictorial file of important historical characters. The secondary sources include the films themselves and photographs from the films that are published in various film guides and journals. Motion picture stills are also available from several major dealers, and these can be collected and filed in the media center. Some sources are listed at the end of this chapter (see posters, stills, and press kits).

Fashions and Film

Costumes are particularly important in creating a sense of the period. Sometimes meticulous research is done to re-create the time. Other films are full of historical inaccuracies in terms of the look they assign to a period. Look at the list of films that have won Academy Awards for Costuming (below) and you will get some sense of how often the award has gone to a historical or period film. Working with some of the following examples, help students understand the concept of historical accuracy in the way a film looks. Teachers can also point out the fact that films have often influenced fashion and set trends.

Writing in *Hollywood and History: Costume Design and Film*, Edward Maeder noted: "When we try to re-create historical costumes, a problem arises. Our vision is so influenced by contemporary style that we cannot be objective, and the result is always interpretation" (1987, 9). Maeder's comments are made in what served as the catalog for a major exhibit mounted by the Los Angeles County Museum of Art. Below is a list of several historical films, some with the catalog's comments on the costumes featured in that film.

- *Cleopatra* (1963). Elizabeth Taylor has 65 costume changes. "It evoked the past while incorporating the stylistic influences of the day."

- *The Egyptian* (1954). Two years of research on the costumes.

- *Gone with the Wind* (1939). Vivien Leigh's hats were not in style during the Civil War and actually reflect 1930s fashion. During the 1860s, women's dresses would have been cut to conform to the corset. In this film they are cut to the bosom, also reflecting 1930s fashion.

- *The Great Gatsby* (1974). "The costumes on both the men and women appear to be historically correct."

- *Romeo and Juliet* (1968). "The costumes are probably the most accurate ever produced for a film of this period."

- *Spartacus* (1960). Kirk Douglas appears as a Roman slave, sporting a very contemporary 1960 hairstyle.

- *The Three Musketeers* (1974). "A triumph of historical accuracy."

- *The Virgin Queen* (1955). This story of Elizabeth I is described as "a stand-out for its historical accuracy." It "broke new ground in Hollywood make-up and hairstyle."

The following films all influenced contemporary fashion at the time they were shown.

Cleopatra (1963)
Tom Jones (1963)
Dr. Zhivago (1965)

Bonnie and Clyde (1967)
The Great Gatsby (1974)
Saturday Night Fever (1977)

(MID/HIGH) — Advanced level students could be assigned the task of researching fashion and film. Select one of the films listed above or another film that had an impact on fashion, and have students examine old copies of *Life, Look, Ebony, Saturday Evening Post, Esquire*, and so on to find evidence of these trends in advertising or in articles. The cover of *Life* (January 12, 1968), for example, featured a story on *Bonnie and Clyde* fashions.

Partial List of Academy Award Winners for Best Costumes

Cyrano de Bergerac (1990)
Henry V (1989)
The Last Emperor (1987)
Room with a View (1986)
Ran (1985)
Amadeus (1984)
Fanny and Alexander (1983)
Gandhi (1982)
Chariots of Fire (1981)
Tess (1980)
All That Jazz (1979)
Death on the Nile (1978)

Star Wars (1977)
Fellini's Casanova (1976)
Barry Lyndon (1975)
The Great Gatsby (1974)
The Sting (1973)
Travels with My Aunt (1972)
Nicholas and Alexandra (1971)
Cromwell (1970)
Anne of a Thousand Days (1969)
Romeo and Juliet (1968)
Camelot (1967)

What's Wrong with This Picture?

(ELEM/MID/HIGH) — Have you ever seen a film in which something struck you as being completely out of place? Sometimes this can be a problem with continuity. In *Camelot*, for example, a montage sequence shows King Pelinore, even though he has not yet arrived in Camelot at this point of the story. In *Jagged Edge*, Glenn Close appears in one courtroom sequence in which she inexplicably goes through several changes of clothes. In *Presumed Innocent*, Harrison Ford is interviewed on the courthouse steps by a reporter with no tape in the recorder. In *Die Hard 2*, Bruce Willis makes a call from a Pacific Bell phone, despite the fact that he's in Washington, D.C. In *Born on the 4th of July*, Tom Cruise is shown in a hospital in 1968 while the soundtrack features Don McLean's "American Pie," which was not released until 1971. These are all minor problems with continuity editing or props, but they can be useful and intriguing examples that can encourage students to be more alert and become more visually literate. Sometimes the problems deal with historical accuracy. When a television miniseries about Napoleon showed a character with a cigarette lighter, viewers called to ask how that was possible. Apparently a rudimentary form of lighter was developed around this time. The incident demonstrated that audiences will note small things that seem obviously out of place. It also demonstrated that if historical accuracy is used, our knowledge of even small things can be improved. One scene in *Gone with the Wind* shows lightbulbs in street lamps, despite the fact that they were not in use at the time. Ask students if something they have seen in movies about the past has ever seemed to be impossible, untrue, or inaccurate. If they have few ideas, you might want to offer one or two examples.

- Jousting sequences in medieval films: Do we ever see the knights lifted onto their horses? Isn't the armor too heavy for them to climb back up when they fall off? Why is this ignored?

- Cleopatra's entry into Rome in the 1963 film *Cleopatra* is incredible for its sheer excess. Who are all these people? Where did they come from? How far is Rome from Egypt? Consider the logistics of moving all of these people, animals, and equipment this distance.

In *God Bless You, Buffalo Bill* (1983), Wayne William Sarf provides intricate detail of historical inaccuracies and anachronisms in westerns. These include the use of cavalry costumes and flags that either were never used or were used in a different era than the one being depicted. Sarf draws particular attention to the number of westerns featuring the Colt .45 Peacemaker, even though the gun had not been available during the period in which the films are set. Mistakes with weapons are common in westerns because the producers either had not done their research or because the drama would have been undermined if characters had to constantly reload their guns.

(MID/HIGH) — Collect a series of images of the American West, using photographs from the period and paintings by Charles Russell and Frederic Remington, and have students compare these to the images from movies. The movie images can come from brief film clips or from movie books or stills. Develop a list for students to work on including such things as clothes, hairstyles, towns, homes, furnishings, tools, and so on. Are there any groups of people that seem to be overrepresented or underrepresented? Remember that in all media analysis, it is important to draw the attention of students to what is left out of the frame as well as to what is put into it. (*Premiere* magazine regularly features a section called "The Eyes Have It" that notes mistakes in continuity and accuracy.)

Mirrors, Windows, and Frames

(HIGH) — *From Caligari to Hitler* popularized the notion that movies were somehow mirrors that reflected society. Although the mirror metaphor raises interesting possibilities for historians, it is often forgotten that mirrors can conceal as well as reveal, can reverse reality, and can even distort the image they reflect. If movies supposedly reflect the society that creates them, we have to be very careful in determining just how that reflection occurs. Two useful examples serve to demonstrate the latent nature of this reflection.

The first example is juvenile delinquency. When it comes to the movies and juvenile delinquency, most people think immediately of the 1950s and films such as *The Wild One* and *Rebel without a Cause*. Actually, juvenile crime was very evident in movies of the 1930s. *Dead End* and *Crime School* are two examples. In 1938, Warner Brothers made *Angels with Dirty Faces*. The following year, with the outbreak of war in Europe, the studio made *Angels Wash Their Faces*. This was an attempt to create a patriotic, positive image of U.S. life. This mood created an artificial image of U.S. life that actually concealed the growing problem of juvenile delinquency. From 1939 to 1945, while juvenile delinquency increased in the United States, images of it in movies declined. As historical evidence, then, the movies do not accurately reflect this problem in U.S. society. What they do reflect is the desire to create a very positive view of U.S. life. Movies such as *Yankee Doodle Dandy* (1942), although set in another age, are clearly part of the U.S. war effort.

The second example is the Vietnam War. With the rare exception of *The Green Berets* (1968), the Vietnam War was largely invisible in U.S. movies of the time despite the fact that it dominated society and filled the nation's newspapers and television screens. To find reflections and references to Vietnam, we need to look beyond the manifest meaning and investigate the latent presence of the war in movies of the time. Westerns made during this time can often be read as allegories of Vietnam. *The Wild Bunch* (1969) certainly reflects the increasingly violent nature of a country bogged down in Vietnam and the Kennedy and King assassinations. *Little Big Man* (1970) depicted the Washita River massacre of 1868, and *Soldier Blue* (1970) dealt with the Sand Creek massacre of 1864. In both cases, the Indians can be interpreted as Vietnamese and the cavalry as less than virtuous U.S. soldiers. The controversial court martial of Lt. William Calley, Jr., for the My Lai massacre in South Vietnam provides a backdrop against which these films can be analyzed. In *The Western*, Phil Hardy makes the link very specific, calling *Soldier Blue* "a displaced reaction to the revelations of American atrocities in Vietnam" (1983, 372).

Civil Rights in Cinema and Society: A Case Study

(HIGH)—The civil rights movement and racial attitudes in general provide a rich and rewarding area for students to investigate. Using motion pictures as historical evidence, students can be exposed to films from *Birth of a Nation* (1915) to *Do the Right Thing* (1989) and *Jungle Fever* (1991) and asked to analyze the content of the films in terms of developments in U.S. society at the time. Although the examples given in this case study deal mainly with images of Blacks in U.S. film, it must be noted that changes in the depiction of one minority often bring changes in the depiction of another. There are certainly parallels between the improved image of Blacks in U.S. films and improved images of Native Americans. The following timeline provides significant dates for developments in civil rights and cinema and should be used as a reference when dealing with this topic.

Civil Rights, Cinema, and Society: Timeline

1863   13th Amendment abolishes slavery.

1868   14th Amendment makes former slaves citizens.

1896   *Plessy* v. *Ferguson* decision by Supreme Court upholds the concept of "separate but equal." Precedent is used to justify segregation.

1909   National Association for the Advancement of Colored People (NAACP) formed.

1915   *Birth of a Nation* made. Remains highly controversial because of its depictions of Blacks and the Ku Klux Klan.

1927   Al Jolson appears in blackface in *The Jazz Singer*.

1930s   Major images of Blacks include the song-and-dance man Bill Robinson (*The Little Colonel, The Littlest Rebel*) and the comic Stepin Fetchit.

1934   *Imitation of Life*. Mulatto stereotype that depicts a Black girl's desire to "pass" as White.

1939   *Gone with the Wind*. Hattie McDaniel wins Academy Award for Best Supporting Actress for her stereotypical role of Mammy.

Daughters of the American Revolution (DAR) bans Black singer Marian Anderson from singing at Washington, D.C.'s Constitution Hall. Eleanor Roosevelt invites Anderson to sing at the Lincoln Memorial and resigns from the DAR.

1940s	Two-and-a-half million southern Blacks move north. Blacks serve in World War II, usually in segregated units.
1947	The film *The Gentleman's Agreement* deals with anti-Semitism.
1948	Paramount Case ends with a legal ruling forcing separation of film distribution from film production, allowing independent film producers to find theaters to show their films.
	Stanley Kramer makes *Home of the Brave*, which openly addresses Blacks' service in the war and the prejudice they faced.
	By an Executive Order, President Harry Truman desegregates the military.
1949	*Pinky* and *Intruder in the Dust*, two of the new "Black problem" films that give a new visibility to the issue of racial prejudice, are released.
1950	*No Way Out*, starring Sidney Poitier, is a breakthrough film because Poitier plays a doctor and middle-class Black life is represented.
	Delmar Daves makes the western *Broken Arrow*. The broken arrow of the title is an Indian symbol of peace. Despite the fact that Cochise is played by a White (Jeff Chandler), the film represented a major improvement on the traditional image of Indians as bloodthirsty savages.
	Ralph Bunche becomes the first Black to win the Nobel Prize for Peace.
1951	Sidney Poitier stars in *Cry, the Beloved Country*, which deals with conditions for Blacks in South Africa.
1954	*Brown* v. *Topeka Board of Education* Supreme Court decision makes segregated schools illegal.
1955	Rosa Parks refuses to sit at the back of the bus in Montgomery, Alabama.
	Bad Day at Black Rock examines small-town prejudice.
1956	*The Searchers*, a John Ford western, continues to look more sympathetically at Indians.
	The King and I is released, a lavish and successful musical with an interesting anti-slavery subplot (note *Uncle Tom's Cabin* sequences).
1957	Civil Rights Act passed, the first such legislation since Reconstruction.
	Miscegenation theme appears in *Island in the Sun*.
1958	Stanley Kramer makes *The Defiant Ones*, with Sidney Poitier and Tony Curtis. The message is that Blacks and Whites must work together. Nominated for best picture, it wins Oscars for cinematography and screenplay.
1960	John F. Kennedy elected president.
	Formation of Student Nonviolent Coordinating Committee.
	Civil Rights Act aimed at helping Blacks register to vote.

1961   Freedom Riders active in attempts to improve conditions for Blacks in southern states.

Raisin in the Sun examines Black life and housing conditions in the North.

James Meredith registers at University of Mississippi supported by troops sent by President Kennedy.

1962   *To Kill a Mockingbird* made into motion picture. Nominated for best picture, it wins Oscars for best actor and best screenplay.

1963   Martin Luther King, Jr., leads march on Washington, D.C. and delivers "I have a dream" speech.

Sidney Poitier becomes first Black to win the best actor Oscar, for his role in the film *Lilies of the Field*.

President Kennedy assassinated; Lyndon Johnson becomes president.

1964   Civil Rights Act passed, outlawing discrimination in public facilities and hiring.

Martin Luther King, Jr., wins the Nobel Prize for Peace.

John Ford makes *Cheyenne Autumn*, dealing with White treatment of Indians.

1965   Black Muslim leader Malcolm X is assassinated.

Voting Rights Act ends literacy tests for voting in some southern states.

Major riots and destruction in Watts (Los Angeles, California). Kerner commission later blames White racism for many conditions in the Watts area.

1966   Black Panther movement formed. A more militant group than the civil disobedience devotees of Dr. King, they asserted "Black power" and "Black is beautiful."

1967   Thurgood Marshall becomes the first Black appointed as a justice of the Supreme Court.

In the Heat of the Night wins best picture Oscar for its story of a Black detective's struggle with racism in the South.

Guess Who's Coming to Dinner nominated for best picture. It wins two Oscars. Directed by Stanley Kramer, it deals with a romance between a White woman and a Black man.

Blacks represent 30 percent of box office receipts in major cities.

1968   Martin Luther King, Jr., assassinated.

Race riots.

Robert F. Kennedy assassinated.

Riots at the Democratic National Convention in Chicago.

Richard Nixon elected president.

Passage of the Civil Rights Act for fair housing.

1969   Gordon Parks becomes first Black to direct a major motion picture for a major studio when he makes *The Learning Tree*.

1970   *Little Big Man* and *Soldier Blue*, both westerns, depict White atrocities against Indians.

1971   The movie *Shaft* develops the image of "superspade."

Melvin Van Peebles makes *Sweet Sweetback's Baadasssss Song*.

1972   Sympathetic treatment of Blacks in *Sounder* and *Lady Sings the Blues*.

1973   Tom Bradley becomes first Black mayor of Los Angeles.

This timeline deals with the major period of civil rights changes and legislation in the United States. It provides some evidence of a relationship between the issues and images in movies and the events taking place in society at the same time. Although some of these relationships can no doubt be dismissed as coincidence, it seems likely that broader patterns do suggest a correlation between social attitudes and the views and values expressed in movies. This concept suggests that history teachers and students could find films to be an interesting area for exploration and analysis as historical evidence, whether dealing with civil rights or any other topic. The 1980s provided useful examples to update this approach in films including *A Soldier's Story* (1984), *The Color Purple* (1985), *Do the Right Thing* (1989), *Glory* (1989), and *Driving Miss Daisy* (1989). Also during this period, the Oscar for best supporting actor was awarded to Louis Gossett, Jr. (*An Officer and a Gentleman*), and to Denzel Washington (*Glory*) and the Oscar for best supporting actress was awarded to Whoopi Goldberg (*Ghost*).

The scenes in the following exercises have been selected to help teachers develop strategies for integrating the film-as-history approach into the curriculum. The film clips can be shown individually or they can be shown in a group. If only one clip is used, teachers should introduce it as an exercise in reading historical documents. Based on their reading and classwork, students would be asked to draw on prior knowledge and analytical skills to name the period in which the film was made and to provide evidence to support their answer. Students could note simple factors such as fashions, furnishings, cars, or vocabulary. In addition, they would be expected to recognize that the themes and ideas expressed in the film belong to a particular period. If two or more clips are used, they should be sufficiently different so that students can be asked to compare and contrast them and place them in chronological order.

Comprehension questions help students to analyze characters and understand their motivations. When students watch the clips, this method provides a context in which they can understand the material. Teachers might focus attention on what happened, whom it happened to, how it happened, and why it happened. This context can be applied to the study of almost any period to help students respond both affectively and cognitively to history.

Cinema and Civil Rights: Additional Case Studies

(MID/HIGH) — *Raisin in the Sun* (1961). This particularly strong and important film makes an interesting companion when compared to *To Kill a Mockingbird*, which was made the following year. The latter film looks at Blacks through the eyes of children and liberal White society. *Raisin in the Sun*, on the other hand, is essentially a Black film in which Whites are only incidental to the plot.

The film is set in Chicago and provides an interesting insight into the extended family. The central characters of the Younger family include Lena, the matriarch; her adult son, Walter Lee; his wife, Ruth; his sister; and Travis, his young son.

Lena's husband has recently died and she is expecting a $10,000 insurance check. For the first time in their lives, the family will have money and be able to realize some of their dreams. It becomes evident, however, that they do not see eye to eye on how to spend the money. Although the family appears in danger of breaking apart, they find unity in their response to the White prejudice they are forced to endure.

The first 10 minutes of the film provide a strong sense of the difficult conditions the family lives in. Have students make a list of these conditions. They include sharing a bathroom with other tenants, no bedroom for Travis, and lack of money.

Walter Lee is a complex and interesting character. He is also prejudiced himself, particularly toward women. He is very unhappy that his sister wants to be a doctor. Walter Lee considers that man's work and tells her to be a nurse. Several times during the early part of the film, Walter Lee argues with his wife, his mother, and his sister. He feels misunderstood and says he lives in the "world's most backward nation of women." Teachers can use this to discuss different levels of prejudice or the status of Black and White women in the United States in the early 1960s.

At one point in the film, Walter Lee, feeling depressed and misunderstood, goes to a bar to drown his sorrows. Fast-forward to this scene and show the sequence when he arrives home drunk. He finds his sister about to go out on a date. She is wearing Nigerian clothes and playing tribal music. Her date is a successful, conservative Black man who does not share her view of her rich ancestry: "Let's face it, baby, your heritage ain't nothin' but some bunch of raggedy spirituals in some grass huts." How does she respond to this claim? Teachers can link this episode to the growth of the concept of Afro-American culture in the 1960s. Phrases such as "Black is beautiful" can be discussed. The musical *Hair* has some interesting songs about Black self-image during this period that could be used to provide further examples of the image of Blacks during the 1960s.

The same sequence provides further evidence of Walter Lee's prejudice. Have students watch for his conversation with his sister's date. What prejudices do they detect? "How come all you college boys wear all them faggoty-looking white shoes?" Walter Lee says. He does not hold education in high esteem, saying all it teaches is "how to read books and talk proper and wear faggoty white shoes." Why would Walter Lee be so negative about education and the way George dresses?

Later in the film, the family decides to use the insurance money to buy a new home. Scan to the scene when a White man knocks at their door. He is balding and seems rather meek and timid. He is a representative of the improvement association for the housing subdivision they are moving to. At first, Walter Lee thinks the man is a form of welcoming committee. His sister is more suspicious and cynical. The White man tells them: "We feel that most of the trouble in this world exists because people don't sit down and talk to each other. We don't try hard enough in this world to understand the other guy's point of view.... You've got to admit that a man, right or wrong, has the right to have the sort of neighborhood he lives in a certain kind of way." Although he assures them that "race prejudice simply doesn't enter into it," he points out that the White community of the subdivision does not want them to move in, saying, "Negro families are happier when they live in their own communities." Use this scene to discuss the notions of prejudice and bigotry. Have the students discuss what they think the Younger family should do in the face of this opposition. Remind students of the passage of the Fair Housing Act in the late 1960s. On November 9, 1953, *Life* magazine ran an article on the riots in Chicago at the Trumbull Park housing project that resulted when Blacks moved into a White neighborhood. Refer to this story as a background to this incident in the film.

Do the Right Thing (1989) also features characters who think races and nationalities would be better off if they stuck to their own kind. One or two scenes from that film could be used for comparison. Students might also be directed to recent events that illustrate this problem. In the late 1980s, for example, the city of Yonkers, New York, clashed with the courts over an issue related to racial themes.

In the Heat of the Night (1967). This scene begins shortly after the start of the film. The police officer, Warren Oates, arrives at the railway station at night and finds Sidney Poitier waiting for the train. Start the clip as the policeman says, "On your feet, boy." The main scene centers on the interrogation of Virgil Tibbs (Sidney Poitier) at the police station by the senior officer, Gillespie, played by Rod Steiger. The clothes, the cars, the salary, and the racial attitudes will help students identify the period in which the film is set. Those who are familiar with *Mississippi Burning* (1988) will recognize the depiction of southern law officers. It is important, however, that they note the subtle indications that Gillespie is not completely negative. There are several developments in his response to Tibbs both before and after he discovers that Tibbs is also a police officer. Stop the scene when Gillespie says, "Because I'm not an expert, officer!"

- How does Gillespie react to Virgil's name?

- Virgil corrects his interrogator's speech, replacing *who* with *whom*. What insights does this give us into the two lead characters?

- Why is it important for the audience to hear the train whistle during this sequence, and how does Gillespie respond to it?

- Why does Gillespie think the money that Tibbs has is stolen?

- Why is the phrase "162 dollars and 39 cents a week" repeated several times during the scene?

- What evidence is there that the arresting officer did not follow proper procedure during the arrest?

- Tibbs turns out to be "the number one homicide expert" in his division, and Tibbs's boss wants him to work on Gillespie's case. How does he respond and why?

- Gillespie reluctantly turns to Tibbs for help. Why? How does this mutual need and cooperation reflect the time in which the film was made?

- Compare Tibbs to Poitier's character in *Raisin in the Sun*, made at the start of the decade.

Guideline to Historical Figures on Film

(ELEM)—Elementary school children can be introduced to some of the historical figures they would study by showing brief 5- or 10-minute clips from some of the following films. Remember, textbooks may tell them who people were and what they did, but films can bring these people to life and make them more meaningful and memorable for young children.

U.S. Figures

Bean, Judge Roy	*The Westerner* (1940), *The Life and Times of Judge Roy Bean* (1972)
Bell, Alexander Graham	*The Story of Alexander Graham Bell* (1939)
Billy the Kid	*Billy the Kid* (1941), *The Left-Handed Gun* (1958), *Pat Garrett and Billy the Kid* (1973), *Young Guns* (1988)
Bonnie and Clyde	*Bonnie and Clyde* (1967)
Buffalo Bill	*The Plainsman* (1936), *Buffalo Bill* (1940), *Buffalo Bill and the Indians* (1976)
Calamity Jane	*The Plainsman* (1936), *Calamity Jane* (1953)
Capone, Al	*Al Capone* (1959), *The Untouchables* (1987)
Cassidy, Butch	*Butch Cassidy and the Sundance Kid* (1969)
Cochise	*Broken Arrow* (1950)
Crockett, Davy	*Davy Crockett, King of the Wild Frontier* (1955)

U.S. Figures (*continued*)

Custer, Gen. George Armstrong	*They Died with Their Boots On* (1942), *Custer of the West* (1967), *Little Big Man* (1970)
Earp, Wyatt	*My Darling Clementine* (1946), *Gunfight at the O.K. Corral* (1957), *Cheyenne Autumn* (1964)
Edison, Thomas Alva	*Young Tom Edison* (1940), *Edison the Man* (1940)
Flanagan, Father	*Boys Town* (1938)
Geronimo	*Geronimo* (1960)
Hickok, Wild Bill	*The Plainsman* (1936)
Holliday, Doc	*Cheyenne Autumn* (1964), *Doc* (1971)
Jackson, Andrew	*The President's Lady* (1953), *The Buccaneer* (1958)
James, Jesse	*Jesse James* (1939), *The Long Riders* (1980)
Kennedy, John F.	*P.T. 109* (1963), *Missiles of October* (1974)
Kennedy, Robert F.	*Missiles of October* (1974)
King, Martin Luther, Jr.	*King: A Filmed Record* (1970)
Lincoln, Abraham	*The Plainsman* (1936), *Young Mr. Lincoln* (1939), *Abe Lincoln in Illinois* (1940)
Lindbergh, Charles	*Spirit of St. Louis* (1957)
Long, Huey	*All the King's Men* (1949)
MacArthur, Gen. Douglas	*MacArthur* (1977)
Mitchell, Billy	*The Court Martial of Billy Mitchell* (1955)
Nixon, Richard	*All the President's Men* (1976)
Patton, Gen. George	*Patton* (1970)
Reed, John	*Reds* (1981)
Roosevelt, Franklin D.	*Sunrise at Campobello* (1960), *Brother, Can You Spare a Dime?* (1975)
Sherman, Gen. William	*How the West Was Won* (1963)
Sitting Bull	*Sitting Bull* (1954), *Custer of the West* (1967)
Truman, Harry	*Give 'Em Hell, Harry* (1975)
Twain, Mark	*The Adventures of Mark Twain* (1944)
Wilson, Woodrow	*Wilson* (1944)
Young, Brigham	*Brigham Young, Frontiersman* (1940)

Foreign Figures

Alexander the Great	*Alexander the Great* (1956)
Antoinette, Marie	*Marie Antoinette* (1938, 1955)
Antony, Mark	*Julius Caesar* (1953), *Cleopatra* (1963)
Arthur, King	*Camelot* (1967), *Excalibur* (1981)
Becket, Thomas	*Becket* (1964)
Boleyn, Anne	*Man for All Seasons* (1966), *Anne of a Thousand Days* (1969)
Caesar, Julius	*Julius Caesar* (1953), *Cleopatra* (1963)
Castro, Fidel	*Che* (1969)
Churchill, Winston	*Young Winston* (1972)
Cleopatra	*Cleopatra* (1963)
Cromwell, Oliver	*Cromwell* (1970)
Danton, Georges Jacques	*Danton* (1982)
Elizabeth I, Queen	*The Private Lives of Elizabeth and Essex, Young Bess* (1953), *The Virgin Queen* (1955), *Mary, Queen of Scots* (1971)
Freud, Sigmund	*Freud* (1962), *Seven Percent Solution* (1976)
Gandhi, Mohandas K.	*Gandhi* (1982)
Guevara, Che	*Che* (1969)
Helen of Troy	*Helen of Troy* (1955)
Henry II, King	*Becket* (1964), *The Lion in Winter* (1968)
Henry V, King	*Henry V* (1945, 1989)
Henry VIII, King	*The Private Life of Henry VIII* (1933), *Man for All Seasons* (1966), *Anne of a Thousand Days* (1969), *The Six Wives of Henry VIII* (1973)
Hitler, Adolf	*Mein Kampf* (1961)
Ivan IV, Czar	*Ivan the Terrible* (1943)
Joan of Arc	*Joan of Arc* (1948)
Khan, Genghis	*Genghis Khan* (1965)
Khrushchev, Nikita	*Missiles of October* (1974)
Lawrence, Thomas Edward	*Lawrence of Arabia* (1962)
Livingstone, David	*Stanley and Livingstone* (1939)
Luther, Martin	*Luther* (1974)

Foreign Figures *(continued)*

Marat, Jean-Paul	*Danton* (1982)
Mary, Queen of Scots	*Mary, Queen of Scots* (1971)
Michelangelo	*The Agony and the Ecstasy* (1965)
More, Thomas	*Man for All Seasons* (1966)
Mozart, Wolfgang Amadeus	*Amadeus* (1984)
Napoleon	*Desire* (1954), *Waterloo* (1971)
Nelson, Lord Horatio	*The Nelson Affair* (1973)
Nicholas II, Czar	*Nicholas and Alexandra* (1971)
Pasteur, Louis	*Story of Louis Pasteur* (1936)
Polo, Marco	*Adventures of Marco Polo* (1938)
Raleigh, Sir Walter	*The Virgin Queen* (1955)
Richard III, King	*Richard III* (1956)
Richard the Lionhearted, King	*The Crusades* (1935), *King Richard and the Crusaders* (1954)
Robespierre, Maximilien	*Danton* (1982)
Robin Hood	*The Adventures of Robin Hood* (1938), *Robin and Marian* (1976), *Robin Hood, Prince of Thieves* (1991)
Tchaikovsky, Peter	*The Music Lovers* (1971)
Trotsky, Leon	*The Assassination of Trotsky* (1972)
van Gogh, Vincent	*Lust for Life* (1956)
Yi, Pu	*The Last Emperor* (1987)
Zapata, Emiliano	*Viva Zapata* (1952)

FILM AND SOCIAL STUDIES

In March 1990, the Academy Award ceremonies were watched by a worldwide audience of 1 billion people. Symbolizing the international nature of the film industry, awards were announced in Buenos Aires, London, Moscow, and Sydney. Karl Malden, the president of the Academy of Motion Picture Arts and Sciences, took the opportunity to comment on the impact of movies on society.

> This is one of those nights when one world is more than a philosophical dream; it's a reality.... So here we are poised on the edge of the final decade of the twentieth century; dazzled by the swift changes that are taking place all over the world. And films have leapt across national boundaries, overcome disparate languages, brushed aside political differences and brought people closer together by depicting our common shared humanity.

Although Malden's enthusiasm for the film industry may be biased, his claims draw our attention to the relationship among movies, society, and social studies. Through the production and projection of images, the film industry influences our perceptions and attitudes.

Image and Influence

Almost from its inception, the motion picture industry has attracted attention and controversy because of the impact it potentially has on people. In the early 1930s, the Payne Fund Studies investigated the influence that movies had on children and youth. The researchers were particularly interested in the values and content of the movies and how they might influence attitudes and behavior in the areas of sex, violence, and crime. Both German and U.S. filmmakers during World War II used motion pictures to influence the attitudes and beliefs of audiences. Film and other mass media were particularly successful in Germany in creating and promoting negative attitudes about Jews, which helped make the Holocaust possible. In the United States, the House Committee on Un-American Activities (HCUA) investigated the film industry, looking for communist influence both behind the scenes and on the screen. In the 1950s, movies such as *The Wild One* and *The Blackboard Jungle* were accused of inciting juvenile delinquency. Similar charges were made about *The Warriors* in the late 1970s. In 1991 *Boyz 'n' the Hood* and *New Jack City* were both blamed for violence following screenings. After the attempted assassination of President Reagan, claims were made that the assailant had been influenced by the motion picture *Taxi Driver*. When Clark Gable wore no undershirt in *It Happened One Night* (1934), undershirt sales in the United States declined. *American Gigolo* (1980) was said to have contributed to the sale of anti-gravity boots. The film *10* (1979) apparently contributed to a renewed interest in Maurice Ravel's *Bolero*.

Often, however, we have no idea what impact movies have on impressionable young audiences. We do not know whether or how film affects their views, values, and perceptions of others. The impact can be very subtle. In *Reel Politics*, Terry Christensen argues that movies have created negative impressions of the political process and actually serve as a form of narcotic by distracting us from issues of the day: "They have disparaged politics in general, presenting it as evil and corrupting.... This image reflects and reinforces popular prejudices but it also helps to entrench alienation and apathy. Movies that reinforce, reassure, or warn us to stay away from politics keep us passive" (1987, 222). Like most media, the movies are capable of creating our ideas and impressions of individuals, institutions, and issues. It is also evident that they do not affect everyone in the same way. How do movies exert an influence on audiences? Communication theory indicates that film and other media messages are likely to have their greatest impact when:

1. The idea is simplified.

2. The idea/image is repeated.

3. The audience has little or no context in which to place the information and no way of judging it.

4. The image is given social sanction by being screened in the family home.

We need to be aware of several things as we consider these points. The messages of movies need to be considered both individually and cumulatively. A negative image of a Native American in one film may have little or no influence. When that image is repeated in hundreds of films and reinforced in other media, however, it is likely that the stereotype will become accepted by many people. If our students have had no contact with the stereotyped group, they are likely to accept media messages as valid. Teachers, librarians, and media specialists can counteract negative messages by giving students opportunities to find out about different groups. The issue of movies and minorities can be an interesting and informative study of social, racial, and occupational stereotyping in the media. Areas studied could include the depiction of women, Blacks, Jews, Hispanics, Asians, the elderly, the handicapped, and homosexuals. Parents also need to be involved in what their children view at home and encouraged to discuss programs with their children. This is particularly important, because it is known that young people often watch a lot of film and television without supervision. The VCR permits them to see images over and over again. Many students rent and watch films containing extreme violence and other scenes that they could not see at the movies, protected as they are by the rating system. Repeated viewing of acts of violence is a potentially harmful process that requires monitoring.

Some of the leading social problems of the last ten years have centered on health issues. AIDS, adolescent pregnancy, and substance addiction have all focused attention on Hollywood and the messages and models it provides for young people. If schools, churches, and parents send one message to students and the film industry contradicts that message, it makes our jobs much harder. Recognizing that the movies and the media in general can influence the attitudes and behavior of our young people is the starting point for integrating these materials into the curriculum. It must also be acknowledged that although some films might be potentially harmful, many other films are potentially helpful.

Today there are a growing number of books and articles about the impact of motion pictures on U.S. society. These sources provide teachers with important insights into the film industry and can be useful tools for planning ways of integrating movies into the social studies curriculum. By studying the social impact of movies, we stop thinking of them as mere entertainment and look instead at the behaviors and attitudes they model. If U.S. society has a problem with violence, for example, is it possible that this is because violence is given social sanction by its prevalence in the cinema? In 1991 a nationally syndicated columnist raised this issue, criticizing Arnold Schwarzenegger's position as chairman of the President's Council on Physical Fitness and Sports: "Does he [Schwarzenegger] see no link between his roles as a gunman and head-basher and the real-life homicide rates that are at record levels in American cities? The actor who now wants to make kids be physically fit worked for a decade to show them how to be morally unfit" (McCarthy 1991, 7A).

Issues and Images: Movies as Myth

In *Movie-Made America*, Robert Sklar argues that "movies have historically been and still remain vital components in the network of cultural communication, and the nature of their content and control helps to shape that character and direction of American culture as a whole" (1975, vi). If we regard movies as myth, the cinema assumes a shamanistic role in society. Joseph Campbell said that "myth helps to put your mind in touch with the experience of being alive" (1988, 6). Campbell makes a distinction between the world of the classroom and the world beyond: "What we're learning in our schools is not the wisdom of life. We're learning technologies, we're getting information" (9). Mass media and the movies have assumed the role of electronic storyteller. They convey meaning that often eludes educators who regard them as popular culture and therefore insignificant. Yet for film audiences, particularly young audiences, these movies tend to assume mythic proportions.

In *The Power of Myth*, Campbell says: "There is something magical about films. The person you are looking at is also somewhere else at the same time. That is a condition of the god" (15). Campbell describes myths as having several functions, including mystical, cosmological, and sociological. The last is of interest to social studies teachers, as it is described as supporting and reinforcing a certain social order. A central question is then raised: How do movies support and validate a social order? Can movies be regarded, as Schlesinger says, as a social cement providing a common dream life "to a society divided by ethnic distinctions and economic disparities" (1979, xii)?

If, as Campbell asserts, movies are "making and breaking lives," what areas do they assume importance in and how can we deal with this in social studies? One way is to develop a list of issues and themes that films commonly address. Having defined these areas, we can begin to analyze the ways Hollywood treats these topics and provide students with a broader context in which to view films.

Stereotypes, Conventions, Clichés, and Social Attitudes

A stereotype is a hackneyed or unoriginal representation of a group. The stereotype attributes characteristics and qualities belonging to some members of a group to *all* members of that group. These can include physical characteristics and appearances as well as the views, values, beliefs, and behavior of the group. Stereotypes are exaggerations and generalizations. Although no harm may be intended by those who repeat the stereotype, the impact can still be detrimental.

The film industry does not invent stereotypes. It repeats existing stereotypes, but in the process reinforces and perpetuates them. This is potentially harmful because it prevents us from understanding other members of our society and robs them of dignity and self-respect. Perhaps the worst stereotyping was the way the Nazi Ministry of Propaganda depicted Jews in films such as *The Eternal Jew.*

Although it is clear that stereotypes can be damaging, the media still use them because they are immediately recognizable. In a short television program or a motion picture, there is not always enough time to flesh out a character. Using a stereotype permits the creators to present the audience with a familiar character type. Stereotypes are therefore part of the codes and conventions of filmmaking. Attempting to break those codes can often be very controversial.

One such controversy exploded in 1991 following the release of *Thelma and Louise.* The depiction of women in the movies has been the subject of several outstanding books, including Molly Haskell's *From Reverence to Rape* (1973) and M. Rosen's *Popcorn Venus* (1974). More recently, feminists such as Ann Kaplan have focused attention on Hollywood's depiction of women as sex partners, mothers, and workers. Kaplan notes, for example, that although films such as *Sex, Lies and Videotape* and *9½ Weeks* give new honesty to expressions of female sexuality, they continue to do so "within a patriarchal imagry" (1991, 5). Into this arena came *Thelma and Louise,* a buddy movie in which the buddies were women. Screenwriter Callie Khouri said she wanted to see what would happen when women were placed in positions traditionally occupied by men, with control of the car, the gun, and the action. Haskell called the film "a breakthrough … very radical in the way it threatens men." Not all critics, however, were as enthusiastic. John Leo wrote an essay in "The Society" section of *U.S. News and World Report* describing the film as "very disturbing … toxic feminism" that espoused "nihilistic and self destructive values" (1991, 20). He concluded by saying, "This is a quite small hearted, extremely toxic film, about as morally and intellectually screwed up as a Hollywood movie can get" (20). Throughout the summer, the debate about women in the movies continued. *Time* said women's roles "fall into three stereotypes: butch, babe and babysitter" (*Time* 1991, 66) and concluded that "actresses may have better body tone, but most of their roles are dispiriting to anyone who harbors the hope that American movies will some day grow up" (67). The depiction of women on screen should always be considered in terms of their roles in the film industry. As of January 1992, *Premiere* magazine indicated that only 18 percent of top billed actors were female; only 15.5 percent of screenwriters at movie studios were women; on average female directors received an annual salary of $40,000 while men were paid $85,000; and women writers received 63 cents for every dollar earned by male writers (17). If the depiction of a group that constitutes more than half of U.S. society can be so constricted, and so controversial, stereotyping of other groups in the culture provides an important avenue for promoting both critical thinking and critical viewing skills. Several films in recent years have generated controversy because of stereotypes and negative depictions. These include *The Color Purple, Sixteen Candles, Big Trouble in Little China, A Fish Named Wanda,* and *Crazy People.* Make a list of others.

(ELEM / MID / HIGH) — Have students create a list of particular groups that are often seen in the movies and describe each group's characteristics. This can include both their physical appearance as well as the way they act and behave. Give students the following list and have them describe the way each group is depicted in films and provide some specific movie titles to support their assertions.

Australians	jocks
dumb blondes	Native Americans
feminists	nerds
Hispanics	southerners
homosexuals	Teamsters
Italian Americans	teenagers

Some films actively attempt to examine and expose these stereotypes. *The Breakfast Club* centers on a group of high school students who are locked into various cliques. They are prisoners of their perceptions, and in the course of the film they come to understand each other better. Unfortunately, the same movie that asks teenagers to judge each other fairly tends to stereotype their parents. *Pretty in Pink* is another teen film that deals with peer pressures and perceptions. The story concentrates on a working-class girl and a wealthy boy and the misconceptions they have about each other. Brief scenes from each film could be used to help middle school and high school students deal with stereotyping on a level that would be very relevant to them.

Sometimes clichés and conventions also subvert our understanding of individuals, issues, or institutions. Adult movie-goers would recognize the unhappy homosexual who will die by the end of the film, the racist southern politician or policeman, and the alcoholic or drug addict miraculously saved by the "love of a good woman." Neat endings, happy or otherwise, may be good box office but they can prevent us from seriously examining our society and the issues that confront it. Here are a list of issues, institutions and groups that can be studied through film. Consult a TV movie guide for descriptions of the films or look for them in a video store.

Adolescents

In *The Cinema of Adolescence*, David Considine examines the ways the film industry depicted adolescent life from the 1930s to the 1980s. In the process the study looked at the changing images of U.S. parents, schools, and teachers. Issues addressed in the book include adolescent sexuality, adolescent self-image, and juvenile delinquency. The author concludes, "For some adolescents, the film industry's repetitive images and stereotypes offer the opportunity for a pre-packaged identity that subverts the natural emergence of an authentic self. Touching upon such vital issues as sex, family, marriage, schooling and the law, the cinema of adolescence serves as a potentially powerful source of information, providing young people with a vision of society and what they can expect from it" (1985, 276). Because most films deal with adolescents in the family context, the conflicts and problems can be useful in counseling, health education, and social studies. Obviously, these films can also often be linked to English and the study of young adult literature. The following is a list of recommended films.

Bless the Beasts and Children (1971)
Blue Denim (1961)
The Breakfast Club (1985)
Breaking Away (1979)
The Chalk Garden (1964)
Dead Poets Society (1989)
The Effect of Gamma Rays on Man-in-the-Moon Marigolds (1972)
The Great Santini (1979)
Hud (1963)
Jeremy (1973)
Last Summer (1969)
Lord of the Flies (1990)
Member of the Wedding (1953)

Me Natalie (1969)
Mosquito Coast (1986)
My Bodyguard (1980)
Ordinary People (1980)
The Outsiders (1983)
Pretty in Pink (1986)
Rebel without a Cause (1955)
A Separate Peace (1972)
Stand by Me (1986)
The Sterile Cuckoo (1969)
Summer of '42 (1971)
Tell Me That You Love Me, Junie Moon (1970)
Tex (1982)

Alcoholism and Addiction

The treatment of alcoholism and drug addiction in movies and the mass media extends back at least as far as the cult classic *Reefer Madness*, made in the 1930s. Throughout the 1980s, as these social problems attracted more and more attention, Hollywood found itself under pressure to change the way it depicted drug use. Casual and recreational use of drugs can be seen in popular films such as *Annie Hall* (1977) and *The Big Chill* (1983). When it was claimed that such images glamorized and endorsed drug use, films began to change their depiction of drugs. *Less Than Zero* (1987) and *Bright Lights, Big City* (1988), both aimed at the teen market, presented very bleak images of the impact of drugs on young people. The adult market has also been targeted by Michael Keaton's *Clean and Sober* (1988). Teachers wishing to work with the issue of society and drugs, whether in social studies, counseling, or health education, can now locate many of the important films that have dealt with these topics in the last fifty years. These include Academy Award-winning films such as *The Lost Weekend* (1945) and *The Days of Wine and Roses* (1962). Teachers are reminded that such themes can be integrated into English and literature classes. Of particular interest, for example, are Eugene O'Neill's *Long Day's Journey into Night* (1962) and Edward Albee's *Who's Afraid of Virginia Woolf?* (1966). In what way do these films confirm or change social and cinematic stereotypes of the alcoholic or drug addict? How might these stereotypes shape public perception and social policy in this area? The following films are recommended.

Barfly (1987)
The Boost (1988)
The Boy Who Drank Too Much (CBS, 1980)
Bright Lights, Big City (1988)
Clean and Sober (1988)
The Country Girl (1954)
The Days of Wine and Roses (1962)
The Death of Richie (1977)
Desert Bloom (1986)
Easy Rider (1969)
A Hatful of Rain (1957)
A Hero Ain't Nothin' but a Sandwich (1978)

Ironweed (1987)
Lady Sings the Blues (1972)
Less Than Zero (1987)
Long Day's Journey into Night (1962)
The Lost Weekend (1945)
The Man with the Golden Arm (1955)
Panic in Needle Park (1971)
Sarah T.: Portrait of a Teenage Alcoholic
    (NBC, 1971)
Sid and Nancy (1988)
Wired (1989)

Blacks

Writing in *From Sambo to Superspade: The Black Experience in Motion Pictures*, Daniel Leab says the "human dimension has been lacking in the movie treatment of the black ever since the 1890s, when the first motion pictures were produced" (1975, 5). The racial stereotypes that Hollywood has perpetuated were also documented by R. Maynard (1972), who noted prejudicial depictions of Africans, South Sea Islanders, and American Indians. In 1985, *The Color Purple* generated an enormous amount of controversy in the Black community. Although the book was written by Alice Walker, a Black woman, the film was made by White director Steven Spielberg, a man with no previous background in making an essentially Black movie. Although many Blacks applauded the highly successful film and saw it as a chance to get more Black stories made, thereby creating more work for Black actors, others were highly critical of the film. Some groups objected to what they regarded as the negative stereotypes the film presented of Black males. When Margaret Avery was nominated for an Oscar for best supporting actress for her work in the film, she took out an ad in the trade papers, essentially hyping the movie. Controversy surrounded the fact that she used patois, which was completely out of character with the role she played in the film. Finally, when the movie failed to win any of the ten Oscars it was nominated for, many people felt that Blacks were being slighted by the film industry. The year before, *A Soldier's Story* lost the best picture award to *Amadeus* and Adolph Caesar lost the best supporting actor award to Haing S. Ngor (*The Killing Fields*). In 1989, Denzel Washington won the best supporting actor award for his role in *Glory*, an outstanding film about the first Black unit to fight in the Civil War. The same year, however, Morgan Freeman lost as best actor and Spike Lee's controversial *Do the Right Thing* was almost totally ignored by the academy.

Stereotyping onscreen should be considered in both a social and an industrial context. Can a dominantly White, male film industry, for example, accurately represent minorities? In a 1989 article, Joy Horowitz noted that although Blacks are highly visible in every sphere of U.S. pop culture—including Eddie Murphy at the box office, Bill Cosby on television, and Michael Jackson in music—"it is a stunning irony that there are no major black executives or agents in the motion picture industry. No one says it out loud but race is a dirty little secret in Hollywood power politics" (1989, 56). Clearly, the structure and organization of the film industry affect the products it produces. That is one reason that media literacy focuses attention on the industrial and ideological origins of the message, rather than isolating it as a single work. The following films are recommended.

Autobiography of Miss Jane Pittman (1974)
The Color Purple (1985)
Cry, the Beloved Country (1951)
Cry Freedom (1988)
The Defiant Ones (1958)

Do the Right Thing (1989)
Driving Miss Daisy (1989)
Glory (1989)
Guess Who's Coming to Dinner (1967)
Home of the Brave (1949)

Imitation of Life (1959)
In the Heat of the Night (1967)
Intruder in the Dust (1949)
Jungle Fever (1991)
Mississippi Burning (1988)
Native Son (1986)

A Patch of Blue (1965)
Pinky (1949)
Ragtime (1981)
Raisin in the Sun (1961)
A Soldier's Story (1984)
To Kill a Mockingbird (1962)

Countries and Cultures

The study of another culture is often done from a textbook with an overemphasis on size of the population, square miles of land, gross national product, political system, religions, chief products, and key exports. Although this information can be interesting and important, little in it helps students understand the people of this culture. Bringing those people to life helps students to understand their views and values and recognize that not all cultures embrace the same value system as the United States. Motion pictures are one way of bringing the rites, rituals, and lifestyles of others into the classroom. Teachers might use something as simple as a Polish wedding scene from *The Deer Hunter* (1978) or a bar mitzvah or Jewish rite (*Bless the Beasts and Children*, 1971; *The Chosen*, 1981). Perhaps it could be something as simple as a folk dance (*Zorba the Greek*, 1964) or Chinese costumes and customs (*Dim Sum: A Little Bit of Heart*, 1984; *The Last Emperor*, 1987; *Fifty-Five Days at Peking*, 1963).

Films can also provide new insights into other cultures. The hostility faced by the Pakistani community in England is well presented in *My Beautiful Laundrette* (1985), for example. In looking at other cultures, teachers can distinguish between U.S. films made about another country and films produced by the country itself. Clearly, the depiction of the Soviet Union in U.S. films is significantly different from the way the Soviet Union depicts itself in its own film industry. The India depicted in *Salaam Bombay* is considerably different from Western stereotypes of India. Although responsible films such as *A Passage to India* (1984) and *Gandhi* (1982) reveal much about the culture, it is always seen through White eyes. Western images of India can be found in *Gunga Din* (1939), *Kim* (1950), and *Indiana Jones and the Temple of Doom* (1984), among others. Western representations of Third World countries invariably create pictures for Western eyes. *American Film* noted that "current iconography dwells on Third World terror and violence. It tends to give a bogus and melodramatic picture of life there" (Powers 1984, 43). Given U.S. involvement in the Middle East, teachers and students could benefit from examining the way Hollywood representations affect public perceptions and national policy. Jack Shaheen's 1987 article "The Hollywood Arab" provides interesting insights into this process.

The Elderly

One of the most important social trends now affecting the country is the aging of the population generally referred to as the "graying of America." The Baby Boom generation (1946-1964) is now aging. Just as that generation had a major impact on the country in the 1950s and 1960s, they will exert a huge influence for the rest of the twentieth century and into the twenty-first. Medical science and generally improved living standards will keep these people alive for many, many years, and the United States will have a huge number of senior citizens. But what will the quality of their lives be? The 1980s witnessed major moral, legal, and ethical arguments centered around this issue and related concepts such as mercy killing. As "gray power" exerts an influence on the political process through the ballot box, it will also influence the entertainment industry through the box office.

By 1990, the film industry was beginning to talk about "Daisy demographics," noting the large number of nontraditional movie-goers who went to see *Driving Miss Daisy*. The film won an Oscar for best picture in 1989, and Jessica Tandy, at the age of eighty, joined George Burns and Don Ameche in winning an Oscar late in life. We can expect to see more films dealing with the elderly and the issues they face with images that are less stereotypical and more respectful. Curiously enough, there is some evidence to suggest that Hollywood now has a "gray list" that makes it difficult for older writers, directors, and actors to find employment in the movie industry. This issue was the topic of *Power and Fear: The Hollywood Gray List*, a video produced by the Caucus for Producers,

Writers, and Directors (Zeitlin 1992, 33). On television, "The Golden Girls" was a ground-breaker for programs dealing with issues concerning seniors, making it clear that to be a senior was to be neither senile nor sexless. Teachers can select examples from some of these films to help young people understand the issues facing the elderly and to think about their relationships with their own parents as their parents age. For children without grandparents, these films might provide their only real understanding of the elderly. Teachers might also consider taking a class to a senior citizens home or inviting seniors in. Remember, senior citizens are a human resource! Grandparents and great-grandparents are living history! Listening to their experiences can bring the past of the textbook to life and illuminate the present. In Colorado and other locations, senior citizens are being used as teachers' aids, bridging a gap between generations. In the process, the young invigorate the elderly and the elderly share their wisdom and experience with the young. The following films are recommended.

Cocoon (1985)	*Stevie* (1978)
Driving Miss Daisy (1989)	*Tell Me a Riddle* (1980)
Harold and Maude (1972)	*Travels with My Aunt* (1972)
Harry and Tonto (1974)	*The Trip to Bountiful* (1985)
Hud (1963)	*Voyage around My Father* (1983)
On Golden Pond (1981)	*The Whales of August* (1987)

The Disabled and the Impaired

How a society responds to its infirm, disabled, and impaired citizens is in part a measure of the greatness of that society. If students are to learn tolerance, patience, sensitivity, and compassion, they need to recognize and respect the rights of those less fortunate than themselves. One way they can do that is by being helped to understand that being different is not the same as being inferior. The media do have a role to play in this area, and teachers can select films and programs that help students understand such individuals. One critically acclaimed television program of the early 1990s was "Life Goes On." The show centered around a family who had a teenage son with Down's syndrome. The program helped viewers recognize the boy's dignity, his sense of self, and his many abilities and strengths. For some viewers, this was probably the first opportunity they had to really understand Down's syndrome and to change some of the misconceptions they had about the condition.

Motion pictures also provide increasing opportunities to help our students recognize these individuals, whether in social studies classes or in special education. Clips from some of these films also could be successfully used with teachers, parents, and other adult groups. Hollywood's increasing sensitivity to individuals with special problems can be seen in a number of important films. In 1990, Robert De Niro was nominated for an Oscar as best actor and the movie *Awakenings* was nominated as best film for the true story of individuals struggling against an illness that trapped them in sleep for years. In 1989, *My Left Foot* received Oscar nominations and Daniel Day-Lewis won best actor for his role as Christy Brown, an Irish artist with cerebral palsy. Dustin Hoffman won the 1988 Oscar for best actor for his work in *Rain Man*, which also won the best picture award. Marlee Matlin won the 1986 Oscar for best actress for her work as a young deaf woman in *Children of a Lesser God*, which was also nominated for best picture. *Mask* (1985) and *The Elephant Man* (1980) both received Oscar nominations. John Mills won the best supporting actor award in 1970 playing a misshapen mute in *Ryan's Daughter*. When Louise Fletcher accepted her 1975 Oscar for best supporting actress for *One Flew over the Cuckoo's Nest*, she drew attention to the hearing impaired by signing her acceptance speech. In 1968, *Charly* won the Oscar for best actor, which went to Cliff Robertson for his portrayal of a retarded man. Patty Duke won the Oscar for best supporting actress for her 1962 role as Helen Keller in *The Miracle Worker*.

These and other films provide good resources for any study of the impaired and disabled. They can also be integrated into literature by studying handicapped and impaired characters. Some useful comparisons could be made to Captain Ahab in *Moby Dick*, to Long John Silver in *Treasure Island*, or to Quasimodo in *The Hunchback of Notre Dame*. Art teachers could use *Moulin Rouge* (1952) to show that Henri de Toulouse-Lautrec's impairment did not prevent his artistic success. Finally, the treatment of this subject matter in film could be studied against a social background such as the 1975 Handicapped Children's Act. The following films are recommended.

Awakenings (1990)
The Best Years of Our Lives (1946)
Born on the 4th of July (1989)
The Boy Who Could Fly (1986)
Charly (1968)
Children of a Lesser God (1986)
Coming Home (1978)
The Deer Hunter (1978)
The Elephant Man (1980)
Ice Castles (1979)
Johnny Belinda (1948)

Mask (1985)
The Men (1950)
The Miracle Worker (1962)
My Left Foot (1989)
Rainman (1988)
Ratboy (1986)
Ryan's Daughter (1970)
Tell Me That You Love Me, Junie Moon (1970)
Voyage around My Father (1983)
The Whales of August (1987)

Hispanics

Writing in *The Latin Image in American Film*, Allen Woll says, "Americans receive a dominant picture of Latin society populated by murderous banditos and submissive but sensual peasant women" (1980, 2). The growing number of Hispanics in the United States requires that the rest of the population understand their culture and the contributions they are making to U.S. society. Although Hispanic influence is evident in music, food, and fashion, much of the media coverage tends to center on negative stories that reinforce stereotypes. Too often the bad guys in the movies and on television turn out to be Hispanic characters or, at the very least, are Hispanic looking. Several motion pictures in the last few years have, however, shown fascinating aspects of the Hispanic culture. *Under the Volcano* (1984) has some extremely interesting scenes dealing with the ritual of the Day of the Dead in Mexico. *The Milagro Beanfield War* also touches on some of the customs and beliefs of Hispanic culture. Other films, such as *Latino* (1985), *Salvador* (1986), and *Missing* (1982), provide disturbing images of U.S. foreign policy in Latin America. *Stand and Deliver* (1987) earned a best-actor Oscar nomination for Edward James Olmos for his role of a teacher striving to encourage Hispanic students. It provided an exceptionally strong role model for dedicated young people who are often invisible in the media. The following films are recommended.

The Border (1982)
Boulevard Nights (1979)
La Bamba (1987)
Latino (1985)
The Milagro Beanfield War (1988)
Missing (1982)

The Old Gringo (1989)
Salvador (1986)
Stand and Deliver (1987)
Under the Volcano (1986)
Viva Zapata (1952)
Walk Proud (1979)

The South

The image of the South has been strongly invoked in motion pictures since their inception. But how accurate has that image been? What stereotypes are imbedded in these films, and what effect, if any, do they have on the way others see the South? Teachers dealing with this aspect of U.S. society can draw students' attention to these images and their roots in literature (*Tobacco Road, The Sound and the Fury, Gone with the Wind*) as well as their presence and proliferation on television ("The Dukes of Hazard"). Students can be asked to examine key stereotypes in images of the South including the redneck, the good old boy, the southern belle, and the Black mammy. Although these images may have some validity in reality, teachers should ask students to consider whether they are really representative of all of southern life. The entire richness of southern life might also be explored by pointing to the difference between the Old South and the New South. Today, for example, students need to recognize the cosmopolitan, corporate nature of Atlanta as well as the Hispanic influence in Florida and the Cajun and Creole cultures of Louisiana. In *The Celluloid South*, Edward Campbell acknowledges the powerful role the film industry has played in shaping the public's perception of the South.

Whatever the image, benign or evil, the cinema insured that the South was a distinct section which drew unrelenting curiosity ... despite the growth of urban centers and heavy industry in the region. The survival of the South in the popular imagination owes more to the cinema than any other force (1981, 191).

The following films are recommended.

All the King's Men (1949)
Angel Baby (1961)
The Big Easy (1987)
Cat on a Hot Tin Roof (1958)
Cool Hand Luke (1967)
Crimes of the Heart (1986)
The Defiant Ones (1958)
Deliverance (1972)
Driving Miss Daisy (1989)
Everybody's All-American (1988)
Glory (1989)
Gone with the Wind (1939)
I Am a Fugitive from a Chain Gang (1932)
Inherit the Wind (1960)
In the Heat of the Night (1967)
Intruder in the Dust (1949)

The Little Foxes (1941)
The Long Hot Summer (1958)
Macon County Line (1974)
Mississippi Burning (1988)
Places in the Heart (1984)
Shy People (1987)
Smokey and the Bandit (1978)
Song of the South (1946)
The Sound and the Fury (1959)
Sounder (1972)
Southern Comfort (1981)
Steel Magnolias (1989)
Sweet Bird of Youth (1962)
Tobacco Road (1941)
Winter People (1989)

Other Themes

In working with film in the classroom, we are limited only by our imagination. It is not possible in this chapter to look at every issue or theme the motion picture industry has addressed. We consider many issues and provide film and print resources to help teachers integrate feature films into the instructional process. Here are films in several other areas you may want to explore.

Ecology and the Environment

The Emerald Forest (1985)
Mosquito Coast (1986)
Star Trek: The Voyage Home (1986)
Turtle Diary (1985)
Where the River Runs Black (1986)

Leadership and Management Styles

The Caine Mutiny (1954)
Mister Roberts (1952)
Norma Rae (1979)
Silkwood (1984)
Wall Street (1987)

Mental and Emotional Illness

Agnes of God (1985)
Birdy (1984)
The Boy Who Could Fly (1986)
Charly (1968)
Equus (1977)

Frances (1982)
Harvey (1950)
I Never Promised You a Rose Garden (1977)
Lust for Life (1956)
'Night Mother (1986)
Nuts (1987)
One Flew over the Cuckoo's Nest (1975)
Orphans (1987)
Snakepit (1948)
Splendor in the Grass (1961)
Stoneboy (1984)

Religion

Agnes of God (1985)
The Cardinal (1963)
Catholics (1973)
The Chosen (1981)
Mass Appeal (1984)
The Mission (1986)

Sports

Breaking Away (1979)
Champions (1983)
Chariots of Fire (1981)
Everybody's All-American (1988)
Hoosiers (1986)

One on One (1977)
Personal Best (1982)
Raging Bull (1980)
Take Down (1977)
Vision Quest (1985)

A Case Study in Cinema and Society: The Movie as Modern Myth

(ELEM/MID/HIGH) — One of the most popular and successful films of all time was *Star Wars*, created by George Lucas in 1977. The film was nominated for nine Oscars and won six. The special effects developed in the movie would set the standard by which all other films would be judged. But there was more to *Star Wars* than high-tech gadgetry. The message of the film touched a responsive chord in audiences around the world. What was it about *Star Wars* that had such an impact on society at the time it was made?

In part *Star Wars* succeeded because, although it appeared to be innovative with its computer-generated images and the effects created by the company Industrial Light and Magic, its essence was traditional myth and fairytale. In creating *Star Wars*, George Lucas consciously drew upon the myths of the past to illuminate the present by reaching the child within each of us. Lucas has said, "There's a whole generation growing up without fairy tales.... I wanted to make a kid's film that would strengthen contemporary mythology and introduce a kind of basic morality" (Pollock 1983, 138-39).

Although *Star Wars* appealed to the young, it also reached inside many adults and reminded them of their past and some universal, even cosmic, truths. In *The Power of Myth*, Joseph Campbell, who worked with Lucas, talked about the message and myth in *Star Wars*: "That movie communicates. It is in a language that talks to young people, and that's what counts.... *Star Wars* is not a simple morality play; it has to do with the powers of life as they are either fulfilled or broken and suppressed through the action of man" (1988, 144-45).

In studying *Star Wars* with students, teachers can integrate the film into such diverse areas as social studies, children's literature, mythology, comparative religion, and language arts. The following approaches might be usefully investigated.

1. Compare and contrast *Star Wars* with *The Wizard of Oz*. Dorothy lives with her aunt and uncle on a farm and wishes herself over the rainbow. Luke lives with his aunt and uncle on a farm and also wishes for a different life. Both characters travel to a distant world with a group of friends they meet along the way. The Cowardly Lion resembles Chewbacca, the Wookie. Dorothy's Tin Man has his counterpart in C3-PO. Darth Vader might be interpreted as the Wicked Witch of the West.

2. Compare and contrast *Star Wars* to the Arthurian legends. Luke can be interpreted as a young knight in search of a quest. The Holy Grail is parallel to the Force, which Luke must learn to embrace. Like many knights, Luke begins his journey with the mission to rescue a princess in distress. King Arthur's powerful weapon is Excalibur, the sword; Luke learns to use the light saber. Obi Wan ("Ben") Kenobi is a Merlin figure. Traditional fairytales begin with "once upon a time." *Star Wars* opens with "a long time ago."

3. Compare and contrast *Star Wars* with the western genre. The settlements in *Star Wars* look like parts of the Desert Southwest where many westerns are set. The intergalactic saloon is an extension of the dangerous cantina across the border where refugees, outlaws, and desperadoes gather. Han Solo acts like a western character, with his gun on his hip and a tough phrase on his lips. He also finds himself pursued by a bounty hunter. The sequence in which Luke's aunt and uncle are killed and he returns home to find them is deliberately reminiscent of *The Searchers*, a classic 1950s western by John Ford.

4. *Star Wars* abounds with biblical references and symbolism. The entire presence of the Force in the film suggests that the movie is essentially about religion, not in an institutional sense but in the sense of spirituality. Much of the movie centers on the inner struggle between good and evil. Darth Vader succumbs to the dark side of the Force. He is a Lucifer character—a fallen angel. Ben Kenobi (later,

Obi-Wan Kenobi) has messianic overtones. The name Ben means "from within," which is what much of the film deals with: the need to find goodness and truth within us rather than placing it in the hands of an external political structure and ideology. When Ben is about to be killed, he warns Vader that he will become more powerful if he is killed. When Vader strikes him down, Ben's body vanishes, leaving just an empty robe. Both of these developments have ties to the life of Jesus Christ. In the Bible, Luke is a disciple of Jesus; Luke Skywalker learns from Ben and carries Ben's message when he is gone. Various Bibles indicate that the name Han means "a revival of learning," and both Skywalker and Solo begin to discover the ways and wisdom of the old Jedi masters.

It is also important to acknowledge that although there are Christian references in *Star Wars*, there are references to Eastern religion as well. Ben is like a Japanese samurai master, and in the sequel, Yoda brings much of Eastern religion and mysticism to the film. The success of *The Karate Kid* series demonstrated the U.S. audience's receptiveness to such philosophy.

5. The influence of *Star Wars* continues to be felt in many areas. *Star Wars* became one of the highest grossing films in movie history and skyrocketed the career of George Lucas. The movie created renewed interest in movie merchandising, which remains powerful today. Although Lucas dislikes the term *science fiction* to describe his movie, the success of *Star Wars* resulted in a number of new sci-fi films and television programs. Expressions such as "May the Force be with you" found their way into everyday language. United States foreign policy in the Reagan years drew upon images and phrases from the film. For example, the president referred to the Soviet Union as "the evil empire," and his high-tech strategic defense system in space became known simply as Star Wars. Finally, the special effects company Industrial Light and Magic continues to pioneer techniques in movies such as *Terminator II*.

REFERENCE LIST

Bergman, Andrew, (1971). *We're in the Money: Depression America and Its Films*. New York: Harper Colophon.

Bogen, D., (1974). *Toms, Coons, Mulattoes, Mammies and Bucks*. New York: Bantam.

Browne, Ray, (1983). Introduction. In Peter C. Rollins (ed.), *Hollywood as Historian: American Film in a Cultural Context*. Lexington: University of Kentucky Press.

Brownstein, Ronald, (1991). Hollywood Hardball. *Mother Jones*, January/February, 32, 34, 85-87.

Campbell, Edward, (1981). *The Celluloid South: Hollywood and the Southern Myth*. Knoxville: University of Tennessee Press.

Campbell, Joseph, (1988). *The Power of Myth*. New York: Doubleday.

Caputi, Jane, (1988). Films of the Nuclear Age. *Journal of Popular Film and Television*, 16:3, 101-8.

Cawelti, John G. (ed.), (1973). *Focus on Bonnie and Clyde*. Englewood Cliffs, N.J.: Prentice Hall.

Christensen, Terry, (1987). *Reel Politics: American Political Movies from The Birth of a Nation to Platoon*. New York: Blackwell.

Christian Century, (1989). *Do the Right Thing*: A Jarring Look at Racism. August 16-23, 739-40.

Collins, Robert, (1977). *Star Wars:* The Pastiche of Myth and the Yearning for a Past Future. *Journal of Popular Culture*, 11:1, 1-10.

Conlon, James, (1990). Making Love Not War: The Soldier Male in *Top Gun* and *Coming Home*. *Journal of Popular Film and Television*, 18:1, 18-27.

Considine, David M., (1985). *The Cinema of Adolescence*. Jefferson, N.C.: McFarland.

Eisner, Lotte, (1969). *The Haunted Screen*. London: Secker and Warburg.

Fraser, G., (1988). *The Hollywood History of the World*. New York: Beach Tree.

Giannetti, Louis, (1976). *Understanding Movies*. Englewood Cliffs, N.J.: Prentice Hall.

Hardy, Phil, (1983). *The Western*. New York: William Morrow.

Haskell, Molly, (1973). *From Reverence to Rape: The Treatment of Women in the Movies*. New York: Holt, Rinehart & Winston.

Higson, Don, (1979). The China Fantasy. *Metro*, 49.

Hillier, Jim, (1973). Arthur Penn. In John Cawelti (ed.), *Focus on Bonnie and Clyde*. Englewood Cliffs, N.J.: Prentice Hall. Pp. 7-14.

Hirsch, Foster, (1981). *Film Noir: The Dark Side of the Screen*. New York: Plenum.

Horowitz, Joy, (1989). Hollywood's Dirty Little Secret. *Premiere*, March, 56-64.

Jackson, M., (1979). The Uncertain Peace: The Best Years of Our Lives. In J. O'Connor and M. Jackson (eds.), *American History/American Film*. New York: Ungar.

Kaminsky, Stuart, (1974). *American Film Genres*. Dayton, Ohio: Pflaum.

Kaplan, E. Ann, (1991). Sex, Work and Motherhood. *Metro*, 85, 3-11.

Koppes, Clayton, and Gregory Black, (1987). *Hollywood Goes to War: How Politics, Profits and Propaganda Shaped World War 2 Movies*. New York: Free Press.

Kracauer, Siegfried, (1947). *From Caligari to Hitler*. Princeton, N.J.: Princeton University Press.

Leab, Daniel, (1975). *From Sambo to Superspade: The Black Experience in Motion Pictures*. Boston: Houghton Mifflin.

Leo, John, (1991). Toxic Feminism on the Big Screen. *U.S. News and World Report*, June 10, 20.

McCarthy, Colman, (1991). Schwarzenegger the Role Model. *Charlotte Observer*, August 6, 7A.

McFarlane, Brain, (1987). *Australian Cinema 1970-1985*. Richmond, Australia: Heinemann.

Maeder, Edward, (1987). *Hollywood and History: Costume Design in Film*. New York: Thames and Hudson.

Mandelbaum, Howard, and Eric Myers, (1985). *Screen Deco*. New York: St. Martin's.

Mapp, E., (1974). *Blacks in American Film: Today and Yesterday*. Metuchen, N.J.: Scarecrow.

Maynard, R., (1972). *Africa on Film: Myth and Reality*. Rochelle Park, N.J.: Hayden.

Mellen, Joan, (1977). *Big Bad Wolves: Masculinity in American Film.* New York: Pantheon.

Monaco, James, (1977). *How to Read a Film.* New York: Oxford University Press.

Murray, L., (1979). Hollywood Nihilism and the Youth Culture of the Sixties: *Bonnie and Clyde.* In J. O'Connor and M. Jackson (eds.), *American History/American Film.* New York: Ungar.

Natale, Richard, (1990). And the Cameras Rolled On: Why You Are Not Seeing Movies about AIDS. *Village Voice*, February 20.

Pitts, Michael, (1984). *Hollywood and American History: A Filmography of over 250 Films Depicting U.S. History.* Jefferson, N.C.: McFarland.

Pollock, Dale, (1983). *Skywalking: The Life and Times of George Lucas.* New York: Harmony.

Powers, John, (1984). Saints and Savages. *American Film*, January/February, 38-43.

Premiere, (1992). F.Y.I., January, 17.

Reffit, A., (1980). *Images of Mexican Americans in Fiction and Film.* College Station: Texas A & M University.

Rollins, Peter C. (ed.), (1983). *Hollywood as Historian: American Film in a Cultural Content.* Lexington: University of Kentucky Press.

Rosen, M., (1974). *Popcorn Venus: Women, Movies and the American Dream.* New York: Avon.

Russo, Vito, (1981). *The Celluloid Closet: Homosexuality in the Movies.* New York: Harper & Row.

Sarf, W., (1983). *God Bless You, Buffalo Bill: A Layman's Guide to History and the Western Film.* Rutherford, N.J.: Fairleigh Dickenson University Press.

Schlesinger, Arthur, (1979). Introduction. In J. O'Connor and M. Jackson (eds.), *American History/American Film.* New York: Ungar.

Shaheen, Jack, (1987). The Hollywood Arab 1984-86. *Journal of Popular Film and Television*, 14:4, 148-57.

Sklar, Robert, (1975). *Movie-Made America: A Cultural History of American Movies.* New York: Vintage.

Smith, Julian, (1975). *Looking Away: Hollywood and Vietnam.* New York: Scribners.

Spoto, D., (1978). *Camerado: Hollywood and the American Male.* New York: Plume.

Stryker, Roy, and Nancy Wood, (1973). *In This Proud Land.* New York: Rapaport Printing.

Time, (1983). *The Outsiders*, review. April 4, 78.

Time, (1991). Why Can't a Woman Be a Man? August 5, 66-67.

USA Today, (1988). Where Are the Blacks in Race-Issue Films? July 27, 4D.

Woll, Allen, (1980). *The Latin Image in American Film.* Berkeley and Los Angeles: University of California Press.

Zeitlin, Marilyn, (1992). To Old for Hollywood. *The Progressive*, 33-34.

RECOMMENDED READING

Bookbinder, Robert. *The Films of the 70s.* New York: Carol, 1982.

Bordwell, David, and Kristin Thompson. *Film Art.* Reading, Mass.: Addison-Wesley, 1979.

Bordwell, David, Janet Staiger, and Kristin Thompson. *The Classical Hollywood Cinema.* New York: Columbia University Press, 1985.

Brode, Douglas. *The Films of the 50s.* Secaucus, N.J.: Citadel, 1976.

_____. *The Films of the 60s.* New York: Carol, 1980.

_____. *The Films of the 80s.* New York: Carol, 1990.

Brownstein, Ronald. *The Power and the Glitter: The Hollywood-Washington Connection.* New York: Pantheon, 1990.

Cohen, Daniel. *Horror Movies.* Greenwich, Conn.: Bison Books, 1984.

Davies, Philip, and Brian Neve. *Cinema, Politics and Society in America.* New York: St. Martin's, 1981.

Gable, Neal. *An Empire of Their Own: How the Jews Invented Hollywood.* New York: Crown, 1988.

Jarvie, I. C. *Movies and Society.* New York: Basic Books, 1970.

Jowett, Garth. *Film, the Democratic Art: A Social History of the American Film.* Boston: Little, Brown, 1976.

Kohn, Alfie. Parenthood Pabulum. *Psychology Today* (July-August 1988), 64-65.

Miller, Randall (ed.). *Ethnic Images in American Film and Television.* Philadelphia: Balch Institute, 1978.

Peary, Gerald, and Roger Shatzkin (eds.). *The Classic American Novel and the Movies.* New York: Ungar, 1977.

Pickard, Roy. *Who Played Who on the Screen.* New York: Hippocrene, 1988.

Pye, Michael, and Lynda Myles. *The Movie Brats: How the Film Generation Took over Hollywood.* New York: Holt, Rinehart & Winston, 1979.

Quart, Leonard, and Albert Auster. *American Film and Society since 1945.* New York: Praeger, 1984.

Richards, Gregory. *Science Fiction Movies.* Greenwich, Conn.: Bison Books, 1984.

Thomas, Tony. *The Films of the 40s.* New York: Citadel, 1975.

Thompson, Robert. American Politics on Film. *Journal of Popular Culture* (1986), 20:1, 27-47.

Tudor, Andrew. *Image and Influence: Studies in the Sociology of Film.* New York: St. Martin's, 1975.

Vermilye, Jerry. *The Films of the 30s.* New York: Citadel, 1982.

White, David Manning, and Richard Averson. *The Celluloid Weapon: Social Comment in the American Film.* Boston: Beacon Press, 1972.

Wood, Robin. *Hollywood from Vietnam to Reagan.* New York: Columbia University Press, 1986.

Wright, Basil. *The Long View.* New York: Knopf, 1974.

Journals

Film and History
Historians Film Committee
c/o History Faculty, New Jersey Institute
    of Technology
Newark, NJ 07102

Journal of Popular Film and Television
c/o Heldref Publications
4000 Albemarle St., NW
Washington, DC 20016

Posters, Stills, and Press Kits

Cinema City
P.O. Box 1012
Muskegon, MI 49443
(616) 722-7760
Regular catalog available.

Movie Star News
134 W. 18th St.
New York, NY 10011
(212) 620-8160 or 620-8161
Catalogs available.

Appendix—Photographs

The Gods Must Be Crazy—When is a Coke bottle not a Coke bottle? Cultural context influences the way we read artifacts and symbols. This movie offers students an opportunity to look at life through different eyes. (Photograph used with permission. © 1984 Twentieth Century Fox Film Corporation. All Rights Reserved.)

Index

About the Authors

      Dr. David Considine developed one of the first media studies courses in an Australian high school before moving to the United States. He has an M.L.S. from the University of North Carolina at Greensboro and a Ph.D. in Instructional Technology from the University of Wisconsin-Madison.

      He is coordinator of the Media Studies program in the Reich College of Education at Appalachian State University in Boone, North Carolina. His writings have appeared in numerous journals including *School Library Journal*, *School Library Media Quarterly*, *Instructional Technology*, *Language Arts*, and *The Journal of Popular Film and Television*.

      A frequent keynote speaker at conferences, Dr. Considine conducts V.I.E.W. (Visual Information Education Workshops) throughout the United States and North America.

      Gail E. Haley is one of the country's most distinguished authors and illustrators of children's books. She has the distinction of being the only person to have won best children's book awards in both the United States and England—the Caldecott Medal and the Kate Greenaway Medal. In her Caldecott medal acceptance speech she warned of television's impact on children, and she has become increasingly involved in creative applications of imagery in instruction, including puppets as teaching tools.

      She teaches Writing and Illustrating for Children and Puppetry in Education in the Reich College of Education at Appalachian State University.

      Ms. Haley is a frequent visitor to libraries and classrooms throughout the United States and overseas, stressing the creative process involved in writing and researching children's books.